FOUNDATIONS OF CRIMINAL JUSTICE

OUR POLICE
EDITED BY
GEORGE M. ROE

with a new preface by
Thomas A. Johnson

AMS PRESS
NEW YORK
1976

FOUNDATIONS OF CRIMINAL JUSTICE

General Editors

Richard H. Ward
Austin Fowler
 John Jay College of
 Criminal Justice

Advisory Board

Arthur F. Brandstetter
 Director, School of Criminal Justice
 Michigan State University

Kenneth Braunstein,
 Law Enforcement Program
 University of Nevada, Reno

Nils Christie
 Institute for Criminology
 University of Oslo

Vern L. Folley
 Director, The Urban Institute
 Harrisburg Area Community
 College

B. Earl Lewis
 D'Anza College
 Cupertino, California

William J. Mathias
 Coordinator of Criminal
 Justice Program
 Georgia State University

Gordon Misner
 Administration of Justice Program
 University of Missouri

James W. Osterburg
 Administration of Criminal
 Justice Curriculum
 University of Illinois

Brian Parker
 Senior Criminalist
 Stanford Research Institute

Donald Riddle
 President, John Jay College of
 Criminal Justice
 New York, New York

Herman Schwendinger
 School of Criminology
 University of California, Berkeley

Jerome Skolnick
 Center for the Study of Law
 and Society
 University of California, Berkeley

John Webster
 Administration of Justice
 Curriculum
 University of Illinois

Leslie T. Wilkins
 School of Criminal Justice
 State University of New York,
 Albany

A DREAM—OUR PROTECTORS ALWAYS.

OUR POLICE.

A HISTORY OF THE CINCINNATI POLICE FORCE, FROM THE EARLIEST PERIOD UNTIL THE PRESENT DAY.

EDITED BY

G. M. ROE.

ILLUSTRATED WITH PORTRAITS AND ETCHINGS.

CINCINNATI, OHIO.
1890.

Library of Congress Cataloging in Publication Data

Roe, George Mortimer, 1848-1916.
   Our police.

   (Foundations of criminal justice)
   Reprint of the 1890 ed. published in Cincinnati.
   Includes index.
   1. Cincinnati—Police—History. I. Title. II. Series.
HV8148.C5R63   1976   363.2'09771'78   77-156024
ISBN 0-404-09125-3

Reprinted from an original in the collections
of the University of Connecticut Library

From the edition of 1890, Cincinnati

Foundations of Criminal Justice Series
General Editors: Richard H. Ward and Austin Fowler,
John Jay College of Criminal Justice

Copyright © 1976 by AMS Press, Inc.
All rights reserved.
Published in the United States by AMS Press, Inc.
56 E. 13th Street, New York, N.Y. 10003

Manufactured in the United States of America

Border Town Beginnings

A Preface to the New Edition of

OUR POLICE

The development and emergence of the police system in the city of Cincinnati lends insight into the effects of historical events upon a segment of growth in the field of criminal justice. One should approach this volume as an attempt at journalistic reporting rather than an academic treatise on the emergence of a police organization.

The impact of the Civil War was more pronounced on Cincinnati than on many other cities. The police organization was significantly altered at an important point in its development since Cincinnati was a "border town" with enormous factions of North and South sympathizers. This created a tenuous situation and sparked riots. Since the citizens of Cincinnati were fearful of the Confederate Army marching upon Lexington, Kentucky, and then onward toward Cincinnati, the unique situation developed in which civilians formed their police organization into an infantry unit and directed it to leave the community to meet an advancing foe.

Even prior to the Civil War, a continual series of incidents structured the police organization into a very partisan political force. Similarly, the organization was removed from the control of local authorities due to corruption and was replaced by an authority deriving from a Board of Police Commissioners, which ultimately saw the governor of the state making the appointments to the board. In addition, the police organization felt a severe impact by the "American Party" or "Know-Nothing Party."

There was a major police reorganization following the political influence of this party.

The police organization also had to contend with severe labor-management disputes which erupted into riotous situations. Moreover, Cincinnati was visited by an extensive natural disaster, namely the great Cincinnati floods of 1883 and 1884. The reader should bear in mind the difficulties of policing a community today should such natural disasters occur, even with the existence of contemporary police practices and organizations. Perhaps this partially explains some of the earlier instabilities of our police organizations.

From its earliest development, the police organization, along with its contemporary counterparts, commonly shared in the phenomenon of very rapid turnover of administrative leadership. This is noted by the short term of tenure for each police chief. Even today this is a structural weakness of our police organizations which has a significant effect upon police practices as well as police innovations. Closely related to problems of administrative leadership in the Cincinnati Police Department, at critical times in its development, was the introduction of military leadership and discipline by former officers who excelled in the Civil War, the Sioux campaigns, or earlier battles. This has had an impact upon the emergence of our police organizations and the semi-military managerial styles of leadership.

Finally, the Cincinnati Police Department experienced the impact of technological developments that altered previous methods of organizing and of accomplishing designated duties. Paramount among the improvements were the introduction of the patrol wagon; the development of signal and telegraphic systems; the development of the telephone; the development of Bertillon identification systems and of fingerprinting methods. The Cincinnati Police Department organized the first daytime police department in 1842. Moreover, they were the first police department to install telephones.

The reader will also discover certain weaknesses in the methodological approach used by the author in approaching the subject matter. First and foremost is a very weak historical methodology. This observation should not astonish the student of historical accounts of police organizations as virtually every book published (until Roger Lane's work in 1967) shows an extremely weak academic approach to the subject. In short, some authors are journalists and not academicians, and this accounts for not only the style of writing, but also for the significant omissions. It may well be that the largest contribution of this work lies more in what was not stated than in that which was made explicit. This point is made in all seriousness of purpose. For until one realizes how weak an historical tradition exists within the Criminal Justice field, one will not question the shortcomings of the journalistic accounts which over-dramatize "cop and robber" stories, which are incessantly preoccupied with portraying and extolling the virtues of manliness of the police officer. This type of journalism prevents the reader from grasping the more important points such as relating significant events of the community's development to the organization and development of the police department.

More specifically, one may observe the absence of any analysis into the most significant technological developments of the day. The reader receives no accounting as to the impact of the telephone or how the advent of patrol wagons may have altered existing thoughts and practices on deployment of police personnel. It is reported as though the patrol wagon, telegraph, telephone, Bertillon identification system and fingerprinting had no organizational consequences on the police department. It is points such as these which prevent our understanding and appreciation of the development of insights into structural and organizational weaknesses within the early development of our police heritage.

Therefore, it is hoped that the authors of tomorrow will more properly appreciate the contribution of this author and commit themselves to writing works which are less dependent upon developing portraits of individual men and their individual acts. This is not meant to imply one should not relate significant biographical accounts which invariably may be desired. It is merely hoped that future authors will go beyond this level and make contributions which help to describe the police organization not as an entity in and of itself as though it resides in a vacuum, but as a subsystem within a larger system that is both affected by and in turn affects the larger constellation in which it resides.

In conclusion, if the systems concept is utilized in reporting the historical development of police organizations, the readers of tomorrow will not only appreciate the events which occurred, but will also understand possible causations for such events, and the possible consequences boded for the present and future of police organizations and all society. Therefore, when writing about the Criminal Justice system and each of its components, future authors would be well advised to relate more of the human, organizational and technological aspects of community living in which police organizations operate.

Thomas A. Johnson, D. Crim.
University of Wisconsin—Milwaukee

PREFACE.

To fulfill modern requirements, a model Cincinnati police officer must at least approach the versatility of an "Admirable" Crichton. In the first place, he must be a perfect specimen of physical manhood, able to pass a physical examination more exacting than that required of the West Point cadet; as symmetrical as an Apollo, as strong as a Hercules, as enduring as iron. He must have a knowledge of the English language sufficient to make his written reports intelligible, and be well enough versed in criminal and municipal laws to avoid making any mistakes in prosecuting his duties both for the discovery and the prevention of nuisances, of misdemeanors, of crime. He must be a police-court judge off the bench, a prosecuting attorney on the witness stand, a jury on his beat. He must have a sufficient knowledge of the business of a physician to know what to do for a man who falls on the street in a faint, how to resuscitate the drowned, to stanch the flow of blood from a wound, what to do for a man who has been frozen, and how to treat one dying from overheat. A sanitary officer's business in a search for contagion is always the business of a policeman. He must be as tidy as a "Beau" Brummel, as polite as a Chesterfield, as brave as a Cœur de Lion; as another writer has said, he must be a hero in peace as a soldier is a hero in war. He is expected to exercise something of a mother's tenderness and solicitude when caring for a lost child, to be as immobile as adamant when facing a mob.

He must be a directory for citizens, a guide-board for strangers, and always as valiant as a knight-errant in the defense of the innocent. He must have the eyes of an Argus and the ears of a Cassandra, seeing all, hearing all, and knowing all that is going on around him.

The man who is weighed by such a standard and not found wanting, is entitled to something more than an enrollment at headquarters. He is worthy of having his name placed where it will possess an interest for a period longer than to-day and to-morrow. To give his name such a place a history of the Cincinnati Police is written. To make the history complete, and for the sake of comparison, which in this case so far as the present force is concerned is not odious, it is necessary to hurriedly go over the past and rescue from prospective oblivion many names, dates and incidents which hitherto have had a place only in pioneer memory. The major portion of the volume, however, deals with the present, with the non-partisan metropolitan police, with men as they appear to-day. If the views taken on these pages seem to smack of optimism the most captious will find that a careful investigation will justify them.

CONTENTS.

PREFACE iii
LIST OF ILLUSTRATIONS xi
ADDENDA 397
ROSTER OF THE FORCE 401

CHAPTER I.

THE SETTLEMENT OF CINCINNATI.—DID LOVE LEAD TO THE FOUNDATION OF A GREAT CITY?—THE ENAMORED ENSIGN AND THE JEALOUS HUSBAND.—THE STORY OF HELEN OF TROY REVERSED.—WHEN INDIANS PROWLED WHERE MIGHTY BUILDINGS RISE.—A NIGHT-WATCH CREATED FOR THE YOUNG COMMUNITY.—LAWS THAT WERE WRITTEN IN LETTERS OF BLOOD.—WHEN IT WAS SAFE TO LEAVE DOORS OPEN DAY AND NIGHT.—THE FATHERS OF THE VILLAGE.—DUTIES OF THE CITY WATCH.—GOOD CITIZENS TO BE INDOORS AFTER TEN O'CLOCK AT NIGHT.—THE TOWN MARSHAL, CAPTAINS AND WATCMEN . . . . Pages 1–27

CHAPTER II.

ISAAC G. BURNET, THE FIRST MAYOR OF CINCINNATI.—ESTABLISHMENT OF A WATCH-HOUSE.—MAYOR SAMUEL W. DAVIES.—A CONSPICUOUS FIGURE IN THE EARLY HITSORY OF CINCINNATI.—THE CITY MARSHAL'S OFFICE WORTH FROM $15,000 TO $25,000 A YEAR.—THE PRO-SLAVERY RIOTS OF 1836 CAUSED BY A FIGHT BETWEEN A BLACK BOY AND A WHITE BOY.—NEGROES CRUELLY SLAUGHTERED BY A MERCILESS MOB.—THE GOVERNOR DECLARES THE CITY UNDER MARTIAL LAW.—NUM-

BER OF NIGHT WATCHMEN INCREASED.—SKETCH OF THE BEDINI RIOTS.—A MOB SETS OUT TO ATTACK ARCHBISHOP PURCELL'S RESIDENCE.—THE POPE'S NUNCIO ORDERED TO QUIT THE CITY.—THE POLICE REPULSE THE MOB.—THE MAYOR COMPELLED TO DISMISS THE CHIEF OF POLICE.—THE KNOW NOTHING RIOTS.—WENDELL PHILLIPS ROTTEN EGGED. ORGANIZATION OF THE POLICE FORCE.—A POLICE COMMISSION WITH A BRIEF EXISTENCE. Pages 28–43

CHAPTER III.

THE SUCCESSION OF MAYORS AND COMMISSIONERS.—R. M. BISHOP.—GEORGE HATCH.—L. A. HARRIS.—CHAS. F. WILSTACH.—JOHN F. TORRENCE.—S. S. DAVIS.—G. W. C. JOHNSTON.—R. M. MOORE.—CHARLES JACOB, JR.—WILLIAM MEANS.—THOMAS J. STEPHENS.—POLICE SUPERINTENDENTS.—ORGANIZATION OF POLICE COMMISSIONS, TOGETHER WITH THE NAMES OF ALL COMMISSIONERS.—POLICE FORCE CONVERTED INTO A BATTALION OF SOLDIERS.—INTERESTING EPISODE IN THE NOMINATION OF A MAYOR . . . . Pages 44–58

CHAPTER IV.

THE RIOTS OF 1884.—THE LAX ADMINISTRATION OF LAW WHICH LED UP TO THEM.—THE KIRK MURDER.—THE MUSIC HALL MEETING.—AWFUL SCENES IN THE JAIL TUNNEL.—HEROIC ACHIEVEMENTS OF CINCINNATI POLICEMEN.—THE FLOODS OF 1883 AND 1884.—WORK OF BOAT PATROLS. Pages 59–77

CHAPTER V.

THE HEAD OF THE POLICE.—INTERESTING CAREER OF MAYOR AMOR SMITH, JR.—HIS BOYHOOD IN CINCINNATI.—HIS SUCCESS IN BUSINESS AND IN POLITICS.—RARE EXECUTIVE

ABILITY COMBINED WITH A LOVE FOR HARD WORK.—HIS SERVICES AS REVENUE COLLECTOR, AND AS CINCINNATI'S CHIEF EXECUTIVE.—HIS CABINET.—MAYOR MOSBY.
Pages 78–95

CHAPTER VI.

THE NON-PARTISAN POLICE COMMISSION—HISTORY OF ITS FORMATION—WHAT SUGGESTED IT—PROVISIONS OF THE BILL BY WHICH THE COMMISSION WAS CREATED—DUTY OF THE COMMISSIONERS IN SUPPRESSING GAMBLING—WHO CONSTITUTED THE FIRST BOARD—SKETCHES OF PRESIDENT DODDS, DR. MINOR, MESSRS. BOYLE AND WERNER, EX-COMMISSIONERS MORGAN AND TOPP, AND CLERK WARREN . . Pages 96–130

CHAPTER VII.

HOW A MAN IS MADE A POLICEMAN.—THE EXAMINATIONS THAT ARE NECESSARY AND THE RED TAPE THAT MUST BE UNWOUND.—DESCRIPTION OF THE UNIFORM ADOPTED.—THE PHYSICAL TESTS AND THE MEN WHO MAKE THEM.—SKETCH OF SURGEON C. L. ARMSTRONG.—HIS EXPERIENCE IN A FORLORN HOPE.—DR. ASA B. ISHAM.—DR. N. P. DANDRIDGE AND THE LATE DR. WALTER A. DUN . . . . Pages 131–148

CHAPTER VIII.

POLICE TRAINING.—THE GYMNASIUM.—HISTORY OF ITS ORGANIZATION.—ATTENDANCE UPON IT COMPULSORY.—POLICE ATHLETES.—MILITARY DISCIPLINE AND THE FIRST MILITARY PARADE.—TRIBUTE FROM THE GOVERNOR OF OHIO.—SCHOOL OF INSTRUCTION.—IMPORTANT WORK ACCOMPLISHED BY CLERK WARREN.—THE MENTAL AND MANUAL EXAMINERS.—SKETCHES OF COLONEL KIRSTEAD, CAPTAIN TINKER, AND F. M. COPPOCK.—THE MORGAN MEDAL, AND MEN WHO HAVE CONTESTED FOR IT.—HOW POLICE TRIALS ARE CONDUCTED . . . Pages 149–177

CONTENTS.

CHAPTER IX.

THE CHIEF AND INSPECTOR.—SERVICES OF PHILIP H. DEITSCH, BOTH IN WAR AND IN PEACE.—HIS EXPERIENCE WITH GENERAL SHERIDAN.—CATALOGUE OF THE BATTLES IN WHICH HE FOUGHT.—HIS SUCCESS AS A COMMANDER OF MEN.—THE INSPECTOR'S DUTIES.—CAPTAIN GEORGE D. HADLEY'S CAREER.—CHIEF DEITSCH'S OFFICE CORPS. Pages 178–201

CHAPTER X.

THE DETECTIVE FORCE.—SKETCH OF ITS EARLY ORGANIZATION.—CAREER OF THE CHIEF OF DETECTIVES, LAWRENCE M. HAZEN.—HIS CORPS OF ABLE ASSISTANTS, MESSRS CRAWFORD, SCHUNCKS, WAPPENSTEIN, CALLAHAN, TOKER, MOSES, HUDSON AND JACKSON.—RECORDS MADE BY THE THIEF CATCHERS. Pages 202–229

CHAPTER XI.

PATROL AND MOUNTED POLICE.—THEIR INTRODUCTION INTO CINCINNATI, AND THEIR EFFICIENCY.—TRIBUTE TO EDWARD ARMSTRONG.—EVERY-DAY DRAMATIC SCENES ENACTED BY THE PATROL.—SKETCH OF SUPERINTENDENT DUFFY.—WIDE AREA OF CINCINNATI SUBURBS, AND THE NECESSITY OF MOUNTED POLICE TO PATROL THEM . . . . . . Pages 230–242

CHAPTER XII.

POLICE RELIEF ASSOCIATION.—WHY A RELIEF FUND WAS ESTABLISHED.—HISTORY OF THE ORGANIZATION OF THE PRESENT FUND.—OFFICERS OLD AND NEW.—THE CONSTITUTION AND BY-LAWS.—POLICEMEN'S BENEVOLENT ASSOCIATION.—THE ROLL OF HONOR.—DEEDS OF HEROISM THAT OFTEN MAKE THE RELIEF ASSOCIATION A NECESSITY . . Pages 243–259

CHAPTER XIII.

CENTRAL STATION AND POLICE TELEPHONE.—THE OLD, THE TEMPORARY, AND THE NEW QUARTERS.—DUTIES OF LIEUTENANTS AND SERGEANTS.—THE DISTRICT IN WHICH THE UNSOLVED BALDWIN MYSTERY WAS DISCOVERED.—REVIEW OF THE STARTLING CRIME AND THE PART THE POLICE PLAYED IN IT.—OFFICERS NOW IN CHARGE OF THE DISTRICT.—POLICE SIGNALING THEN AND NOW.—THE OLD DIAL AND THE LIGHTNING TELEPHONE . . . . Pages 260–288

CHAPTER XIV.

SECOND AND THIRD DISTRICTS.—TERRITORY WHICH COMPRISES RAT AND SAUSAGE ROWS AND "OVER THE RHINE," THE TOUGHEST AND JOLLIEST PORTIONS OF THE CITY.—THE NOTORIOUS DEER CREEK GANG.—LIEUTENANT JOE THORNTON'S CLEVER CAPTURE OF A FORGER, AND THE MANNER IN WHICH HE RAN DOWN A "SWITCH."—HOW LIEUTENANT LANGDON TREED A BLACKMAILER.—WHAT A BUNDLE OF RAGS IN A STATION-HOUSE CONTAINED.—ANIMATED APPEARANCE OF VINE STREET SUNDAY NIGHTS.—THE HOUSE OF DETENTION.—SKETCHES OF LIEUTENANTS AND SERGEANTS. . . . . Pages 289–318

CHAPTER XV.

FOURTH AND FIFTH DISTRICTS.—"SHANTY TOWN" DESCRIBED.—BRAVERY OF AN OFFICER IN FOLLOWING A DESPERADO.—INTERESTING INCIDENT IN THE LIFE OF THE NOTORIOUS CORDELIA WADE.—HOW THE QUIETUDE OF THE FIFTH DISTRICT WAS STARTLED IN 1874.—DETAILS OF THE SCHILLING MURDER, THE MOST ATROCIOUS IN THE CRIMINAL ANNALS OF CINCINNATI . . . . Pages 319–345

CHAPTER XVI.

FROM SIXTH TO TENTH INCLUSIVE.—THE DISTRICTS WHICH COMPRISE CINCINNATI SUBURBS WHERE OFFICERS ARE EITHER MOUNTED OR ARE PROVIDED WITH A SUPERABUNDANCE OF

LEG TALENT.—THE UNCANNY EXPERIENCE OF LIEUTENANT HEHEMAN IN ARRESTING A BURGLAR.—"BURKING" AND BODY SNATCHING IN THE SUBURBS.—HOW THE WORD BURKING CAME INTO USE.—THE STEALING OF THE BODY OF PRESIDENT HARRISON'S FATHER, AND THE AWFUL CRIME OF INGALLS AND JOHNSON . . . . Pages 346–378

CHAPTER XVII.

THE ROGUES' GALLERY—A UNIQUE DESCRIPTION OF A DEPARTMENT WHICH OFTEN FURNISHES THE UNMISTAKABLE TRAIL—THE PART INSTANTANEOUS PHOTOGRAPHY IS TO PLAY IN POLICE BUSINESS—HOW IT CAN DEFEAT THE ROGUES WHO OBJECT TO HAVING THEIR "MUGS" PLACED ON FILE.
Pages 379–388

CHAPTER XVIII.

THE POLICE REPORTER.—NECESSITY FOR VERSATILITY IN HIS MAKE UP.—ACTING IN THE ROLE OF CONSOLER AND DETECTIVE.—A VERITABLE GENERAL WHOSE ARMY IS MADE UP OF ONE MAN . . . . Pages 389–394

ILLUSTRATIONS.

	Page
FRONTISPIECE	
Amor Smith, Jr.	79
John Borden Mosby	93
Milo G. Dodds	101
Dr. T. C. Minor	105
James Boyle	111
Louis Werner	119
Robert J. Morgan	123
S. B. Warren	127
C. L. Armstrong, M. D.	143
A. B. Isham, M. D.	143
N. P. Dandridge, M. D.	143
A model gymnasium	151
Jeremiah Kiersted	163
H. H. Tinker	163
F. M. Coppock	163
Morgan Medal	171
Philip H. Deitsch	181
George D. Hadley	189
Dr. J. Draper	193
William J. Byrne	193
Harry Hall	193
Charles S. Vickers	193
J. R. Bender	197
James S. Weatherby	197
Thomas G. McGovern	197
Philip Strieff	197
Lawrence W. Hazen	205
John McGrann	211
W. W. Clawson	211
Peter J. O'Hara	211
Thomas A. Duffy	235
Roll of Honor	253
C. M. Fisher	265
Adolph Schmidt	265
Thomas F. Gill	265
John W. Carroll	273
George Ewbanks	273
William F. Borck	273
Joseph Wilmer	273

ILLUSTRATIONS.

	Page
Joseph Thornton	291
Mark Langdon	291
Eugene Diehl	291
Luke Drout	301
Samuel T. Corbin	301
Edward B. Newman	301
Godfrey Pistner	307
Peter Berg	307
Henry Hambrock	307
Edward Leonard	315
Emil Linhardt	315
Lewis Bedinger	315
Patrick Currin	321
Jesse Lingenfelter	321
John W. Scahill	321
Joseph M. Burman	329
M. C. Brennan	329
Henry Leitz	329
Edwin T. Rockwell	333
Bernard Rakel	333
James J. Hanrahan	333
John H. Kiffmeyer	343
Edward C. Hill	343
Louis Schmitt	343
James M. Brangan	347
M. J. O'Hearn	347
Jeremiah Nagle	347
Henry McMullen	347
Samuel B. Hall	353
Michael Duffy	353
Robert King	353
F. W. Shaffer	353
Edgar Robinson	359
Charles F. Geist	359
Thomas F. Bartley	359
Daniel Adams	359
Newton Kendall	363
William Luckering	363
John J. Nealis	363
W. E. Watson	363
William Heheman	369
William Krumpe	369
Michael Rigney	369
John Winters	369
Fogues' Gallery	383
General Andrew Hickenloper	397

ACKNOWLEDGEMENT.

For valuable aid in the preparation of this book, I am under especial obligations to Messrs. A. C. Sands, Jr., James W. Faulkner, and George C. Brown of the *Enquirer;* to Messrs. Louis O'Shoughnessy, David Graham Phillips, E. H. Anthony, and F. E. Tunison, of the *Commercial Gazette;* to Messrs. James Albert Green and Lewis T. Heck, of the *Times-Star;* Dr. Max Herzog, of the *Volksblatt;* and Mr. Gustav Karger, of the *Volksfreund.* But for the kind co-operation of these gentlemen, this book would never have been written.

THE EDITOR.

CINCINNATI, *1890.*

CHAPTER I.

THE SETTLEMENT OF CINCINNATI.—DID LOVE LEAD TO THE FOUNDATION OF A GREAT CITY?—THE ENAMORED ENSIGN AND THE JEALOUS HUSBAND.—THE STORY OF HELEN OF TROY REVERSED.—WHEN INDIANS PROWLED WHERE MIGHTY BUILDINGS RISE.—A NIGHT-WATCH CREATED FOR THE YOUNG COMMUNITY.—LAWS THAT WERE WRITTEN IN LETTERS OF BLOOD.—WHEN IT WAS SAFE TO LEAVE DOORS OPEN DAY AND NIGHT.—THE FATHERS OF THE VILLAGE.—DUTIES OF THE CITY WATCH.—GOOD CITIZENS TO BE INDOORS AFTER TEN O'CLOCK AT NIGHT.—THE TOWN MARSHAL, CAPTAINS AND WATCHMEN.

ONE HUNDRED YEARS AGO, on the 6th of September, 1788, the following notice was printed in the Kentucky *Gazette*:

"The subscribers, being proprietors of a tract of land opposite the mouth of the Licking river, on the northwest of the Ohio, have determined to lay off a town upon that excellent situation. The local and natural advantages speak its future prosperity, being equal, if not superior, to any on the bank of the Ohio river, between the Miamis. The in lots to be each half an acre, and the out lots four acres. Thirty of each to be given settlers upon paying one dollar and fifty cents for survey and deed of each lot. The fifteenth day of September is appointed for a large company to meet at Lexington, and make out a road from there to the mouth of the Licking, provided, Judge Symmes arrives, being daily expected. When the town is laid, lots will be given to such as may become residents before the first of April next."

The announcement was signed by Matthias Denman, Robert Patterson, and John Filson. Denman was from Springfield, New Jersey, and had purchased a site for a town from John Cleves Symmes, a Jersey Congressman, who had but just become the owner of about six hundred thousand acres, located between the two Miamis. Col. Patterson was of Lexington, Kentucky, and had acquired fame in the Indian wars, and Filson was a school teacher of the same place, and had considerable knowledge of surveying. The original site of Cincinnati was described as being located opposite the mouth of the Licking. It comprised seven hundred and forty acres, and was bounded by what is now known as Liberty street on the north, the Ohio on the south, Broadway on the east, and Central avenue on the west. The price paid for this territory was sixty-six and two-thirds cents an acre, or about five hundred dollars. The capital was furnished by Mr. Denman. Col. Patterson contributed his courage and skill as an Indian fighter to the assets of the firm, while Mr. Filson's capital was represented by his knowledge of surveying, quite an important factor it will be readily conceded in the requirements for a new town.

Pursuant to the plan of the notice just quoted a large party, made up of the three men already named,—Israel Ludlow, John Cleves Symmes, and others, started in a flat boat from Maysville, or what was then known as Limestone, Kentucky, and floated down the Ohio, landing at the mouth of the Big Miami. After a superficial survey of this spot Symmes decided that the proper location for a town was at the point now known as North Bend. The party measured the distance between the two Miamis and returned to Maysville. While on this return trip, and while stopping at North Bend, Filson became separated from the party and disappeared. He was never heard of afterwards. He was believed to have been killed by the savages, who, for years after the settlement of Cincinnati and North Bend, lurked about their vicinity.

At once Ludlow, who had come from the east to act as a surveyor for Symmes, took Filson's place in the firm which Denman had organized, and not later than December of 1788, went, with about twenty other persons, to the spot described as opposite the mouth of the Licking, built a block house, and began a settlement.

The evidence at hand that the site he had chosen had been a favorite one for Indians, that they had selected it in ages gone by as an eligible place for their villages, was looked upon by Ludlow as an important reason why this was a better location for a town than was that of North Bend. This evidence Ludlow found in mounds scattered all over the territory inclosed by the hills, which make of Cincinnati one vast amphitheatre.

To the new town was given the pedantic name of Losantiville, a name that had been urged by Filson as descriptive of its location—"the town opposite the mouth of the Licking." It was a compound of Greek, Latin, and French, and did not find favor among the practical pioneers. In a letter dated at North Bend, January 9, 1790, the change of name is thus described:

"Governor St. Clair arrived at Losantiville on the 2d inst. He could be prevailed on to stay with us but three nights. He has organized this purchase into a county, and has complimented me with the honor of naming it. I called it Hamilton County, after the Secretary of the Treasury. Gen. Harrison has named the new garrison Ft. Washington. The Governor has made Losantiville the countytown, and has given it the name of Cincinnati, so that the name of Losantiville will become extinct."

In Burnet's Notes on the Northwest Territory, another story of the settlement of the city is given, which may not have as much fact in it as the history just recited, but is certainly much more interesting. Burnet says that by request of Judge Symmes, Ensign Luce was sent from Louisville to North Bend with a detachment of eighteen soldiers for the performance of garrison duty, and to act in the capacity of what the settlement did not then have, viz.: policemen. Against the remonstrance of Judge Symmes, the Ensign soon after abruptly left the Bend with his soldiers, went up the river fifteen miles, and on the site of Cincinnati constructed temporary fortifications. The reason given for their sudden departure, and the one which Judge Symmes is said to have indorsed, was that the young, black-eyed and handsome wife of a North Bend settler had been transferred by her jealous husband to the neighborhood of the mouth of the Licking. The jealous husband had moved, and the young military gallant, of whom he was jealous, had followed. Thus in western history was a woman made responsible for the foundation of a great city, as in early eastern annals the beautiful wife of Menelaus was held responsible for a great city's destruction.

The first of the three or four log cabins built by Ludlow was located on Front just east of Main street. By the end of January, 1789, the little town had been pretty thoroughly surveyed and the streets laid out through a thick growth of sugar maple and sycamore which covered the lower table, or what is now known in Cincinnati as the bottoms. The street corners were marked upon the trees. The population by this time consisted of eleven families besides twenty-four unmarried men, all living in about twenty cabins.

About the 1st of June of 1789 Major Doughty arrived with a hundred and forty men from Fort Harmar, on the Muskingum, and built four block-houses, located on the line of Third street, between Broadway and Lawrence street, and thus began the construction of Fort Washington. This was a fortification of hewn logs, was about one hundred and eighty feet in length, and two stories high. It was located near the block-houses just mentioned. General Harmar with three hundred men took possession of it in November of the same year, and with this garrison made a future city possible, for by this time the question of protection had become an absorbing one. It was a protection, however, from foes from without rather than from foes within that was desired. The Indians were troublesome, and constant vigilance became the price of personal safety—of life itself. General Harmar may be said to have been the town's first Chief of Police, and the first force may be said to have been composed of three hundred men, armed and equipped. In spite of this armed protection, many of the inhabitants, if they chanced to wander beyond the range of the muskets of the soldiers in the fort, were killed and scalped by the marauders who, up to the beginning of the present century constantly prowled about the Cincinnati neighborhood.

The early police protection, proper, of the town was meagre. The pioneers for the most part were an orderly and quiet people, and did not, therefore, realize the necessity for anything like a police system. The earliest organization, however, of the village recognized the necessity for preserving order, and conferred upon the Council the power to pass ordinances under which protection to the lives of the citizens and their property could be secured.

On the first day of January, 1802, the Territorial Legislature passed the first Act incorporating the village of Cincinnati. The judicial power of the corporation was vested in a court, which consisted of a Mayor and three Aldermen, appointed by Council, and from among the citizens of the village. The legislative power was lodged with the Council, chosen annually, and made up of a President, Recorder, and nine Trustees. By a second Act, passed thirteen years later, the town was divided into four wards, each electing three Trustees for a term of three years. When they first met the Trustees were to choose a Mayor from their own number, elect a Recorder, Clerk and Treasurer. The Council was empowered to pass and enforce all ordinances necessary and proper for the health, safety, cleanliness, convenience, morals and good government of the town and its inhabitants. The law creating a Council empowered that body to establish a night-watch to guard against fire. It also extended the power to appoint a Marshal. In a directory printed in 1819 by Morgan, Lodge & Co. is found the authority for the statement that the President of Councils, by common consent, was recognized as President or Mayor of the village. The ordinance establishing a "Night Watch" was passed March 29, 1803, and was suggested by a destructive fire which visited the town but a few nights before. To adopt the language of the ordinance "It shall be, and is, hereby made the duty of the President of the said Council to cause a poll of all the citizens residing in the said town, of twenty-one years of age and upward, to be made out immediately, and shall, by the thirtieth day of the present month, divide the said citizens into classes consisting of twelve men each, who shall serve as watchmen in rotation, and it shall be the further duty of the President two days preceding the night the class is to serve as a watch, to deliver or cause to be delivered to one of the said class a list of the twelve persons who are to be on duty as watchmen, and it shall be the duty of the person to whom the list is delivered to immediately summon the class to which he belongs to attend at the watch-house precisely at the hour of 8 o'clock, on the evening they are to watch."

"And be it further ordained by the authority aforesaid, that it shall be the duty of the said twelve persons so summoned as aforesaid, in rotation, when met, to choose one of their class to be the officer of the night, whose order they shall be subject to, and it shall be the duty of the officer, so chosen, to divide his class into two divisions consisting of five men each, which division shall in their turn during the night time, watch and guard the said town by walking to and fro through the streets thereof in a quiet, peaceable manner; and it shall be their duty to apprehend and take into their custody and safe keeping all and every person or persons they may detect during the night in any felonious act, or any person or persons who are behaving in the streets in a noisy, riotous manner."

By the same ordinance any person summoned as a watchman was permitted to send a substitute, provided, that substitute was a "strong, able, discreet, sober man of twenty-one years of age and upwards."

"The homes of Hugh McCullum and David J. Poor, by and with their consent," were considered as the watch-houses, and at these two houses the watch nightly alternated.

Two years later it was found necessary by the pioneer municipal officers to pass an ordinance to protect the "watch" from insult, with the following: "That if any person or persons be found doing any act that will or might make a false alarm, or doing any act that might injure another, or insult one or more of the patrols when on duty, he or they so offending shall be fined in a sum of money not exceeding twenty dollars." The penalty of a fine not to exceed five dollars was at the same time fixed for any person who having been summoned to watch refused to respond. The person who refused to act as a commander of the watch when so elected was fined in a sum not to exceed ten dollars. Thus it will be seen that there was a period in the history of Cincinnati, when men were so indifferent to the honors of an office that it was found necessary to fix a penalty for a refusal to accept them.

Another interesting feature of the early days of Cincinnati was the fact that penalties were much severer than they now are. The old Draconian ideas which were said to have been written in blood, were still more or less popular among the western pioneers. As late as 1815, rape, arson, and treason, as well as murder, were regarded as capital crimes, which the perpetrator could expiate only on the gallows.

The watch carried what was known as a watchman's rattle, which served to call assistance and for purposes of giving signals. Gas or electric lights had not favored these times, and the watch carried large perforated tin lanterns. Everybody went to bed about nine o'clock, and nothing was heard after that save the watch calling half past nine, and every hour thereafter until morning.

Mr. Barnet, the New England traveler, said after he visited Cincinnati in 1817: "The police of the city are respectable; they have, however, no lamps or watch-words, nor do they need any. We boarded in the heart of the town, and our doors were mostly open night and day. Theft is very rare; the lowest characters seem above it."

The city in this year extended from the river to Sixth street, and from Broadway to Walnut street, and not much beyond these limits. It contained nine thousand inhabitants.

It was the Mayor's or President's exclusive duty to decide upon all charges for violations of ordinances, subject to appeal to the Council or Court of Common Pleas, at the option of the party aggrieved by the decision. He also exercised the principal functions of Justice of the Peace within the town limits. The Marshal's duties were defined by an ordinance passed by the village Council in 1802, to wit: "To execute all writs, warrants, summons, and other precepts that may be directed to him by the Council in such manner as is required of the Sheriff by law, and for his trouble therein shall be allowed the same fees as are allowed the Sheriff on writs of a similar nature." The Town Marshal was subject to the suffrages of the people, and like the President of the village or Mayor, as he was called, was chosen annually. The first President of the village elected under these laws and ordinances, was David Ziegler. He was elected in 1802, and served two years; his successor was Joseph Prince, chosen in 1804. A year later, James Findlay succeeded to the Presidency of the village, and he was followed, in 1806, by John L. Gano. In 1807, Martin Baum was President; in 1808 and 1809, Daniel Symmes; in 1810, James Findlay was again elected, and re-elected the year following; in 1812, Martin Baum was again made President; in 1813, William Stanley was elected, and re-elected in 1814; in 1815, Samuel W. Davies was chosen President, but before his term expired, by a new ordinance the selection of a Mayor by the voters of the village became necessary, and in that same year William Corry was chosen, and William Corry continued to be Mayor until 1819, the year Cincinnati was incorporated as a city, when Isaac G. Burnet became the Chief Executive. Even before a city charter was granted, as early as October 18, 1818, better protection than that the citizens' watch could afford was found necessary. Accordingly, an ordinance was passed by the village Council establishing a guard, composed of one captain and six subordinates. They were appointed by the Council and held their office during the pleasure of that body. The captain's duty was to cause the watchmen to trim the street lamps and "light them about dusk." The watchmen were to "repair to the watchhouse at 9 o'clock and continue under the captain's command until daylight in the morning." This dogberry-guard was empowered to arrest any person found abroad after 10 o'clock at night, "in the commission of any unlawful act," take the prisoner to the captain, who should discharge or detain, as he thought proper. If detained, the prisoner in the morning must appear before the Mayor. If the captain in anyway neglected the duties of his office as a vigilant and faithful guardian of the town he was liable to a fine in any sum not less than five dollars nor more than fifty. Any watchman guilty of disobeying the orders of the captain or of neglecting his duty or of "misbehaving himself," was fined in a sum not less than two dollars nor more than ten. His compensation was fixed by Council and could not have been what might be termed munificent, for seven years later, when the town had grown to a city and the guard had been enlarged, Messrs. B. Drake and E. D. Mansfield, in a small book on Cincinnati, wrote : " The Council, in compliance with the wishes of a respectable portion of the community, have recently established a city watch, consisting of two captains and eighteen men, at an expense of about $3,000 per annum." The captain, as a guarantee for the faithful discharge of his duties, was obliged to give a bond in the sum of $500, and each watchman in the sum of $200. The Marshal of the town at the same time was compelled to give a bond in the sum $10,000. The first Marshal under the city charter was Samuel R. Miller. There is no record of his having served but one term; his election occurred at the same time with that of the first Mayor, Isaac G. Burnet; he was succeeded by William C. Anderson, and he in turn was followed by William Doty. Until 1827, the Mayor and Marshal of the City of Cincinnati were chosen annually. On that year the charter was revised and again amended in the Legislative session of 1828–29, when the election of Mayor and Marshal was made bi-ennial, and the day fixed for the first Monday in April.

CHAPTER II.

ISAAC G. BURNET, THE FIRST MAYOR OF CINCINNATI.—ESTABLISHMENT OF A WATCH-HOUSE.—MAYOR SAMUEL W. DAVIES.—A CONSPICUOUS FIGURE IN THE EARLY HISTORY OF CINCINNATI.—THE CITY MARSHAL'S OFFICE WORTH FROM $15,000 TO $25,000 A YEAR.—THE PRO-SLAVERY RIOTS OF 1836, CAUSED BY A FIGHT BETWEEN A BLACK BOY AND A WHITE BOY.—NEGROES CRUELLY SLAUGHTERED BY A MERCILESS MOB.—THE GOVERNOR DECLARES THE CITY UNDER MARTIAL LAW.—NUMBER OF NIGHT WATCHMEN INCREASED.—SKETCH OF THE BEDINI RIOTS.—A MOB SETS OUT TO ATTACK ARCHBISHOP PURCELL'S RESIDENCE.—THE POPE'S NUNCIO ORDERED TO QUIT THE CITY.—THE POLICE REPULSE THE MOB.—THE MAYOR COMPELLED TO DISMISS THE CHIEF OF POLICE.—THE KNOW NOTHING RIOTS.—WENDELL PHILLIPS ROTTEN EGGED.—ORGANIZATION OF THE POLICE FORCE.—A POLICE COMMISSION WITH A BRIEF EXISTENCE.

ISAAC G. BURNET was a man of more than ordinary ability and tact, as was manifest in the fact that he served the new city as Mayor for several successive terms. During his first term in office Samuel R. Miller was elected Marshal, and he was followed by William Anderson, and he in turn by William Doty. In the spring election of 1827, Mayor Burnet, in a city whose population was not less than 22,000, received a majority vote of but twenty. At that election Zebulon Byington was chosen Marshal by a majority of 931. Mr. Byington had been a constable, and had had some police, or "watch," experience, so that he was not altogether a tyro on entering upon his new duties. During the May following his election Council passed an ordinance providing for the appointment of one captain, one assistant, and five patrolmen, whose term of office was to last from May 16 to October 31 of that year. On October 31, however, an ordinance was passed to continue this force until the following April.

The captain of the watch was empowered by the same ordinance to employ additional patrols, if in his opinion they were necessary, by and with the consent of the Mayor, providing the number did not exceed four.

In 1829, Isaac G. Burnet was re-elected Mayor, and William Doty, who seems to have been a popular and efficient officer, was again elected City Marshal, receiving 1,603 majority over Thomas Heckewelder in a total vote of 2,095.

The total police expenses this year were only $977.30.

William Doty succeeded so well in discharging the light duties that were imposed upon him as City Marshal that he was re-elected to the office in 1831.

Elisha Hotchkiss was elected Mayor the same year, after having been repeatedly defeated for that office.

The administration of these two officials was as uneventful as that of their predecessors. There is no record of any epidemic of crime, any riots, or public disturbances to afford them the opportunity to distinguish themselves, and so become entitled to a re-election. The municipal waters ran smooth, notwithstanding which the police expenses for 1831 alone amounted to $6,941.30.

During the second year of the administration of Marshal Doty, an ordinance was passed by the City Council, authorizing the City Marshal to organize a night watch, to consist of not more than twenty persons, and to procure a building in the central portion of the city for a watch house.

The establishment of this watch house was a pronounced departure in the police affairs of the city. It was the first house of the kind in Cincinnati, and from it grew the present system of station houses. It was not at first designed for the lodgment of prisoners, but merely as the place for the night watch to meet at sundown in the evening, and at sunrise in the morning, to answer roll-call, instead of meeting at the houses of private citizens, as heretofore.

The election in 1833 resulted in Samuel W. Davies being chosen Mayor, and Jesse Justice, Marshal. Mr. Davies continued in office for ten consecutive years. He was one of the prominent figures in the early police history of Cincinnati. Those of the old citizens who remember him speak highly of his intelligence and strict integrity, both in public and private life. In his personal appearance there was nothing striking except his queue, a fashion in hair dressing affected by the elderly men of that day. He was nearly six feet in height, and his smooth shaven face always wore a severe mien. He was a Whig in politics, and an Episcopalian in religion. Public spirited or nothing, he was one of the first in a company to establish the city water works, from which grew the present extensive system of water supply. His death occurred December 22, 1843.

Jesse Justice held the office of Marshal but one term. During the last year of his official life an ordinance was passed fixing the Marshal's salary at $1,000 per annum. He was succeeded in 1835 by James Saffin, who had been identified in a subordinate way with the police force for many years. Mr. Saffin was a natural detective. He was a shoemaker by trade, but seems to have been as deft in catching a thief as he was in driving a peg. Though he held the office of City Marshal for twelve consecutive years, he laid down its responsibilities as poor as he was when he took them up. In those days the office was a "fat" one, and all that a man who wanted to get rich easily and quickly had to do was to secure an election to it. The fees were numerous and liberal. It was a common thing for a City Marshal, from Saffin's time until the office was abolished by legislative enactment, to make from $15,000 to $20,000 a year, and sometimes as high as $25,000. This was in addition to the regularly fixed salary, which, by comparison, was but a bagatelle.

In the pursuit of criminals, Mr. Saffin is described as a sleuth-hound. Few ever escaped him. In subsequent years he occupied a place as Police Court Judge, and then was promoted to the Common Pleas Bench; and whether as an expounder of law or as minister or executioner, he was always the same shrewd, honorable, and energetic man.

The amount paid the police force at this period was ridiculously small. On June 18, 1834, the City Council passed an ordinance levying one mill on the dollar for the support of the night watch. This was the first instance on record where any tax provision was made for a watch fund. Six years later the same body formally fixed a watchman's nightly compensation at one dollar. The same year the tax levy for a watch fund was made, the first idea of a police commission was conceived. It consisted in a committee selected by Council, whose power it was to both appoint and dismiss watchmen. But its life was short. The ordinance providing for it was after a few weeks rescinded.

The great pro-slavery riots which began April 11, 1836, and raged unremittingly for several days, occurred during Marshal Saffin's first term. At that time, the most bitter feeling existed against the negro in Cincinnati, and it required but a slight provocation to cause this popular feeling to find vent in mob violence. Two boys, one black and the other white, became involved in a quarrel from some trivial cause, when the white boy was bested by his companion. The cause of the former was championed by those who wanted to rid the community of the negro, and a mob soon collected. Violence began at the intersection of Broadway and Sixth streets, known as "The Swamp." The houses of many negroes were burned to the ground, and their occupants shot down like dogs. Marshal Saffin called out his watch, and made heroic efforts to put down the rioters, but without avail. Members of the force were compelled to stand and see unoffending colored men killed, without lifting a hand to save, so overwhelmed were they by the mob. Finally, the Governor of the State declared the city under martial law, and fixed his headquarters in Cincinnati. The stringent measures adopted by him soon quelled the mob, and restored law and order. On July 30, of the same year, several men clubbed together and destroyed the philanthropist newspaper, breaking up the press and throwing it into the river, and were threatening further acts of violence, when Marshal Saffin called out his watch and broke up the incipient riot. A remarkable feature connected with these pro-slavery demonstrations was the eminent respectability of the men who acted as their leaders, and it was probably owing to this fact that the subordinates of Marshal Saffin were not more radical in their efforts to restore order. They hesitated to strike at a man whose influence could easily remove from them the means of making a livelihood.

A change took place in the manner of selecting the city watch in 1840. Prior to this time, Council had had the appointment of the force, but by the change, that power was delegated to the people, each ward selecting a certain specified number of watchmen. James Ewan, Peter Early, John Redhead, Robert Cappin, Jesse B. Bawlin, Aaron G. Dodd, and John Cordeman, were selected by the first popular vote under the new law. For thirteen years thereafter, from 1840 to 1853, the city watch was thus chosen, when the mode was again changed, and when the power of appointment again fell to the lot of the City Council and to the Mayor, whose duty it was to share in the responsibility. In 1840, Ira A. Butterfield was captain of the watch, and James Wise, lieutenant. They were subordinate to the City Marshal, whose authority, at this period of Cincinnati's history was well-nigh supreme in all matters affecting the police.

Up to 1842, Cincinnati had no day police, but on May 27, of that year, Council passed an ordinance creating a day watch to consist of two suitable persons to be elected by that body. The compensation for each was fixed at $1.25 per diem.

In 1843 Henry E. Spencer succeeded Samuel W. Davies as Mayor of Cincinnati. He held the office for four consecutive terms, and won the admiration of all parties for his honesty, ability, and public spirit, He was born and reared in Cincinnati, and was a lawyer by profession. In politics he was an old line Whig, but became a Democrat in 1856. He was methodical and business-like in his habits, and by the introduction of certain reforms made the police force much more efficient than it had ever been before. His presence was commanding, his executive ability exceptional. It was during his administration that the Marshal temporarily lost his control of the city watch, and the Mayor assumed it and immediately delegated it to a captain. During Mayor Spencer's eight years there were two captains of the watch—William Small and Jacob Jacobs. When Mr. Spencer was chosen Mayor for the third time, the veteran Marshal, James Saffin, was succeeded by Ebenezer Hulse, who served but one term, when James L. Ruffin, son of the old city clerk, became Marshal, an office he filled for three successive terms. Ruffin was a good prototype for the Lecoq of Gaboriau. His scent for crime was as keen as was the scent of the dog with which Artemis fortified Procris. He was a native of Cincinnati, born December 22, 1813, and in his youth was given to those agricultural pursuits known as "sowing wild oats." The tradition has been handed down to the present generation that he was once prominently identified with a gang of young toughs who terrorized the western portion of the city, and who were known as the "Fly Market Rangers." It is possible that the training he received at this time made him better able to cope with the difficulties he was destined to surmount in his subsequent warfare on crime. Certain it is that his short experience as a clerk in the mercantile house of Nesbitt & McCullough, as a clerk on a river steamer, as an apprenticed bookbinder, or as a deputy under County Clerk William Henry Harrison, was not at all congenial to him, as was shown by his rapid change from one place to another. Early in the '40's he was chosen a constable, and, for the first time in his career, found employment that was to his liking. From serving civil processes, the change to serving those of a criminal nature was both easy and pleasing. His efficiency as a constable made him conspicuous, and finally necessary as a marshal, upon whom power over the police had again been conferred by Council. Those familiar with the old Marshal found many sterling qualities under his rough exterior. He was shrewd to a degree, and succeeded in his long career as Marshal, and subsequently as Chief of Police, in accumulating a large fortune, which he left to an estimable wife. He never had any children.

In 1849 Council recognized the increasing importance of the night watch by raising the salary of the captain to $1.75 a night; first and second lieutenants to $1.50 a night, and watchmen to $1.35.

March 29, 1850, an ordinance was passed by Council increasing the number of night watchmen by providing that six should be elected from each of the wards of the city. On April 22d, of the same year, Council passed another ordinance, providing for the appointment of a Chief of Police and six lieutenants. This ordinance does not seem to have been put in force, however, until 1853, when David T. Snelbaker became Mayor. The same ordinance provided that of the six watchmen elected in each ward, five were to be designated to serve at night, and one in the day-time. The same ordinance also provided that no watchmen or officer was to engage in any other business without special permission from the Committee on Watch in writing. This clause would seem to imply that the watchmen of the city had hitherto considered their office as of secondary importance, fulfilling its duties at odd intervals, when they had nothing else to do.

In 1851, M. P. Taylor succeeded Henry E. Spencer as Mayor. Peter Early was his first captain of the watch, succeeded by David Hoke, and he, in turn, by Chauncey Couch.

An ordinance was passed on June 25, 1851, reducing the number of lieutenants to one, with three assistants. The same ordinance provided that the Committee on Night Watch should select one watchman from each ward to act as sergeant of police, who was to be recommended by the trustees of the ward.

In 1853, Mayor Mark P. Taylor was succeeded by David T. Snelbaker, under whom the first Chief of Police, so-called, was appointed. The first man to fill this place was Jacob Kiefer, whose official life lasted but a few weeks when he was succeeded by Thomas Looken. The latter was deposed after a short term of office under rather sensational circumstances, and was succeeded by David Hoke, who had been captain of the watch under Mayor Snelbaker's immediate predecessor. About this time the salaries of lieutenants of the police, watchmen, and station house keepers were raised to $1.60 per diem.

The Bedini riots, among the most notable events in the police history of Cincinnati, occurred in December, 1853.

At that period quite a large colony of Germans, who had taken part in the rebellion of 1848, and who were known as "Forty-eighters," resided in Cincinnati, having been compelled to fly from their native land. In this country they organized a "Society of Freemen," made up of bold, determined men, whose hatreds engendered five years before still rankled in their breasts. They believed in the universal equality of man, and it was the attempt to put their doctrines on this point into practical operation that had caused their banishment to America. With them the belief was popular that they had been betrayed, and among their betrayers they thought they recognized Father Bedini, who had in some way got mixed up with their affairs in Europe. When, therefore, in 1853, as the Pope's Nuncio, he reached Cincinnati, and took up his residence with Archbishop Purcell, they were confident that his coming had something to do with the rebellion in which they were prime movers. They called an indignation meeting, the result of which was the framing of a request for the Nuncio to leave the city.

Upon the adjournment of this meeting, a crowd of the Forty-eighters, to the number of two hundred or more, started for the Archbishop's residence, where it was known Father Bedini was stopping. In the meantime Mayor Snelbaker had heard of the threatened disturbance, and had issued an order to Chief of Police Looken to take steps to prevent it. When, therefore, the "Forty-eighters" reached the intersection of Eighth and Plum streets, and had started to cross the open space in front of the City Buildings, the entire police force, which had been rendezvoused in the buildings for the purpose, sallied forth under command of Chief Looken, and advanced upon the mob. Several shots were fired and one policeman was mortally wounded, when the Chief gave his celebrated command, "Pitch in," and the police "pitched in" and clubbed the rioters right and left. The purposes for which the indignation meeting had been called, and the request for the Nuncio to depart, were for the nonce forgotten in the mad haste to escape the clubs of the "pitchers in." The mob was dispersed almost before it could catch a glimpse of the archiepiscopal residence.

Here is the account of the affair as printed in the *New York Herald* at the time:

"CINCINNATI, December 25, 1853.—Our city is the scene of terrible excitement, caused by a threatened demonstration by an organized band, calling themselves the Society of Freemen, toward Cardinal Bedini, the guest of Archbishop Purcell. Five hundred of them assembled in front of the Archbishop's residence and threatened to do personal violence to the Nuncio. The Chief of Police received an intimation of the movement, and the entire police force at the watch-house were stationed in front of the Archbishop's residence. As the Freemen approached, setting up a dismal groan, accompanied with shouting and discordant music, the police rushed on the Freemen and arrested a man. A general melee followed and many shots were fired. The rioters fled.

"MIDNIGHT.—The parties arrested last night have been held to bail for an appearance on Friday next. Fourteen people were wounded, one of whom, a policeman, died this morning. All is quiet."

As indicated in the foregoing, those who were arrested appeared for trial the following Friday, but at the popular behest were promptly dismissed. A great deal of indignation was expressed against the police, Mayor, and Chief of Police, for the rough usage the rioters had received, which it was claimed was wholly unwarranted and uncalled for. One of the rioters afterwards died from blows he had received from the clubs of the policemen. His funeral was one of the largest ever witnessed in Cincinnati. On this occasion the Society of Freemen issued flaming handbills denouncing the "brutal and tyrannical police," and calling upon the people to rise in their might and put them down.

The Forty-eighters and their partisans claimed that it was their intention to do no personal violence to Father Bedini, that they had simply determined to go to the residence of the Archbishop and express their disapproval of the Nuncio's presence in the city, by means of groans, hisses, and hooting; all this popular out-cry and expression of resentment finally resulted in the call for another indignation meeting. A Committee of One Hundred was appointed to wait upon the City Council, and request that body to compel Mayor Snelbaker to resign. This the committee did, but Council took no notice of the request. Thereupon the members of the committee held a meeting, and sent word for Mayor Snelbaker to appear before them. This he refused to do, replying that he was busy, but that he would receive any communications the committee saw fit to transmit to him. This action of the Mayor added fuel to the flames, and Judge Spooner, of the Police Bench, sprang to his feet and moved that since the Mayor had refused to comply with a polite request, he be compelled to come, and that a sufficient force be sent to bring him. Foreseeing the result of such action, Hon. Bellamy Storer, who was present, arose and poured oil upon the troubled waters by saying that they were American Sovereigns, assembled together for the performance of a public duty. That that duty was to express their disapproval of the conduct of a servant of the people, and to induce him to mend his ways. To do more than this was to violate law. Since the Mayor had not seen fit to come before them, the best thing they could do was to adjourn and go home. The meeting took this view of it, and adjourned. The popular indignation was such, however, that the Mayor was compelled to dismiss Chief of Police Looken, although the latter had done nothing but obey his orders. For years shafts of humor and ridicule were leveled at ex-Chief of Police Looken for the order he gave the police, to "pitch in" on this occasion. Popular music was composed and named "Pitch in waltz," and was thumbed on every piano and blown by every brass band of the city. The anti-Bedini prejudice spread throughout the western country, as a result of the Cincinnati demonstration, so that during the following January the Nuncio's arrival in Wheeling was the signal for another outbreak. Inflammatory hand-bills were scattered throughout that city, and only by the efforts of the coolest heads was bloodshed averted. The bitter feeling was not allayed in Cincinnati, even after Father Bedini had departed for Wheeling, for on the 15th of January the "Forty-eighters" and their coagitants assembled on a vacant lot on Elm street and marched thence, several thousand strong, through the city to the home of the Archbishop, in front of which an effigy of the Nuncio was burned. James L. Ruffin, then the Marshal, with two or three officers and Deputy-Sheriff Thomas Higdon, sought to quell the disorder when Higdon was stabbed and mortally wounded, and the Marshal knocked down and clubbed.

Another riot, famous in the police annals of Cincinnati, was that of the "Know Nothings," of April, 1855. About this period the feeling between foreign-born citizens and what was known as the "American Party," was bitter, and there were frequent clashes between them. Especially was this true in Cincinnati, where so many of the inhabitants were aliens or naturalized citizens. At the spring election of 1855 this feeling was high, and at an early hour on the morning of voting it became apparent that there would be serious trouble before the day was over.

The Eleventh Ward was a German stronghold, and in this ward the trouble began. It was started by the "Know Nothings," who were aiming to get possession of the ballot-box. The Germans resisted, and in the struggle that ensued, the foreman of Link's brewery was shot down by a member of the Know Nothing party, named William Brown. The wound was fatal; the unfortunate man died on the spot. The Know Nothing party, which in the meantime, by preconcerted signals, had assembled its partisans from all over the city, finally obtained possession of the ballot-box and destroyed it. Shortly after this had been done the police, under command of Chief of Police David Hoke, appeared on the scene, and succeeded in restoring order.

It has been claimed that this riot was really caused by professional gamblers, who had large sums of money staked on the election; that they had obtained admission to the Know Nothing Society, and gained possession of its signs and passwords; that when they saw the election was going against them gave the signal, calling the members of the Know Nothing party together, resulting in the destruction of the ballot-box in the strongest German ward of the city, and a consequent count which saved for them the money they had hazarded. The *New York Tribune*, of April 7, 1855, thus spoke of this outbreak:

"Despatch from Cincinnati—The result of to-day's election is not determined, but the Know Nothings are probably ahead. Several serious rows have taken place, the Americans having taken possession of the ballot-boxes and destroyed the tickets. The Know Nothings turned out en masse, and, taking a cannon from the Dutch and Irish, turned it upon them and fired. It is thought ten or twelve persons have been killed and many wounded.

"CINCINNATI, April 6, 1855.—There has been another riot in this city. A party of rowdies went to a German drinking-house and were handed some beer. They broke up everything in the house, knocked the proprietor senseless and assaulted his wife and children. They then left the premises, and meeting four Germans on the sidewalk, they knocked down three and fatally stabbed the fourth. The Germans have armed in self-defense. The militia are out."

Another riot of some note, occurring in ante-bellum days, was that occasioned by the attempt of Wendell Phillips, the great abolition orator, to lecture at Pike's Opera House. A pro-slavery mob gathered, and interrupted the speaker with hoots, yells, and catcalls, and finally smeared him with a shower of rotten eggs. They were charged and dispersed by the police, under command of Chief John W. Dudley.

In 1855 James J. Faran was elected Mayor, and William Craven City Marshal. Edward Hopkins was made Chief of Police. The police force at this time numbered 101.

In 1857 N. W. Thomas became Mayor and Benjamin Robinson City Marshal. Robinson was a Democrat, but slipped in through a split in the Republican party, which was in the majority in the city at the time. James L. Ruffin, who had been City Marshal, was Mayor Thomas' Chief of Police. The force had been cut down until it only numbered ninety.

In 1859 R. M. Bishop was elected Mayor and John S. Gano City Marshal. Mr. Gano was the last of the City Marshals. He is described as an exceptionably able business man and a conscientious public official. Lew Wilson was Mayor Bishop's Chief of Police.

Up to this date the police force had been an undisciplined body of men. They had no more manual training than so many constables. In fact it was not until 1863, when Colonel Lew A. Harris became Mayor, that any attempt was made at discipline. Colonel Harris, a military man himself, introduced military discipline into the force with salutary effect. Up to this period police were ununiformed, with the exception of the wearing of a badge and a blue blouse, which was cut in a style to suit the taste of each officer's tailor.

The first attempt at an organization of the police force of Cincinnati upon police principles, similar to those that prevailed in other metropolitan cities, was made in 1859, when the Legislature, March 14, passed an Act to provide for the appointment of Police Commissioners in cities of the first class having a population exceeding eighty thousand inhabitants. This Act provided, in the first section, that in such cities it should be the duty of the Mayor, Police Judge, and City Auditor to appoint from among the qualified electors four persons who were to be styled Police Commissioners, and who were to act with the Mayor, and constitute the Board of Police Commissioners. At the first meeting of the Board they were to draw lots to determine who should remain in the Board five years, four, three, and two. Vacancies in the Board were to be filled by the same authority that appointed it, and any two of the Board constituted a quorum.

The duties of the new Board of Police Commissioners were to appoint a Chief of Police, lieutenants, and as many watchmen as were needed. They were to appoint not more than two stationhouse keepers for each station, were to formulate rules and regulations for the force, and to hear and determine all complaints against any member thereof. They were to receive no pay and hold no other office under the City, County, or State.

Section 3d authorized the Council to provide for the monthly pay of the police out of the City Treasury, and Section 4th provided that the monthly certificate of the Chief to the President of the Board should be certified to the Auditor. Section 5th abolished the office of City Marshal, and imposed its duties on a Chief of Police. He was to execute all processes of the Mayor or Police Judge, designate the lieutenant who was to attend the Police Court, suppress riots, breaches of the peace, and have power to arrest fugitives from justice. His salary was to be $1,500 from the city and not less than $500 from the county. Section 6th provided for the creation and maintenance of a city prison and workhouse, and the appointment of a superintendent of the same. This bill was called the Dobmeyer Bill, and under it Charles Rule, Dr. Joseph S. Unzicker, Elbert Marsh, and William P. Hulbert were appointed Police Commissioners. N. W. Thomas was the Whig Mayor, A. J. Pruden the Democratic Judge of the Police Court, and S. McGibbon was the Democratic City Auditor. Pruden and McGibbon got together and appointed the Commissioners, as they could do under the law, two constituting a quorum. The Spring Election, April, 1859, went Whig or "Opposition," as it was called. D. P. Lowe was elected to the Police Court, R. M. Bishop was elected Mayor, and Emanuel Wassenick City Auditor. Influences were brought to bear upon W. P. Hulbert, which frightened him off from the Commission. He was told that the law creating the Commission was unconstitutional, and that if he went on and appointed the police he would be individually liable for their salaries. Being a wealthy and responsible man, he promptly resigned, and the rest of the Commissioners followed suit. Mayor Thomas, the day before Judge Pruden's time expired, brought forward the newly elected Judge Lowe and introduced him to Judge Pruden, who bowed, and at once ordered the Marshal to open Court.

Mayor Thomas went to the late Ben. Robinson, who was then Marshal, and asked, "Ben, is Judge Pruden going to appoint a new Commission?"

"Yes; you bet your life he will, if it's the last act of his life."

Sure enough Judge Pruden and the City Auditor that day appointed a new Commission,—George Hatch, five years; Charles W. West, for four years; George C. Sargeant, for three years, and Francis Beresford, for two years. The new Commissioners were to meet at the Mayor's office on the 7th, but this they found closed. Nothing daunted, they assembled around his door. Frank Beresford was elected chairman, and George Hatch secretary. They then adjourned to the Council Chamber, and adjourned to meet at the call of two members, or the president. On the 9th of April of that year, which was on Saturday, the Commissioners met in the office of the City Marshal, and Wm. S. Hudson was appointed lieutenant of police, and detailed by the new Chief for duty at the Police Court. Deputy Marshals Reagon and Lawless, John Banker, and Phineas Hudson were appointed policemen, the two former assigned to Police Court service, the two latter to take charge of prisoners at the City Prison.

Ben. Robinson was qualified as Chief of Police, and served as such in the Police Court. In the course of the day John S. Gano, claiming to be the Marshal-elect, called upon Robinson and made formal demand for the books and papers belonging to the City Marshal's office, which Robinson refused.

On Monday, the 11th, a writ of habeas corpus was served on Ben. Robinson, the new Chief of Police, to produce the body of William Reckford, committed to the City Prison, before the Superior Court. The Chief answered that he had no such person in his custody, and the writ was dismissed at the cost of the complainants. The fact was the prisoner was in the custody of the policemen who had charge of the City Prison.

Meantime the Police Court had organized, with D. P. Lowe as Judge, and John S. Gano as Marshal. On the 7th of June the new Commissioners managed to hold a meeting in the Mayor's office, but both Mayor Bishop and his clerk declined to act with them. James L. Ruffin was appointed a policeman, and then Mayor Bishop said it was time to close his office, and that he would be under the necessity of having it cleared. They left without going through the formality of an adjournment.

Early in November the District Court ruled, in reference to the right of John S. Gano to exercise the function of City Marshal, an office abolished by reason of the passage of the Police Bill. Judge Dickson sustained the bill so far as the abolishing of the office of Marshal was concerned, but declined to decide upon its constitutionality.

The Whig lawyers claimed that the new Commission was an unconstitutional one. The District Court decided that the appointment of the first Board of Commissioners, all of whom had resigned, was legal. It also held that no power had been extended to reappoint a Commission, and ruled that the appointment of the Chief of Police was legal.

There is an interesting bit of history, referred to before in these pages, which was connected with the origin of this first Police Commission. The father of the Commission idea was Judge A. J. Pruden. To him belongs the honor of having originated and drawn the bill, in the interest of honest reform and economy. One summer day in 1858 the Judge and Ben. Robinson, who was the City Marshal, were out driving. Ben. was somewhat "in his cups" and disposed to be loquacious. Slapping the Judge on the shoulder, he said,—

"Judge, I made $25,000 last year."

The person addressed dropped the reins and exclaimed—

"What, $25,000!"

"Yes, sir; made it and salted it down."

"Why, how pray?"

"Out of my office as Marshal."

"That 'll never do," said Pruden; "why that's a robbery of the tax-payers. I shall at once draw a bill to stop such a proceeding."

"Oh, for Heaven's sake," said Ben, who saw that he had gone too far, "don't do anything like that till my term expires."

Judge Pruden put on his thinking cap and began investigating. He soon found that Ben's talk was no idle boast. As Marshal, Robinson was getting constable fees for every arrest made by a police officer, while the officers or watchmen were paid by the city, he was boarding the prisoners and making a handsome profit, so that altogether he had discovered a gold mine, and didn't have to go to California to work it either. Judge Pruden conferred with Hon. J. J. Faron, ex-Mayor of the city, and the Dobmeyer Bill was the result.

At the next session of the Legislature. on the 8th of March, 1860, so much of the Act by which the Police Commission was appointed was repealed, although the office of City Marshal was abolished, and the Chief of Police appointed by Mayor Bishop remained. During his term of office the Mayor was the head of the police force. He made all the appointments, and discharged officers at will. Three of the policemen that he discharged brought suit against him for damages, and R. B. Hayes, afterwards President, was his attorney. The Mayor won.

CHAPTER III.

THE SUCCESSION OF MAYORS AND COMMISSIONERS.—R. M. BISHOP. —GEORGE HATCH.—L. A. HARRIS.—CHAS. F. WILSTACH.— JOHN F. TORRENCE.—S. S. DAVIS.—G. W. C. JOHNSTON.— R. M. MOORE.—CHARLES JACOB, JR.—WILLIAM MEANS.— THOMAS J. STEPHENS.—POLICE SUPERINTENDENTS.—ORGANIZATION OF POLICE COMMISSIONS, TOGETHER WITH THE NAMES OF ALL COMMISSIONERS.—POLICE FORCE CONVERTED INTO A BATTALION OF SOLDIERS.—INTERESTING EPISODE IN THE NOMINATION OF A MAYOR.

POLICE affairs settled down into the old tread-mill order under Mayor Bishop and his chosen chief of police, Lewis Wilson, after the little flurry of a commission had come and gone. Mr. Wilson was a good drill-master, and during his term, succeeded in giving the force such a military training that it was able at least on dress parade to exhibit a good deal of power.

Mayor Bishop was succeeded in 1861 by George Hatch, who chose for his chief of police, Col. J. W. Dudley, a thoroughly conscientious man who, because of a lack of executive ability, was inefficient as an officer. He remained in office during only a part of Mayor Hatch's administration, and was succeeded by Col. Lawrence Hazen, now the Chief of Detectives of Cincinnati. Col. Hazen very soon brought order out of chaos and restored the police force to a semblance at least of its efficiency under former administrations.

The formation of the police force into a body of infantry, to do military duty, is unique in the history of any city. The Cincinnati police force was thus formed during the administration of George Hatch as Mayor. It was during the summer of 1862, when the city was kept in a constant state of dread owing to a threatened raid from the army of the Confederate Chieftain,

John Morgan. A border city, it was thought he would make his first descent upon it. When, therefore, word reached Cincinnati that Morgan was marching upon Lexington *en route* for the metropolis of Ohio, almost as much consternation prevailed in the Queen City as is said to have filled Jerusalem when Titus sat down before it. A public meeting was held in the Fifth street market space to consider what should be done in the emergency, and Benjamin Eggleston was the principal speaker. He urged that as the police was an organized body, sworn to preserve the peace of the city, and protect the property of the citizens, it should be converted into a battalion of infantry armed and equipped as such, and sent to assist in opposing the march of Morgan's army. The suggestion was at once acted upon. Armed with muskets the patrolmen were sent to Lexington under the command of Chief of Police Dudley. During their absence an extra force was sworn in, and for the time being Mayor Hatch did double duty, acting in the capacity both of mayor and chief of police. The force was absent on military duty for about ten days. Its military experience consisted exclusively in manœuvering about Lexington, and the Blue Grass region; before the bobbies could hear a report from many guns or could shed any Confederate blood, they were recalled to resume their place on their respective beats.

In 1863, Mayor Hatch was succeeded by Col. L. A. Harris, who served two terms, and made one of the best of Cincinnati's mayors. He at once developed a splendid executive ability. Though elected as a Republican, he did not allow partisan motives to influence him in the least. James L. Ruffin, the old and experienced marshal, he at once appointed at the head of the police force which he himself individually commanded. Mayor Harris was *de jure* and *de facto* the commander-in-chief of the police force during his entire administration, and Col. Ruffin was simply his lieutenant, compelled to execute all orders without question. A great many of the rules and regulations that now govern the police force, were first introduced by Mayor Harris. He was a stickler for military drill, and thus transformed his men from a body of ordinary constables to a regiment of soldiers. He was the first to prohibit the police from taking any part in politics. A violation of this rule, no politics, or the wilful disobedience of any rule, meant immediate discharge, and once discharged a policeman could never be reinstated under Mayor Harris. No consideration, personal or political, could induce him to overlook and forgive insubordination or disobedience. To carry out his idea of reform, he found it necessary to remodel the force. To this end, whenever it was possible, he appointed as patrolmen discharged soldiers, of whom there were many in the city at the time. This was done because the soldiers were accustomed to obey, were well drilled and disciplined, and out of politics, free from the restraints of local political influence. The excellence and efficiency of the police force under Mayor Harris was largely due to this fact. So well were the reforms received by the citizens of Cincinnati that to overcome the reluctance Col. Harris felt to holding the office a second term, the City Council raised the salary of the mayor to $4,000 per annum. In addition to this he was presented with a valuable house and lot by the business men of the city. Prior to the time of Mayor Harris, the saloons were allowed to have full sway on election day, no attempts being made to close them. As a result, on days appointed for voting a great deal of drunkenness and disorder prevailed, and the policemen in consequence were given a great deal of trouble. The first election after Col. Harris became mayor was the one in which C. L. Vallandigham was a candidate for governor. With grave apprehension the people of the city looked forward to this contest at the ballot box, so heated was public sentiment and so bitter were the political animosities that then divided the two great parties of the country. It was feared that bloody collisions would occur, ending possibly in riots; Mayor Harris, however, was alive to the gravity of the situation and issued a proclamation ordering all the saloons to close their doors on election day. He also issued positive instructions to the police to arrest on the spot any saloon keeper found violating this order. This action had the desired effect. The order was generally obeyed, very few saloon keepers being arrested, and as a result Cincinnati never held a more orderly or decent election.

During Mayor Harris' first term, on July 15, 1863, an ordinance was passed authorizing the mayor to appoint four additional policemen for each ward in the city. This it was found advisable afterwards to change, and another ordinance was passed December 18, 1863, reducing the number of additional policemen to two for each ward.

Charles F. Wilstach succeeded Mayor Harris as mayor in 1867. Robert Megrue was his first chief of police. It was soon found that Mr. Megrue was not fitted for the office. Under him the police force began to retrograde, and it looked as if Col. Harris' good work was to go for naught. The political machine was again revived and used to influence elections, necessitating the early displacement of Megrue and the reappointment of James L. Ruffin. John W. Torrence was elected mayor in 1869 and continued Col. Ruffin as the chief. He served but one term, when, in 1871, S. S. Davis was chosen his successor, and David Bleeks, long a private watchman in the S. S. Davis banking house, became chief. The administration both of Mr. Davis and his lieutenant was clean and creditable.

The next commission to be intrusted with the management of the police was created by an act of the Ohio Legislature, passed during the winter of 1872 and '73, toward the close of the mayoralty term of Mr. Davis. Its purpose was taking the police from the hands of the mayor and placing the body in the care of a commission of four men, to be chosen at the spring election of 1873. The men elected at that time were Wesley Cameron, for a term of four years, Gustav Hof, for three years, Henry Kessler, for two years, and Hugh Campbell for one year. Mr. Campbell, who was elected for the shortest term, was a native Irishman, who came to America as soon as he had attained his majority. He became a contractor, naturally falling into the line of business of his father, who was a civil engineer. After about five years he came to Cincinnati. He here accumulated a large fortune, on which he has now retired to live the remainder of his days at Harrison, Ohio. He only served a short term as police commissioner, resigning to be succeeded by Gus Neather. His only other public position was that of work-house director, to which he was appointed by Mayor Johnston shortly after his resignation from the Police Board. Gustave Hof, the three-year man, was a wealthy German citizen, owner of a large part of the stock of the Volksblatt. His position as Police Commissioner gave him a taste for politics, and shortly after his term expired he sold his newspaper stock and went into the saloon business on Freeman avenue. This became unprofitable and swallowed up all his money. He held several insignificant clerkships, the last being in Auditor Brewster's office. Soon after leaving this place, he died in miserable poverty.

Henry Kessler, elected for two years, was at the time of his election President of the Eagle Insurance Company, a position which he held until his death, four or five years ago. He also carried on a large buckskin glove manufactory. His first political position was that of sheriff, to which he was elected in 1854. He was afterward sent to the State House of Representatives, and after being Police Commissioner to the State Senate. He only remained in tne Police Board during two or three meetings, a dispute arising as to the division of the appointments among the Democrats and Republicans, which caused him to resign. James L. Ruffin, ex-marshal and ex-chief of police, was appointed to fill the vacancy.

Wesley Cameron, the member for the long four-year term, was a builder, and retired at the age of seventy-four. He is a wealthy and honored citizen and has never held any public positions with the exception of this one and one other—trustee for the rebuilding of the court-house. Mayor G. W. C. Johnston was also a member of the board, ex-officio. He was in many respects one of the most surprising mayors Cincinnati ever had. Previous to his election to office he had been "one of the boys," in the sense in which that term is ordinarily used. When he came into office, in 1873, every one thought he would continue as he had been. But his accession to the dignified office of mayor was the dividing line between the old life and the new. Those of his former associates who appeared before him for recognition were as much astonished and chagrined as was Jack Falstaff when he discovered the difference between Prince Hal and King Henry.

Johnston made a splendid mayor and was triumphantly re-elected for a second term. It was during this term that he arranged what is known to history as "Johnston's jamboree"—a magnificent, perhaps the most magnificent celebration Cincinnati has ever had. It was in honor of the Centennial of American Independence. This was of course in 1876. Mayor Johnston was born, reared and died in Cincinnati, and aside from the position of mayor held one public office—trustee of the water works.

Under this Board of Police Commissioners the title of chief of police was abolished and that of superintendent of police established. This latter has been the proper designation of the head of the Cincinnati police ever since. Jeremiah Kiersted was the first man to hold it, being appointed to the office by the new board. His term as superintendent was interrupted for a month by his being removed from office, and Eugene Dayler, a man who had been a constable and also a guard at the work-house. But Kiersted was reinstated and finished his two years of service.

The Legislature of 1874 repealed the act establishing the Police Commission, and the police rule now fell under the direct supervision of the mayor. Col. Kiersted held over until February, 1875, when the mayor appointed Thomas E. Snelbaker in his place. Snelbaker had been secretary of the water works. He was a Cincinnatian by birth. He has been dead about two years. He was succeeded in the police department by Captain Jake Johnson, who was appointed upon the accession of R. M. Moore to the office of mayor in 1877 as successor to Johnson. Johnston had been a policeman for a good while, and was a fair man for the place. He had held the highest rank under the superintendent—captain of police, and had acted as chief at one time. Mayor Moore, who appointed him, had never held any public position but that of mayor, which he held but one term. He was quite an old man when elected to the office, and died soon after he left it. Under his administration, the Legislature of 1877 re-established the Board of Police Commissioners, and the following men were appointed to it by Governer Hayes, who afterwards became President Hayes: Enoch T. Carson, Charles Jacob, Jr., Charles Brown, George Ziegler, and S. F. Covington. Mr. Zeigler was the only Democratic member. After some difficulty, the Board induced Ira Wood to accept the position of chief of police. He had already been superintendent of the work-house, and in that way had obtained much knowledge which fitted him for the position. He lived but a few months after his appointment, dying early in 1878. George Ziegler, a member of the Board, was then appointed. He had been and is still a butcher, and, though he held several offices, never abandoned his stall in market. He has been both sheriff and superintendent of the work-house, and always made an excellent officer.

With the accession of Charles Jacob, Jr., to the office of mayor, Enoch T. Carson became head of the police under appointment from the board. He is now President of the Knight Templar and Masonic Mutual Aid Association. It was from the position of commissioner that he was appointed superintendent of police. He filled that position most honorably for nearly two years. Charles Brown is a prominent Mason, a wholesale grocer on Second between Vine and Walnut, and made a good commissioner. He is now on the shady side of middle life. The most prominent member of this board was Charles Jacob, Jr., a prominent German citizen, and a man who has filled many public positions with honor and even with distinction. He is a wholesale pork packer, has been a councilman, and more recently a member of the Board of Public Affairs. He was elected to the mayoralty in 1879, from the office of police commissioner. He is as fearless as a lion, and has many times distinguished himself in this way. Once during the election riots of 1877, he walked into one of the most desperate precincts of this city, where the "gang" had threatened to kill him on sight, and single-handed quelled a disturbance. His public services have been of the most valuable character.

During the term of Hon. Samuel F. Covington as Vice President of the Chamber of Commerce, Prof. Cleveland Abbe, then in charge of the Observatory at Mt. Adams, laid before the Board of Managers a suggestion that the approach of storms and of great changes in temperature could be predicted some hours in advance of their coming, and thus preparations could be made to meet their arrival. Mr. Covington and Mr. S. C. Newton, now deceased, were appointed a committee to confer with Prof. Abbe in relation to his theory and make report. A careful study of the subject convinced the committee of its practicability. A report of their views upon the subject was made to the chamber, and an appropriation of $300 was asked for the purpose of experimenting. The appropriation was made more for the purpose, it is believed, of having a good joke on the committee rather than through any faith in their recommendation. Before the appropriation was all expended, however, it was demonstrated, notwithstanding the difficulties attending experimental efforts, that a valuable service was being rendered especially to slaughterers and packers, and when a second appropriation was asked for, it was granted with a hearty good will. This was the commencement of what is now a National institution—the weather predictions by the United States Signal Service.

Mr. Covington's action in forming this nucleus of a service which has become National, was characteristic of all his actions in life, and of his short term as commissioner. He has been nothing if not radical. Never satisfied with being abreast of the times he has always striven to be a little ahead, and he has generally succeeded.

A party of friends, eight or ten in number, were assembled about a round table in the Grand Hotel, one evening, early in 1881, discussing champagne and the local political situation. Mr. William Means, whose family lived at Yellow Springs, Ohio, but whose business had made him a guest at the hotel named, was one of them. The verdict was unanimous that Mayor Jacob would secure what it was clear he wanted, viz., a renomination at the hands of the Republicans.

"Whom shall we put up against him?" asked one of the party as he raised a glass of the "sparkling" to his lips.

"Let's nominate Means," answered another; and again the champagne was quaffed.

"Why, he is not a resident of the city," suggested a third. "It wouldn't do to elect him."

"Who cares for the residence? Let's nominate Means!" exclaimed two or three others in concert; and then they all broke in with "Means! Means! Here's to Means, Cincinnati's next mayor! Hurrah for Means!" and again the glasses clinked together, more corks popped, and then the cabal joined hands, marched around the round-table singing a pæan to Means. The nomination thus made was not declined by the nominee. The next morning a communication, written in the midst of champagne glasses and champagne corks, appeared in the old *Cincinnati Gazette*, a Republican anti-Jacob organ, suggesting William Means as Democratic candidate for the mayoralty. The Democrats seized upon the suggestion, and without any special Means' organization hoisted their banner with his name on it. Disgruntled Republicans endorsed this action of the Democracy; Means was elected by a pronounced majority, and the Board of Police Commissioners was then abolished. Mr. Means never held any political office except this one. He had been prominent in financial circles, and had been a member of this Board of Exposition Commissioners. His latest business connections were most disastrous to his fortunes, and he is at present suffering from a probably fatal sickness.

Jacob Gessert was his first appointee to the office of superintendent of police, and served but a few weeks, when he resigned. He was a man of good character, but for some reason, which has never been discovered, was quite generally supposed to have suffered temporary mental aberration, as he committed suicide a few months after his resignation was accepted. Mayor Means appointed Col. M. F. Reilly to succeed him. Col. Reilly had been a sergeant in the United States army, went on the police force in 1873 as patrolman, and stood for a good while as special officer at Fifth and Vine streets. He then became lieutenant, and finally Captain. His term of office lasted until the close of Mayor Stephens' administration, and was marked by many exciting events. He filled the office with credit to himself and to Cincinnati. He is now at the head of the Merchant's Police System.

Mayor Means was succeeded by Thomas J. Stephens, a glue manufacturer, and one of the landmarks of this city. Mr. Stephens has led a respectable and useful life, full of good deeds and stainless in all respects. He has been a strong Democrat, and has borne the brunt and heat of many an unsuccessful battle. As mayor he was irreproachable, discharging his duties blamelessly. Mayor Stephens was succeeded in office by the present incumbent, Amor Smith, Jr.

The Board of Police Commissioners of 1885 was created under the act of the Legislature empowering the Board of Public Works to appoint the original members. It was the first commission to receive any compensation, the salary of each member being $1,500 per annum. Col. Morton L. Hawkins, its president, William A. Stevens, and Julius Reis were appointed; of these the first and the last named were Democrats, and Mr. Stevens a Republican. Mr. Stevens was appointed for the short term of one year; Mr. Reis for the two year term, and Col. Hawkins for the three year or long term. Colonel Edwin Hudson, who had been inspector of police under Mayor Stephens and Chief Reilly, was, shortly after the organization of this Board, made superintendent, Colonel Reilley retiring and assuming command of the patrol wagon service.

There had been strong rivalry between Hudson and Detective Chas. Wappenstein for the superintendency, but a compromise was effected by making Wappenstein chief of detectives. Jim Dunn, who had been superintendent of the patrol and detective forces was made inspector, and John Bender was made clerk of the department.

Only a few weeks elapsed before Wappenstein and Dunn were relieved from duty. Lieutenant Thos. Meara was then made inspector *pro tem.*, and Captain Grannan chief of detectives. A month later Lieutenant Mike Mullen was elected inspector. Mr. Mullen had done some excellent service as a police officer. Within two hours after Pete Dolan, and a man named Wicher, had "stood up" and robbed Morris Moses of a large sum of money, as he was making his way up town from the Covington bridge, one night in 1884, Mr. Mullen, assisted by the present superintendent of patrol, Duffy, had collared the miscreants and had secured sufficient evidence against them to send them on a seven years trip to the penitentiary. It was owing to his vigilance that the notorious "Kid" Walker got ten years for breaking into a store, and that Bill Taylor and Aaron Carter, both murderers, were convicted and sent up for long terms. To him as much as to any officer, the public owed the final abatement of the "fence" which Mike Lipman for years ran in Cincinnati, and called a pawn shop, still his appointment created dissatisfaction, and was the forerunner, if not, indeed, the direct cause, of numerous charges which were filed against the Board collectively, and the members individually. The Board had been in existence less than a year, when these charges assumed formidable proportions. The most serious was that the Board was using the police force for political ends, and in favor of the Democratic party, just then not in majority in the city. This charge undoubtedly sprung out of the appointment of Mike Mullen, who had gained some notoriety at the previous election, on the charge, that as lieutenant of police, he had abused his authority by imprisoning a number of colored men in Hammond street station house, thereby depriving them, it was alleged, of their right to vote.

At the time the charge against the Board gained such prominence, the Democratic party was largely in control of the city departments, the police force especially, under Col. Edward Hudson, the chief elected by this Board. The mayor, Amor Smith, Jr., and the governor, J. B. Foraker, were Republicans, however. As stated before, the tide of public opinion was at this time setting strongly in favor of the Republican party, owing to some alleged abuses on the part of the men in power, and it was an easy matter to still further stir up opinion, and incite it against the Democrats. The press especially, was bitter, and the object of all the denunciations was the Board of Police Commissioners. They were charged with almost every conceivable offense not directly criminal, and the title of the "Boodle Board," however unjustly gained, clung to it for some time. In this state of affairs, it was not long before the rumors and allegations that the police force was being used as a political instrument took definite shape in charges against the Board, which were filed with Governor Foraker. That official, who, under the law creating the Board, was vested with the right to dismiss any or all of the members thereof, took prompt action, and the dismissal of Col.

Hawkins, Julius Reis and William A. Stevens followed. Col. Hudson was a cool, level-headed chief, and possessed good judgment. He had been on the force for a long time, having been successively patrolman, sergeant, lieutenant, and captain. His long experience, combined with an upright and fearless character, made him an excellent superintendent. He remained in office until the appointment of the new board under the non-partisan act. Since his retirement from this office he has done some police business, having in charge the police at Coney Island.

After the old board had been ousted, Mayor Smith assumed charge of the police, and ordered Col. Hudson to report to him. This the chief refused to do, stating that he had been appointed by the Board of Police Commissioners, and proposed to retain control of the police until a new board was elected or appointed. The matter was carried to the Supreme Court, which sustained Hudson, who continued as chief. Then followed a couple of months of uncertainty. The law had provided that in the event of the resignation or removal of a member, the remaining members should appoint his successor, but made no provision for the appointment of members in the event of the removal of the entire board. Finally both parties nominated good men for the vacant positions in the Board, to be voted for at the spring election of 1886.

The Legislature, however, with a Republican House and a Democratic Senate,* passed a bill on the eve of the election, creating the non-partisan Police Board, consisting of four members, to be appointed by the governor.

Col. Morton L. Hawkins was born in Cincinnati in 1843. A few years later, his widowed mother took him with her other children to the little village of Bantam, Clermont county, Ohio, where he remained, going to school part of the time until 1860, when he returned to the city, and began as "devil" and "copy holder" in the book publishing house of Morgan, Overend & Co. Remaining nearly a year, he enlisted in Co. F. 34th Ohio Infantry, and served four years. He passed through all the grades

---

* The Senate was subsequently Republican, the four Democratic Senators from Hamilton county having been unseated.

from private to the command of his company. He was wounded in the right shoulder at Winchester, Va., September 19, 1864.

At the close of the war, Hawkins returned to Cincinnati and took a desk in the Adams Express Company. He afterward entered the Journalistic field, first on the staff of the *Evening Star*, and then to the *Enquirer*, and in a few years rose from "fire and station-house reporter" to the position of City Editor, succeeding John B. McCormack. He afterward resigned to accept the nomination for sheriff of Hamilton county, and was elected. Col. Hawkins, who gets his title from his active connection with the 1st Regiment Ohio National Guard, as its Lieutenant-colonel, was on duty at the jail the night it was attacked by the Berner mob, an account of which is found in another part of this volume. He was surrounded by a few of his deputies. Instead of sleeping at his own home, as all sheriffs are supposed to do in Hamilton county, he had cots for himself and men in the jail office. The demands made by the rioters to deliver Berner into their hands, was answered by the statement that Berner had been taken to the penitentiary. The mob angered by the sheriff's cool refusal to open the jail door, battered it down. Vain attempts were made to reason with the attacking party. A few hundred rioters finally made their way to the cells on the upper floor. With the assistance of the police, the mob were pushed down the stairs and finally into the street, without the firing of a shot. Sheriff Hawkins now sent to the Armory for assistance. After considerably delay, Captain John Desmond, with a company of militia, reached the jail, and it was not until that building was almost demolished, and its defenders as well as prisoners at the mercy of the mob, that the order to fire was given. Governor Hoadly afterward sent Sheriff Hawkins a personal letter, thanking him for his "courage and distinguished gallantry."

A year after Sheriff Hawkins' retirement from office, he was appointed President of the Board of Police Commissioners, and later assumed the managing editorship of the Cincinnati *Telegram*, a position which he now holds. He also held a responsible position in the advertising department of the Centennial Exposition. Col. Hawkins is a member of the military order of the Loyal Legion; of the Duckworth Club, the commandership of which he held for several years, and is one of the charter members of the Cincinnati Press Club. He has been married twice, his first wife being the eldest daughter of the late Philip G. Weatherby, his last the eldest daughter of Charles S. Weatherby, a prominent dry goods merchant of Cincinnati.

Julius Reis was born in Baden, Germany, in 1841. His parents were farmers of humble means. His early education was such as the schools of his native town afforded. Later he went to the High School of Heidelberg, graduating from the schools of Frankfort-on-the-Main. He entered commercial life there, in a large shipping firm that sailed ships to all parts of the world. He continued there for several years, and on the Fourth of July, 1857, amid the booming of cannon and shooting of firecrackers, and a general hurrah, he sailed into New York harbor, and gazed with astonished eyes on all the strange bustle. His first impression of the country, and it was strengthened by the glowing accounts he had read at home, was that it was a land of continual jubilee, and he set foot on land with a glad heart. From New York young Reis went to Columbus, Ga., where he remained until the outbreak of the civil war, when he removed to Cincinnati, where he has since resided. He has amassed a competence here, and is now connected with the banking firm of Seasongood, Sons & Co., Third street. Mr. Reis married a daughter of Jacob Seasongood, deceased, and is the father of six daughters, the eldest the wife of Dr. Sigmar Staub. Mr. Reis was for fifteen years a member of the Board of Aldermen, and for five years president of that body. He is an ardent Democrat, and was a delegate to the National Convention of 1880, that nominated General Hancock. He is a member of the Duckworth and of the Phœnix Clubs, a director in the Young Men's Mercantile Library Association, and a member of the Chamber of Commerce. His home is on Gilbert avenue, Walnut Hills.

Will A. Stevens was born in Aurora, Ind., August, 14, 1853. When he was six years old his parents moved to Cincinnati, in the public schools of which young Stevens acquired his early education, graduating from Chickering Institute in 1871. He immediately entered the dry-goods business, in the employ of Chamber, Stevens & Co., remaining with that firm until 1879, when the house of Weatherby, Stevens Co. was established, and in which firm Mr. Stevens is still an associate. Mr. Stevens is a Republican, and one of the life members of the Lincoln Club. At the time of his appointment to the Board of Police Commissioners, he was Vice President of the Blaine Club, but has since severed his connection with that organization. He is an Odd Fellow, and a member of Magnolia Lodge, No. 53, and also a member of the Ancient Order of United Workmen, and connected with U. S. Grant Lodge, No. 24. Though still a young man Mr. Stevens has established a reputation both as a business man and as a steadfast adherent to party principles.

CHAPTER IV.

THE RIOTS OF 1884.—THE LAX ADMINISTRATION OF LAW WHICH LED UP TO THEM.—THE KIRK MURDER.—THE MUSIC HALL MEETING.—AWFUL SCENES IN THE JAIL TUNNEL.—HEROIC ACHIEVEMENTS OF CINCINNATI POLICEMEN.—THE FLOODS OF 1883 AND 1884.—WORK OF BOAT PATROLS.

ORIGINATING with some writer whose comprehensive thought should have given greater prominence to his name, is a trite and proverbial phrase concerning the ingratitude of corporations. The genius of the press for absorbing and adapting to constantly recurring needs the good things that fall from the table of literary luxuriance, has gained for this observation world-wide circulation and credence, and, as need be, for corporation one can read municipal, state or national government; these last comprising some of the changes that have been rung upon the virgin refrain for effect's sake, and in order to secure harmony between the transient thought and its application. This simple truth, that corporations and municipalities are ungrateful, was never better exemplified than in the rapidly-shifting action of the machinery of local government during the few years that have elapsed since the memorable three-days' rioting in March, 1884, and, in so far as that action applies to the sweeping changes made in the Police Department. Men who had faced death in its most desperate and most deplorable shape; who had been sorely wounded in the discharge of a duty that brought them into direct, personal, and frequently fatal conflict with erstwhile friends and neighbors; who at heart could not but sympathize with the popular indignation against criminals and the amazing looseness of criminal jurisprudence, which looseness tended to promote those vices that rendered their retention as peace guardians necessary; men who had accomplished all this were cast aside as a garment that is soiled, their good points forgotten in order that election promises might be fulfilled. To-day the names of many of them have no more significance than may be discovered by a study of the roster of the district wherein they were assigned to duty. A few found favorable mention in the columns of the newspapers, which particularized with astonishing exactitude upon the reign of terror and fiery purification. The majority can only be honored with the distinction of being the unknown heroes in an episode which finds few parallels in history. The police force as constituted at the time of the riots was a notable result from the frequent and damaging evolution of politics. The then mayor, Thomas J. Stephens, was the appointing head. The chief, and hence the mayor's executive officer, was Colonel M. F. Reilly. Second in command was the inspector, Captain W. H. Devine, who, just prior to the riots, was displaced by Edward Hudson for political reasons and made senior lieutenant of the central district.

At control were the customary number of detectives, commissioned officers, specials and patrolmen. The chief and his assistant were men of enlarged experience in the labor and responsibility of guarding the commercial and private interests of a great city. They knew from continued observation that any one properly enthroned under the law, can make a policeman, but that nothing short of divine power can endow him with the brains necessary to the intelligent exercise of the functions of his office. Both had come up from the ranks. They had learned the lesson of obedience, and were all the better fitted to command. Having so risen, they carried with them into office an accurate estimate of capability as reflected in individual members of the force, and, in so far as was possible, filled the vacancies with veterans, men of decision, firmness and unquestioned bravery. Among the commisioned officers was more than a sprinkling of those familiar with military tactics, under whose guidance the district squads had been steadily and intelligently instructed in the manual of drill. While in such a hurly-burly conflict as the rioters of necessity imposed, there was little opportunity of presenting ocular proof of the benefits of the system, still it was of incalculable value, giving the officers confidence in their leaders and in each other, and securing ready acquiescence in an order when delivered. Had the case been contrariwise, had the men in blue been unsophisticated and raw, the result of the first night's engagement wonld have been far different. As it was they offered implicit obedience and not one, through all that trying ordeal, swerved from the plain path of duty. The evils of a system of political domination over one of the vitally important branches of a city's government had for once at least, and at a time of imminent danger produced an unforeseen element of good. It has been said that the policemen, at heart, had reason to place themselves in sympathy with the energetic expression of public opinion, and this is worth brief examination before passing to the subject in chief.

The jail was filled with criminals of almost every shade of offense, whom police activity and vigilance had placed at the ready disposal of the courts. An epidemic of crime, which had culminated in the worse than causeless murder of the stableman Kirk, by Berner and Palmer, and the burking horror in Avondale by the negro Ingalls and his accomplice Johnson had been making destroying inroads upon the peace of the community. All police efforts to prevent its further spread were ineffectual because of the law's delays. To secure an offender bed and board at the general expense seemed the end of justice, whose mandate it was policemen's aim to serve. They were discouraged and naturally so, and may be excused the forcible enunciation of ideas to which they would perhaps have lent active enforcement had they not worn the municipal garb warranting protection and the abatement of wrong. While in no sense responsible for the condition of things leading up to the outbreak, they felt the rebuke in all its keenness, being as they were an integral part of the machinery that was proving so ineffectual. Many is the bluntly-worded disquisition on the inefficiency of courts and the technical redundancy of criminal lawyers those owls of the press—the police reporters—have been regaled with, while pacing the beat with some patrolmen who mingled philosophy with duty or while seated round the long table, in the old central station, during the dull hours of the last watch after the one o'clock call. The case is plain to them from actual personal experience, and they seldom grasp the necessity of extending the benefit of doubt until the burden of proof has been properly laid.

The guilt of the miserable wretches who had ended the life of their employer Kirk, was so clearly shown as to silence controversy, the manner of committing the crime so atrocious as to render any argument in their defense a hollow mockery. The hardened indifference of the accused, caused a perceptible increase in the public resentment against them. From the moment that the fact of the murder was made known, through the gradual development of the accompanying details, the arrest of the murderers and the trial of Berner, the interest was intense and feverish. The police prosecuted the portion that fell to them with unexpected promptness, each step that they advanced, strengthening the web of testimony. The evidence as presented went to show that the murder was done for the sake of a trifling sum of money, that Berner had first entertained thought of the crime and had persuaded the mulatto to aid him, that they beat their victim into insensibility and then strangled him. Afterwards they took the limp body, put it into a wagon and driving to a point in the outskirts of the city, dumping it into a thicket with as little regard as might be displayed for a dog that has had his day. Cumminsville and Central district officers were most nearly concerned in the investigation, but the arrest was made by the veteran sergeant, Phillip Rittweger, and officer Mitchell, in whose territory the crime had been committed. The confessions were wrung from the bloodstained pair by Lieutenant Devine.

The trial of Berner, whose indictment had been separated from that of his associate, for obvious reasons to those who are acquainted with the race animosity that still holds on the turn of separation between North and South, came to an end at last. He was found guilty of murder in the second degree, and, after courteous deliberation the court sentenced him to twenty years confinement in the penitentiary. The rage of the people, which had been smoldering and gathering headway in anticipation of just such a result knew no bounds. The death sentence should have been the prisoner's portion was the general verdict, and that the jury had been corrupted was but supplementary to that inflammatory opinion. Feeling that scant respect had been shown for the law by its ministers, it need hardly be deemed beyond the bounds of possibility that those, unlearned in the law and composing the mass should rush headlong to the same extreme and themselves precipitate—with far more serious consequences—the very offense they could not condone in others—namely, wilful disregard of statutory enactment. But the immediate cause of the riot was much more innocently grounded than it could thus be made to appear. It sprang from what, to all intents and purposes, was a peace meeting, a meeting in which it was purposed to respectfully, but firmly protect against the watery consistency of the judicial system. The distinguished originators of that never-to-be-forgotten assembly had not closely scanned their Testaments, for they would there have read of a great flame that a little fire kindleth. Had they thought, it would have been plainly noted that they were standing about the open throat of a powder magazine, each with a lighted fuse in his hand in the shape of well-meant but ill-advised speeches. The Music Hall meeting on that Friday evening, the 28th of March, 1884, was, as one writer has aptly expressed it, a terrific commentary upon the prevalence and fatality of that peculiarly American disease, the "gift of gab." With all this the result of the massed protest could not have been foretold, or if a prophet had arisen he would not have been believed. Ropes that would pliantly caress and expeditiously strangle throats held within their noosed embrace were freely displayed; but with more of empty bravado on the part of the bearers than evident intention to put them to practical use. The feeling existed, and all that was needed was the confidence inspired by numbers to lead a few to raise the cry "on to the jail." This was taken up with the ready responsiveness of an echo, and the march to anarchy and death was begun. A few were determined. Many more thought it a grim joke, while the majority were simply curious; but all were violators of law. The whole movement then had the effect of a complete surprise. And the time of the authorities for preparation to resist the uprising was limited to the space that would require the crowd to march from the great temple of music on Elm street, to the jail on Sycamore and Court. The riot alarm—621—sounded at five minutes to ten o'clock, followed by the number of the jail fire-call. So nicely regulated was the disposition of the police force that the first posse anticipated the tumultuous arrival at the jail; but they were not armed, as was afterwards the case, with the long navy sixes, having only clubs and pocket weapons. It took but a few moments for an improvised battering-ram in the hands of muscular agents to break open the doors leading to the office. It was the work of an instant to demolish the netting that served the purpose of a separating medium from the stairway leading up to the cells. Then the crowd swarmed in and swept up to the galleries like a destroying wind; but massive barred doors, with well forged locks, baffled them again, and before they could recover from their discomfiture at this and their failure to find Berner, who had been removed, they were made the victims of moral suasion, and lost the advantage they had gained. Just as the last of them were being good naturedly driven into the office reinforcements arrived. The patrol wagons, which had proven to be powerful aids in the enforcement of law, began to arrive; but for once the rattle and crash of their advance, and the clang of the alarm gong had no terrors for wrong-doers. The crowd had swelled into thousands, and in so far as the final result is concerned, it is not argument to urge that the real offenders, the active working agents could easily have been counted. In such a case the man that lends the endorsement of passive presence, is just as guilty as the wielder of weapons. Patrol No. 3, of which Adam Mechley was the driver, was the first to attempt an entrance into the dense mass, but was turned back. The driver, Mechley, was afterwards disabled by a blow on the head from a boulder hurled by one of the rioters, and had to be conveyed to the hospital. A few moments later, Patrol No. 1, driven with a little more care, was permitted to reach the main entrance to the jail. The vehicle contained Colonel Reilly and a detail of ten officers, among whom were Shortall, Schuler, Thomas Duffy, Hudepohl, Nunn, Roff, and Von Seggern. Just as the wagon stopped and while the inmates were alighting, a half dozen or more shots were fired by reckless pistol carriers in the crowd, and the first blood was shed, a youth of seventeen sinking to the sidewalk with a bullet in his brain. Whether or not this initial waste of ammunition was indulged with intent to harm, or whether it was of a piece with the bravado spirit that has already been noted as characterizing the movement of the mob was never known. As for the police, against whose persons the shots were supposed to be directed, they paid not the slightest regard; but acting under the quickly uttered order of the chief, formed by twos and marching around on North Court street to Main, passed to the entrance and disappeared from the gaze of the crowd. They were wise enough to take advantage of a method of entrance, known to but few, and that was the tunnel by which prisoners are given quiet transfer from jail to court room and back again. A newspaper representative walked beside the chief, whose actions were marked by a determination and calm precision never noticeable before. The measured tramp, tramp, tramp of the stalwart men at his back, echoed and re-echoed through the deserted building, and ever and anon above it all rose a hoarse cry from the clamorous multitude without. Reaching the tunnel they found the outer door, of heavy iron, bolted against them. Through the restricted field of vision afforded by the keyhole, it could be seen that the jail was filled with men, who, at the distance, seemed struggling for life against overwhelming odds. The few minutes that ensued before Jailor John Brady gave them ingress were a veritable eternity. Everybody was given a chance to think, and not a man but made full time. Once in the tunnel the rest was easy, and in a brief period thought had given place to the liveliest kind of action. The men in the jail were inclined to be good natured, veiling real intentions—after they had been baffled—under a laughing indifference. Sheriff Hawkins placed himself on the stairs that led up to the cells, and tried his power of speech. He succeeded in convincing those nearest him that the leading object of their vengeance had been removed. Many of those who gathered the full purport of his words turned away disgusted. A few were inclined to parley; but all were forced outward, and a feeling of thankfulness that the worst was over was ringing in every breast, when a new and totally unanticipated factor for harm made its appearance.

Of the solid mass of people that glutted the square but a few could take advantage of the common entrance to gain admission. The fact, however, that a few were within, woke the spirit of desperate emulation in others and from these came the warning that the end was not yet. On the south side of the circumscribed space known as the well, stood a heavily barred iron door. The room into which this opened had been taken possession of by a motley crowd of men and boys, who had forced an entrance from the gallows yard. First was heard the crash and clatter of broken and falling glass; then a rush of hurrying feet, and faces were glued to the bars, hard and cruel enough to make an honest man blush for his kind. There was not one open manly countenance in all the array, simply a bundle of common rogues, and when they saw what they had now to face, the police smiled grimly while each one gripped his club of straight-grained maple the tighter. Leaving a sufficient number to guard the stairs to act as a reserve, the remainder ranged themselves in a semi-circle about the latest point of attack. The command was given to them to use the clubs but no pistols which was in the line of reason and common sense, because in the confined space they would have been a menace unto themselves had firearms been brought into play. For a moment those repulsive faces remained glued to the bars. Then they gave place to one of their number, a man of tremendous muscular development, who, wielded a sledgehammer with the skill of one practiced in the trade. As need be he paused in his work, and bending over scrutinized with care the progress he was making. Behind him the gang of ruffians that acknowledged his lead, maintained a portentous silence. Within the defenders circled round the point of siege, and watched this man who had the hardihood that compels admiration. There has always existed a notion, however, that he felt perfectly secure, when he should have been shot down without ceremony. All things have an end, and at the expiration of ten minutes or more the lock yielded. It was seen to be going, and those within braced themselves with a deep drawn breath. Then it fell, the door swung back upon rusty hinges with many a creak and grumble of discontent, and through it sprang the leaders, confident that they would have no more painful method of ejectment applied to them than had been directed to their fellows a few moments before. They forgot for the moment that once inside they would stand face to face with a familiar foe—and not the county's deputies whose mettle they had never tested, and hence had no fear. That gate was their Thermopylæ. The dozen or more clubs sounded a veritable tatoo for a full minute. Each one, as he received his little reminder that he was arraigned against law and order, was thrown headlong into the tunnel, where many of them remained the rest of that terrible night. It was an excellent place to indulge repentant thoughts. In the midst of the *melee*, and just as the crowd in front was becoming restive, the lights were suddenly turned out. So unexpected was the move that every hand was palsied, every voice stilled. The silence could be felt for an instant. Then arose a hoarse cry for lights. The gas was relighted, and the crowd pouring through both doors precipitated itself upon the little band of officers and sheriff's deputies. Several policemen were hit with bowlders, one with an axe thrown at him.

It was midnight when this last assault was made. Meanwhile, the sheriff had sent for the militia, who marched across from the armory, and were admitted to the tunnel, just as the last of the rioters were flying from before the determined front of police and deputies. The club had again proved its superority as a weapon of offense and defense in a rough and ready conflict; and the mob had not yet established its right to exist, which right comes of conquest. There is no room here, nor is it perhaps the place to discuss the question of the condition of the militia. Imagination had been at work with them as with hundreds of others. They formed in the long tunnel by threes, and filled it from end to end. To attempt the task of firing over the heads or across shoulders of comrades, under such conditions was like courting self destruction, and especially when an arched roof, but nine feet in height, formed a deflecting plane for the bullets of those in the rear. The order to fire was never explained, and the statement of that period, that they were first fired upon, creates a smile now, for the reason, that, entombed as they were in the tunnel, with a bullet and bomb proof door behind them, and the police in full possession of the jail in front, there was absolutely no chance to expend powder for their discomfiture. Special policeman Von Seggern, who was standing near the inside entrance witnessed the preparations, and with horror in his voice exclaimed.

"For God's sake don't shoot in here, you will hit some of your friends."

As well argue with sheep that have seen one of their flock pass through an opening in wall or fence. The order was delivered, and a crash as of cave-confined thunder followed that made the building shake to its foundations. A few of the militia men were wounded. Von Seggern sustained a wound in the cheek, and poor Phil Nunn, one of the bravest of all that brave phalanx, fell to the floor with a shot in the groin. In a few moments he passed out through the tunnel between two of his comrades, his face drawn with suffering but with no complaining word upon his lips for the ill considered haste that almost cost his life. For weeks he hovered between life and death, returned to duty looking the ghost of his former self, and then fell a victim to the epidemic of politics. A man who should have been given a pension, received not even a word of thanks for service that was priceless in support of law against anarchy.

Narrow escapes were numerous through all that trying time. Joe Thornton, then sergeant in the Hammond street district was deputized, shortly after midnight to make his way through the crowd to the private office, there secure the cell keys and return with them. He did not complete one half the journey before he was assaulted by cowardly mobsters from behind. They defeated their own ends, for had he once secured the keys or they learned the location, desperate measures would have been employed to use them to advantage before the soldiery arrived. Joe Sturm, the driver of patrol No. 2, was standing by wagon No. 5, directly in front of the jail at 2 o'clock on the morning of the 30th. The mob had just poured petroleum down the steps, the militia sprang forward to avert the devilish stratagem and delivered a shattering volley, unaware of the nearness of friends. Sturm fell dead, pierced with five balls.

All day Saturday—the 30th—the police force bore their full measure of anxiety and responsibility. Heavy details waited in Central, Hammond, and Bremen street districts, convenient for concentration upon any given point. Others were with the troops behind the barricades. These were in charge of Lieutenants Devine and Welsh. All sorts of rumors were afloat, one of which was that forty kegs of powder had been concealed in a stable on South Court street, with which it was intended to blow up the jail as soon as night had arrived. Welsh, with a detail of officers soon established the fallacy of this. With the descent of night the hundreds emerged from homes and hiding places and sought the jail and court house. The barricades looked sullen and uninviting, and only the more venturesome of the crowd braved a near approach. All day the crowd had been dense about the County building; but it was composed in the main of sight-seers, who possessed no interest other than curiosity. A few looked loweringly upon the fast hastening preparations for protection being taken by the authorities, but held their thoughts within reasonable bound. The socialists tried a pronunciamento in the shape of an inflammatory circular. It raised not a ripple, and the police and military against whom it was intended to operate, laughed at its raving, rabid impotency. The decent element of the population retired with evening, leaving the field to a still more heterogeneous assembly than that which forced the jail on the preceding night. The preliminary act was to hurl rocks through the front of the court house. Not being molested in this diversion the crowd acquired courage sufficient to enter the offices on the ground floor, beginning with that of the Treasurer. They piled the furniture up, applied the torch, and so worked their way from room to room until the great structure was a mass of flames. The firemen were not allowed to work. If the rioters debouched on to either North or South Court street they were fired upon by the militia. With this exception they followed the bent of their own lawless inclination until the arrival of the Fourteenth Regiment from Columbus, when, under a storm of leaden hail, and before a line of gleaming bayonets they learned the lesson of obedience by compulsion. This relieved the police who were thereafter assigned to outside duty. But they had slight chance to rest, for the lawless element was liable to reveal itself in a new destructive capacity at any moment and in an unforseen direction. The point of most serious danger was the gun stores, one or two which were ransacked for loose ammunition. At Powell's such ammunition was found, but propelled with such liberality from a prepared battery, manned by the proprietor and his clerks that those who received its benefits did not wait to examine into its merits. This was at nine o'clock on Saturday night.

Three hours later word reached the Hammond street station that a squad of rioters had taken two cannon with caissons in Power Hall of the Exposition buildings, and were on their way to the Main street gun stores. Lieutenant John Burke, then in charge, sent one of the patrolmen out, who returned shortly with news that the noise of their advance could be plainly noted. With a "fall in men" and buckling on his revolver as he went the lieutenant sallied forth. By the time he and his men reached Fourth and Main streets, the noisy rabble of possibly thirty men and boys had advanced up the latter thoroughfore nearly to the stores. Slipping quietly along in the shadow of the buildings the police posse made its way and suddenly pounced upon crowd and guns. A volley from the heavy revolvers and the lawbreakers were specks in the darkness. A few were captured, nearly all of whom were found to have come from across the river.

It was earlier in the evening that Devine, and detective Williams had a narrow margin for life at the court house. They had been ordered, with Captain John J. Desmond and Sergeant Malone, to pass through with a small detachment of militia and save, if possible, the Treasurer's office which had then just been invaded. Desmond was killed, shot down at the side of the police lieutenant, and Malone was wounded. Sunday was a day of feverish unrest. There were threats that Music Hall would be destroyed, the newspaper offices, the public library and Hunt's hotel. Music Hall was approached; but the soldiers disposed of the handful of turbulent citizens, who were after the

Power Hall cannon, before Lieutenant Austin of Bremen street station could bring his forces to bear. The same crowd, which was warned in time and so escaped the clutches of the soldiery, moved down Central avenue, and the next news to reach the chief operator at police headquarters was in effect that they were gutting the numerous pawn shops. The real rioting had ended, the thieving was now to begin. Private watchman McCaffery, whose life nearly had been passed in the district, delivered the timely warning. With a detail of forty policemen, Lieutenants Devine and Langdon, double quicked to the scene and dispersed the band, which was composed of petty thieves. Many were arrested. One who had possessed himself of an Enfield rifle discharged it at Langdon and Devine at a distance of less than ten paces, missing them both. Then he turned and ran as if for life, but was neatly apprehended by officer John Altevers, since deceased, and held to answer. Thus during that notable three days the police force of Cincinnati was put to such a test as few are called upon to pass through, and it won a lasting reputation for undying courage, patience, and ready obedience. Old things have passed away; all things have become new. The men of that period no more, except in widely separated examples, wear the blue of the regulars, but it is pleasant to note that under their old commander many of them find place and welcome on the merchant's force.

Rarely was the efficiency of a police department more thoroughly tested than was that of Cincinnati, during the terrible floods of 1883 and 1884, strangely occuring each year in February. No American city of its size has ever suffered from inundations as has the metropolis of the Buckeye State. The overflows of the Ohio river in the years described were especially damaging. The high water records of the past were completely submerged. The busiest parts of the wholesale portion of the city were shut off from active operations in both years and incalculable injury therefrom done to both trade and buildings. The immense stretch of waters from whose tossing waves arose the peaks and roofs of houses and of factories, steeples of churches, and the towering structures of huge establishments looked like a city lost to the world. The extent of the encroachment of the torrents was fully one third of the city. The southern portion of Cincinnati, called "the bottoms," is mostly occupied by mercantile houses, but in the southwestern, western, and northwestern, factories and places of residence prevail. It can therefore readily be understood that the field of operations for the lynx-eyed protectors of the law was wide. M. F. Reilly was at the head of the force both years, and to his executive ability was due the success of the brave and hardy men under him. He was blessed in having most competent aids to carry out his instructions, and the force itself was in excellent condition. Who can tell of all the sufferings relieved, of the assistance rendered, and of the hardships endured by that heroic band? Subject to the frightful changes of temperature that marked the periods of both floods, and repeatedly drenched to the skin while performing their mission of duty and mercy, no words of praise can overdo the matter in the attempt to express the extent of their services to the afflicted city and her citizens. During 1883, the boats with which the police were able to maintain their vigilant watch against crime and accident, were not as worthy as they should have been considering their important usage. Many a brave officer can trace his chronic rheumatism or some other permanent physical disability to the exposure to which he was subjected in those boats. Many of their courageous acts at that time were not heralded through the public press. Scores of people whose names were never reported, were saved from watery graves by the timely appearance of the blue-coated representatives of justice. In the night and during the day, they floated through the floods, up alleys and down the streets, carrying joy to imprisoned families or preventing the daring thief from executing his criminal designs. The police stations were repeatedly filled with poor families rescued from their homes, driven to retreat by the rising waters. Especially was this true in 1884, when the Ohio, just as all danger was supposed to be passed, suddenly changed, and, aided by a continuous fall of rain, unprecedented in the history of the valley, swelled so rapidly that many unfortunates had to be rescued by the over-worked police and aiding boatmen. They were found standing on beds and tables to keep out of the reach of the liquid enemy. So swift was the upward tendency of the river, that Chief Reilly was compelled to draft into use all the serviceable boats he could find. Many poor families, driven from their homes by the invading water, themselves sought refuge at the police stations, being moneyless and in most cases without protecting friends. In nearly every instance, so hasty had been their retreat that they had left everything to the destroying element, and were indeed in a pitiful condition. The bare floors of the cell rooms were all that the police, whose sympathies went out to the fugitives, had to offer, but even such accommodations were better than the streets, for they were warm and dry. If they could do naught else to relieve the suffering of the thinly-clad refugees, the station house keepers could keep the fire blazing, and this they did with a hearty good will. The daily papers teemed with such deeds of heroism, as "a family named Fisher consisting of a mother and five children was taken from the second story of West Front street, in a skiff by officer Duffy," and " officer Knox patrolled his beat in a skiff yesterday going from house to house, lending assistance to people moving out." In addition to the refuge which the station houses furnished, the school houses were closed for school purposes and thrown open to the homeless. At one time during the distress, they sheltered more than 5000 people, all of whom were fed at the expense of the city, and by charity which poured in from every section of the country. Thousands more were fed from the same bountiful source in their homes where the floods made them close prisoners, and where the boat-patroling officers found them. At noon on Tuesday, February 13, 1883, the flood of 1847 was passed, and at eleven o'clock in the evening of the same day, the supposed unapproachable deluge mark of 1832, was covered with 66 feet in the channel. At four o'clock on the morning of Thursday, February 15, 1883, the flood reached the tremendous depth of 66 feet and four inches, and was at a stand.

As with every such calamity, the city was filled with gangs of thieves and pirates ready to take advantage of the general distress—villians who would rob and plunder the suffering people, and steal goods from the sidewalks of the hapless merchants whose cellars and store rooms had been filled with water—they would in the darkness of the night garrote peaceful citizens on their way home, and burglarize the residence of those whom the violence of the waters placed at their mercy; the presence of these buzzards had been foreseen by the authorities, and Mayor Means on the evening of the 13th, ordered out the First Regiment, 400 strong, to aid the police in patroling the semi-drowned city. This seemed particularly necessary since the gas works had been partially submerged. Thus as the gas lamp sentries went off duty the home guard came on. Mayor Means and Chief Reilly were sleepless in their work, and were busy every night until early in the morning, issuing orders to the various stations in regard to the placing of patrolmen, the distribution of aid, and the caring for people who were homeless. Lanterns were distributed among the men and the strictest injunctions issued to arrest all suspicious characters. The officers at the station houses, especially at the Third street, Hammond street, Fulton, and Cumminsville, were kept busy caring for the poor that thronged those places of refuge. All available space was given up to them. The scenes thus presented were interesting and often sorrowful in the extreme. There were men, women, and children, white and colored, and of all ages, huddled together on the floor and benches. A majority were poorly clad, and with no clothing or blankets except what they had been able to snatch from their homes in the hurry of their departure. As soon as better accommodations could be secured, they were each day removed.

There were many romantic incidents connected with the police work, on the third day of the flood. Officers Conroy and Conroy discovered an old lady, who was confined to her bed. The water had already reached the floor of the room, and her joy, when she saw the two officers entering, can better be imagined than described. The people in the tenement building where she lived, had been caring for her, but in taking their hasty departure seemed to have forgotten her. Just across the river is Newport. On the morning of February 11, 1883, Joseph Hilton, a patrolman lost his only child. His home was completely surrounded by water, and the first floor of it was covered. There was little time to notify friends and less to wait the accustomed time for a funeral, as the floods were slowly but surely creeping up to the chamber of death. Two o'clock on the day of the death, was the hour appointed for a burial service, which was necessarily simple, for no minister could be found. A few only gathered in boats entered the house through the second story windows, and an hour later left in a train of boats which down one street and up another followed all that was left of Hilton's darling, which was also borne over the water in a skiff. The aquatic funeral procession broke up at the Covington and Newport bridge, where a hearse received the remains.

When the flood of 1883 was at the worst, the cellars on Wilstach street were partially filled with water, much of which was poisoned by the contents of sewers, the mouths of which were not far off. One of these cellars, at No. 50, was covered by a three story brick house, occupied by three or four families. On the second floor lived Special Officer Ben Macke, one of the handsomest policemen in Cincinnati, with his wife and one child. On the morning of February 15, two boys named Brown, sons of the owner of the premises, went into the cellar to discover what progress the water was making on its way up to the first floor. They carried a candle with them; no sooner had they scratched a match for the purpose of lighting the candle, than there was a frightful explosion. The house was literally lifted from the foundation, the boys were blown into the street unconscious, and then the walls went tumbling into the cellar and on the sidewalk. Three hours later the lifeless and mangled remains of the officer and his family were dug from the *debris*.

While at J. V. Nicolas' cement and lime establishment on the lower side of Water street, near the Suspension bridge, a fire was started by the rising flood creeping in among the lime, another contradiction equally unique was in a threatened water famine. The most careful economy was enjoined. Incongruous as it may appear, had an extensive fire broken out in the heart of the city, at this time a water famine would have been inevitable. Indeed, a year later, on the morning of February 13, 1884, the papers printed the following ominous paragraph:

"Superintendent Moore, of the water works is now of the opinion that the water supply will not last longer than six days. It was thought several days ago that the supply in the Eden Park reservoir would last ten days, but since the pumping has ceased the supply can now be more intelligently measured. Should the river come to a stand-still at this time, and the water recede as slowly as it arose, which, in all probability will be the case, the pumping at the works can not be resumed for ten days." The river was 69 feet 2 inches that morning and still rising. With water, water everywhere, there was a likelihood of there not being, when it was most needed, one drop to drink.

On the third day of the 1883 flood, the station houses on Third street, and stores were abandoned on account of the presence of the water in them.

With the bitter and thrilling experience of 1883 before them, the police were in much better shape for the terrible flood of 1884, which was far more disastrous than was its predecessor. Chief Reilly was alive to the situation, and determined to do more effective work, and he did it. The police were vigilant, and the strictest watch was maintained over the devastated district. Much valuable property was thus saved. Families that remained in the upper portion of buildings in the deluged parts were kept supplied with provisions by the activity of the police. Thieves found very little opportunity to ply their nefarious trade, so numerous were the swiftly moving police-boats. There was no chronicler of their kindness and noble deeds, but the people remembered them. It was a singular circumstance that the maximum depth of water in 1884, was reached just one year to a day from the maximum depth in 1883. It was on the morning of February 15, 1884, that water in the channel measured 71 feet and three fourths of an inch, and was at a stand. As if it had been determined from the start, that the losses and fatal accidents in the second flood, should exceed in magnitude those of the first, just as the volume of water of the second exceeded that of the first, just one year from the terrible Macke explosion, the cause of which could be directly traced to the influence of the flood, the walls of a tenement house standing on the corner of Pearl and Ludlow streets, weakened by the surging waters, gave way and fell. The next day ten human bodies were recovered from the ruins, all dead. As in the first flood, the city was in darkness, and as a consequence the assistance of the First Regiment was again required. It was necessary that the police should be reinforced, and so the mayor made the call.

The losses incident to these inundations, particularly those of 1884, can only be guessed at. The total will never be known. In the little City of Newport opposite to Cincinnati, more than two thousand houses were under water. This number was more than trebled in Cincinnati. The loss of cattle pens, and drowning of hundreds of head of cattle in the Mill Creek bottoms, were but incidents in the thousands of heavy losses. The utter stagnation of business during the time all railroad traffic was suspended, and the far-reaching influence of that stagnation, the loss of orders, destruction of machinery, the countless number of unfulfilled contracts, all went to swell the general aggregate until it could be represented only in the tens of millions column.

CHAPTER V.

THE HEAD OF THE POLICE.—INTERESTING CAREER OF MAYOR AMOR SMITH, JR.—HIS BOYHOOD IN CINCINNATI.—HIS SUCCESS IN BUSINESS AND IN POLITICS.—RARE EXECUTIVE ABILITY COMBINED WITH A LOVE FOR HARD WORK.—HIS SERVICES AS REVENUE COLLECTOR, AND AS CINCINNATI'S CHIEF EXECUTIVE.—HIS CABINET.—MAYOR MOSBY.

A man of forty-eight, in whose dark brown, almost black glossy hair and beard, carefully, but not closely trimmed, are only a few gray threads to testify against a fresh complexion that argues a dozen fewer years; a stature of five feet eleven inches, over which 175 pounds are compactly but nowhere prominently distributed; a pair of cordial grey eyes that always welcome a caller and yet somehow suggest that their owner would never hesitate to say "no" when necessary; a frank, open countenance, prominent in which is a nose of the kind classed by some physiognomists as "the American," and by others as "the business" nose; a figure that is erect, but more fitly described as alert than as soldierly; a general air of being thoroughly yet quietly wide awake, and which somehow gives the impression that the man would obey orders unflinchingly or enforce swift and utter obedience to his own commands, that is Amor Smith, Jr., Mayor of Cincinnati for his second term, and the head of the city's police department. Mr. Smith owes his office less to his knowledge and practice of political arts than to the confidence of the people in his fitness for the executive chair of the municipality. Coming to the mayorality at a time when municipal affairs were at the traditional sixes and sevens—and in some departments confusion, was the least of the shortcomings—he has so managed that Cincinnati is fast being recognized as a model municipality. It is true that this is largely due to the pressure of a long outraged, and finally

AMOR SMITH, JR.
Ex-Mayor of Cincinnati.

aroused community, it is none the less creditable to Mayor Smith, that much of the improvement is the direct result of his common sense methods and straightforward execution of his duties. It requires rare executive ability to secure a second term as mayor of a city of more than 300,000 thinking, criticizing, often fault-finding people, and if Amor Smith, Jr., is any thing he is an executive. Long and arduous business training have well developed a trait in which he naturally excels most men. Without that finish of a full course in college, which is supposed to veneer its recipient with "polish," Mr. Smith is a man of culture. Blessed with a fine physique, which he has cared for by temperate habits, and the cultivation of an even temper, he finds himself in the prime of life, able to smile easily and affably. No official is more easy of access, but whether his visitors are rich or poor, whatever their object may be, they are received with the same courtesy, and their business is attended to with the same thoroughness—and, it may be added, with the same celerity. He has great capacity for hard work, and he can be relied on to find the best and quickest way to do a difficult thing. Few people could tell after meeting him, whether he wore a stand-up or a lay-down collar, but all would be sure he was well dressed. Nobody would be afraid to ask him for a favor, but it would be an exceptional man who would care to hear him say "no" a second time.

Amor Smith, Jr., was born at Dayton Ohio, October 22, 1840. His father, Amor Smith, who still lives and is at the head of two prosperous firms, consisting of Amor Smith, Leander and Amor Smith, Jr., came from Delaware in 1819. His mother, Sarah Spencer, was born at Hull, England, and some members of the family still keep up acquaintance with their English relatives. When he was seven years old the Smiths moved to Cincinnati, and the future mayor acquired his education in the public schools, and was clannish and pugilistic as became a hearty school-boy of forty years ago. The family lived in what was then the East end; it took stout nerves or fleet legs to maintain individual integrity or a whole suit of clothes in the frequently forays, by the different juvenile bands of that day. "Each boy had to fight his way," the mayor has said in recalling school-day reminiscences.

At the age of seventeen, young Amor entered the Swedenborgian university at Urbana, Ohio, but left before completing the full course, to enter business with his father, who was a candle manufacturer. In 1865 he became a partner in the house of Amor Smith & Co., manufacturers of fertilizers, located at Cincinnati, with a branch house at Baltimore, where it is known as Amor Smith & Sons. In 1863 he married Mary Jane, daughter of Henry Kestler, who died at Baltimore, in 1873, Mr. Smith having removed to that place for a short time.

In politics Mr. Smith has always been a Republican of the stalwart kind. He was chosen to the first Board of Aldermen, elected in Cincinnati, and was the youngest member of the chamber. Always an active partisan, Mr. Smith's ability as an organizer was recognised in 1875, by election to the chairmanship of the County Executive Committee, and that year he carried Hamilton county for the whole Republican ticket, in face of the tidal wave of Democracy which had swept over Ohio the year before. Next year he helped carry the county for Hayes for President. Shortly after, he was very active in assisting to carry the county for the first loan voted to build the Cincinnati Southern road, the greatest railroad enterprise ever projected by a single city. In 1878 he was appointed by President Hayes Collector of the First Internal Revenue District of Ohio, which handled larger collections than any other district in the country, amounting to $12,000,000 per annum, or $44,000,000 during his administration of three and one-half years. He received a formal letter of thanks from Commissioner Raum for the splendid administration of his great trust. He was succeeded in 1881 by W. H. Taft, now judge of the Superior Court.

Relieved of his official duties, Mr. Smith resumed active participation in the business of his father's two firms, of which he still remains a member. But in 1882 he was nominated by the Republicans of the Second Ohio District for Congress. That was the year in which the Sunday law and the Pond law had been enacted by a Republican legislature. This had caused many Germans to repudiate the Republican party. The "Liberals," in the matter of Sunday observance, and saloon taxation became very strong, and, casting their votes with the Democracy, Mr. Smith was defeated at the polls by Isaac M. Jordan. Beyond attending to his regular business, and taking active interest in the conduct of each campaign as it came along, Mr. Smith was not in public life for the next two and a half years. But in 1885, he was nominated by the Republicans for mayor of Cincinnati, and elected in April, by a majority of more than 4,000 over George Gerke. As mayor he became Chairman of the Advisory Committee on Specifications, an adjunct to the Board of Public Works, in the matter of expending $4,000,000 in improving the streets of Cincinnati. When the Board of Public Works was superseded by the present Board of Public Affairs, the Advisory Committee ceased to exist. Yet its work was practically done, and it may be remarked that it had been well done, as the streets of the city bear eloquent testimony to-day to the care and and thoughtfulness with which this Committee, serving wholly without pay, performed its honorable duties.

In the spring of 1886, occurred one of these crises which come to every large city now and then, and of which American cities have not yet seen the last one. Labor troubles broke out in Cincinnati, as they did at St. Louis, at Chicago, at Milwaukee and elsewhere. That the scenes of East St. Louis, of the Chicago Hay-market and the Milwaukee brewery troubles, were not duplicated at Cincinnati, is due partly to the greater intelligence and conservatism of Cincinnati workmen, but no less praise is due to the cool head, the wise forethought, and the indomitable will of Cincinnati's mayor. Just two years and a month before the city had marvelled at the phenomenon of a mob in her streets, the memory of which had been made perpetual by the loss of more than a million dollars to the tax payers, with consequent incalculable damages, which are not measured by dollars and cents. Coming so soon after the riot of 1884, with the report of the anarchist bombs at Chicago in their ears, conservative citizens may well be pardoned, for fearing that Cincinnati might furnish a companion picture to the scenes in the Hay-market. Fortunately there was nothing of the kind.

The first symptom of possible trouble arose one day early in

May. The freight handlers of the Cincinnati, Hamilton and Dayton railroad, had struck for increased wages. In a body of 300 or more, they marched from the western to the eastern part of the city, intending to force the freight handlers of the Little Miami railroad to quit work also. The authorities were informed of the movement, which was open and above board, and Col. Moore, then chief of police, was ordered to take a sufficient force and prevent any interference with the men at work. A cordon of police intercepted the strikers, who were ordered to halt. Three of the leaders, who refused to stop and endeavored to break through the lines, were arrested, whereupon the main body, like sensible and law-abiding American citizens, countermarched away from the scene. The police acted with moderation, but with firmness; the strikers with discretion. This was the nearest approach to an actual conflict, yet the whole affair would not have attracted more than passing attention at another time, so quietly was it attended to.

But, in spite of the quiet, it was felt that the situation was worthy of the gravest consideration. The workingmen of Cincinnati, are and always have been, free from any appreciable taint of Anarchism or Communistic tendencies. Left to their own consideration, there was little doubt that the labor troubles would have found a peaceable, if not a speedy solution. The streets were as full of working people—largely in holiday dress and sightseeing—as the factories were empty. Thirty thousand men were "on strike." But there is always danger from malcontents at such times; always enough tow to catch from a malicious brand. The Governor was called on for troops, not to put down a mob, not to quell a riot, but as a preventitive. That "an ounce of prevention is worth a pound of cure" was readily conceded—with a glance at the now re-building court house. Five regiments of militia were sent here, and Adjutant General Axline was ordered to place the entire division at the command of Mayor Smith. Three regiments were encamped for several days at Carthage or at Burnet Wards, while the First Regiment—from Cincinnati—was put in barracks at Industrial Hall, a part of the great exposition buildings.

This action of the mayor was denounced by the more turbulent element of the strikers in their meetings, as intimidation, and as a wanton waste of money. The mayor then called a meeting, through the press, of all representatives of the various labor organizations engaged in the strikes, to meet at his office, for conference. It was duly held, the mayor in the chair, and James M. Morley of the strikers, acting as secretary. The situation was amicably and fully discussed. The mayor took the ground, that as between the strikers and their employers, the differences were matters to be settled between themselves, but that as to the interference of one man with another, which should take the shape of a breach of the peace, that was a matter in which it became the duty of the authorities to interpose in the interest of law and order. That the mayor promised emphatically should be done. There was no mistaking the firmness of his intention. After a full interchange of views the meeting adjourned, and the fact that no occasion offered to test the disposition and the power of the mayor to keep his word in this respect, proved the wisdom of his action in calling the meeting.

In the outset of the strikes, the men laying the new streets had been driven from work by the strikers. The contractors at work on the very extensive improvements then in progress called upon the mayor for protection, saying frankly that they should hold the city responsible for heavy damages if their work was stopped. The mayor issued a proclamation assuring protection to all who should resume work. Immediately following this he was visited by two men, who said they were delegates from a meeting of strikers, and protested against his action in promising protection to these street improvers, whom they characterized as "foreigners" because some, as claimed, came from Louisville and other cities, and held places which should have been given to citizens of Cincinnati, closing by assuring the mayor that if his course was persisted in "bloodshed would follow." Mr. Smith heard them patiently, combatted their assumption that the workers on the street contract were "foreigners," even if they did come from other cities, and closed by answering their threat as to bloodshed, with the stalwart declaration: "If you start it I'm prepared to end it, and I'll do it, too, and support my proclamation!" The delegation retired, and it is presumed that cooler counsels prevailed, for not a drop of blood was spilt, though the street-laying went calmly on. The mayor, to use the trite phrase of military historians, "preserved an armed neutrality" between the strikers on the one hand and the employers on the other, with the result that he had the happiness of preserving perfect order, and, in the end, the hearty thanks of both sides.

In March, 1886, the bill creating the non-partisan police force for Cincinnati passed the Legislature. Under it the mayor is the executive head of the police department. He also makes all appointments to the force, nominating to the Board of Commissioners, which has the right of confirmation or rejection. The design was to take the department quite out of the influence of politics, which, more than anything else, had contributed to its demoralization in many respects. It was determined to insist upon rigid physical requirements, and to this end, a Board of Examiners was appointed. Then came the selection of men. There were thousands of applications, every one of whom had more or less grounds on which to base a claim for nomination. All of these had to pass through the hands of the mayor, who soon found what a Herculean task had been imposed upon him. But a great capacity for hard work stood him in good stead, and this task, together with all the other details necessarily accompanying the organization of a great police force almost *de novo*, was finally accomplished, with such fortunate results that the board has never had cause to complain of the mayor's appointments.

On taking office, Mr. Smith appointed Col. Arthur G. Moore chief of police, who held the place only a short time, and until his selection to the office of superintendent of the water works. His successor was Col. Philip Deitsch, the present incumbent.

One of the greatest tasks which has occupied Mayor Smith, since his accession to office, and one in which a very great service was rendered the tax payers, was in the year 1886, when as chairman of the Board of Revision, the rottenness in the City Infirmary was brought to light, and the guilty parties prosecuted.

All the steps necessary to these ends were ordered by the Board of Revision, which found a great task upon its hands. As a result of the investigation ordered by them, according to the report made by an expert accountant, thirty-six indictments were found, and $50,000 were saved to the tax payers of Cincinnati.

It was through the energy and push of the same officer, that the difficult task of redistricting Cincinnati from twenty-five to thirty wards was finally accomplished.

For some years there have been complaints about the water supply of Cincinnati, the more annoying because of the confessedly great difficulties in the way of remedying the matter. In the winter of 1887-8, the Legislature passed an act providing for the consideration of this subject, under which the governor appointed as a Board of Commissioners, Mayor Smith, Dr. T. W. Graydon and W. P. Anderson, the first being chosen president of the board. The question for consideration involved not only the expenditure of several millions of dollars, but the health of the citizens, and the protection of their property from fire. The recommendations of the board called for the most thorough investigation, and the most careful weighing of widely divergent views from sources equally eminent and trustworthy. The board secured the services of five of the best expert hydraulic engineers in the country, who made a thorough examination in the premises and prepared a preliminary report for the Legislature. That report, however, was not acted upon. The Chamber of Commerce and Board of Trade, sent committees to confer with the Senate Committee, which had the matter in charge, with the result, that, as all agreed a new source of water supply should be had, it was deemed advisable that the Commission should continue its investigation during the rest of the year 1888, which is being done, with the view of reporting more fully to the Legislature by January 1, 1889.

At the same session of the Legislature, was enacted what is known as the "Owen law," which provides a punishment for the keeping open of saloons on Sunday. This was passed in April. It was bitterly but unavailingly opposed by the saloon keepers, who immediately set about finding a way to circumvent it. An exciting time was anticipated. It was known that many citizens, not saloon keepers, were opposed to the law. The action of the mayor was awaited with great interest. That officer pondered on Davy Crockett's maxim: "Be sure you're right; then go ahead." He notified the saloon keepers that he should enforce the law. They protested, but without avail. A day was set—as soon after the passage of the law as was practicable—on which the saloons must be closed. The chief of police was ordered to instruct his men to carefully note all offenders, and to arrest them on Monday, on warrants sworn out. All of them were so arrested. Seven arrests were also made Sunday, "on sight," because of disorderly conduct connected with the opening of their saloons. This course was strictly followed for seven Sundays, until more than 1950 arrests in all had been made. The trial of the offenders was pushed in the Police Court. By ordinance defendants there have the right to trial by jury, which was, by advice of their counsel, strictly insisted on. The first case tried was that of Henry Munzebrock, who had been arrested on Sunday, because of disorderly conduct connected with the keeping open of his saloon. After a long trial he was found guilty, and sent to the work-house, from which he was almost immediately released on a writ of *habeas corpus* and brought before Judge Robertson, of the Common Pleas Court, and the case renewed upon its legal aspects. The result was that Judge Robertson released him, because it was shown that Munzebrock had been arrested without a warrant having been sworn out as was contemplated by the law. Twelve other offenders against the Sunday law were also tried, all of whom demanded juries, with the result that the juries all disagreed. These thirteen cases were regarded as being that of the most flagrant violations of the law. Then the public prosecutor in the police court, refused to put the city to the expense of further prosecutions, saying it was useless to expect convictions under existing circumstances. Meantime, under direction of the mayor, the police had kept steadily on with the work of making arrests, until, as stated, more than 1950 had been made. Of these 758 cases had been docketed and 745 still remained before the court. But with this action on the part of the prosecutor, further efforts by the police department were useless, and the making of arrests were suspended for the time being. The result is that the question of Sunday observance in Cincinnati, remains in the same condition that it was in before the passage of the Owen law, though the mayor has done all in his power to enforce it—the same failure to enforce the closing of saloons, having followed the enactment of the Smith and Stubbs Sunday laws (still unrepealed) of a few years ago. Throughout the period between the passage of the law and the suspension of arrests, the conduct of the mayor was marked by dignity and cool judgment. A demagogue would have done less, a hypocrite would have done more. Mayor Smith's course was that of the sworn executive, acting without fear or favor.

Mayor Smith is a 32° Mason of the Scottish rite, a member of the A. O. U. W., and belongs to the order of Cincinnatus. His mother was a Swedenborgian, and he was baptized in that church. Though always too busy to mingle much in society, he is very companionable, a good story teller when it comes to "point a moral or adorn a tale," and fond of a few choice, rather, than of many indiscriminately chosen friends. That region of the head assigned by the phrenologists to the social faculties is well developed, hence he is fond of home, of family and of country. At the breaking out of the war, he was prostrated with the only serious ailment of his life, rheumatism of the heart, which prevented him entering the army, though he took as active part as a young man could, in raising funds for the soldiers, and in the management of the many Sanitary Fairs held in Cincinnati, matters of a kind in which he always took delight.

By his first wife he had three children, two sons, Kessler and Alvin, each standing six feet four inches, and one daughter, Leonora, aged seventeen. In the fall of 1887, after remaining a widower for fourteen years, he was married to Miss Ida Sennett, a charming lady. But few knew of the approaching wedding, until the morning it took place. The groom applied for the necessary license, and an hour or so later he and a friend met the bride, her mother and two sisters, at the minister's house, where the ceremony was performed. The only other witness was an enterprising newspaper man, who, hearing of the issuing of the license, had managed to locate the officiating clergyman.

One familiar with the mayor's life was asked to what he attributed his success. He replied: "To constant application, hard work, good health, and to enough common sense to apply the sound teachings of my father, who brought me up from a child, my mother having died when I was only seven years old."

The salary of the Mayor of Cincinnati is $4,000 a year. Every incumbent who performs anything like his duties earns his wages. The "honor" attached to the office may, in some degree and to some people, partly compensate for the shortcomings of salary, but it would hardly satisfy a practical man for the onerous demands upon his time, his patience, and the waste of the gray matter of his head. Most of the time from three to a dozen people are waiting to see him, refusing to be comforted by the well-meant offers of the clerks to attend to their wants, though nine times out of ten their business is turned over to the clerks to finish. There is a delegation to see "His Honor" on the needs of Ward 87 for an additional policeman. A poor widow comes to see if the mayor can get her a pass to Pittsburgh, where her relatives live. Aldermen from another city are piloted in to pay an official call of courtesy on the head of the municipal government. A big, awkward, tender-hearted policeman comes up from the police court with a plea from some poor soul, who has known the mayor in more prosperous days, to stave off a conflict with Justice *in re* Wilkins *vs.* a brace of chickens, on account of suffering innocence in wife and children. A lady in black complains of the cruelty of Policeman No. 0094 toward her son and heir, who persists in stealing rides on street cars, and has been soundly spanked by the practical conservator of the peace. Another lady calls with a subscription paper for the relief of a burned-out family, whose head is in the hospital with a broken leg. Still another lady, who deftly conceals her sample-book under her shawl until the moment she springs it on the suffering mayor, who surrenders at discretion and signs his name with horrible illegibility in his haste. A man who wants to get on the police force. Ditto for the Fire Department. Ditto for a letter of recommendation for a place in a store. The chief of police wants instructions as to a recalcitrant railroad magnate. Member of the Police Commission drops in to talk over plans for enlarging the force. Old friend, rotund and broad-faced, rushes in to pay his respects, and leaves the memory of a hand shake that will last half an hour and a reminiscence of "the night we fought all the Deer Creek boys single-handed!" The mayor must "go on 'Change" at 1 o'clock to meet a committee raising funds for the yellow fever sufferers; has an appointment for 3 o'clock to meet the Water Supply Commission at the Burnett House; must help inspect the workhouse at 5 P. M.; is announced to attend a banquet at 9 o'clock, and respond to a toast; promised his wife to drop in at a church social at 11 o'clock and take her home; gets to bed at 12.30 A. M., and for three hours suffers from a nightmare, the result of an internal conflict between the *pate de foi gras* and champagne of the banquet with the ice cream and oyster of the church militant. Yet that is only a fair sample, "by and large," of a day in the mayor's office in Cincinnati or any other large city. The office demands men of large capacity and reliable digestion.

All on the police force are appointed by the mayor. In addition to these, Mayor Smith has made the following appointments in other departments and boards, as follows:

Infirmary Directors: John D. Caldwell and A. M. Strang, to fill vacancies occurring before election.

Workhouse Directors: Sam W. Trost, Dan Weber, Charles B. Wing, Lewis Werner, and Charles F. Smith.

Fire Commissioners: Joseph R. Megrue, Charles Fleischmann, and John Goetz, Jr.

Emil Rehse, Clerk of Police Court, in place of George Richards, removed.

Inspector of Fire Escapes and the Consumption of Smoke: John Fehrenbatch.

Inspector of Buildings: Walter R. Forbush.

City Sealer: Michael Gramp.

City Treasurer: Henry M. Zeigler, to fill a vacancy caused by the death of Albert F. Bohrer.

Inspectors of Engines: A. D. Bateman, John Rahn, and James Ross.

City Weigher: W. Robinson.

The mayor is *ex-officio* a member and president of the Board of Revision and the Tax Commission, and a member of the Cincinnati Museum Association and of the Board of Trustees of the Cincinnati Hospital.

JOHN BORDEN MOSBY, who was elected Mayor of Cincinnati, and thus became the head of the police department in April, 1889, was born in Cincinnati, Ohio, December 4, 1845, on Third street, between Vine and Race, opposite old Shires' garden. His father, Napoleon Bonaparte Mosby, was a well-known wholesale grocer of this city and came here from his birthplace, Petersburg, Va., at an early age. Mayor Mosby attended the public schools of Cincinnati as far as the intermediate, when, at the age of fourteen years, he went to work. During the first two or three years after leaving school he worked for Geo. C. Kerr, hatter, on Fifth street, near Vine; Chas. Howland, photographer, Fifth and Main; and Ballenberg and Black, cigarists, on Vine, above Fourth. He then entered the grocery house of A. Luddington, 32 East Pearl street, where he clerked eleven years, with the exception of one hundred days' service in the army in the 137th Ohio Volunteer Infantry. On August 1, 1872, he formed a partnership with A. J. Hodson, and embarked in the wholesale grocery business at 106 East Pearl street, where he prospered, and in May, 1885, the firm removed to its present location, 17 and 19 West Second street. His partner, Mr. Hodson, dying in July, 1889, Mr. Mosby succeeded to the entire business, which had been the third largest in Cincinnati in that line during the previous year.

He is a great secret order man, being a charter member of Cincinnati Lodge, No. 2, K. of P.; Palmetto Lodge, No. 175, I. O. O. F.; N. C. Harmony Lodge of Masons; Cincinnati Chapter of Masons; Cincinnati Commandery, K. T.; Scottish

JOHN BORDEN MOSBY.
Mayor of Cincinnati.

Rite; A. Shriner; Fred. C. Jones Post, G. A. R.; a veteran, and a prominent member of both the Blaine and Lincoln Clubs. He was one of the organizers and moving spirits in the Order of Cincinnatus, which was organized by the business men of the city, and which in the first seven years of its existence, spent $300,000 in wages to workingmen of Cincinnati. He was president of the order four years. Mayor Mosby is married, and resides, with his wife and four children, at 369 Park avenue, Walnut Hills. He has been active in politics for a number of years, and was nominated and, as before stated, elected Mayor of Cincinnati in April, 1889.

Since assuming the duties of his office Mayor Mosby has proved himself an indefatigable worker, and, although burdened with a multiplicity of cares, has devoted himself heart and soul to business, and accomplished what would seem almost impossible. The death of his active partner shortly after his election, threw the care of an enormous business on him, and caught him in the midst of several very important investigations of other officials, notably the Work-house Board, and several employees of the Board of Public Affairs, which demanded several weeks of the closest application on his part, as *ex officio* member and chairman of the Board of Revision or investigating board. At the same time he had the bulk of the business of the Order of Cincinnatus, preparing for its annual exhibition, on his shoulders, and several other important duties, all of which he managed successfully.

As head of the police department, Mayor Mosby has wrought a great reform in Cincinnati by closing places of business, notably saloons, on Sunday, after a terrific struggle with the latter element, who succumbed only after failing by open defiance of the law to discourage the mayor.

CHAPTER VI.

THE NON-PARTISAN POLICE COMMISSION—HISTORY OF ITS FORMATION—WHAT SUGGESTED IT—PROVISIONS OF THE BILL BY WHICH THE COMMISSION WAS CREATED—DUTY OF THE COMMISSIONERS IN SUPPRESSING GAMBLING—WHO CONSTITUTED THE FIRST BOARD—SKETCHES OF PRESIDENT DODDS, DR. MINOR, MESSRS. BOYLE AND WERNER, EX-COMMISSIONERS MORGAN AND TOPP, AND CLERK WARREN.

In the hands of an unscrupulous partisan, a police force can be made an engine for much harm in any municipality. An ambitious mayor, refusing to be governed by right impulses and having a large body of men to obey his beck and nod, could come pretty near subverting the rights of any community before his arm could be staid by the slow process of an appeal to the courts. If to him is given the prerogative to add to and take from a police force, his unrestricted power becomes a constant menace. This condition of affairs has existed in Cincinnati; fortunately it exists no longer. The legislative power in Ohio, as in many other States, early showed a disposition to avert this danger by distributing the control of the peace conservators. This, as has already been shown in these pages was done in various ways. It was first given into the keeping of men selected by judicial authority, then it again lapsed into the hands of a mayor, next elective officers assumed the responsibility of appointing and directing a police force, and again the chief executive of the city took command. A board was created to be filled by the Governor of the State, and for lack of many of the characteristics which has made the present Board of Commissioners a brilliant success, its history, too, was soon written, then there came a commission appointed by a political organization, and, like its predecessor, its days were quickly numbered. It remained for the Ohio Legislature of the winter of 1885–86, to bring into existence an organization which should steer clear of the mistakes of its numerous predecessors, that, in a word, should adopt their virtues and shun their vices. That organization was known as the "Non-partisan Police Board," with principles as follows:

1st. That there should be one person exclusively responsible for the actions, direction and control of the force.

2d. That the admission to or expulsion from membership should not be left to the caprice or political bias of the person so controlling.

3d. That the members of the force should be relieved of any fear that their connection with it is in any way dependent upon any other condition than that of good conduct.

4th. That the commands of the several branches of the force should not be granted on the ground of personal friendship, but through ability, fitness and adaptability only.

5th. That faithful service should always be recognized and rewarded.

6th. That there should be continual supervision of the force by others than the executive officer relative to its rules, regulations, duties, education and progress in police knowledge.

7th. That when the controlling officer fails to exercise his duties, somebody should be ready and lawfully authorized to promptly take his place.

The particular events that led to the formation of the non-partisan police department are illustrations of the power of a police force when misdirected or not directed at all, and when used as part of the machinery of a political organization. In the fall of 1885 it was very evident that a large amount of false registration had taken place, and there were signs that the coming election would be affected by illegal voting. From this and a desire for changes in the administration of local affairs sprang what is known as the Committee of One Hundred. This committee was composed of citizens from all political parties, so that any attack upon recognized evils or endeavors to reform the methods of local government could not be met with the cry that the efforts were to benefit one party or another. The committee took a lively interest in the preparations for election. The registration was carefully scrutinized, the residence of voters verified by personal inspection, and several flagrant cases of a violation of the election laws were discovered. A prominent citizen made the proper affidavits, and the warrants for arrest were issued. These warrants were taken to the old Board of Police Commissioners, and by that body entrusted to the superintendent of police, but he failed to obtain a prompt execution of the service.

Events followed quickly that led to the removal of the old board by the governor of the State. It was discovered that the existing law provided no means for the filling of places when all the seats were declared vacant, so that if the members of the board should be removed from office the police would be deprived of an executive head. It was evident that the governor would remove the commissioners, and a dilemma must be avoided. The Committee of One Hundred placed the matter in the hands of Colonel D. W. McClung, with the instructions that a draft of a law must be prepared and be in the State Legislature for approval in two days. There was a necessity for sharp action, for there was now an opportunity for engrafting all the features that experience had taught would be beneficial. The draft was ready at the time named, and, almost simultaneous with the decree of the removal of the commissioners, was presented to the Legislature and on March 30, 1886, became a law. Under that law the police force of the City of Cincinnati is now organized and controlled.

The first feature of the law is that all police powers and duties are vested in the mayor and four police commissioners, who shall be electors of the city, well known for their intelligence and integrity, not more than two of whom shall be of the same political party, two retiring at the end of each four years. These commissioners are appointed by the governor, and may be removed by him in case of any unofficial conduct. The appointment of two from each political party renders it impossible for any strictly partisan measure to be carried out in the deliberations of the board, a fact which has already been proved in its short history.

The mayor alone has the power to appoint all policemen and officers for the police force, but before an appointee can assume the responsibilities and duties of the office he must be approved by the Board of Police Commissioners, it being expressly stipulated that all appointments shall be made without reference to political opinions or affiliations.

That the police force shall be freed from any political influence it is further provided that any commissioner who, during the term of his office accepts, any other place of public trust or emolument, or who, during the same period, knowingly consents to his nomination for an office elective by the people, or fails publicly to decline the same within twenty days succeeding his nomination, shall be regarded as having vacated his office, and the governor shall appoint a successor. The effect of this provision is to place a commissioner where it is impossible for him to use his office by threat, fear or promise among policemen through whom he might hope to gain influence or to affect in any way an honest and impartial election.

But the law does not stop with the commissioners. It is unlawful for any member of the force to be a delegate to, or otherwise take part in, any primary or other political convention or election, except to cast his vote. If any officer or member of the force interferes in elections or conventions for or against any political party or candidate, the law commands immediate dismissal of the offender.

That the responsibility shall not be divided, the mayor possesses full power and authority over the police organization, government and discipline. This is absolute, there being only two provisions of law which in any way limit this power. One portion of the law prescribes that the commissioners shall cause to be prepared a convenient manual containing a compend of all the laws and ordinances which the police force is required to obey and enforce, and such instruction as shall aid in the intelligent discharge of duty. To each member of the force is given this manual. With its directions, rules and prescribed duties he is to become familiar. Until these rules and directions are changed, an obedience to any order from the mayor, running counter to them, would be a violation both of the spirit and letter of the law.

If at any time the mayor shall, after request from the Board of Commissioners, either refuse or, for three days after notice, fail to authorize and direct the superintendent of police to enter a common gaming house, or a place of lewd or obscene public amusement, or place for the deposit or sale of lottery tickets or lottery policy, and forthwith arrest all persons found offending against any law, and seize all the implements connected with the named violations, then the Board of Commissioners shall undertake to exercise the powers of the law.

The first members of the non-partisan Board of Police Commissioners met in the office of the Mayor, Hon. Amor Smith, Jr., April 1, 1886, and there the following gentlemen, Hon. Milo G. Dodds, Dr. T. C. Minor, Robert J. Morgan, and George R. Topp, took and subscribed to an oath to support the Constitution of the United States and of the State of Ohio, to obey the laws, and in all their official actions and judgments to aim only to secure and maintain an honest and efficient system of police, free from partisan dictation or control.

The board immediately convened and elected Robert J. Morgan president, and James S. Gordon clerk, the latter retiring October 19, 1886, when S. B. Warren was elected to the vacancy.

The personnel of the board remained the same until January 1, 1887, when R. J. Morgan, influenced by business reasons, retired from the board and was succeeded by James Boyle, and August 1, 1888, G. R. Topp retired and was succeeded by Louis Werner.

In 1886, for some time after the formation of the board, its sessions were thrice a week, and during the labor strikes daily, but at present are on Tuesdays and Fridays at 3.30 P. M., with such additional adjourned and special meetings as may be necessary. Besides these meetings, under the law, at the request of the mayor, conferences are frequently held with him.

In January, 1887, Dr. T. C. Minor was elected president, and filled the position with marked ability until January, 1888, when George R. Topp was chosen president, holding the office until August 1, 1888, when he was made a member of the Board of Public Affairs. He was immediately succeeded in the presidency

MILO G. DODDS.
Commissioner of Police.

by Hon. Milo G. Dodds, who had been the board's vice-president. James Boyle was then elected vice-president.

Arthur G. Moore, a former superintendent of the city water works, was the first chief chosen by the new board. His nomination by the mayor did not meet with the unanimous favor of the commissioners, and the confirmation therefore did not take place until after several successive meetings. He served only from April 1st till June 19th, when he resigned to resume his old position in the water works, and Philip H. Deitsch was appointed his successor.

The house on East Third street, just east of Pike and opposite to the old Longworth gardens, in the old flatiron ward, still stands where Milo Gilbert Dodds was born, September 3, 1847. His father, William B. Dodds, was a native of Pittsburgh, Penna., and came here in 1835. After following his trade as a shoemaker a short time, besides being engaged in various other business enterprises, he united with E. Hall and his son, Joseph L. Hall, in 1851, and established the firm of Hall & Dodds, safe and lock manufacturers, a business house whose fame has gone into every part of the civilized world where people have had valuables they cared to preserve safe. Six years later he helped to establish the Urban, Dodds & Co. safe manufactory, a house that came to be known equally well with the one with which he was first connected. The elder Dodds was an organizer, as has already been indicated, and a man of great determination, two traits which the subject of this sketch inherited.

Young Milo was educated in the Cincinnati public schools, which he left abruptly to go into the hundred-day service, in the 137th Ohio Volunteer Infantry, under Colonel Len. Harris. This was in 1864, near the close of the late war between the North and the South. At the expiration of his term of service young Dodds returned to his home and was an assistant to his father until 1870, when he went to St. Louis and embarked in the same business in which his father had acquired a fortune. Six years later he returned to his native place and established a successful insurance agency under the firm name of Long & Dodds. His partner was Albert A. Long, for years a popular public school principal. The partnership was subsequently dissolved by the death of Mr. Long.

In the fall of 1877, Mr. Dodds was elected a member of the sixty-third Ohio General Assembly and served one term. He was chairman of the Committee on Corporations, other than Municipal, and second on the Committe on Insurance. It was Mr. Dodds who introduced the bill, which afterwards became a law, making women notaries public, thus placing Ohio among the states first to recognize the right of the gentler sex to "swear."

Mr. Dodds was one of the organizers of the Committee of One Hundred, which committee was for the most part responsible for the non-partisan police bill, under which the present efficient police force was organized. Mr. Dodds was also prominently identified with the work of the Committee of One Hundred in establishing for the State the admirable election laws under which voting in all Ohio municipalities is now conducted. He was appointed a member of the non-partisan police board by Governor Foraker in the spring of 1886, and is now its efficient president. In politics he is an uncompromising Democrat. He belongs to that class of men who are so thoroughly interested in the future welfare of their party that they would rather lose an election on a good platform than win on a poor one; would rather submit to temporary defeat, believing that the right will finally triumph. He is an enthusiastic fraternity man, having for years been prominently identified with the Masons, Odd Fellows, and Knights of Pythias.

As a member of the commission there is none better posted on police law and its requirements than Mr. Dodds. No one is more painstaking in his duty, no one gives the business in hand more careful attention. The qualities of this officer may be estimated by a remark recently volunteered by his old associate on the board, Mr. Robert J. Morgan, who said: "I believe Milo G. Dodds' services as a police commissioner to be second to the services of no police commissioner, past or present, either in Cincinnati or in any other American city."

There was an anxious conference of prominent citizens one evening in the summer of 1886, when the business of all but one

T. C. MINOR, M. D.,
Commissioner of Police.

of the railroads centering in Cincinnati had been paralyzed by the railroad strikers. The road still operating was the Little Miami. Among the private gentlemen present at the conference were General Hickenlooper, Hon. Samuel Bailey, Jr., Dransin Wulsin, and the superintendent of the Little Miami. Several municipal officers were also present, among them Commissioner Morgan and the subject of this sketch, the latter by the especial invitation of the Little Miami superintendent, whom he had chanced to meet in Central Police Station after the conference had been in session for an hour or more. The superintendent had explained that the men in the employ of the railroad he represented had been threatened with personal violence if they attempted to go to work on the morrow, and they had notified him that they would not go to work unless assured of police protection. For this assurance he therefore petitioned the municipal officers. The sentiment appeared to be unanimous among the private citizens, as well as among the officers, that it would not be safe to send a company of policemen, which would necessarily be small, to thwart the plans of several hundred determined strikers. Commissioner Morgan expressed the belief that this was the only proper thing to do, but his counsel was overruled by that of men more timid, when Mr. Dodds was given the floor. He urged that for the city to show the white feather at this particular juncture was to virtually give it up to fire and pillage. If the men of the Little Miami were not protected in the inalienable right to earn a livelihood there was no reason for hoping that citizens would be protected in the possession of their property. He was satisfied that he could select six lieutenants from the police department, who in turn could choose their men, and that at once a company of officers could be sent to the Little Miami railroad shops and depots that would successfully resist the threatened encroachments of ten thousand lawless strikers. This expression of determination, this show of combativeness at once changed the drift of the sentiment of the meeting. Called upon for some advice, General Hickenlooper said: "Mr. Dodds has made my speech." Mr. Bailey and Mr. Wulsin, and, finally, the rest of the company endorsed the view the two commissioners had taken, and the police officers went to the Litte Miami, and the Little Miami employes kept right on with their work. The strikers kept their word, so far as going to the scene of industry is concerned, but the presence of a battalion of blue coats, with faces hard set, like statues of stone, deterred them from commiting, or even attempting to commit, any overt act. Mr. Dodds had won.

There have been few committees in the commission on which he has not served with credit to himself and the board, whether as an auditing committee where all the thousand and one bills of the board must be scanned carefully, as an important aid in organizing the present relief association, as a presiding officer, as a member fertile in resource, he has never been weighed and found wanting.

In 1881, Mr. Dodds was united in marriage to Miss Charlotte Crawford. Three children have blessed the union, two of whom are still living. His home is on Alpine Place, East Walnut Hill, and is one of the pleasantest in Hamilton County.

A few years ago a company of boys were whiling away a hot afternoon in the shade of an old sycamore tree, near Chillicothe, this State. One of them was lying on his back with his eyes closed, and was apparently sound asleep. The others were seated where they could look down into his face.

"I wonder what makes Tom limp?" whispered one of the boys, as he furtively glanced at his prostrate companion.

"Cork leg," laconically replied another.

"No cork about it," put in a third boy, "it is made of flesh and bone and blood same as yours."

"Bet cher a dime," was the answer of the youngster, who could not have been more positive if he had stood by and seen the supposed artificial limb whittled into shape.

"My money is up," came back from the boy who scouted the cork leg theory.

The first speaker was made custodian of the stakes, who, as he received the money, inquired, "How shall the question be decided?"

"With a pin," answered the amateur anatomist, at the same time producing one, sharp and shining, from one of his numerous pockets.

"You are not going to stick that into him, are you?" asked the stakeholder.

"'Course; he will not feel it. Can't. It's cork."

All this conversation had been heard by the subject of it. Not one syllable had been missed, and while the companions discussed the manner of deciding the bet, he resolved that the cork leg advocate should win, and nerved himself accordingly. The point of the pin touched the sensitive skin of his leg, but not a muscle moved. It pierced the skin and entered the flesh, still there was no sign that the sleeper was disturbed. The mischievous little wretch who handled the pin drove it into the yielding flesh clean to the head, and still there was no apparent awakening. The two dimes were then turned over to the boy who had backed his opinion on the artificial character of the limb with his money. And for years thereafter Tom Minor was pitied as the boy who limped with a cork leg.

This incident in the early life of Dr. Thomas Chalmers Minor was a pretty faithful index of the disposition and character which have made him one of the most useful of Cincinnati's citizens. Once determined upon a certain line of policy he ha always been as indifferent to public criticism as he was stoical when the boys tortured him with a pin.

Dr. Minor was born at Cincinnati, July 6, 1846. His early education was received at Herron's Seminary and Chickering Academy for Boys—private schools of instruction of this city. At the age of sixteen he entered the office of Dr. J. Baird Smith as a medical student, and soon after matriculated at the Ohio Medical College, from which institution he was detailed to act as *interne* at the old St. John's Hospital, by the late Prof. George C. Blackman. Entering this hospital in the early part of 1865, he remained through the cholera epidemic of 1866; and, graduating from the Ohio Medical College in the spring of 1867, he went to Europe, where he visited the various hospitals of Paris, London and Wurzburg, Bavaria. Returning in the late fall of the same year, he assumed charge of the Good Samaritan Hospital as an *interne*, where he remained until the summer of 1868, when he finally embarked in private practice.

On November 1, 1871, Dr. Minor was assigned to duty as outdoor poor physician for the Fourteenth Ward, on account of the then prevailing epidemic of small-pox, over 1,100 deaths from that disease having occurred. He remained on duty under the health officer, Dr. M. Clendennin, until the subsidence of this memorable outbreak, and then retired. In the spring of 1873 Dr. Minor was elected a member of the Board of Health, and performed active service during the cholera outbreak of that year, being re-elected for the long term of three years the following spring (1874). It was while holding this position that Dr. Minor attempted to regulate the social evil by the adoption of the French system of registration. He was back of the Harries Ordinance, and most of the articles *pro* and *con* appearing in the newspapers of that date were from his pen. Failing to accomplish what he considered a valuable sanitary work, he retired again from the Health Department.

In the spring of 1878, on the eve of the yellow fever outbreak at New Orleans and Memphis, Dr. Minor was elected Health Officer of Cincinnati, and, at the outset of the epidemic, established at Cincinnati the first regular inter-state quarantine ever undertaken in America, his agents and inspectors going through the railroad trains of Kentucky and Indiana, and also examining the boats on the Ohio river. It was probably owing to these precautions which were undertaken, not without a great deal of adverse criticism, that the city owed its escape from the ravages of the plague.

Re-elected health officer in 1879, he again ran the Ohio river quarantine stations during the prevalence of yellow fever in the South. Tendered a unanimous re-election in the spring of 1880, he declined, and returned once more to private practice, having also served in the meantime as trustee of the Cincinnati University for the space of six years. In July, 1884, Dr. Minor was re-elected health officer by the unanimous vote of the then newly elected Board of Health, but positively declined to enter the public service in an office that would occupy his entire time and attention to the injury of his private practice.

In the spring of 1886 Dr. Minor was appointed one of the

JAMES BOYLE.
President of the Board of Police Commissioners.

four non-partisan Police Commissioners named for Cincinnati by the Governor of Ohio. It was on his introduction to this board that he presented a resolution advocating a physical standard for the reorganization of the new metropolitan police force. It was on his recommendation that the standard devised by the Board of Medical Examiners was adopted. In the spring of 1888 Dr. Minor was again appointed police commissioner for the long term of four years by his excellency, Governor Joseph B. Foraker.

In politics Dr. Minor is an old time Democrat, a believer in hard money, a pronounced free trader, but an independent in local politics. For many years the doctor has been an active worker on medical journals, and there are few numbers of the Cincinnati "Lancet and Clinic" that do not bear evidences of his literary work. He has been the French and Italian translator of this journal for over fifteen years.

Dr. Minor is the author of a number of medical books and pamphlets. Among his principal professional works may be mentioned "Erysipelas and Childbed Fever," "Scarlatina Statistics of the United States," "Epidemiology of Ohio," "Sanitary Survey of Cincinnati," "Yellow Fever in the Ohio Valley," and sanitary papers too numerous to mention. Dr. Minor has also published many short stories and translations in various papers, and two works, i. e., "Her Ladyship" and "Athothis"—the latter a medical satire on modern medicine. He is also the author of three copyrighted librettos, viz.: "The New Don Juan," "Old Lallah Rookh," and "Frosquita."

James Boyle, the youngest of Cincinnati's Police Commissioners, has his heart thoroughly in his work. He is an enthusiast in the matter of increasing the efficiency and raising the standard of the police force. Being of a thoroughly practical turn of mind his efforts are not wasted in intangible theories, but are made to tell in directions where reform is possible. Mr. Boyle belongs to that profession which is said to embrace all other professions— journalism. Certain it is that the career of an active newspaper man covers so many varying interests that he comes at last to know all sides of the world and to know them most intimately. It is hard to imagine any better preparation for public position than that given by general newspaper work. The opportunities for observation are unequalled, and the range of experiences is almost unbounded. Thus it is that Mr. Boyle has a special fitness for his work in the police department. His life has been an eventful one. He was born in Essex county, England, in 1854, though he came as a mere boy across the Atlantic, his parents going to Toronto, Canada. There he learned the art of type-setting and the more difficult art of phonography. Before he was twenty he was counted the most rapid and accurate short-hand writer in Canada. His first newspaper work was for the *Ontario Workman*, published in the interests of the reform labor movement. Later he was a reporter on and then city editor of the *Montreal Herald*, where he did such excellent work that a similar position, and one better in a financial sense, was tendered him on the *Toronto Mail*. His excellence as a stenographer soon became known, and it brought him the position of official stenographer in the Canadian House of Commons. This was an admirable position, but it was confining. Mr. Boyle found the hard, close work telling on him, and he gave up his place, going to St. Louis, where for four years he was on the *Globe-Democrat*. He was tempted away from there by an offer from the old *Cincinnati Gazette*. That was nine years ago; and since that time he has been in Cincinnati, going on the *Commercial Gazette* as staff correspondent at the time of the consolidation of the two papers. He is a constant and vigorous writer, and all readers of the *Commercial Gazette* are familiar with the initials "J. B."

Mr. Boyle takes to himself the credit of having proposed Judge Foraker's name through the press to the people of Ohio for Governor. In 1883 and 1885 he was the Governor's shadow through the campaign. Where the former went, the latter went too; and J. B.'s letters advocating Foraker's election, and his report of his speeches, were powerful factors in the canvass. Mr. Boyle is not a writer who looks on all sides of a question in a calm philosophical style; on the contrary, he is a warm and eager partisan. What he does he does, with his whole might; and not only did he fight for his party on paper, but he was one of the organizers of the Blaine Club, a potent factor in Cincinnati politics. He was also a prime mover in forming the League of Republican Clubs in Ohio, as well as chairman of the Committee that arranged the National League of Republican Clubs.

As a newspaper man Mr. Boyle is noted for his tremendous energy and rapidity. For instance, he once wrote a whole page of the old *Gazette* in half a day. It was a report of the Indiana State Republican Convention in the fall of 1882. He left Cincinnati on the early morning train, got into Indianapolis by 11 o'clock, and spent the afternoon at the convention. He reported its proceedings as they occurred, taking down the speeches in short hand. When the convention was over he took a late afternoon train for Cincinnati, transcribing the speeches on the cars. When he reached the office every line of his report was complete, even the head lines having been written. Next morning the account of the convention, gotten up in the most admirable style, too, filled a solid page of the *Gazette*. This was a great feat, as any one who has ever filled even a column of a newspaper can testify.

Mr. Boyle's copy, by the way, is a model of cleanliness and legibility. He writes a hand that would do credit to a clerk who toils to round his periods, shade his curves, cross his t's and dot his i's to a nicety. The majority of hard working journalists find that years of hurried work play the mischief with their chirography, as all the world knows was the case with Horace Greely.

As a police official this youthful commissioner has been unrelenting in his warfare upon gamblers and the other parasites that prey upon society. When he was a reporter in St. Louis he first had his attention called to the evils of gambling, and he fought the faro banks and keno establishments vigorously in the columns of the *Globe-Democrat*. It was partly on account of the notice his attacks on the gamblers received that he was called to Cincinnati, and the first notable work he did in the Queen City was an exposure of the game of "policy." The city authorities and the police had, for a long time, left the "policy" dealers unnoticed. The *Gazette*, as a paper with a right standard of morals, had time and again protested against the dealers. Mr.

Boyle was given instructions to investigate the seductive game, and he went at his work after the manner of a detective. Policy shop after policy shop was discovered, and everything about them carefully noted. Cases where the game had brought ruin and distress were found out and investigated. No stone was left unturned. The result was the expose was complete, even to showing how the police had favored the policy dealer more than the gambler of a better type. As a result the mayor issued an order shutting up the shops during the rest of his administration.

This experience is only given to indicate the constant and versatile activity of the man. His short, sturdy, well-knit figure, and the face that has a nervous look in it, tell the same story. And when Governor Foraker appointed Mr. Boyle to fill the unexpired term of Robert J. Morgan as police commissioner, ending in 1890, he devoted himself to his new duties with all the energy that he had shown in other fields of endeavor. The first thing that he did which was notable was to carry into execution a plan for the establishment of a police gymnasium. As a young man he was a great athlete. He personally knew and appreciated the value of systematic muscular training.

"Then," to use his own words, "there is no sight much more displeasing than that of a big, lumbering, bowel-heavy policeman, whose limbs have suffered a fatty degeneration, and who could not run half a square without being utterly winded. Policemen are not expected to cultivate their paunches, yet the history of all police forces is that the majority of the men show a tendency to grow unduly stout. Then the lack of special exercise often renders them unfit to cope in a hand-to-hand struggle with evildoers."

And so Mr. Boyle perfected the plan of the police gymnasium, and drew up the stringent rules making it compulsory for the men on the force to be constantly in systematic "training." To say that this gymnasium has done as much as any one thing to change the Cincinnati police for the better is stating the exact truth. It has done for the men physically what the high standard of admission to the force has done for them otherwise. Of course Mr. Boyle is fond of being the father of the "Gym," as it is familiarly called, though he disclaims any originality in the idea of such an institution.

"It is not a new thing," he said; "and here it had been discussed for a year."

Still, it was not until Mr. Boyle took the matter in charge that it assumed definite shape and become the success that it is.

It is almost needless to say that the subject of this sketch finds that Cincinnatians appreciate his work. They recognize in him an official who does his duty without fear or favor, and they regard him as one of the rising young men of the State. That a fair future is before him cannot be doubted.

Mr. Louis Werner is the most recent addition to the Cincinnati Board of Police Commissioners, having been appointed a member of it in July, 1888, to fill the vacancy caused by the resignation of Mr. George Topp, who was at that time made a member of the Board of Public Affairs. The new member is not a man who says much, but "he does a deal of thinking." At the meetings of the board he will keep silence for long periods, then he will suddenly come out with something apt and to the point. In the trials of men charged with various offenses, Mr. Werner will allow his colleagues to ask the great majority of the questions, but when he does come out with an inquiry, it will be one that shows how keenly he has followed the details of the matter, and what an ability he has for getting at the truth in the most direct way.

It is almost unnecessary to say that Mr. Werner is a self-made man. He was born in Bavaria in 1839, and is therefore in his fiftieth year. In 1844 he came to Cincinnati with his parents, and so he is as near a native as a man can be who has had the misfortune to be born outside the corporate limits of the Queen City. Until he was twelve years old he attended the public schools, then his father died, and the lad had to do all he could for the support of his widowed mother and of his sister. He went to work for George W. Scholl & Co., trunkmakers, and remained with them for fifteen months. After that he secured employment from Samuel Coleman, a maker of bolts. This did not suit him, however, and he resolved to learn the trade of the cabinetmaker. He went at it with a will, served his time regularly, and became an expert workman. But he was not robust enough to stand the confinement of the factory, and he felt his health breaking down. Not afraid of any hard work so it was honest, he left his trade and went in the employ of Adam Beck, well known to Cincinnatians, and became a butcher. He found this profitable, and in 1866 he went into business for himself at 66 East Fourth street. Mr. Ison was his partner, and finally Mr. Werner sold out to him, opening a grocery and daily market at George and Mound streets, which turned out to be a remarkably prosperous establishment. A careful man of business it is not a great wonder that Mr. Werner succeeded. But his health continued to trouble him, and in 1880 he resolved to go out of business altogether, his affairs being in such a condition that he could easily do this. He purchased a fine residence at 173 York street, where he now lives, and the release from daily cares has made him feel that he is another man.

Since his retirement from business, Mr. Werner has taken an active part in politics, being a stalwart Republican. He is a member of the most prominent of the political clubs of his party, and does not hesitate to give them his money and services. He is not above practical politics, and he therefore is a power. In April, 1887, he was elected from his ward, the Twenty-third, to the Board of Education, and that body chose him to be one of its representatives in the Union Board of High Schools. In the former board he is a member of the Building Committee of the Buildings and Repairs Committee, and chairman of the responsible Committee on School Lots. He has personally looked after the erection of a number of new school buildings, and superintended additions and repairs, seeing for himself that the city got a dollar's worth of work for every dollar expended. He brings into the affairs of the public the same square, exact methods that are used in private business. Mr. Werner was also, up to the time of his present appointment, a member of the Board of Work-House Directors.

Those who are acquainted with Mr. Werner's record as a successful and upright business man, and as a conscientious public

LOUIS WERNER,
Commissioner of Police.

officer, know that he is a valuable addition to the Police Board. He has the opportunity to devote his time and energies to the public service, and his admirable work speaks for itself.

The existence of the present efficient Police Commission is probably as much due to the individual exertion of Robert J. Morgan as to that of any other citizen of Cincinnati. He was one of the first to urge the organization of the Committee of One Hundred. He was one of the first fourteen Cincinnati gentlemen to meet to plan for that organization, and when there was a clamor for a change in police management in Cincinnati, Mr. Morgan's name was the first to be urged as a candidate for the office of manager. When in 1886 it became Governor Foraker's duty to appoint a Police Commission under a reorganization act, Mr. Morgan had already been nominated as a commissioner on the old board. His name was therefore among the first to be selected by the Governor, and he became the Commission's first President.

Mr. Morgan was born at Bandon, County Cork, Ireland, June 24 1838. When only nine years old he came with his father to the United States on the first screw steamer that ever crossed the Atlantic, and on May 24, 1847, reached Cincinnati, coming a part of the way via the old Erie canal. Three years later he began his career as a printer, with the old firm of Foster & Corwin, publishers of the *Chronicle and Atlas*. With that firm he served six months. Then he was indentured by his father for five years to Caleb Clark & Co., owners of the Ben Franklin Job Office. He had served only a part of his time with this company when he became the pressman. Later he went to the *Enquirer Office* and finished his apprenticeship. There he first made the acquaintance of Mr. Russell, his future partner. In 1858 he went to Memphis and took charge of Hutton & Freligh's press-room, and through his influence Mr. Russell was sent for to take entire charge of the establishment. There Mr. Morgan remained until the beginning of the war, when he returned to Cincinnati and became a member of the printing firm of Johnson, Stevens and Morgan. Selling his interest in this establishment he went into the army. At the close of the war he began business, in which he remained for a few months only, at Easton, Ohio, and then with Mr. Russell bought the *Enquirer Job Rooms,* and established the Russell and Morgan Company, of which he is now Vice President and one of the most active managers.

For two terms and a half Mr. Morgan served the city as a member of the Board of Education, and was one of the most influential men in that body.

When he became a police commissioner he exhibited the same energy and tact in the business of reorganization of the force that had characterized his conduct of his own private interests through his entire business career. He made repeated trips to eastern cities for the purpose of observing how metropolitan policemen were there selected and trained, and the Cincinnati commission at once profited by his observations. He was a stickler for an observance of the letter of the law in the appointment of officers, constantly insisting that each candidate for position should come up to all the requirements both mental and physical. Finally, when his own private cares made it necessary for him to retire from the board, January 1, 1887, to encourage the maintenance of the high standard for which he had contended, Mr. Morgan offered a fifty dollar gold medal for five years, to be awarded on the first of each year, to that officer who shall become the most proficient in all that appertains to a policeman's duties. The influence of the emulation which his offer has excited has been most salutary. At the first examination made of officers contending for this prize there were ten to enter their claims. The award was made to John McGrann, a member of Patrol Company, No. 2.

The second contest occurred on the first of the current year. Fifty-four men were entitled to enter, but only eleven availed themselves of their rights. William W. Clawson received the medal.

Though retired from any active management of the Cincinnati police system Mr. Morgan still continues to entertain a lively interest in its success, and to feel a just pride in the fact, that it is now the best the city has ever enjoyed.

Mr. George Topp, one of the best-known young men in Cincinnati, was one of the original members of the Non-partisan

R. J. MORGAN.

Police Board, and he had much to do with establishing the code which has made it so effective. He was chairman of the Committee on Law, and solved many of the knotty legal questions that came up to perplex the board. So thorough and conscientious was he in his work at the critical time when Cincinnati made over her police force, that he examined personally the bonds presented by the new officers. He took no bond for granted, but carefully went over the tax duplicate to make certain that the signers were responsible. This in itself was a gigantic task, and that it was done faithfully and well the number of bonds rejected will testify.

Mr. Topp is a native Cincinnatian, born May 9, 1852. He went through the public schools of the city, and when he was ready to enter the High School his parents sent him to Germany to finish his studies. Hanover, in Brunswick, was the place where he "polished off," and he has always regarded the years spent there as all but wasted. When he returned to this country he found that he had to go to work and learn many things that he had forgotten before he could begin the practical work of life. He studied law in the office of Colonel Gustav Tafel, and, on being admitted to the bar, became Interpreter of the Courts of Hamilton county. This office was created by the General Assembly especially for him, and he filled it acceptably for ten years. In 1881 he established the "Law Bulletin," the official paper of the courts, and made it a success. He was meanwhile taking the utmost interest in politics, and, as a recognition of his party services in 1886, Governor Foraker appointed him on the Police Commission. Early in 1888 he was called higher by an appointment as a member of the more important Board of Public Affairs. He has always displayed great executive ability and an energy that is inexhaustible. Over his recent troubles, the public can but draw the mantle of charity.

Mr. Samuel B. Warren was born in Detroit, Michigan, January 10, 1840, and, when two years old, became a resident of Cincinnati. The school over which Auntie Wright presided, and which was located back of St. Paul's Church, the present site of the St. Paul building, was where the ideas of the young Wolverine were first taught to shoot. When but four years of age he became one of the Auntie's pupils, and continued to be one until 1848. At this time there were no stores on the south side of Fourth street, west of Walnut. The street was given up for the ultra fashionable residences, and the school referred to was among the most select and the best. From Auntie Wright's school young Warren was promoted to a seminary on Seventh street, between Walnut and Vine streets, conducted by Joseph Herron, where he remained until he was twelve years old, when he was sent to a semi-military school at Springfield, Ohio, where he prepared for admission to college. At the age of fifteen he entered Trinity College at Hartford, Conn., where four years later, when only nineteen years old, he graduated with the highest honors of his class. He was the valedictorian of the Class of 1859. The same year he connected himself with the wholesale house of J. T. Warren & Co., a firm then known throughout the South and entire western country. Two years later, or just as he obtained his majority, he became a partner, and remained one until in 1882, when the firm was finally dissolved. Mr. Warren was once one of the most efficient members of the Board of Education, and was once its vice-president. His constituents urged him to become a candidate for re-election, but he declined.

The club that has a commanding influence in Cincinnati is known as the Commercial Club. Mr. Warren was one of its organizers, and was most prominent in shaping its constitution and policy. He was the club's first president, and continued to hold that office for two successive terms. In social circles for years no name has been more prominent than has that of Samuel B. Warren. The fact that Mr. Warren was an enthusiastic student of Trinity College is circumstantial evidence that his mind had a leaning towards the tenets of the faith taught by the Protestant Episcopal Church. For successive years he was the superintendent of the Sunday School of Christ Church, and is still the teacher of a Bible-class there. In connection with this work he is much sought after as a public speaker.

In 1886, October 19, Mr. Warren was chosen the clerk of the Board of Police Commissioners, *vice* James Gordon, resigned.

S. B. WARREN.
Secretary to the Board of Police Commissioners.

In February of 1888 he became official police instructor. No one connected with the police department has the work and interests of the peace conservator more thoroughly at heart and knows more about the needs of that department than Mr. Warren. He is a man for detail, and peculiarly fitted therefore to occupy the place he has so acceptably filled during the last two years.

An important feature of the police department, is that relating to its money affairs. The sources of revenue are fixed by law, and the amount can be readily estimated within a few thousand dollars each year except under extraordinary circumstances. It is a truism that no municipal department has an income equal to its supposed necessities, and therefore, there is always before the managers of a fund, the question as to how to make the expenditure of each dollar productive of the greatest results. The provisions of the law of 1886 permitted to the board certain expenditures for which, if they had been carried out, would have caused the department to enter the year 1887 considerably in debt. One source of revenue was from the tax imposed by the Dow law upon the sellers of intoxicating liquors. This law was vehemently opposed, forcing the board in its own defence to assume the responsibility of defeating the opposition, for, pending a judicial decision on the law, the revenue of the department was not equal to the necessities for salaries. The board was determined to procure rapidly and promptly a judicial decision, and so employed two attorneys, Thomas McDougal and C. B. Mathews, who succeeded, upon an action carried to the Supreme Court of the State, in securing a satisfactory ruling upon the constitutionality of the law.

Under the law for expenses necessary to carry on the department, the commissioners have the power, on the recommendation of the mayor, to appropriate money, to pay the same out of the police fund, by an order signed by the president and countersigned by the clerk of the board, drawn upon the city comptroller, payable to the person to whom such sum is due, specifying the purpose for which the appropriation is made, after which the city comptroller gives his warrant upon the city treasurer.

When a bill is sent to the board, it is referred to the **auditing** committee, who, carefully examines it to see that it is properly made out in the particulars of address, dates, purposes, prices and calculations. The auditing committee in 1886, was Dr. T. C. Minor, and from January, 1887, to August, 1888, Hon. Milo G. Dodds filled the position. From that date, Dr. Minor has done the auditing. The examination of the expenditure of a half a million of dollars in sums varying from the petty purchases of pins to the pay roll involves no small amount of care and labor, making necessary knowledge of the commercial value of a horse and its equipments, of stationery, groceries, hardware, feed, medicines, household goods, painters' materials, upholstery, furniture, and hundreds of other items. Such a committee must know the value of labor, whether that of a horse-shoer, carpenter or plumber. In order to practice the greatest economy, there has been established a repair department, by which much work is performed under the supervision of the superintendent of patrol. By this branch all the patrol boxes are manufactured, station-houses painted, their needed incidental repairs made, and the wires, connections, etc., of the telephone service kept in a proper condition.

The estimate of expenses for 1888 was $433,000; the actual, $432,418.85. The estimate for 1889 calls for $504,337.

CHAPTER VII.

HOW A MAN IS MADE A POLICEMAN.—THE EXAMINATIONS THAT ARE NECESSARY AND THE RED TAPE THAT MUST BE UNWOUND.—DESCRIPTION OF THE UNIFORM ADOPTED.—THE PHYSICAL TESTS AND THE MEN WHO MAKE THEM.—SKETCH OF SURGEON C. L. ARMSTRONG.—HIS EXPERIENCE IN A FORLORN HOPE.—DR. ASA B. ISHAM.—DR. N. P. DANDRIDGE AND THE LATE DR. WALTER A. DUN.

THE discontent among the laboring classes, which was made manifest by the wide-spread strikes of 1886, and which the anarchists in the community were at pains to foment, convinced the commissioners that the force as constituted by the Act of March 30, of that year, was entirely inadequate to probable emergencies; through their efforts, therefore, the law was amended May 19, 1886, and the maximum number of the patrolmen raised from three hundred to four hundred. It was while this amendment was being considered and the exciting scenes attendant upon the strikes were being discussed, that a system was planned and adopted by which a man was regularly made a patrolman. Inasmuch as a candidate for position was applying for that which, when acquired, was not to prove of precarious tenure, but to last through life or good behavior, the commissioners proceeded in their work with deliberation and the utmost care. They made examination, mental and physical, compulsory, and scrutinized certificates of character from persons of repute with the vigilance of a West Point Examining Board. The preliminary step taken by the candidates for position, in conformity to the rules which now obtain, is the filing with the mayor of an application signed by several reputable citizens, obliged to name their residence and the number of years they have personally known the applicant. Each signer attests intelligently to the applicant's character, habits and associates; that he is a man of "good moral character, orderly in his deportment, and not in any respect a violator of law and good order; that he is of sober, temperate and industrious habits, and not addicted to the habitual use of intoxicating drinks, or to any other hurtful excesses; that he has never seen him drunk, or known or heard of his having been drunk; nor of his having been guilty of, or convicted of, any criminal act; nor of his having been convicted of any misdemeanor within the past three years; that he is a man of truth and integrity, of sound mind, good understanding, and of a temper, habits and manners fit for a policeman."

With the foregoing paper on file the applicant is then obliged to fill a blank on which questions are asked as to name, place, and exact date of birth; if naturalized, when and where; if an elector of Cincinnati, how long he has been one; place of residence, street and number; whether or not he can write the English language understandingly; whether he is a man of sobriety and integrity; if always a law-abiding citizen; if ever arrested, and if so, for what; if ever engaged in any unlawful calling; what has been his occupation, and what is it now; if married, how many persons in his family; height and weight; any chronic disease; subject to fits; done any military service, if so, where and when, and whether honorably discharged; ever been a policeman; has he promised to pay any money or other consideration to any person, directly or indirectly, for any aid or influence to procure his appointment on the force?

If the mayor regards the application with favor he addresses a note to the commissioners, stating that Mr. —— has been requested to ap ear before the board for medical examination, and the examination is made, and is as elaborate and as rigid as any made by the most carefully managed life insurance association. Indeed the medical blanks used by the police examiners have the appearance of having been copied from those prepared by some first-class actuary. The medical examiners for its commissioners even go further than those for most insurance companies, for they not only examine the candidate when clothed, but make a second examination, when he is stripped to the skin. They take no chances on his having some chronic disorder hidden under a fair exterior. If the physical examination proves satisfactory, the candidate is ordered to the gymnasium race track, where his speed is tested. If all the requirements are met by him, a note saying as much is signed by the three medical examiners and sent to the mayor, who in turn transmits it to the Board of Commissioners, together with all papers relating to the candidate, and supplements the same with the following:

"CITY OF CINCINNATI, MAYOR'S OFFICE.
"POLICE DEPARTMENT.
.... 188........

"*To the Hon. Board of Police Commissioners:*

"GENTLEMEN:

"I hereby nominate for your consent and approval.. to be a .... on the Police Force.

"Very respectfully,

....
"*Mayor.*"

This nomination is read to the board and ordered laid over till the next meeting. Meantime it is given to the press and published, so that if there are any objections to a confirmation they may become known. At the next meeting the applicant appears before the board, accompanied by two reputable citizens, who are questioned as to his character, temper, and fitness for the position. If the questions are satisfactorily answered and there are no objections filed, the candidate is questioned upon his citizenship, legal record, and habits, especially as to the use of intoxicants, and, finally, as to the use of weapons as a policeman. If nothing appears that would justify the contrary he is confirmed, and ordered to procure a bond in the sum of one thousand dollars, guaranteeing to pay any damages that may be adjudged against him by any competent tribunal for the illegal arrest or imprisonment, or injury by him of any person, and to pay all indebtedness which may have arisen against him in favor of the City of Cincinnati from any cause whatever during his continuance in office.

This bond is carefully examined by an expert, to determine whether or not the bondsmen severally possess realty to double the amount of the bond, and whether or not they have signed a bond for some other member of the force. If a bondsman is found to have signed for some other officer, he is rejected, unless his property, represented on tax duplicate, is of such a value as to cover all losses in all possible contingencies. If his bond is approved, the patrolman takes an oath of office, as follows:

"I, —— ——, do solemnly swear that I will support the Constitution of the United States of America, and the Constitution and Laws of the State of Ohio, and the Laws and Ordinances of the City of Cincinnati, and that I will well and faithfully discharge the duties of the office of ——, to which I have been appointed, according to law and to the best of my ability.

"Sworn to and subscribed before me.

"In testimony whereof, I have hereunto set my name and affixed the seal of the City of Cincinnati, this — day of —, 188–.

"—— ——, *Mayor of the City of Cincinnati.*"

The oath is filed with the Board of Commissioners with the rest of the application papers, and the candidate is then sent to the School for Instruction four hours each day for seven successive days, and to duty with an old patrolman for practical lessons. At the expiration of the seven days the new patrolman begins two hour lessons twice a week for three months, and at the end of six months the mental and manual examiners put him through the policeman's catechism and fix his grade accordingly. Gross ignorance of an officer's duty developed in this examination is considered ample reason for a prompt dismissal from the force. The grades are:

"1. Officers of the first grade and first class, and officers of the first grade and second class.

"Officers of the first grade and first class shall be those whose average percentage on examination was ninety and over—men who have never been punished by the Board of Commissioners for any dereliction of duty.

"Officers of the first grade and second class shall be those who, while having a percentage of ninety and over, may have violated rules of the Department.

"2. Officers of the second grade and first class, and officers of the second grade and second class.

"Officers of the second grade and first class shall be those whose average percentage on examination was eighty and over—men who have never been punished by the Board of Commissioners for any dereliction of duty.

"Officers of the second grade and second class shall be those who, while having a percentage of eighty and over, may have violated rules of the Department.

3. "Officers of the third grade and first class, and officers of the third grade and second class.

"Officers of the third grade and first class shall be those whose average percentage on examination was seventy and over—men who have never been punished by the Board of Commissioners for any dereliction of duty.

"Officers of the third grade and second class shall be those who, while having a percentage of seventy and over, may have violated rules of the Department."

The advancement of officers depends entirely upon examinations and conduct. No favoritism is possible, neither is dismissal except for cause. Concerning the examinations the Manual of the Cincinnati Police Department says:

"Officers whose average is below seventy per cent. shall appear before the board for re-examination within sixty days, and, if failing to reach the required percentage, shall be suspended from duty until such time as they may meet the standard fixed by the board.

"Officers whose percentage on Manual falls below seventy shall reappear before the board thirty days thereafter, and if they then do not reach seventy per cent. they shall thereupon be dropped from the rolls of the force, after the termination of the fortnight's salary term pending.

The officer's probation ends with the first semi-annual examination, or when his grade is first determined, and at that date his life as a regular officer to last during good behavior begins. His calling and election as an officer made sure, the question of a uniform at once becomes important. It was determined by the commissioners at the start that the Cincinnati guardian of the peace should not only be a perfect specimen of physical manhood, but that his handsome form should be set off with a handsome uniform. They insisted that fine feathers must not be overlooked in the business of making fine birds, and so rules were adopted by which the new officer should be clothed, as follows:

"All members of the department shall wear dark blue overcoats, double-breasted, with short rolling plain collars, buttoned close up to the neck; the waist two and one-half inches below the natural waist; skirt, four inches below the knee-pan; one pocket on the right breast outside, one pocket on the left breast inside, and one in each skirt; a row of eight police buttons on each side, four buttons behind with side edge, and three small police buttons on each cuff. The Superintendent and Inspector may wear velvet collars, and extra buttons on the cuffs.

"The superintendent, inspector, and lieutenants of police shall wear a dark blue double-breasted frock coat, plain collar, with a row of six police buttons on each side, made so that it can be buttoned up to the neck; skirt to be one inch above the centre of knee-pan; breast pockets inside, and a pocket in each skirt; three buttons on each cuff, and two on each skirt behind. The superintendent and inspector may wear velvet collars, and extra buttons on the cuffs.

"Sergeants and patrolmen shall wear dark blue, single-breasted, straight frock coats, buttoned up to the throat, with plain jacket collar and straight skirt, with nine police buttons on the breast, two on each cuff and four behind; side edges half the length of skirt; edges double stitched, one-eighth of an inch wide; sleeves to match, plain around bottom; two inside breast pockets, cash pocket outside on right side; waist two and one-fourth inches below the natural waist, and skirt one inch above the centre of knee-pan.

"All members of the department shall wear dark blue, single-breasted vests, made without collars, and with seven police buttons, to button up to within three inches of the neck.

"All lieutenants, sergeants, and patrolmen shall wear dark blue pantaloons, with a white welt in the outer seam.

"The superintendent, inspector, and lieutenants shall wear a blue cloth cap, with a gold bullion wreath in front, encircling gold bullion letters indicating the rank of the officer.

"Sergeants shall wear a blue cloth helmet, with a gold bullion wreath in front, encircling gold bullion letters indicating their rank.

"Patrolmen shall wear a blue cloth helmet, having in front a white metallic wreath, encircling silver figures indicating the officer's number. Covers may be worn over caps and helmets in stormy weather.

"The superintendent, inspector, and lieutenants shall wear upon each shoulder a gold bullion strap indicating their rank.

"The summer uniform shall consist of a blue flannel sack coat, and blue flannel pantaloons. The coat of patrolmen to be a single-breasted sack, with short turn-over collar, to button close up to the chin, and to reach to a point four inches above the bend of the knee, with four buttons on the front; no pockets to show on the outside, and the pantaloons to be made same as winter pantaloons.

"White gloves shall be worn in the summer when on special duty, and dark gloves in the winter.

"The uniform of the station-house keeper shall be the same as the summer uniform of the patrolmen.

"There shall be gossamer covers for the helmets and caps, and a rubber overcoat for rainy weather."

The supervision of the uniforms was placed under the charge of Commissioner Dodds, and he took the greatest interest in seeing that the materials were of the proper character, recommending changes when evidently necessary for the wear and tear, giving especial attention to the actual results as seen by service. Mr. Dodds continued in charge until July, 1887, when the board made the following modification:

"The coat of the mounted police and patrol-wagon men shall be made like the U. S. cavalry jacket, single breasted, with nine small regulation buttons on the breast; length to be two inches below the natural waist.

"The overcoats for patrol-wagon men shall be made a double breasted sack, skirt to reach the first joint of the thumb, the arm hanging naturally.

"The addition to overcoat of the mounted men shall be a cape, the length to extend to the wrist, the arm hanging naturally, to be fastened under the collar with six small regulation buttons in front."

The cloth for all the uniforms was a matter of much and careful examination, and finally the board accepted that known as "The Metropolitan Police Cloth," a change being made later in the cloth for the pantaloons, substituting one heavier and more serviceable.

"When a policeman is fully equipped for duty he is in full dress, carrying self-cocking pistol in his hip pocket; a rosewood baton, with red cord and tassel, hanging in the socket of his belt, on which is hung a cartridge-box containing six fixed charges for the pistol, and fire, patrol-box, and release keys; on the left breast a badge, to which by a chain is attached the whistle; and in his inner coat pocket the manual, fire card, and memorandum book."

The members of the Legislature, when they created a Board of Medical Examiners to co-operate with the Police Board, builded wiser than they knew. The provisions by which it was brought into existence were few and trifling. They only prescribed that the board should examine and pass upon all applicants for positions, either as patrolmen or lieutenants, and on the cases of any members of the force claiming an allowance for any temporary or permanent disability. The only other duty named was that of furnishing certificates of physical fitness. It was stipulated that the board should consist of the police surgeon and two physicians who have had five years' experience in the practice of medicine.

The board is now made up of Drs. C. L. Armstrong, A. B. Isham, and N. P. Dandridge.

On April 6, 1886, the nomination of C. L. Armstrong, M. D., was presented to the board, and on April 7, 1886, he was approved as police surgeon, taking the oath of office April 8, 1886.

On April 6, 1886, Walter A. Dun, M. D., and A. B. Isham, M. D., were nominated and confirmed as medical assistants. These gentlemen then organized the Board of Medical Examiners, by the election of Dr. A. B. Isham, President, and Dr. W. A. Dun, Secretary. This organization continued until the death of Dr. Dun, which occurred November 9, 1887. Dr. N. P. Dandridge succeeded him in the board seven days later.

The benefits arising from a rigid medical examination of the applicants for position is manifest, not only in the light mortality rate, from natural causes, but in the few sick patrolmen; and thus has the wisdom of the law, creating the Board of Examiners, been established. This board does not find much favor with the politicians in insisting that every appointee shall have not only a sound mind, but a sound body as well. It stands like a stone wall against any effort to overlook a physical infirmity as a reward for political services.

The first work the board had in hand after organizing was the adoption of a physical standard. At the suggestion of Dr. T. C. Minor, the main features of the requirements of the United States Army for regulars were accepted as the requirements for a Cincinnati policeman. These were:

"1. That patrolmen and substitutes be selected between the ages of 21 and 40 years, the Board of Police Commissioners, however, reserving to itself the right to make such exceptions in reference to age that in its discretion may be necessary in the interest of the public service.

"2. That lieutenants be selected between the ages of 21 and 50 years.

"3. That the minimum stature be fixed at 5 feet 7½ inches, and the minimum weight correspond to that opposite the stature as set forth in the following table:

5 feet 7½ inches......................Minimum weight, 140 pounds.
5 " 8 " .... " " 144 "
5 " 9 " .... " " 148 "
5 " 10 " .... " " 152 "
5 " 11 " .... " " 156 "
6 " " .... " " 160 "

"Five pounds additional for every inch in stature above 6 feet. Weight to be taken stripped.

"4. That the minimum chest measurement, taken during quiet respiration, shall correspond to the following table of heights:

5 feet 7½ inches	34 inches.
5 " 8 "	34½ "
5 " 9 "	35 "
5 " 10 "	35½ "
5 " 11 "	36 "
6 "	37 "

"An inch additional in chest measurement for every inch in height over 6 feet.

"5. That three inches difference between forced inspiration and forced expiration be required in chest measurement.

"6. That applicants be graded according to their power of speed and endurance as shown at various distances tested on a track.

"Measurements of the circumference of the chest are to be taken on bare skin, on level with nipple."

The Board of Medical Examiners are to reject all who fall below this standard, and are to hold all doubts in favor of the department. No applicant shall be nominated or confirmed as a member of the police force unless he is able to procure a certificate showing that he in all respects complies to the physical standard adopted in the department; said certificate to be signed by all the members composing the Board of Medical Examiners.

The Board of Commissioners reserve the right to make some slight exceptions to the standard in case of old soldiers and marines, and members of the old police force who had served the city faithfully and well. Subsequently the standard was raised, by placing the maximum age of the candidate for position at thirty-five years, and the minimum height at five feet nine inches, other measurements to correspond. To be convinced of the wisdom of this standard one has only to see the force on dress parade. No better types of manly beauty and strength were ever seen on Campus Martius or in the midst of the old Olympian games.

Dr. Clinton Lycurgus Armstong, the senior member of the Board of Medical Examiners of the police force, comes of most excellent old American stock. His great-grandfather, Captain John Armstrong, was killed bravely fighting on the bloody field of Monmouth, N. J., June 28, 1778. By his side fought and fell his eldest son. On the maternal side his great-grandfather was John La Boiteaux, one of the earliest of the Ohio pioneers. He settled in Hamilton County when its hills and valleys were still unbroken woodland, and owned and cleared all the land upon which Mt. Healthy was afterwards built. A man with an ancestry like this may well be proud of it. Brockville, Ind., was Dr. Armstrong's native place, his birthday being March 3, 1844. When he was but eighteen he joined the army, going into Company D, of the 83d Regiment, Indiana Volunteer Infantry, which served in the 15th Army Corps, under Sherman. He was a mere boy, yet he made an admirable soldier, cool and ready at all times and brave to the point of recklessness. He fought in all of the ten assaults upon Vicksburg, and was in the thick of some of the hardest fighting of the war. There is no private who can boast of a more glorious army record than was that of Dr. Armstrong, for he was an actor in one of the most gallant and yet disastrous enterprises of all the long struggle. There has been no poet laureate to sing of it, as the "Charge of the Six Hundred" was sung, but on the rolls of fame it deserves to be celebrated with as lofty praise. Around Vicksburg was a chain of forts. They were eight hundred yards apart, and connected by an embankment ten feet high, in front of which was a deep ditch. Sherman intended to attack a part of this chain, break through it, and then drive the enemy from their guns by a charge in their rear. It was necessary that some one lead the way, and Sherman called for one hundred and fifty volunteers. They were to rush across the open space in front of the rampart—the road leading to it was called by the soldiers "Grave-yard road"—half of them carrying planks twelve feet long, with which to bridge the ditch, the other bearing ladders, to scale the steep bank. Every one knew the frightful danger of the attempt, yet the volunteers came forward, and Dr. Armstrong was the first to report at Sherman's headquarters for this duty.

It was the 22d of May, 1863, and the hour set for the charge was 10 A. M. As the volunteers stood ready with their planks and ladders Sherman, in order to encourage them, though they needed no encouragement, said: "Soldiers, remember that the enemy always over-shoots, and the larger body behind you is sure to draw the heaviest fire." Then the word of command was given, and they started on a run for the Confederate works. There was no firing until they were within two hundred feet of the bank, and then it seemed as if the thunders of the universe were let loose at once. By some means the enemy had heard of the contemplated charge, and were ready for it. The two nearest forts delivered a galling cross fire upon the gallant band, and a solid regiment in front rose on the embankment and emptied its muskets at them. That volley meant annihilation to the volunteers. One hundred and thirty-eight of them fell dead, eleven were wounded, and but one man escaped unscathed. A more frightfully fatal fire was not delivered during the entire course of the war. Dr. Armstrong received three bullets, two in his right leg and one in his abdomen. All day he lay upon the field, and at night he dragged himself to the Union lines. For months he lay between life and death, and all through life he will bear the marks of his wounds. The only other living survivor of this "forlorn hope" is Mr. William Orr, of Eaton, Ohio. General Sherman is endeavoring to have Congress award these two heroes of that fatal day gold medals, and doubtless their bravery will yet be recognized in this way.

After the war Dr. Armstrong came to Cincinnati and studied medicine. He graduated with honor, and is now one of the best known and most successful physicians in this city. Mayor Jacobs appointed him police surgeon about ten years ago. At that time the surgeon was ranked simply as a patrolman, and received the same salary. Dr. Armstrong really created the position which he has filled with such signal ability. Among other things he is the inventor of the medicine chest that is carried on all patrol wagons, and which is a wonderful exemplification of *multum in parvo*.

As one of the Board of Medical Examiners of the non-partisan

C. L. ARMSTRONG.
A. B. ISHAM.
N. P. DANDRIDGE.
Medical Examiners.

police force, he has been instrumental in introducing the present high physical standard. He is also one of the trustees of the Cincinnati Hospital, surgeon for the Cincinnati, Washington & Baltimore Railroad, and has been President of the Lincoln Club, the oldest Republican organization in Cincinnati.

In 1878 Dr. Armstrong married Miss Mary Cotton, of Winchester, Ind., and he has found in her the completeness that his life lacked as a physician.

Among the police there is no man more popular than Dr. Armstrong. He knows them all, is ever ready with a word of advice or the ringing words of cheer that often mean more to the sick man than medicine, and is indefatigable in his duty. No night is too dark, and no distance too far, if there is suffering to be relieved. A hater of sham, he is a model of frankness and sincerity. His success has been thoroughly deserved.

If Dr. Asa Brainard Isham were to be seen in a crowd on the street, the stranger would not have a moment's hesitation in picking him out as a physician. He is the typical doctor. With keen eyes, a serious face, beard and hair sprinkled with gray, and a slight stoop in the back, he carries the marks of his profession all about him. Like many of the men who have risen to fame and fortune, he began life as a printer's devil. He was born at Jackson, Jackson Co., Ohio, in 1844, and after going through the county schools he started for Marietta College. But his collegiate career was cut short, and he went to Marquette, Mich., where he secured the position as devil in the office of the *Lake Superior Journal*. It was not long until he showed the stuff that was in him, and he was made a reporter, and finally manager and associate editor. He made such a stir in his new position that, when only eighteen, he was offered the position of city editor on the *Detroit Tribune*. He accepted the place, and was just beginning to shine in city journalism when he was seized with the war fever. In 1862 he enlisted in the 7th Michigan Cavalry, which went into Custer's Brigade in the Army of the Potomac. A year later he was wounded in a sharp contest near Warrenton, Va. Recovering, he again joined his regiment, distinguished himself, and was made a first lieutenant in 1864. He was with Grant during the campaign before Richmond.

After the war he came to Cincinnati and began the study of medicine at the Ohio Medical College, where he graduated in 1869. For a time he occupied the chairs of Physiology, Materia Medica and Therapeutics in the Cincinnati College of Medicine and Surgery, and was greatly liked by the hundreds of young men whose good fortune it was to be in his classes. The outside world knows him as a frequent contributor of vigorous articles to the medical journals. His home is on Walnut Hills, but his practice extends all over the city. As a member of the Medical Examining Board of the Police Department he takes the keenest interest in his work.

In Dr. N. P. Dandridge a worthy successor to Dr. Dun was found. The place made vacant by the latter was a hard one to fill. His enthusiasm and faithfulness, and his successful work in establishing a proper physical standard for patrolmen, have already been related. Upon Dr. Dandridge, fell the duty of bearing up the high standard established by his predecessor. And the mayor made a wise selection. Dr. Dandridge is a member of one of the oldest families in Cincinnati. His high character places him beyond the reach of undue influences, while his experience and care make him well able to discharge the important duties of his position.

Nathaniel Pendleton Dandridge, was born on the 16th of April, 1846, which makes him at present a little over forty two years of age. After a course in the schools of this his native city, he entered Kenyon College at Gambier, Ohio, with the class of 1866. He graduated with the highest honors, which he had well won and well deserved. Immediately afterward he entered the College of Physicians and Surgeons in New York city, to fit himself for his profession. He graduated from there in 1870, and began the practice of medicine in this city. It was not long before he was found in the front rank of the surgeons. He made that branch of medicine his specialty, and worked hard at it. But his labors in this line did not prevent him from winning the admiration and esteem of a large circle of friends. This latter triumph was due to these excellent qualities of heart, for which the doctor is no less distinguished than for mental ability.

During his eighteen years of practice in this city he has written and published many papers, which have been valuable additions to surgery. Whenever he speaks on the subject of surgery he is sure to command attention, because he has spared no pains to be accurate, while his deep love and study of science makes him original. In recognition of his abilities, he now occupies the chair of surgery in the Miami Medical College, and is a surgeon at the Cincinnati Hospital, at St. Mary's Hospital, and at the Episcopal Hospital for Children. On November 17, 1887, he received from the mayor the appointment to the Board of Medical Examiners, and his manner of discharging the duties of this place has been in perfect accord with what he has done before.

In the formation of the conditions which have brought about these results, as well as in arranging matters so that they should be lived up to, no one was more untiring or more active than the late Dr. Walter A. Dun. He became a member of the Board of Police Examiners at its beginning, and worked faithfully in it until his fatal sickness.

Walter A. Dun was born near London, Madison County, Ohio, March 1, 1857. His early education was conducted at his father's home, under the care of a tutor. Afterward he entered the Ohio State University at Columbus, from which he graduated in 1878, at the age of nineteen, with high honors. He then came to this city and entered Miami Medical College in the fall of '79. After a three years course he graduated at the head of his class, receiving the faculty prize. Soon afterward he left for Europe, and spent several years in the London Hospitals, taking, in 1882, the degree of Licentiate of the Royal College of Physicians. In the same year he also became a member of the Royal College of Surgeons. He returned home in 1883, and declined the position of resident physician at Girard College to become a trustee of Miami Medical College. During his years of study he had prepared himself to at once take a place among the first physicians of this city. He was not only an exceedingly popular man socially, but in his profession; his zeal, extended study and acuteness of mind made him looked upon as one of the coming men. His work in the Board of Police Examiners was like his work everywhere else. He neglected nothing, attending to the slightest details of his many interests. He formulated a system of physical examinations for applicants, and carried it out to the letter. In addition to this position, he occupied a clinical chair in the Miami Medical College, was a trustee of the Cincinnati Society of Natural History, a member of the Staff of the Episcopal Hospital for Children, which owes much of its success to his efforts, a member of the American Association for the advancement of science, of the American Medical Association, of the Ohio State Medical Association, of the Cincinnati Medical Society, and of at least half a dozen social clubs besides. With all these things to attend to, and with his social duties which his popularity made imperative, he was never guilty of neglecting anything. It was this young man, barely thirty years of age, entering upon a career which was certainly bright and radiant with promise of success, that a deadly attack of brain fever laid low. His death on the 7th of November, 1887, was a genuine shock to the entire community. When it was heard that he was sick, every one remarked that he was young, and had a good constitution and that he would surely recover. But overwork had sapped his energies, and after four weeks of sickness the end came. No greater tribute can be paid to him than the fact that the community at large, outside of his immediate circle of friends, yet vividly remembers and regrets his loss.

CHAPTER VIII.

POLICE TRAINING.—THE GYMNASIUM.—HISTORY OF ITS ORGAN-IZATION.— ATTENDANCE UPON IT COMPULSORY.— POLICE ATHLETES.—MILITARY DISCIPLINE AND THE FIRST MILITARY PARADE.—TRIBUTE FROM THE GOVERNOR OF OHIO.—SCHOOL OF INSTRUCTION.—IMPORTANT WORK ACCOMPLISHED BY CLERK WARREN.—THE MENTAL AND MANUAL EXAMINERS.—SKETCHES OF COLONEL KIRSTEAD, CAPTAIN TINKER, AND F. M. COPPOCK.— THE MORGAN MEDAL, AND MEN WHO HAVE CONTESTED FOR IT.— HOW POLICE TRIALS ARE CONDUCTED.

A few years ago the idea of attaching a fully furnished gymnasium to a police department would have been regarded as chimerical, and even now the number of cities that have made use of the sensible idea can be counted on one's fingers. But it is to the credit of Cincinnati that not only was she among the first to introduce this improvement, but that she has one of the best in the country, and that the police authorities believe in and mean to keep improving it.

At first thought it would not strike the average individual that a gymnasium was of any particular use to a police force that, ordinarily, is on duty from eight to twelve hours each day, largely spent in "walking a beat." But it is of use, nevertheless. The policeman usually has been a hard working man, whose daily labor has kept off all superfluous flesh and hardened all his muscles. When he dons the police uniform his mode of life is changed. He no longer walks briskly for any length of time, he mostly saunters on his beat, or stands quietly at his post on a street corner, where his only exercise comes from an occasional stroll across the street as convoy for a bundle-laden lady among the piratical teams and dashing cable cars. Except for the swinging of his club by his side, his arms get no exercise, save in an infrequent battle with a muscular and recalcitrant law breaker. He may have had the best of wind when he first put on his silver badge, but his official duties are not likely to give him a chance to use it once in three months in chasing a fleeing burglar. All these things have their influence upon his physical welfare, and they begin to make their mark in a year's time, and keep on to his deterioration. It is only a matter of time when the most stalwart gets weak in the arms, asthmatic from accumulated adipose tissue, flabby in the muscles of the body, bilious, and suffers from indigestion, until at last he has a rotundity that in comparison would make Falstaff himself look lank, and the erstwhile Apollo degenerates into plain, wheezy Podger. All this and more can be prevented by a judicious course of "work" in a well-appointed gymnasium, and the policeman's health be preserved, while his physical proportions may remain a joy to those susceptible people who delight in masculinity, surrounded by well-fitting blue flannel and garnished with brass buttons.

The police department of Cincinnati was organized under the non-partisan act on a broad basis, and with every safeguard to insure permanency. Men who join it have a life situation, unless they misbehave, and are assured of a pension if injured in the line of duty, or if they are retired from old age. Hence the advantage of keeping them in good physical condition, if only on the score of economy. The importance of a gymnasium was early recognized by the Board of Commissioners. The medical board informed the commissioners that many of the men who had just passed the very rigid physical examination to which they are all subjected, would, in a year's time, fall below its requirements unless meanwhile subjected to a course of training different from what they could get in the ordinary line of their duty, for the reason that they had heretofore been leading very active lives, quite different from what they would encounter as policemen. The matter was talked over with more or less earnestness in the Board of Commissioners, but without any action until the advent of Mr. Boyle, who took his seat January 1, 1887. Mr. Boyle had all his life been a lover of athletic exercises and a constant patron of gymnasiums. In fact, some years before, when a newspaper worker—as he still is—without a thought of holding such

A MODEL GYMNASIUM.
Front from Staircase.

A MODEL GYMNASIUM.
Rear from Staircase.

an office as he now fills, Mr. Boyle was a successful contestant in a walking match at St. Louis, and won a fine gold watch which he still carries. He at once grasped the full value of the idea, and soon brought up the subject by resolution to the board. The board favored it. The medical examiners urged it as a physical necessity for the maintenance of the physical standard of the men. There was doubt as to the authority of the board to establish and maintain a gymnasium. Finally the city solicitor gave his opinion that it might be properly done by the board if necessary to maintain the efficiency of the force. That settled it and thereupon the entire matter was referred to Mr. Boyle, with power to act, and he went to Council for the money necessary, and got it.

But resolving to make a gymnasium and making it were two very different things. Economy was absolutely essential. The coat must be made of a very small quantity of cloth. Many plans as to details were suggested, most of them proving impracticable, because of the too great expense contemplated. It was very hard to find a suitable place within the means allowed. Finally the second floor of Hammond street station-house was selected. For a long time it had been devoted to the storage of the Gatling gun belonging to the department, and the room itself was in a generally dilapidated and untidy condition. The Gatling gun was moved elsewhere. Carpenters, plasterers, and plumbers were set to work and the room was made respectable, even inviting.

Hammond street station-house is on Hammond street, half way between Third and Fourth streets, and a half square east of Main street. Climbing up the clean, broad stairway to the second floor, a placard on the door cheerfully announces: "Please wipe your feet. Shut the door. No smoking or chewing." The door is closed with a night catch, to which every policeman has a key. Entering one finds a room about 100 by 40 feet. Two large windows in the front and two in the rear, and five upon each side in the rear two-thirds of the room, give ample light and ventilation. The ceiling is high, with ventilating flues. Not a speck of dust or dirt is to be seen. On the north wall hang numbered hooks for clothing. In the southeast corner is a small office, occupied by the janitor, in which are kept the towels and other supplies, the registers, etc. In the south wall open out two doors. These were formerly the doors to closets, which had little or no use in the former occupation of the room. In the fitting up of the gymnasium the question of providing bath-rooms was a difficult problem. There seemed to be no place to put them. Finally the two closets were thrown into one, a window was let into the end, the doors were taken off and in their place were hung half curtains sliding on rods, which gave at once concealment and light and ventilation. Inside, instead of bath-tubs, were placed five large porcelain-lined basins, by the side of which are racks for sponges and towels, with a faucet for the water, and all accessories for a sponge bath. The floor is covered with lead, over which is laid a false floor of slats. There is thus given abundant room for five men to take each a sponge bath in a space that could have afforded but two bath tubs.

The room was fitted up under the direction of Mr. Edward Murphy, superintendent of the Cincinnati gymnasium. All around the room is a running track, said by experts to be the finest of the kind in the country. It is of felt, the kind used for covering boilers, an inch thick, and covered with canvas, treated with three coats of paint. At each of the four corners the outer edge is raised, the object being to prevent the men from falling when running rapidly. This makes the track not only safe, but very "fast." Just inside the end of the track nearest the door is a false ceiling, eight feet square, from which depends a striking ball, which is the particular pet and admiration not only of the janitor, but of all the policemen as well. It is the most popular implement in the room, and is said to be the best in the country. The ordinary striking balls would last but a short time here, for the reason that the men who fondle it are bigger men and stronger hitters than those who usually manipulate such affairs in ordinary gymnasiums. They knocked so many ordinary rubber balls to smithereens that the wits of those in charge of the room were sorely tried to devise something to withstand the stalwart blows of the gigantic policemen of the Queen City. Finally, the manufacturers made a rubber ball of extra strength, which was covered with stout leather, and now the ball withstands its daily assaults with perfect equanimity. Six combination pulleys, the invention of Mr. Murphy, are ranged near the centre of the room. These are so constructed as to provide for the exercise of about every muscle of the entire body, and may be graded to suit any strength by the addition of weights of any desired burden. Then there is a vaulting horse, of Mendart's patent, and the very best construction, and a pair of Mendart's parallel bars, vaulting and tumbling bars, a climbing rope, climbing ladder, a wrestling bed, of sawdust covered with canvas, one of the best in the country, and a full complement of Indian clubs, dumb-bells, ranging from one to sixty pounds in weight, boxing gloves, etc. The total cost was well on to fifteen hundred dollars, and improvements are constantly being made.

When the gymnasium was first opened, the men had little disposition to attend. Some of them thought it was designed as a playground, and they came to it just as they felt inclined; and, when duty was hard, the inclination was usually lacking. The board felt bound to insist by strict orders upon attendance. It was hard, even then, to induce attendance. But now nearly all come cheerfully, and, on the part of some, there is an eagerness that might even call for repression but for the fact that the requirements of duty do not allow too much of this kind of dissipation. The rules, which are carefully laid down, require attendance of one hour each week, except in the cases of certain officers in the patrol and mounted service, who are excused every other month. Voluntary attendance is without restriction. In times of long extended hard duty, such as has been involved by the Centennial Exposition for instance, this rule is relaxed, and the attendance is wholly voluntary. The rules are carefully formulated to meet all ordinary requirements. In wrestling, boxing, etc., good nature on the part of the participants is insisted upon. The first thing to be done by an officer when he enters the room is to give up his pistol to the janitor. This is to prevent accidents, and is strenuously enforced by the men themselves. Clothes must be hung upon a hook, designated by a check received for the pistol. Shoes must not be worn at exercise, nor must a shoe be set upon the track or the wrestling bed. The men furnish their own costumes for exercising in, but the entire outfit is furnished and maintained by the Board of Commissioners, so that it is the only institution of the kind in the country supported free of expense to the men. The whole place is heated by hot air, and hot water is furnished the bath-room. When the police annex is completed at the new City Hall, a bigger and better gymnasium will be among its appointments. But by that time it is altogether probable that the police force of Cincinnati will be so enlarged that both the new and the old gymnasiums will be found necessary.

When the gymnasium was opened the men were for three months under the instruction of A. C. Brendamour, attaché of the Cincinnati gymnasium. Since then they have been in charge of officer Charles Folger, who has been specially assigned to this duty. Mr. Folger is a thorough athlete, not muscular, but very wiry, supple, and strong. He was formerly a contortionist in the shows of Robinson, Sells Brothers, and others. He is an ingenious young man, and is perfecting a system of police alarms which promises to be of great utility. Mr. Folger devotes a great deal of attention to exercise of the arms and shoulders, points to which the ordinary work of the policeman does not contribute any benefit, the idea being to develope the lungs and spread the shoulders. Two pound dumb-bells are used rather than heavier ones, Mr. Folger's experience showing that it is better to gradually build up the muscular system by them than to use the heavy weights, which retards the quickness of the muscular movement so necessary to a policeman, and in the end gives as much muscle as the larger bells. Work on the vaulting horse, on the horizontal bars, the ladder and the climbing rope, wrestling and boxing, are particularly encouraged. The men are divided into classes, and about forty at a time can be drilled. Some of the men have become very proficient, and would compare well with those attending any gymnasium in the country. Officer Curry is a fine boxer and wrestler, and has thrown every man he has met. In a contest with Wittmer, of the Cincinnati gymnasium, a noted local athlete, he threw him in the first bout in four and one-half minutes; was thrown in the second in fourteen minutes, while the third bout was declared a draw at the end of fifteen minutes. Otting, of the mounted police force, has become a very proficient all-around athlete. Dennis Ryan has made the best time on the track. Sergeant Corbin is a fine boxer, and learned all he knows in the police gymnasium. Officer Casey, who weighs over two hundred pounds, is the fastest heavy weight on the track. Kelly, of the patrol service, is an expert wrestler. So are officers Wunskump and John McCarthy, while many others are above the average attendant on gymnasiums in proficiency in athletic exercises. From the gymnasium to a military drill is but a step. The one is an excellent trainer for the other.

In this history probably no more striking fact will be discussed than the change from the old watchman to the new policeman. It is not many years ago that the only evidence of authority worn by an officer was a badge, and his only weapon a club. Even after the adoption of the uniform there was still something lacking—and that military drill. It is due to the present board that a drill has been made a prominent feature of discipline. This branch of service is under the charge of Inspector of Police George D. Hadley, ably assisted by Sergeant John W. Carroll as drillmaster. The board, early in 1887, determined to have annual parades, and fixed upon April 30 as a date for the first one. There were some fears that perhaps at this time the force would not exhibit the precision of movement desired, but the result exceeded expectation. At this review there were present the Governor of the State and numerous National and State military officials, upon invitation made by the department, and many citizens personally interested, or whose curiosity had been aroused by such an unusual event. A pleasing incident in connection with this parade was the following letter received from Hon. J. B. Foraker, Governor of Ohio:

"COLUMBUS, O., May 2, 1887.
" HON. AMOR SMITH, JR.,
Mayor of Cincinnati.

" DEAR SIR:—I knew by general repute, and from what I had from time to time casually observed, that the police force of Cincinnati was composed of a fine body of men, but I did not know until the review and inspection of last Saturday what an exceedingly creditable organization you have. I do not refer alone to the splendid physical proportions of the men, the neatness of their uniforms and equipments, evident good discipline, or the steadiness and precision with which they marched and executed all movements. All these movements were necessarily apparent to every spectator, and are no doubt appreciated. I was pleased with something else I observed, which may not have been noticed. I carefully scanned the face of every man and officer, and view it of the highest credit to yourself and the Board of Police Commissioners, and all others connected with the organization of the force, to be able to say, as I gladly do, that every man had a clear face, an open, frank, manly, and intelligent countenance, that indicated gentlemanly instincts and trustworthiness of character. The force, one and all, is to be congratulated upon splendid appearance and manifest efficiency. The people of Cincinnati are to be especially congratulated upon the assurance so given them of peace, order, and good government.

"Very truly yours, etc.,

"J. B. FORAKER."

The School of Instruction was established in 1888, and is intended to cover some of the deficiencies which would naturally arise were the gaining of police knowledge left to experience only. The Board at first planned for a school to be held twice a week at each station. It soon became evident to the clerk of the Board, however, that the pupils from station schools held views widely different as to police laws and regulations. Some central point of instruction, therefore, was found necessary. His attention was first called to a direct personal effort in this direction by the application of a lieutenant to prepare a series of questions upon the police manual. Being desirous to aid the officer, he began the work, and found that he could not fully prepare these questions without careful examination of the criminal laws and city ordinances, if he wished to do justice to the topics presented by the manual. About three hundred general questions were prepared at first, and for the time being were useful, being employed by the mental and manual examiners as a basis upon which they built up their own system. Becoming interested more and more in the matter, upon the suggestion of Commissioner Dodds, Mr. Warren prepared an exhaustive series of questions, designing to present to the Board a plan for issuing this series to each station. After months of preparation it became evident that the work intended would be of so extensive a character that it would involve more than was originally intended, and the subject was presented to his Honor, Mayor Smith, who cheerfully presented Mr. Warren's name to the Board as an official instructor. Mr. Warren entered upon the work with enthusiasm, devoting all his leisure time, day and night, to his classes.

The general divisions of the instruction are upon such United States and State laws and city ordinances as pertain to police duties; upon the powers, privileges, duties, discipline and exercises of patrolmen as may be prescribed by the Board of Police Commissioners; upon explanations of the principles, causes, and modes of action under the general orders issued by the mayor and the superintendent of police, and upon the topography of the city, which includes in general the location of all prominent places of interest, such as parks, amusements, buildings, and places of business, and especially in each district its prominent places of interest, even to the location of residences of citizens of any prominence. One additional branch that is not specified by any order of the board, or laid down by any rule, the official instructor has steadily kept in view, and that is the principles that should actuate each officer in the performance of duty, that he must be vigilant, active, and courageous.

The law provides that "the commissioners shall cause to be prepared a convenient manual, containing a compend of all the laws and ordinances which the police force is required to obey or enforce, and such instructions as shall aid them in the intelligent discharge of their duties. The annual report by Dr. T. C. Minor, when he was President of the Board, gives the following brief description of the lamp by which an officer's feet are guided:

"The new manual was completed June 17, and approved and

put in force on July 1, 1887. The credit for the compilation and systematic arrangement of the manual is largely due to Messrs. Topp and Boyle, who spent much time in preparing the manuscript for the printer. Each rule in it was duly approved by the Mayor and the Board of Commissioners. The work contains, in addition to the rules governing the force, a list of the offenses against the city ordinances, and a very complete synopsis of the principal crimes against the laws of Ohio, prepared by Fred. Hertenstein, a prominent young lawyer of Cincinnati. A manual of instruction in military tactics is also included in this policeman's guide, the latter being the work of Captain George D. Hadley, inspector of police. The instructions as to the 'care of the sick and injured' are clear, concise, and briefly-worded notes of medical advice, compiled by the Board of Medical Examiners for the use of patrolmen in medical emergencies. One of the most important articles in the manual is the advice of Judge S. R. Matthews, of the Court of Common Pleas of Hamilton county, on the 'general principles of law relating to arrests and the use of fire-arms.' The new manual is a model of clearness as to the details of police business, and a work in which the department may well take pride, being without exception the most perfect manual in use in the United States to-day, and will be considered the standard by which other cities must model."

With a body well trained in the gymnasium, and by a drill-master, a mind filled with information imparted by Instructor Warren and gleaned from the manual, the officer is then fitted for a mental and manual examination.

The police law provides: "It shall be the duty of the Board of Police Commissioners, at least twice in each year, to require the examination and inspection of the entire force, and for this purpose the commissioners may appoint an examiner or examiners, and prescribe the methods of examination. Gross ignorance of the laws and regulations governing and directing the police after six month's service as officer or member, shall be deemed conclusive proof of inefficiency, and shall require the removal of such officer." The semi-annual examinations of the force under these provisions began December 3, 1886, and was continued under the super-

F. M. COPPOCK.
H. H. TINKER.
JEREMIAH KIERSTED.
Mental Examiners.

vision of the commissioners until April 23, 1887, when Colonel Jeremiah Kiersted and Frank M. Coppock were duly appointed, and assumed the duties of mental and manual examiners. F. M. Coppock was afterwards appointed special clerk, and Captain H. H. Tinker succeeded to the vacancy June 21, 1887. The examinations are rigid in proportion to the length of service of the officer examined. The examiners have adopted the following method of procedure: Each man on appearing before them must submit a letter of not less than ten lines, and must read any paragraph printed in English offered to him. He is asked such number of questions as are deemed necessary on the laws of the State relative to crimes, ordinances under police supervision, rules and regulations of the department, knowledge of drill, and the topography of the city. After each examination an officer is graded upon a standard of 100 in reading, writing, spelling, and the manual, as has been indicated on these pages. As an evidence of the character of attainments by the force, only two members fell to seventy per cent., and these two subsequently attained a higher percentage, one even passing into the coveted position of Grade 1, Class A.

Probably no man now living in Cincinnati is more familiar with the police matters of the city, from the infancy of the system down to the present time than Deputy U. S. Marshal Jeremiah Kiersted.

Colonel Kiersted is a Cincinnatian born and bred, and has been closely identified with the affairs of the city for nearly half a century. The fact that he has led a pure and blameless life, both as a public official and as a private citizen, is shown by the number of offices and important public trusts he has held by the choice of his fellow townsmen. Colonel Kiersted was born on Fourth street, between Race and Elm, December 16, 1822. He received a common school education, entering the public schools on the first day they were opened.

In 1835 he entered Woodward High School, from which he graduated with honor. After leaving Woodward young Kiersted served an apprenticeship as a sheet iron worker, and followed that trade up to the spring of 1850.

In the fall of 1850 he was appointed deputy sheriff under C. J. W. Smith, in which capacity he served for two years.

In the spring of 1853 he received the Democratic nomination for marshal of the city and was defeated by James L. Ruffin. He then entered Bartlett's College to take a course in book-keeping. He had been in the college but a short time when he was appointed clerk in the County Treasurer's Office, under Charles Thomas. Here he remained but two months, when he was appointed to fill a vacancy in the Board of City Commissioners. This appointment was made by the city council against the earnest protest of Colonel Kiersted. At the solicitation of friends, however, he was induced to accept the proffered honor.

He filled this responsible office in an acceptable manner until the expiration of his term in the spring of 1854, when he was nominated to succeed himself by the almost unanimous vote of the Democratic City Convention, and was elected.

In the spring of 1858, his term of office having expired, he was nominated and re-elected for one year.

At the expiration of this term Colonel Kiersted received the appointment of local mail agent under Postmaster James J. Faran.

In the spring of 1860, while discharging the duties of mail agent, he was again elected city commissioner for a term of three years, being with one exception the only Democrat elected that year in Hamilton County.

While holding this office the rebellion broke out, and Col. Kiersted was appointed Superintendent of Fatigue force. This was during the Kirby Smith raid.

In 1864, feeling it his duty to go to the front, Colonel Kiersted enlisted in the Union army, was elected second lieutenant of Company A, 129th O. V. I., and was stationed at Point Lookout, in Maryland.

After coming out of the army he returned to Cincinnati, and entered the employment of the Columbus Accident Insurance Company. From there he went into the United States Internal Revenue service, being appointed to the position of store-keeper in 1867, under Colonel Stephen J. McGroarty, Internal Revenue Collector. In this service he remained two years. In 1873 he was appointed superintendent of the police, in which capacity he served during parts of the years 1873 and 1874. In the interval between 1874 and 1880 he served on the Board of Education. In 1880 he was elected decennial assessor in the Fifth Ward, and was chosen city sealer during Mayor Mean's administration in 1881, for a term of two years, by a unanimous vote of the city Council. In May, 1885, Colonel Kiersted was appointed deputy United States marshal under Henry C. Urner, which position he still holds, together with the respònsible one of mental and manual inspector of the police force of Cincinnati.

Henry Harris Tinker was born in New York city April 15, 1836. When five years old he removed to New London, Connecticut, and eleven years later, or in August, 1852, to Cincinnati, where he has since lived continuously. For a long time he was in the dry goods business, and before the war was a sergeant of the old "Guthrie Greys." The proclamation of war was issued on the twenty-fifth anniversary of Mr. Tinker's birthday, and he enlisted for the three months service the same day. Afterward he re-enlisted for the three-years term. He went out elected captain of Company H, Sixth Regiment O. V. I., and served in that position during his entire war experience of three years and two months. Captain Tinker was wounded in his head the second day of January, 1863, at Stone River, and at Chicamauga, September 19, the same year. Here he was captured, and his name was stricken from the roll as "dead or missing." He was, however, laid up more than a year by the injuries he then sustained. In 1866 he was appointed a deputy clerk of the Court of Common Pleas, under Benjamin Horton, and clerk of the courts by the county commissioners in 1870, to fill the vacancy caused by the death of Col. Stephen J. McGroarty, his opponent for the same position for election before the people.

The same year he was elected by the people to the same position, and for three years succeeding the expiration of his term of office was an attaché therein. He was one of Revenue Collector Amor Smith's staff of storekeepers, and September 15, 1881, was appointed special deputy surveyor of the port, under Colonel D. W. McClung. He was appointed a member of the Board of

Mental and Manual Examiners of the police force June 1, 1887. Captain Tinker is an unmarried man.

The records do not do justice to the relation of Mr. F. M. Coppock with the police department. Ostensibly he is only a clerk therein. Really he is the legal adviser, the solicitor of the department, the man who prevents the authorities running amuck through the statutes and ordinances. His ministerial duty is simply the drawing up of legal matter. Everything in law connected with the police department that does not come within the scope of the city solicitor is placed in Mr. Coppock's hands. Hence, he is seen as often in the county criminal courts as in the civil rooms. His duty at the former tribunal is the defense of officers under charges growing out of the performance of the obligations of a member of the force. The office, as can be seen, is an important one. It is of comparative recent creation. The pushing aggressive policy of the new police department made such a tributary to its power a necessity. The incumbent must be a man who is always alive to the situation, and Mr. Coppock is that sort of a man. His full name is Francis Marion Coppock, after the revolutionary war general. He was born in the country, near Troy, Miami County, Ohio, August 10, 1851. His parents were Joseph C. and Sarah A. Coppock. His boyhood days were passed on his father's farm. Young Frank ploughed sunshine during the summer season, and cultivated the seeds of ambition in the Troy public schools in the winter, until he was seventeen years old.

At this age, with an excellent common school education, "well ground in," young Coppock started on a course in Miami University, at Oxford, Ohio, where he remained five years, including one year in the preparatory department. Then he went to Europe to polish off. The succeeding three years were passed at hard work at the Universities of Gottingen, Leipsic, and Heidelberg, and from the last named institution he graduated in 1876, as a doctor, not of duelling, but philosophy. Returning home the same year he entered the Cincinnati Law School, and two years afterward graduated and hung out his shingle. For two years he practiced law alone—not as to clients—and later formed a partnership with his brother, W. T. Coppock, and William Caldwell, the recent surveyor of customs. The subsequent retirement of Mr. Caldwell made the firm Coppock & Coppock. Young Coppock's ability began to be recognized, and in 1885 he was elected city solicitor. The trust he managed with signal ability. In this connection he was attorney for the Board of Revision. At the expiration of his term of office he formed a partnership for the practice of law, taking in John D. Gallagher and Frederick Hertenstein, his assistant solicitors. Mr. Coppock was for a time a member of the Board of Manual Examiners of the police force, but resigned to accept the position as clerk to the department on his nomination by Mayor Smith, and election by the Board of Police Commissioners, about a year ago.

On October 22, 1885, he was married to Miss Jennie Williams, daughter of Mr. and Mrs. Francis Williams, of Walnut Hills.

Mr. Coppock's professional life has been very successful. No attorney stands higher at the Cincinnati bar than he. His public administrations have been pure. His domestic life is a happy one. Altogether he is a good example of an energetic young man, with bright years behind him, and with years still brighter just ahead.

There is one reward which stands highest in appreciation by the force. The first president, Robert J. Morgan, gracefully emphasized his retirement from the board in an address to the force at an inspection made at the close of 1886, by offering as an incentive to proficiency in police duties a gold medal, of the value of fifty dollars. This offer he renewed in the following letter to the board:

"CINCINNATI, January 11, 1887.

"*To the Honorable the Board of
    Police Commissioners of the City of Cincinnati*:

" GENTLEMEN,—In taking leave of the police force of this city, in the organization of which I had taken an active part, as an incentive to stimulate them in the performance of their duties, I promised to the patrolman who should be declared by your honorable board as having been the most efficient in the discharge of his duties during the past year a gold medal, of the value of fifty dollars; this to occur for five years. In furtherance of this object, I propose to have such medal designed and executed, you furnishing me the name of the patrolman not later than December 1st of each year.

"Respectfully,
"ROBERT J. MORGAN."

Upon the receipt of this communication the thanks of the board were immediately sent to Mr. Morgan, and it was ordered that a copy of the letter be read at the several station and patrol houses at roll-call, and that the medal should hereafter ke known as the Morgan medal.

In September, 1887, the board was notified that the medal was ready, awaiting the name of the successful person. The board immediately established the following rules:

1st. That every patrolman, including sergeants, who has attained ninety-five per cent. at his semi-annual examination shall be considered a competitor for the Morgan medal.

2d. That such competitor shall present himself before the Mental and Manual Examiners for examination.

3d. That the Mental and Manual examiners shall, from the competitors, submit to the board a list of ten names of men, whom they shall consider the best in mental proficiency in the rules and regulations of the department.

In accordance with these requirements, the examiners presented, in 1887, the following list: W. F. Borck, L. Biedinger, M. J. O'Hearn, Joseph Wilmes, E. F. Rockwell, W. W. Clawson, W. Brockman, J. W. Scahill, John McGrann, and E. C. Hill. These officers appeared separately before the board to answer a list of questions previously prepared, and after careful scrutiny of claims the honor fell to John McGrann, captain of Patrol Company No. 2.

The board in making this selection, also made the matter the subject of a general order, and added that the other named patrolmen were entitled to an honorable mention.

It is a noteworthy fact that of the above names W F. Borck, L. Bedinger, M. J. O'Hearn, Joseph Wilmes, and E. C. Hill are

MORGAN MEDAL.

now acting sergeants, and J. W. Scahill has been promoted to a lieutenancy.

The medal, as will be seen from the sketch attached, bears upon its face the picture of Mr. Morgan, and on the reverse the proper inscription. The engraving is in the highest art.

In 1888 the same rules were adopted, but it is to be noted that while, in 1887, thirty-six patrolmen were entitled to compete for the honor, in 1888, fifty-four were proffered the privilege.

John McGrann, winner of the first Morgan medal, is of Scotch-Irish descent, and was born in Cincinnati, on the 17th of August, 1848. He has lived here ever since, having spent most of his life in and about livery stables. For ten years before going on the force he was fireman at Zumstein's. On the 20th of October, 1886, he was appointed to the police force and stationed at the Hammond street station. Two nights after his appointment he was transferred to the patrol division, where he has remained ever since, serving first on the Four's wagon, and then on the Two's. He is an excellent patrol-wagon man, and fills his position as captain of the Two's squad in a most satisfactory manner. He has been offered a sergeantcy, but has refused it, preferring his present branch of the service. He is a veritable mine of information on the history of Cincinnati, and also on the locations of buildings and streets. This fact is due to his long and uninterrupted residence here and to his powers of observation. His capture of the medal was well deserved, and the higher honor because he bore it away from some of the best officers on the force.

On September 11, 1888, it was ordered by the Board of Police Commissioners that all patrolmen and sergeants of the police force who had received ninety-five per cent. or over at their last semi-annual examinations previous to November 1, 1888, be qualified to compete for the second Morgan medal, and that examinations of the competitors should take place during the month of October, by the mental and manual examiners; it being further ordered that no patrolman should be permitted to compete who had been disciplined by this board within one year previous to November 1, 1888. It was also provided that the mental and manual examiners should select ten from among the competitors and forward their names to the Board of Commissioners, from which number there should be selected one whose name should be transmitted to R. J. Morgan, Esq., as entitled to be the recipient of the second medal under his generous offer.

Each competitor was ordered to write a letter of not less than fifteen lines upon a topic which should suggest improvements, modifications, additions, or any other matters the adoption of which would, in the view of the writers, be worthy of the consideration of the department. This rule was complied with by each competitor, and his standard of writing and spelling thereby determined by the examiners. Before the examiners each competitor presented himself, and was required to read aloud a printed paragraph of ten lines, in order to determine his improvement in reading. Twenty-five questions were then asked upon manual rules, State laws, and city ordinances, and fifteen questions upon localities, officials, and other points connected with the topography and government of the city.

On November 1, 1888, the examiners reported to the commissioners, submitting the following names: F. W. Arnim, W. T. Bebb, William Copelan, William W. Clawson, William Finn, John Grimm, E. C. Hill, J. H. Kiffmeyer, E. Leonard, J. J. Nealis, and M. J. O'Hearn as entitled to appear before the commissioners. The board thereupon ordered that the named officers be cited to appear before the board on November 9, 1888, at 7.30 P. M., for final examination. It was further ordered that the rules for the final examination be the same as those for the one held in 1887, and that S. B. Warren, the clerk of the board, be requested to prepare a list of questions. At the time appointed the clerk announced that he had prepared a list of one hundred questions, of which by lot he had selected forty. It was then ordered by the board that forty numbers, corresponding to those of the questions, be deposited in a hat, and that the clerk should draw twenty-five therefrom, which twenty-five were used in the competition, each competitor being asked the entire number. The named competitors appeared before the board and separately answered the several questions. The examination being completed, it was found that three competitors had been selected by the different members of the board as entitled to the sought for honor. It was thereupon ordered that sixty numbers corresponding to those of the questions which had not been selected in the previous drawings be again deposited in a hat, and the clerk instructed to draw five therefrom which should be asked of the three persons selected. They duly appeared before the board and answered the questions.

It was then ordered that a vote be taken by which it should be decided who of the three officers, in the judgment of the board, was entitled to the medal, each member of the board voting *viva voce.*

The roll being called each commissioner named William W. Clawson, who was declared the successful competitor. The decision was then communicated to R. J. Morgan, Esq. The decision was also communicated to the mayor, who issued a general order announcing the result, and then congratulated the other competitors who had appeared before the board upon their splendid records made in the competition.

Officer William Wheeler Clawson was born in this city on July 18, 1849. Previous to going on the police force he was employed in the printing department of James L. Haven & Co. On August 16, 1885, he was appointed to the force and assigned to the Oliver street station, where he remained until April 1, 1888, when he was transferred to Bremen street—his present station. His success in the Morgan contest speaks for his abilities as an officer.

The world is made up of the antithetical. "Like bodies repel" is one of the axioms of natural philosophy. That a description of the process by which the best officers compete for and receive medals for efficiency and proficiency should be abruptly followed by the detailed formalities observed in a police trial, need not therefore be a matter of surprise to the reader. The two fit together at this place in the volume as the fingers of the competent right hand fit between those of the incompetent left.

The share the board has in the immediate government of the force is limited, but it has placed upon it, by the law of 1886, one of the most important duties. The statute says: "No member or officer of the police force shall, after his appointment, be removed, or reduced in grade or pay, for any reason except inefficiency, misconduct, insubordination, or violations of the law." "Any person may present charges against an officer, which shall be filed in the office of the mayor, and by him communicated, without delay, to the commissioners, whose duty it shall be to investigate and decide upon them." The law further provides what punishments the board may inflict.

The usual course of procedure is simple. A member of the force charged with an offense by any person is summoned before the superintendent, who investigates the matter, and if the person so charging insists upon a trial by the board, the superintendent has a proper form drawn up, which he submits to the mayor, and says that the charges, "if true, are prejudicial to the good order and discipline of the Cincinatti police force, and in violation of rule No. —." The mayor, on receipt of the charges, refers them for final disposition to the board. The accused appears at the next meeting of the board where, together with the prosecutor, he is allowed four witnesses. In cases of great importance where more testimony may be needed this number may be increased. No attorneys are allowed to appear before the board on either side, and no witness is allowed more than fifteen minutes time in giving testimony. The hearing is summary and without pleading. No witness except the one prosecuting is allowed to be present while another is testifying. The president puts the question to the prosecutor: "Are you willing to abide by the decision of this board, whatever it may be?" Upon an affirmative answer the president continues: "Are you, prosecutor and defendant, ready for trial?" Should either answer be in the negative, a date is fixed to which the hearing is continued. Upon an affirmative answer, the charges are read and the witnesses sworn. Upon the conclusion of the testimony all persons interested are compelled to retire. The president asks: "Shall the charges be sustained?" to answer which requires not less than three votes. If the charge is sustained, then by a vote equally pronounced, the penalty is decided upon. Each charge is voted upon separately.

The decision of the board is communicated to the mayor in writing, and the penalty duly executed. The penalties are a reprimand either by the president of the board or the superintendent of police; a suspension usually not beyond thirty days; a fine not to exceed sixty days pay; forfeiture of pay due; reduction in rank, or a dismissal from the force. The limit of fines, by a tacit rule, is one hundred dollars, and when the offense seems to demand this punishment it is understood that the offending member escapes dismissal from the force on account of previous good conduct. There is a satisfaction in recording the fact that the largest number of police trials occurred during the first year of the existence of the present board, and the least number during the year which has just been brought to a close.

CHAPTER IX.

THE CHIEF AND INSPECTOR.—SERVICES OF PHILIP H. DEITSCH, BOTH IN WAR AND IN PEACE.—HIS EXPERIENCE WITH GENERAL SHERIDAN.—CATALOGUE OF THE BATTLES IN WHICH HE FOUGHT.—HIS SUCCESS AS A COMMANDER OF MEN.—THE INSPECTOR'S DUTIES.—CAPTAIN GEORGE D. HADLEY'S CAREER.—CHIEF DEITSCH'S OFFICE CORPS.

SUPERINTENDENT of Police, Philip H. Deitsch, whose efforts have largely contributed towards bringing the force to its present high standard of excellence, is acknowledged to be one of the best chiefs of police the city ever had. He has been in active police service in Cincinnati for twelve years, as patrolman, sergeant, lieutenant, and chief. He has worked his way from the bottom to the top of the ladder.

When Colonel Deitsch took charge of the force it was regarded as about the worst in the history of the city. He went to work quietly and without ostentation and began the weeding-out process. He first started a reform in the uniforms of the patrolmen. Under former administrations the men dressed carelessly, and appeared at roll call in semi-officer's dress. Night after night the chief appeared before the men at roll call and inspected their clothing. His orders were imperative, and whenever any unlucky patrolman appeared with unpolished shoes and soiled clothing he was ordered out of the ranks and sent home. It took weeks and months of careful training, but at last the men were brought to a realization that the new chief meant just exactly what he said. To-day the force is perhaps the neatest, cleanest, and best uniformed outside the famous Broadway squad of New York, and all owing to the work of the chief.

One year after his selection as superintendent of police, Chief Deitsch ordered the first public inspection of the force. The entire department was out, and the scene presented was a revelation to the citizens of the city. The inspection was held at Garfield Place and Race street, and Governor Foraker and nearly all the dignitaries of the state were present. The chief on this occasion was publicly complimented by his excellency the governor.

Colonel Deitsch was born in Rhenish Bavaria, on the seventh day of October, 1840. When quite a young man he came to America and enlisted in the regular army, and was detailed out West for active duty. At this time he was looked upon as raw recruits usually are. A number of the older soldiers treated him with contempt, but the young man attended strictly to his duties, and paid but little heed to the slurs cast at him. One day a son of Erin, who had up to this time been the bully of the camp, took offense at some fancied wrong of young Phil, as he was called, and asked him out to fight. Deitsch quietly told the fellow that he had not enlisted to do that kind of fighting, and asked to be excused. The fellow persisted, however, and finally told young Deitsch that if he did not fight he would brand him as a coward. This was more than the young man could stand, and he stripped off his coat. The other soldiers gathered around, expecting to see the raw recruit get a sound thrashing. Three minutes later they were disappointed. It took Deitsch just that length of time to give the bully a pummelling that he remembered the rest of his life. This act on the part of Deitsch made him the hero of the hour, and from that time on he was treated with consideration and respect by his comrades.

This was in 1856. Although but sixteen years of age, his soldiery qualities began to show themselves, and the then young German boy made his first move in his successful career. He was sent to Washington Territory, and assigned to Company B, Fourth United States Infantry. At Fort Yamhill, Oregon, he served under gallant Phil Sheridan, who was then a lieutenant, and later he served under General Crook, then commanding Company D, Fourth United States Infantry. During the entire year of 1858 his company was continually on Indian expeditions, and at Snake river Captain Taylor and sixteen men were killed. After these campaigns Company B was ordered to Fort Terwah, a fort built in upper California by General Crook. During the many battles in which Company B engaged, the bravery of young Deitsch was recognized, and in the fall of 1858 he was promoted to corporal of his company, and detailed to escort General Mansfield from Fort Garrison to Fort Terwah. During their march the men had a number of skirmishes with the Indians, in the midst of one of which young Deitsch received a painful arrow wound in the left wrist. His valor on this occasion was the means of causing his promotion a few months later, when he was made first sergeant of his company.

At the breaking out of the war in 1861, young Deitsch's time having expired, he re-enlisted, and cheerfully told his old comrades that he would stay with them to the end.

The chief tells an interesting incident in connection with his experience with Lieutenant Sheridan at this time. He was standing near that officer when the news of the firing on Sumter was announced, and the probabilities of an extended war discussed, and he heard the lieutenant say, "Well, I hope in the fight to come I can win a captain's commission." The world knows how successful Little Phil was in this laudable ambition.

The company of which Deitsch was a member was ordered to Washington City, and was a part of the Army of the Potomac. The young man was assigned to the Fifth Army Corps under Fitz John Porter. The following is a list of the battles that he participated in: April, 1862, Siege of Yorktown; May 4, 1862, Battle of Williamsburg; June 26, 1862, Battle of Beaver Dam; June 27, 1862, Battle of James' Mill; Seven Days' Fight at the Battle of Malvern Hill; Aug. 30, 1862, Battle of Manassas; Sept. 16 and 17, 1862, Battle of Antietam; Dec. 13 to 16, 1862, Battle of Fredericksburg; May 1 to 5, 1863, Battle of Chancellorsville; July 1 to 4, 1863, Battle of Gettysburg, at which fight young Deitsch was wounded; May 6, 1864, Battle of the Wilderness; May 16, 1864, Battle of Spottsylvania; May 24, 1864, Battle of North Anna River; June 2 and 3, 1864, Battle of Bo-Botomail Creek; June 17, 18, and 19, 1864, Battles of Petersburg and Siege of Petersburg.

After being wounded at Gettysburg, the following October, on

PHILIP DEITSCH,
Superintendent of Police.

the recommendation of General U. S. Grant, young Deitsch was commissioned ordnance sergeant of the United States army. At the close of the war he returned to Cincinnati, and was soon after appointed on the police force. He served but one month as patrolman, when he was promoted to sergeant, and two months later was commissioned lieutenant of police. During the time Colonel Deitsch was assigned to the Hammond street district, which was then considered one of the worst in the department, Colonel Deitsch took part in two riots, one at Front and Race streets, and the other the election riot during the first Grant campaign. In 1873, Colonel Deitsch resigned to accept a position in the revenue service, which he held continuously until January, 1885. At that time he was appointed clerk in Probate Judge Goebel's office. When it became known that Chief of Police Moore would resign, Mayor Amor Smith, Jr., at once selected Colonel Deitsch for the position. His confirmation followed as a matter of course, and in his service as chief of police he has answered fully the expectations of his friends; and as for enemies he has none except those who are against honest men, and who are opposed to the just enforcement of the laws.

One of the most famous murders in the history of crime in Cincinnati is what is now known as the Teal mystery. No one has ever been convicted of this crime, which was evidently a premeditated affair.

It was in the year 1871, when Colonel Deitsch was a lieutenant on day duty at the Hammond Street Station. One morning word came to the station house that a man had been murdered at a boarding house on Arch street, between Broadway and Ludlow streets. Lieutenant Deitsch at once went over to the place indicated, and found that the story which had reached the station was indeed true. On the floor of a little back room James Teal was lying on his right side. From a bullet hole behind his ear a stream of blood had trickled through his hair to the bare floor, staining the boards a dark crimson. Teal was quite dead. He was dressed in his underclothes, and had a bed-quilt drawn over him. He was about forty-five years of age.

Lieutenant Deitsch at once began the investigation. He found

Mrs. Teal in bed in the next room, suffering, as she claimed, from a severe sickness. She showed very little interest in her husband's death, but stated that she supposed he had gotten out of bed while she was asleep, and going into the next room had been killed by some one who had come in from the outside.

Lientenant Deitsch watched her closely. She was a gloomy-looking, dark-browed, dark-featured woman, with hair of raven blackness. But her striking feature was her eyes, which she fastened on the police officer defiantly. They were jet black, and glistened and glowed like the eyes of a basilisk; terrible eyes which, taken in connection with a firmly compressed mouth, and a smile of strange fierceness, betokened a woman of a strong, turbulent and daring nature.

Deitsch continued his investigations, and found from an examination of Lizzie McBride that there had been a revolver lying on the mantel in the room where Mr. and Mrs. Teal slept. It had been there but the day before, and was now gone. After satisfying himself that there was no revolver in the house, Deitsch ordered the vault to be searched. Success rewarded the effort, and a thirty-two calibre revolver was brought to the surface. All its chambers were full but one, in which an empty shell only was found. After a further examination of Mrs. Teal and of several people in the house, from whom it was learned that she was a woman of a ferociously jealous temperament, Deitsch ordered her placed under arrest and taken to the Hammond Street Station.

She never showed the slightest interest in the proceedings, never asked about her husband's funeral, refused to answer all inquiries, and met every question of the officers with the cold, sardonic laugh and the piercing glance of the midnight eyes.

A strong case of purely circumstantial evidence was built up against her, but the jury found a verdict of not guilty. After the trial she left for Toledo, and a year afterward she met Deitsch in the post office in this city and told him she was keeping a boarding house there, and that if he ever came to Toledo, she would be pleased to have him stop there.

No one else was ever arrested for the murder, and to this day the perpetrator of the crime and the causes which led to it, are unknown. Lieutenant Deitsch, however, was highly complimented for the skill and persistence with which he followed up the crime, even though his efforts were not in one sense rewarded with success.

In the ante-bellum days Colonel Deitsch had many adventures of the most thrilling type during his service as United States soldier in the far west. One, which is told of him, especially illustrates his courage and persistence, qualities in his make up that have caused many a thief's heart to sink within him since. This adventure happened in the spring of 1858. Deitsch was then about eighteen years of age, and a corporal in the troops stationed at Fort Humboldt, near the Bald mountains, in northern California. A detail of men under Captain Collins had been sent out to make a road through the mountains. The region had never been trodden by white man's foot, and the naked Indians observed the progress of the soldiers with rage which their cowardice alone prevented them from venting. The party advanced under positive instructions about ten days' journey. Then the provisions began to give out, and when Round Valley was reached, Captain Collins saw that something must be done. He therefore detailed Corporal Deitsch, with five soldiers, the Mexicans, and the pack mules, to make a forced return march, and bring provisions to the mountain camp. The journey to Fort Humboldt was accomplished without adventure, but on the return with the provision-laden train the trouble began. About two days out from the fort the fires of the Indians began to burn on many mountain sides—a sure sign that a disturbance is at hand. The men continued the march steadily, until suddenly a shot rang out from the thickets, and one of the soldiers dropped dead. Then the unequal contest began in earnest. Corporal Deitsch and his remaining four men defended themselves as best they could. Each hour the attack was renewed, each night the war-whoops of the Indians resounded through the forest. Many a time a mad rush was made for the train, but by Deitsch's skillful arrangement the attack was each time repulsed. The men several times wanted to abandon the train, but Deitsch sternly ordered them to remain at the post of duty. For ten days this incessant fighting was kept up, the Indians never seeming to weary, while the soldiers were ready to drop for want of rest and sleep. Finally, the entrance to Round Valley was reached, and the Indians retreated. Deitsch found the camp destitute of provisions, and almost at the point of starvation. But for his courage and determination, not only himself and his detachment, but the entire camp must have perished.

The superintendent of police in Cincinnati is always subject to the orders of the mayor and of the Board of Police Commissioners. He is the chief executive officer of the police force. He is to devote his entire time to the discharge of the duties of his office. It is his duty to see that all laws of the State and all ordinances of the city are executed, as well as all orders from the mayor or the Board of Police Commissioners. He must keep his office open at all times for the transaction of business, and in it a record of all stolen or lost property, all murders, suicides, and fatal accidents, a record of all suspicious persons and places, such as gambling houses, premises used for indecent public amusements, for the sale of lottery tickets, pawn shops, second-hand stores, and auctioneers, a record of all brothels, and of all persons at large in the city who may have been at some time convicted of crime. He must keep a copy of all general or special orders issued by him, a record of all important telegrams sent by him in or out of the city, and a "report book," giving a summary of all the business of the department for each month. The superintendent must keep a record of all requisitions made by governors of other States for the return of fugitives from justice, and a "secret service book," containing a full and complete record of all detective work undertaken by the "fly force," supplemented with the final result of such work, must also be one of the features of his office. This book is open to the inspection of the mayor, superintendent of police, chief of detectives, and the Board of Police Commissioners. The mayor's orders to the police are issued only through the superintendent, or, in his absence, through the inspector. From first to last Superintendent Deitsch has filled all the requirements herein catalogued to the letter. He has been constant in season and out. His course has been manly and straightforward. When a duty is presented to Colonel Deitsch he never flinches.

In politics the superintendent is a Republican. His height is about five feet eight, and his weight not more than one hundred and sixty-five pounds. His complexion is fair, and his hair dark. His handsome face is ornamented with a heavy mustache. Whether mounted, in full uniform, and at the head of a police column; on foot, in the midst of his men; or engaged in the routine of office business, he looks the soldier—one who has been ever ready to obey, and is therefore the better fitted to command. He has an interesting family and a pleasant home in the Twenty-fifth Ward.

The Inspector of Police stands next in rank to the Superintendent. In the absence of the latter he performs his duties. The care of the force with regard to discipline and training falls upon him. He must visit every police and patrol station at least once every fourteen days. He must instruct the lieutenants in their military and other duties, and must see that they properly instruct the men. He is the drillmaster, and must be versed in military science. In addition to these requirements, he must observe the action of the men on their beats as far as practicable, and note whether the ordinances are properly enforced.

From this outline of his duties it can readily be seen that the appearance and discipline of the force are, to a great extent, dependent upon the efficiency of the inspector. That Captain Hadley, the present incumbent of the position, has well and faithfully discharged his duties, is plainly shown by the fine condition of the police.

George David Hadley was born in New Orleans, Louisiana, on the seventeenth day of July, 1830. His father was an Englishman, and, when young Hadley was a mere child, he went on a visit to England. He showed a liking for military affairs at a very early age, and when only sixteen, by overstating his years, he enlisted in the American army for the Mexican war. This was in the spring of 1846, and he was assigned to the Second Louisiana Infantry. He served the three months for which he had enlisted under General Taylor. At the end of that time he was discharged. But his liking for "the pride, pomp, and circumstance of glorious war" had only increased by experience, and he re-enlisted for three years or the remainder of the war. His fearlessness soon made him a marked man in the regiment. The men, with whom he was a favorite, would have made him a lieutenant-colonel when the opportunity offered, but he refused the honor because he feared his extreme youth would stand in the way of the successful discharge of his duties. He was soon assigned to the regiment of Louisiana Rangers, organized with especial reference to bravery and the ability to endure hardship. It was while campaigning with this troop that he had an experience which few men in the world have ever had. His troop was assigned to escort General (afterward President) Franklin Pierce from the City of Mexico to Vera Cruz. The ascent of the mountains which stand guard around the valley in which the city is situate had just been made, and the men had turned their horses into the road which ran down the other side. It had been raining, and the heavens were spanned by a splendid rainbow. The gorgeous bow extended across the sky, and the end of it touched the mountain side just where a great tree stood. Hadley saw this, and, saying something jestingly to his companions about the pot of gold at the end of a rainbow, spurred his horse forward until the flashing vari-colored lights surrounded both him and his horse. He had stood in the end of a rainbow. The Rangers was a corps which stopped at nothing, and made relentless war on the guerillas. Hadley won much distinction in many desperate hand-to-hand conflicts.

When the war closed he began to learn the trade of coppersmith, but in 1848 followed his father to Cincinnati, where he was superintending the construction of the gas works. In the fall of that year he accompanied his brother to Havana, Cuba, where they put up the great gas works of that city. He returned home to gain, in the Lane and Bodley machine shops, a more minute knowledge of machinery, after which he returned to Havana, coming back to Cincinnati in the fall of 1854, to work at his trade of machinist.

GEORGE D. HADLEY,
Inspector of Police.

With the first threatenings of civil war he began the organization and drilling of men into companies. The great trouble at that time was lack of arms, which difficulty he remedied with his own company by the use of wooden guns. He was thus enabled to drill his men in the manual of arms, and prepare them for muskets when they came. His own company was called the "Iron Greys," because it was composed of iron workers. It did most effective service in guarding the Cincinnati and Marietta Railroad, the great line of communication between the seat of war in Virginia and the West. During the early months of the war Captain Hadley spent his entire time in drilling men, having at one time over 5,000 men to look after daily. The "Iron Greys" were never mustered into active service, but disbanded soon after completing their work on the Marietta Railroad. Captain Hadley then organized another company, which should have been ordered to the front, but which did not go as soon as it was discovered that their captain had been tricked out of his position by some men who were engaged in buying and selling soldiers. Captain Hadley became disgusted on account of this experience, and that fact, combined with several other unfortunate circumstances prevented him from continuing his brilliant record of the Mexican war in the civil war. But his services as drillmaster were invaluable, and many an Ohio company owed its knowledge of military tactics to his teaching.

Shortly after the war he became Overseer of the Poor, and then a member of the Board of Education. In 1878 he was appointed to the police force as patrolman for special sanitary duty. He had charge of all the sanitary force under Dr. Minor, and quarantined the first yellow fever boat, the John Porter. When the necessity for sanitary precautions was at an end, he was assigned to a boat which he ran but two weeks before being appointed sergeant. After six months experience as sergeant he was appointed lieutenant, and in this capacity served through the riots. It was to his foresight that the powder magazines on Beresford avenue, Walnut Hill, were kept out of the hands of the mob. He suggested the advisability of sending a company of militia to guard them at a critical time, when they had been forgotten altogether by the authorities, and his suggestion was acted upon. He was reduced to the ranks early in 1885 by the Police Board, of which Colonel Hawkins was President, and as no cause was assigned, he resigned from the force. He went in again with the accession of the present board, and was on the 16th of April, 1886, appointed inspector of police. The work of drilling, uniforming, and disciplining the men was begun at once, and the new inspector displayed his fitness for the work immediately. The fact that the Cincinnati force to-day presents such a splendid military appearance, is due to his efforts. They are able to execute the most difficult manœuvres with the precision and exactness of trained regulars. In addition to this, they are the admiration of strangers and the pride of citizens, because of their neatness and manly bearing. Inspector Hadley can point to this with pride as his work. He is quiet and mild in manner, but has a mind fitted to command and an energy that knows no discouragement. He performs his duties without bluster or display of harshness, and yet he performs them well. There is no more faithful or valuable officer connected with the force than Captain Hadley.

* * * * * * * * * * *

On January 20, 1844, on the west side of Main street between Third and Fourth, Dr. J. Draper first saw the light of day. His education was obtained from the public schools, from A. J. Rickoff's once famous academy, and from Bartlett's Commercial College. After graduating from the last named institution he was employed as a bookkeeper and cashier, and became an expert as a judge of money, genuine and bogus. Later he studied medicine with Dr. H. H. Barker as a preceptor, and after several courses of lectures at the Cincinnati College of Medicine and Surgery, and at the Cincinnati Hospital, graduated in 1864, and for the five years succeeding practiced his profession. Dr. Draper was a private in the 137th Ohio Volunteer Infantry, and made an excellent record as a soldier. He left the profession of medicine for business that was more congenial, and became the assistant superintendent of the Evansville & Chicago Railroad

DR. J. DRAPER.
WM. J. BYRNE.
HARRY HALL.
CHAS. S. VICKERS.

during the process of its construction, which enterprise was abandoned during the panic of 1873. He finally drifted to the South, where he was appointed a United States commissioner, which position he resigned on account of the sickness of his wife. Dr. Draper had some experience with the Ku Klux organization of the South, and was at one time an unwilling witness to a scene in which a man received seventy-five lashes from a black snake whip in the hands of one of the masked men. While in the South he rendered important assistance to United States officers in bringing to justice illicit distillers and counterfeiters. On his return to Cincinnati he became paymaster and purchasing agent for the Cincinnati Water Works, and served in that capacity for four years. When the present police board was organized, and Arthur G. Moore became chief, Dr. Draper was made his private secretary, and when Colonel Deitsch became superintendent, he was selected to act for that officer in the same confidential capacity. Dr. Draper has been twice married, and has been the father of six children, four of whom are now living.

William J. Byrne is another Cincinnati boy, having been born March 13, 1865, in this city. He received a thorough education in St. Xavier's College, and before beginning the fight of life, added to his other accomplishments a knowledge of stenography. On October 1, 1883, he took the positon of stenographer for Ralph Peters, superintendent of the P. C. & St. L. R. R. Four years after he went into the offices of the O. & M. passenger department in the same capacity. Since March 15, 1888, he has been stenographer in Colonel Deitsch's office, having secured the position after a difficult and hotly contested competitive examination. Byrne is able to write from 175 to 180 words a minute.

Harry Hall, private secretary to Chief of Detectives Hazen, is a Kentuckian by birth, having been born in Cold Spring, Campbell County, of that State, on the 2d of March, 1860. His parents removed to Cincinnati when he was very young, and he received a good education in the public schools of this city. He occupied several clerical positions previous to his appointment to his present position in 1886. Hall occupies a very responsible position, all the secrets of the police department being in his possession. He possesses in a marked degree the power of keeping his mouth closely sealed when it should be. He also has detective ability of no mean quality. He has several times aided in the capture of important thieves by his penetration or knowledge of the workings of police business. To his credit belongs the capture of the notorious George Runyan, one of the most persistent thieves known to the police. About a year ago Runyan finished serving a sentence in the Franklin penitentiary which had been made far lighter than he deserved on account of his miserable health. About a week after he had finished his term, when he robbed the house of a prominent citizen of Covington of a number of books and valuables, Hall traced him down with no other clue than a bit of conversation which Runyan had had with a man to whom he sold one of the books. In the course of that conversation he dropped a remark about a private transaction with another man. Hall went to the man concerned, and after some difficulty, found that he had told this fact to Runyan. Then, afterward, he traced him to the C. H. & D. depot and arrested him. He is now back at Frankfort. Hall is Colonel Hazen's right bower, and knows everything that is working in the mind of that old and imperturbable detective. He has the full confidence of the police department—a well merited mark of esteem.

J. R. Bender, the clerk of the police, though of German parentage, is a native of England, born August 17, 1836. When he was but three months old his parents came to America, and in Cincinnati joined his grandparents, who, eleven years before, had left the Fatherland. Young Bender grew to manhood in the Queen City, and in her public and private schools, and in St. Xavier's College, received a liberal education. In 1850, Anthony Bender, father of the subject of this sketch, failed in business, and though but fourteen years of age, his son was at once thrown upon his own resources. He had the experience of errand boy and salesman common to the youth of those days, and when twenty-two years old went in business for himself in Dayton, Ohio. This was in 1858. A year later he married, and when the spring of 1860 rolled around he emigrated to Leavenworth,

THOMAS G. McGOVERN
Report Clerk.
JAMES S. WEATHERBY,
Property Clerk.

JOHN C. CULLAHAN,
Messenger.
JOHN R. BENDER,
Chief Clerk.

Kansas, whence he went into the quartermaster's department of the United States army, and with a large detachment of recruits accompanied Colonel Phil Cook to General A. S. Johnson's army, at Camp Floyd, near Salt Lake City. Before the year was done, however, Mr. Bender was back in Cincinnati, to remain but a short time, when he enlisted in the 7th Ohio National Guards, of which Colonel L. A. Harris was a member. He returned to Cincinnati with the regiment, and was next found as clerk and bookkeeper for the Excelsior Printing Works, where he remained until appointed a water rent collector by Mayor G. W. C. Johnston. In 1874 he was elected clerk of the Police Court, and re-elected in 1876 by a majority of 1,863, although half the candidates who ran with him on the ticket in that race were defeated. In 1878 Mr. Bender retired from the police court, and was straightway appointed to a clerkship under County Treasurer John G. Fratz. He served through Mr. Fratz's entire term, and then became clerk of the Decennial Board of Equalization. When that Board finally adjourned, he formed a partnership with J. T. Shawhan in the printing business, and had scarcely begun work in this new field before County Treasurer Miller tendered him a responsible place in the county treasury, which he accepted. At the end of Mr. Miller's term, Mr. Bender was nominated by the Democracy for the position of magistrate, but with the rest of the Democratic ticket in the Blaine campaign, Mr. Bender was snowed under. Again he embarked as a job printer, but early in the January following Mayor Stephens tendered him the place of clerk of the police department to succeed Frank Tate, and the tender was at once accepted. When the non-partisan Board of Commissioners came into power they complimented Mr. Bender's efficiency by retaining him. On April 22, 1886, Mayor Smith reappointed him to the place, and the appointment was promptly confirmed by the commissioners.

Mr. James S. Weatherby, the property clerk for the police department, was born in Cincinnati April 9, 1848, and has all his life made his home in his native city. At the age of fourteen years Mr. Weatherby secured a clerical position in the pension agency at Cincinnati, and remaining there continuously until 1877, when he resigned to accept an appointment as United States gauger, under Hon. Amor Smith, who was then the internal revenue collector for the Cincinnati district. He remained in the Government service until August, 1885, when, for political reasons only, he was removed. For nearly a year he was connected with a wholesale grocery house in Cincinnati, when he was appointed to the place he now fills with credit to himself and the department. Mr. Weatherby was married in January, 1885, and is the father of a Weatherby, Jr.

Thomas G. McGovern was but one year old when he first became an inhabitant of Cincinnati. His birthplace was Roundout, Ulster County, New York, and the date of birth was December 26, 1852. When only ten years old he left home, without saying good-bye or by your leave, and for eighteen months followed the United States army. He was in the battle of Nashville, where his father fought, and wholly unknown either to himself or to his father was within a hundred feet of him during the engagement. Later he went to Cynthiana, Ky., and participated in the fight with Morgan's brigade, and after the battle carried water to the wounded and otherwise acted in the rôle of a good Samaritan. Satisfied with this much of a soldier's experience, young McGovern took the first train for Cincinnati, and for one year remained at home. When, in November, 1865, his mother died, the little boy began the battle of life in earnest by making for himself a living. This he succeeded in doing by toiling early and late for Proctor & Gamble. With this firm he remained steadily until 1880, when he went with the Miami Soap and Oil Works, and two years later with the Cincinnati Desiccating Company. In 1885 he became record examiner in the city engineer's office, and a year later assistant clerk of the police. Mr. McGovern has a wife and three children and a pleasant home on Roll avenue, in South Cumminsville.

Phil Strieff, special clerk in Superintendent of Police Deitsch's office, was born March 5, 1848. Phil is a native of Cincinnati, and has never left its boundaries except for a brief visit. He received his education in the public schools, and at fourteen became an employé in a glue factory. He was ambitious, however, and soon entered a business college, where he acquired a thorough knowledge of book-keeping. He utilized the knowledge thus acquired for seven years in the pork-packing establishment of his brother, at Second and Sycamore streets. He then became a "weigher," but soon after gave this up to enter the cigar business. For four years he kept a cigar manufactory in conjunction with a retail store, but sold out to enter the revenue service. On July 2, 1886, Strieff was appointed special clerk in Chief Deitsch's office, where he has remained. He was married in 1874 to Miss Carrie Neighbors, the daughter of a prominent butcher.

Charles S. Vickers was born in Richmond, Ind., on January 9, 1853. When but ten years old his parents left their Indiana home and took up their residence on Eighth street, Cincinnati. The boy's schooling was therefore received partly in Richmond and partly in this city, his education terminating with a course in a well-known business college. Vickers, after leaving school, became a clerk and was employed in various large establishments of the city. When Sam Ramp became county clerk he appointed Vickers to the position of subpœna clerk in his office, a situation which the latter filled for three years. Charley then entered the city delivery department of the post-office. On July 19, 1886, he became special clerk in Chief of Police Deitsch's office, a position which he fills acceptably.

CHAPTER X.

THE DETECTIVE FORCE.—SKETCH OF ITS EARLY ORGANIZATION.—CAREER OF THE CHIEF OF DETECTIVES, LAWRENCE M. HAZEN.—HIS CORPS OF ABLE ASSISTANTS, MESSRS CRAWFORD, SCHUNCKS, WAPPENSTEIN, CALLAHAN, TOKER, MOSES, HUDSON AND JACKSON.—RECORDS MADE BY THE THIEF CATCHERS.

THE police force has a double function with regard to crime—prevention and detection. The former is largely the office of the uniformed officers. To fulfill the latter duty a special department is organized, known as the detective force. The men composing this must be of superior intelligence, in order that they may successfully perform their work. The detective must have keen reasoning faculties, a fair memory for faces, and above all must know the criminal class. The larger his acquaintance in this direction, the greater will be his success. For crime, as a rule, is not the work of untutored hands, but of men to the manner born, bred and trained in vice from earliest infancy, whose ancestors have been thieves before them.

At the bottom of this social strata which make up a great city lies this class, toiling while honest men sleep, preying on their own kind in many ways—keen, cunning, desperate and vicious. To cope with such men the detective branch of police business was organized.

Ever since 1854 there has been a detective branch of the Cincinnati police force. But it never reached anything like a state of completeness until it was organized into a distinct department, with its own chief and its own special machinery. The Board of Police Commissioners, which was appointed in 1886, recognized this necessity, and organized the detective force, placing Philip Rittweger at its head. At the end of six months he was succeeded by Ralph Crawford, and after six months more Colonel "Larry" Hazen took the bureau in charge. He is the present chief of detectives, and with his assistance the organization was fully completed. It now consists of five regular detectives and two clerks who are assigned to detective duty. The five regulars are, Ralph Crawford, Daniel A. Callahan, John Schuncks, Joseph Wappenstein and William A. Toker. The two clerks are Edward Moses and Charles Hudson. In addition to these, patrolmen are from time to time taken from their beats and assigned to special duty.

Colonel Hazen, the head of this force, is responsible directly to the superintendent of police. His duties are to order and assign the work of the detectives, placing them where they can use their talents to the best advantage. He must also keep a record of crime and criminals in general, and of the criminals arrested by his men, together with the disposition of their cases in the courts. For this position a great detective is necessary— one whom years of experience has acquainted not only with criminals and their methods, but also with the best methods of coping with them. He must have great executive ability and a careful knowledge of his force, so that he may dispose his men to the achievement of the best results.

The results of the past year and a half have shown the wisdom of the police commissioners in their choice. "Larry" Hazen's detective experience extends over thirty years, and in that time he has achieved a reputation second to none. He has hunted down criminals in every nook and corner of the United States, and throughout all his career has shown unflinching courage and ability, second to none in untangling the web of mysterious crime.

Lawrence M. Hazen was born in Ireland, on the 14th of June, 1830. When only three years old he came with his parents to this country. They stopped in Philadelphia, but when Larrie was a mere boy they came on to Cincinnati. When he was scarcely twenty years of age he was elected constable of the old Flat Iron Ward. In 1851 he became a member of the volunteer Independent No. 2 Fire Company, and on the organization of the pay department he was appointed captain of the Deluge Company No. 10.

In 1856 he went on the police force, thus beginning a connection that was to last through life and was to bring him a national reputation. He was assigned to patrol the river bank. At that time most of the business of the city came by river, and hence this was a most important and well guarded place. A short time afterward he became a lieutenant at the Hammond street station. It was here that he did his first important piece of detective work, and which was the means of advancing him far along the highway of fame as a detective.

About six o'clock one evening, late in the fifties, Lieutenant Hazen was going home to supper along Third street from the Hammond street station. As he was walking along he saw a colored porter roll a truck containing a small safe out of the Adams Express office, near Sycamore street, dump the safe on the sidewalk, and turn his back on it. Just then a tall, slender man jumped out of an adjacent door-way, walked along past the safe, and stooping down, pressed his hand on it for an instant before passing on. Hazen thought the action looked suspicious, and turned it over in his mind. At length he came to the conclusion that the man was trying to get a mould of the lock of the safe.

The next evening Hazen made it his business to be on hand at the Adams Express office about the same time. As he sauntered along he saw the safe again dumped on the sidewalk, and the tall man once more jumped from the door-way to press his hand on it when the porter was not looking. This time Hazen followed the tall man up Third. At Broadway he overtook him, and recognized him as a certain Colonel Green, to whom he had been introduced some time before.

He said nothing to him, but early next morning went to the express office and asked to see Superintendent Gaither. He related to him what he had seen, and Gaither told him to investigate further. Hazen inquired around about Green, and found that he was from Baltimore. He also discovered that the Adams Express Company had been robbed in that city by a scheme very similar to this one Green seemed to be working here. This was enough, and he set out to find his man. Soon after he met him face to face in the post office.

LAWRENCE M. HAZEN,
Chief of Detectives.

"How do you do, Colonel Green?" said Larry.

"I beg your pardon," said Green, drawing himself up. "I don't know you, and Green is not my name."

"That's all right. Put up your hands; I want to see what you have in your pockets."

Green protested, then struggled, and finally drew a revolver. But Hazen overpowered him, forced him to the wall, and searching his pockets found several wax moulds. Taking him by the arm he led him to the station-house, and then went over to the express office with the moulds. Sure enough, they fitted the lock on the safe exactly. Green was identified as the man who had done the Baltimore "job," and was sent to the penitentiary from there for fifteen years. It was through this piece of work that Hazen became employed as detective by the Adams Express Company. He did not see Green again for nearly eighteen years, when he met him one day walking out of a block of newly-finished houses on Third street. He at once suspected that Green was getting moulds of the locks, so that when people moved in he and his pals could go around and "weed" the houses without any trouble. He spoke to him, searched him again this time without opposition from the Colonel, and found the moulds, as he had expected. He took them away, and told him to leave town at once. Green left within a few hours, and has never been here since.

Under Mayor Hatch, Lieutenant Hazen became Chief of Police. This position he held until Mayor Harris was elected, when he resigned. This was in 1864, and by resigning this position he obtained one which brought him all his reputation. Mr. Gaither, of the Adams Express Company, remembered the keenness displayed by Hazen in the case related above. He had observed his career ever afterward, and had seen many examples of his fitness for great detective work. When the three express companies, the Adams, American, and United States, determined to employ a detective to hunt down all criminals who should make depredations on their property, Mr. Gaither proposed Colonel Hazen. Messrs. Fargo and Kipp, general managers of the other companies, had also observed his work, and were heartily in favor of Mr. Gaither's recommendation. Colonel Hazen accordingly received the appointment, and entered on the long and chequered career, crowded with thrilling incidents and remarkable adventure, more incredible than romance, which makes him at the present time such an interesting figure.

But before beginning his career as express detective, one incident should be related which dates back as far as 1857, the time of the visit to the United States of H. R. H. Albert Edward, Prince of Wales. When the young Prince arrived at St. Louis, under the guardianship of the old and fussy Duke of Newcastle, Hazen was acting as detective at the fair. The royal party visited it and viewed the sights under the guidance of young Hazen, then a handsome fellow of twenty-seven years. The Prince became captivated with him and taking him to one side, proposed that they go out and "see the town" that night together. Young Hazen consented and the affair was arranged. The Prince retired early and thus threw the old Duke off the scent. Hazen and the Prince then met and started out. Next morning the Duke of Newcastle looked high and low for his royal charge, fearing that some one had kidnapped him to hold for a ransom. But Albert Edward was nowhere to be found. The police were alarmed and a thorough search was instituted. Just about the time the old Duke had given up and was taking suicide into serious consideration, the young Prince and Larry walked into the hotel. After that his grace of Newcastle slept across the door of the Prince's bedchamber.

To relate in detail one-tenth of the strange and interesting things which became a part of Colonel Hazen's life in the next twenty years would fill volumes. Only one or two incidents of world fame can be touched upon. Colonel Hazen was the first and only detective who obtained an indictment against the James' boys. In Gallatin County, Missouri, he obtained indictments against Frank and Jesse James and Colonel Younger. His adventures with this gang of desperadoes forms a long and most interesting story. In dealing with them, he had seemingly insurmountable difficulties to overcome. His own life was constantly in danger, the people of the districts infested were paralyzed with fear and often refused to aid him, and even after arrests were made he could scarcely induce those who knew of the facts to testify, because they feared the vengeance of the gang. But despite these difficulties he succeeded in sending several of them to the penitentiary, among others one of the Younger boys, brother of the far-famed bandit, Colonel Younger, who carried his troop to success in many a daring and desperate robbery. Colonel Hazen made the first organized effort against the gang, and the beginning of its downfall dates from his arrival in Missouri. He hounded them through the South and Southwest until they were compelled to adopt caution, when before open and defiant lawlessness had characterized them. Colonel Hazen participated in the capture of the Northampton, Massachusetts, bank robbers. He also brought back Harry Lee, the defaulting cashier of Woodrough and McParlin, who departed for Canada with $15,000. He has taken many noted express robbers and has been remarkably successful in recovering the money also.

In 1883 he established in this city the Hazen Detective Agency, at present under the management of his son William. This agency is among the first in the country, and one of the few that does a strictly legitimate detective business. In May, 1887, he was appointed chief of detectives, elevated by force of superior merit to a position for which he has shown his fitness. The names and faces of great thieves and also of local celebrities in this line, are as the page of an open book to him. He directs his men with energy and ability, furnishing much of the head work and displaying great skill while sitting in his office, and by sheer reasoning power reaching conclusions which the investigation of his men justify.

During his long and fearless life Colonel Hazen has been shot at and shot many times. The midnight assassin has often lain in wait for him. He has engaged in hand-to-hand conflicts with criminals nerved to desperation by the thought of impending punishment. When physical force was necessary he has been able to furnish that, and when intelligence and logical reasoning were demanded, there, too, he has displayed his ability. The romancer cannot weave from the intricate fancies of his brain such plots and stories as Colonel Hazen can read from the pages of his own memory. His has indeed been a long, perilous, useful and notable career.

A more successful detective team than Crawford and Schuncks has never done duty in Cincinnati, or probably in the United States. They are well known all over the country. It would be a difficult matter to give their histories separately, as for the past seven years Crawford and Schuncks have been almost inseparable. One without the other would be apt to prove a hunter without his trusty rifle, but "doubled up," they are a tower of strength in ferreting out crime and bringing criminals to the bar of justice. Crawford and Schuncks have a brilliant record. Their list of criminals who have been sent to the gallows, or who are now serving terms in prison, is a lengthy one. Although frequently called upon to face danger, and, in not a few cases, threatened death, they have never yet been known to flinch. Ralph Crawford was born in Connorsville, Indiana, in 1853, and reared in Richmond. From 1870 to 1879 he was a sleeping-car conductor, running out of Cincinnati. In 1879 he was appointed on the Cincinnati police force by Mayor Jacob, and ran a beat from Central station. He was a patrolman one year, and during that time his shrewd work and keenness attracted the attention of the department, and secured him a place on the "fly" force. He ran six months with Charley Wappenstein, who has been chief of police and chief of detectives, and who is now a Pinkerton detective in Chicago. Then he was doubled up with Schuncks, and, with the exception of one year, when he was chief of detectives, has been with him ever since. Two years ago a law was passed authorizing the appointment of six detectives, subsequently known as the "Big Six." Crawford and Schuncks, notwithstanding the fact that their politics was opposite to that of the administration, were at once selected as two of this chosen number, and have remained two of the Big Six since. The two have run together longer than any other two detectives in the United States.

John Schuncks was also born in 1853, in Cincinnati, which has always been his home. He learned the trade of cabinet and

JOHN J. McGRANN.

W. W. CLAWSON.

PETER J. O'HARA.

chair making, working at it eight years. He then became an inspector in the water-works department, and after two years went into the chief's office, under Chief of Police Gessert, as a messenger. After serving in this capacity about one year, during which time Schuncks developed undoubted ability as a detective, he was put on the detective force, and doubled up with Crawford.

Last summer Crawford was sent to Canada for Frank Hopper, a defaulting bookkeeper. He was gone one month, during which time he traveled back and forth from Toronto to New York, tracing his man, and after a good deal of hard labor, he captured him in Toronto, and two days later had him safely behind the bars in Central station, Cincinnati. During all this time Schuncks was in Cincinnati working on the case, and furnishing information daily to his absent partner. In August, 1883, Crawford and Schunks were detailed to work up a murder case. Walter Norris, colored, had killed a man named Tolbert, also colored, and escaped. The only clue the officers possessed was that Norris had gone South, and the only mark of identity they had to work on was a gray spot on the back of the murderer's head. Crawford went all over the South, and after several weeks of patient search found his man on a steamboat, near Memphis. He brought him back to Cincinnati, but before the trial Norris died in the hospital. In 1884, Crawford and Phil Rittweger, then a sergeant of police, located George Fay and Henry Haney in an alley near Sixth and Elm streets. Fay and Haney were two desperate thieves, and had recently burglarized a large tobacco store. They had their booty, a large quantity, in the alley mentioned, and at midnight the two officers tracked the desperadoes to this alley. In the darkness they pounced upon them, and met with desperate resistance. After a bloody fight Rittweger succeeded in landing Fay in Central station, but Crawford was less fortunate. Haney made several attempts to shoot him, but the latter, after vainly endeavoring to drag his prisoner from the dark alley, shot him in the leg. The next morning both men were given heavy workhouse sentences, but Haney was sent to the hospital for treatment. He refused to allow the surgeons to probe for the ball, and one week later died from blood poisoning. Crawford and Schuncks performed a brilliant piece of work in breaking up a gang of notorious safe-blowers. These were George Iron, *alias* "One-armed George," *alias* Whitney, and Harry Day, *alias* Ed. Jones, *alias* Harry Manion. They were from a family of Detroit safe-blowers, and were known all over the country as the most desperate criminals. When the two officers arrested Iron and Day, the latter fought desperately, and assaulted to kill, but were baffled, and finally landed in prison. The next day they received the largest workhouse sentence ever given in the Cincinnati police court for carrying concealed weapons, both being heavily armed when arrested. After serving their terms Iron went to New York, blew a safe, was arrested and convicted, and is now serving ten years as a punishment. Day went to Richmond, was arrested while burglarizing a business house, shot a policeman, and is now serving seven years at Richmond for the crime. Mr. Crawford was sent to Chicago to look for Bill Dixon, who killed Walter Greaves in Cincinnati. After searching two weeks in Chicago, he found his man, took him to Cincinnati, where he received a sentence of ten years in the penitentiary. About two years ago four New York professionals came to Cincinnati, and burglarized a wholesale clothing house of a large quantity of valuable property. Crawford and Schunks were detailed on the case, and in a week had every burglar arrested and all the goods recovered. Of the burglars, George Carney, George Maloney, and Barney Kelly were sent to the penitentiary, and John Hyde to the work-house.

Some five years ago Owen Adams, a wealthy Cincinnatian, was held up by highwaymen on Gilbert avenue and robbed of $200, and Crawford and Schuncks were at once given the case. Soon after they arrested the men and recovered the money. The highwaymen proved to be Ed Lafayette and Dan O'Neill, two noted burglars. Both were sent to the penitentiary, where O'Neill subsequently died. In February, 1886, this pair of detectives captured Charles Jackson, *alias* Harris, *alias* Lewis, a colored burglar, who had been the terror of Cincinnati, and had but recently burglarized a house in Covington, carrying off a wagon-load of clothing. His arrest occurred in Cincinnati on Saturday. He was taken to Covington on Sunday, bound over on Monday, indicted on Tuesday, and on Wednesday sentenced to the Kentucky penitentiary for twelve years. All of his plunder was restored to the owners. These detectives, about the same time, caught Frank Williams, *alias* Scott, a noted boarding-house sneak thief and had him arraigned in the police court on eight charges. Williams is still in the workhouse. Jerry Woodruff, of Shelbyville, Indiana, a born murderer, who had stabbed no less than twenty men, was captured in this city by Crawford and Schuncks and taken to Indiana, where he was tried and sentenced to ten years in the penitentiary for stabbing a base ball player. Woodruff was a terror all over Indiana. He is still in the State prison.

In October, 1887, while President Cleveland was on his western and southern tour, Mr. Crawford was sent to Montgomery, Alabama, and arrived there the day the President did. The city was filled with an immense crowd of people. A gang of pickpockets and sneak thieves had been following the presidential party, reaping a rich harvest, and were in Alabama's capital on the day in question. Among them was Fred Winters, *alias* "Sharkey," who was at once recognized by the Cincinnati detective and arrested. When searched a valuable diamond pin, belonging to Horace Starr, of Richmond, Indiana, was found on Winters, who had taken the pin from Starr the day previous at Atlanta. The property was returned to the owner and Winters sent to prison.

Dick Berry, who attempted to kill Allen Pinkerton, the Chicago detective, on a boat crossing the Detroit river, was caught in this city by these two officers. It is only about three months since they arrested George Henderson, *alias* Post, and George Walters, *alias* Wilson, two noted bunko men who were wanted in several places.

Four years ago a colored woman was killed in Bucktown, and Schuncks was detailed on the case. He worked about a week, finally arrested a negro named Parker, and worked up the evidence against him. The prisoner was sent to the penitentiary for fifteen years. The same officer also caught William Franklin, who shot his wife in Cincinnati two years ago. This he did by the use of decoy letters. Franklin was sent to the penitentiary for thirteen years. Another good piece of work done by the same vigilant officer was the arrest of Henry Mersman, who shot and killed Ben Ricking. Mersman was landed only after a hot chase and hard fight. He was sent to the penitentiary for life.

Two years ago Jim Moran, a desperate character, knocked an old man down stairs at Seventh and John streets, killing him, and Moran escaped, and after a long search, Schuncks found him on a farm, ten miles from St. Louis. He was brought to Cincinnati and given ten years in the penitentiary. On November 29, 1881, Schuncks arrested Frank Day, a noted burglar and safe-blower. He worked through Kentucky, was arrested for robbing a store in Dover, and sent up for two years. Previous to this Day was in jail in Memphis, Tennessee, and while there made a key out of a spoon and came near letting all the prisoners escape.

On July 11, 1882, Schuncks caught T. J. Jacobs, an advertising swindler, who beat a Cleveland man named Bissmeyer out of $1,200. Besides capturing the man, the officer recovered $1,000 of the stolen money.

On December 27, 1883, Crawford and Schuncks arrested Henry Bowman, *alias* Poindexter, a noted burglar and sneak, and sent him to the workhouse. On his release Bowman was followed to Louisville by the two officers. They found him there in company with a colored burglar named George Thomas, who had but recently been released from the Ohio Penitentiary. The two had committed a number of burglaries in Louisville. Chief Whalen, of that city, through the work of the two Cincinnati detectives, recovered several thousand dollars' worth of goods Bowman and Thomas had stolen. They were tried, convicted, and sent up for sixteen years.

A few weeks ago Schuncks caught George Elliott, the bogus package-game worker. Elliott escaped through a straw bond signed by his own partner. This is but a portion of the good work performed by these two gentlemen. The catalogue can be extended almost without limit. They are both modest and unassuming. They attribute their success to industry, patience, application, and an unbounded confidence in each other. These traits, combined with the natural ability and shrewdness possessed by each, make them a detective team which is equalled by but few in this country and excelled by none.

The man known as "The Boy Detective" is Daniel A. Callahan. He was born on Mt. Adams, Cincinnati, August 5, 1862. At an early age he was compelled to shift for himself, and this he did in a manly, energetic fashion, blacking boots, selling papers, doing anything that was honorable to earn his own way, and thus prevent his being a burden on others. His was a familiar figure for years at the corner of Fourth and Vine streets, where he plied his vocation as newsboy. The lad was always at his post early in the morning selling papers, and at school-time he always disappeared; he was off to his lessons. School over for the day, his duties as a newsboy were resumed. It is said that some of Dan's school-mates, whose parents were wealthy, were disposed to treat him scornfully, because he worked so hard to obtain an education. They undertook to "chaff" him over his morning and evening occupation, but making fun of Daniel Callahan soon became an unpopular amusement with them, for the newsboy had acquired a habit of settling disputes with his fists in a manner which was not conducive to the symmetry of their personal appearance. However this might have been, Callahan worked his own way up the ladder of life, and, very justly, is rather proud of the fact that he was once a boot-black.

Endowed with more than ordinary intelligence, and with an athletic frame, the young fellow, on leaving school, found it hard to decide what occupation to follow through life—whether to engage in a calling of a physical or of a mental character. It was perhaps natural in one of his age that he should choose the former. He decided to learn the trade of carriage trimming, and he entered a factory for that purpose, working for some months. But the boy had a friend in Hon. C. B. Montgomery, of Cincinnati, an attorney, and this gentleman, confident that the pursuit which his protégé had chosen to follow was not on a par with his abilities, persuaded the youth to enter his office as a law student. Callahan read law for two years, and then entered the office of County Prosecutor Outcalt, where he served in the capacity of clerk. When Mr. Montgomery was made internal revenue collector for Cincinnati, his first appointment was that of Dan Callahan to the position of government storekeeper, and the young man filled this place until ousted by a change in the complexion of political affairs, when he became the agent in Hamilton County for the Standard Insurance Company of Detroit.

In 1886 young Callahan began his career as a detective. After serving as a patrolman for three months, he was detailed to do detective work. When Mayor Smith appointed his "fly" corps, in May, 1887, Callahan was made a member, and is now considered one of the most trustworthy men on the staff. He made a reputation in his first cases as a shrewd and nervy officer, and was soon assigned to the most difficult and complicated "jobs" by his chief, Colonel Hazen, with whom he has always been a prime favorite.

One of the first cases of note on which the "Boy Detective" was engaged, and one which brought him into prominence, was that of Bernard Schaff, the "book-swindler." The case became famous not only on account of the magnitude of the swindles practiced in this and other cities by "Professor" Schaff, but because of his tragic death.

Bernard Schaff, the scion of wealthy and prominent citizens of Berlin, Germany, received a classical education at Bonn and Heidelberg, in his native land. A quarrel between young Schaff and his father caused the former to leave his home for America. He spent a short time in several large cities of this country, and five months after his arrival at New York came to Cincinnati. Here he at once began the schemes which he was afterwards found to have practiced with success, under an assumed name, in St. Louis. Representing himself as the president of a Lutheran Evangelical Seminary, Schaff wrote to various publishing firms of New York, Boston, and Chicago, and ordered books by the wholesale, stating that the above-mentioned mythical institution would pay for them as soon as received. The books were generally sent without suspicion, when Schaff sold them to *bona fide* purchasers. In this manner the swindler obtained hundreds of dollars, and was doing a flourishing business when brought to a halt by young Callahan, who was put on the case. By means of a decoy letter and continuous "shadowing" the latter soon had his man "dead to rights." December 20, 1886, was an eventful day for the "Boy Detective," for on that date he arrested "Professor" Schaff, the swindler, and in a few hours afterwards recovered one thousand dollars' worth of books at 124 Smith street, where the prisoner had secreted most of the stolen property. Schaff was bound over to the grand jury, and eleven days after his arrest, unable longer to endure his disgrace and the prospect of a long term in the penitentiary, ended his miserable life in the county jail, by draining of a vial filled with a mixture of morphine and arsenic, obtained for him by a fellow prisoner.

The crime of Mrs. Anna Saulmeyer, who was arrested by Detective Callahan, April 25, 1887, was one which shocked the entire community. This woman was delivered of an illegitimate child, and, in order to prevent her aged and wealthy husband from becoming aware of her misconduct, she thrust the fruit of her guilty love into the flames of a stove. After the arms and part of the legs of the babe were consumed, the mother took the charred remains of the lifeless child into an attic, where they were afterwards found by Detective Callahan and Coroner Rendigs.

The promising career of the new detective came near being brought to an untimely end a few months ago, while he was arresting George Barnes, the alleged murderer of patrolman Mike Welsh. Barnes had been tried for the killing of Welsh, and although circumstances pointed to his guilt, direct evidence was wanting and he was acquitted. Callahan was strolling up Fifth street one night when he caught sight of one Sellman, at that time badly wanted by the police, standing at the entrance of Lodge alley. Barnes was with him. Callahan at once started for them, but the crooks saw him and took to their heels, closely pursued by the officer, who overhauled them in a neighboring restaurant, and a lively set-to followed. Finding that Dan's agility and training was likely to prove too much for them, Barnes and Sellman each drew a revolver which they presented under their antagonist's nose. The latter pluckily grabbed the weapon of Barnes, who was nearest to him, and continued the fight, Sellman taking advantage of this move to escape. Callahan succeeded in preventing his adversary from discharging his pistol, and the struggle was about decided in the former's favor, when Barnes suddenly jerked away and ran off towards Race street. Another pursuit ensued, the detective firing as he ran. Down to Race street and up that thoroughfare to George flew pursued and pursuer, until the former was met by merchant's policeman Sibler, who downed and held him until Callahan came up and secured him. The crook was then taken to the station.

The foregoing are only one or two of the good "collars" made by Dan Callahan. He is probably as near the typical detective of fiction as is found in real life. Young, sturdy, shrewd, he adds to these qualities a good education, pleasing address, the manners of a gentleman, and perfect honesty. Fame and success in the occupation he has chosen are assured.

William A. Toker was born at Columbia, Hamilton County, Ohio, in 1852, and received a common school education at Milford. In 1869 he went to Planeville, Ohio, where he learned the trade of a miller, but this business he never followed. Believing there was money in the saloon business he went to Put-in-bay, where he opened a first-class establishment. Every summer at this favorite resort, brought him in contact with some of the smartest thieves in the country. He finally came to know them all, and many was the "tip" he gave the authorities on the worst of them. Keeping a saloon was not congenial to Toker, and he sold out two years ago and was appointed an officer in the police court in this city. There he remained until January, 1887, when he was detailed for special service, and his good work soon gained for him his appointmant as a regular detective. His career on the "fly" force has been creditable throughout. He is shrewd, conscientious, and ambitious. When sent for a man he has made it a rule to fetch him. Another thing to his credit is the fact that he has never sworn away the liberty of an innocent man. On the witness stand he is always fair. Toker was one of the detectives who captured the notorious pennyweighters, Lizzie McGuire and Mary Smith, who had secured from Clemens Hellebush more than $1,000 worth of jewelry, and it was through his energetic work as much as through that of any other officer that Lizzie McGuire was convicted and sentenced to five years in the penitentiary.

The arrest by Toker of a negro named George Williams was another clever piece of work. Williams, in company with two other negroes named George Hood, of Columbia, Miss., and Bill Carroll, of Nashville, Tenn., had committed a murderous assault on a family named Neighbors, near Memphis, Tenn. After robbing the house, clubbing and shooting its inmates, whom they left for dead, they fled. When the discovery of the crime was made, hundreds of men in vain scoured the woods and surrounding country for the perpetrators, but they had fled to Corinth, Miss. After traveling together for a few days they separated, and Williams made his way to Cincinnati. Chief of Detectives Hazen received word one day that the desperado was probably in the Queen City, and detailed Toker to run him in. The instructions he was not long in obeying. He found his man in a notorious ranch on the levee. Williams weakened after being locked up, told the details of the crime, was taken back to Tennessee, and sent up for a long term of years.

This officer has been assigned to duty in nearly every mysterious killing occurrence since his connection with the detective department. When Louis Brown was so cruelly murdered at North Bend by Harrison Staples and Joe Hall, Toker was sent after Staples, who had been located at Rockwood, Tenn. He got his man and landed him safely in the Cincinnati jail. Assisted by Hudson he ran down and captured in Cincinnati a murderer named Dave Williams, who was wanted at Jellico, Tenn.

It was Toker who arrested Frank Morse, *alias* E. K. Eggleston, a noted silk thief, for a job committed in Cleveland, and for which Morse went to the penitentiary. All of the stolen property was recovered.

Joseph Wappenstein, who for the past two years has been a member of the regular detective force, was born at Sandusky, O., in 1849. He had become quite a lad when his home was transferred to Cincinnati. The late Hon. Fred. Hassaurek was Mr.

Wappenstein's half brother, and so is Colonel Markbreit, manager of the Volksblatt. He is a full brother to Charles Wappenstein, Ex-Chief of Police of Cincinnati, and now one of the most valued members of the Pinkerton Agency. After he left the public schools the subject of this sketch learned the trade of a molder, but a few years later determined to become a policeman. Through the influence of friends he secured a place on the force, and rapidly worked himself up to a lieutenancy, which position he held for several years. When the present detective force was organized he became one of its members. In this position he has been for the most part confined to running down local thieves, who, as a rule, give the authorities more trouble than any other class. By his energy Wappenstein succeeded in breaking up a gang of river pirates, headed by Joe Tromefer and George Brickley. The men lived in a shanty boat on the river, and at night plied their nefarious trade up and down the river, cracking storehouses wherever opportunity offered. They were finally arrested and indicted by the grand jury, but there being insufficient evidence to convict they were released from custody. Subsequently Brickley was caught burglarizing a house and was sent up for three years. Joe Tromefer was arrested on suspicion of having had a hand in the Delhi train robbery and the murder of Baggage Master Ketchum, but he escaped for lack of sufficient evidence to convict. Wappenstein, arrested at the Boone Barracks on Woodward street, the notorious burglar Ed. Johnson, an escaped convict from the Nashville Penitentiary. Johnson was taken back to Nashville and is now serving out a term in the Tennessee Penitentiary. He also arrested an embezzler from Birmingham, Ala., named E. H. Ellis, who was taken back to his home where he is now awaiting trial. George Duncan and Doc McKenzie, who robbed the post office at Lebanon, O., were also arrested by Wappenstein and given fifteen months each in the penitentiary. When Wappenstein "collared" Duncan on Freeman avenue, Duncan showed fight, and drawing a revolver tried to kill the detective, but the latter overpowered him and made him a prisoner. During the excitement McKenzie escaped but was subsequently captured. Breaking up gangs of local thieves has been Wappenstein's special work, however, and in it he has been most successful. Scores of the light-fingered gentry have been landed in the workhouse by him and others driven out of town.

Detective Charles Hudson was born June 27, 1858, on Richmond street near John, and is therefore but thirty-one years of age. He received a good education, passing through the lower grades and the "first intermediate" to high school, when at seventeen he left his books and secured employment in Mitchell's furniture factory, at Second and John streets, where he worked for two years. He left the factory to become a clerk in John Hay's oyster and game establishment, which at that time occupied quarters in the Wiggins Block. On June 2, 1881, Hudson became a member of the Cincinnati police force. Means was then mayor of the city, and Jacob Gessert, who afterwards suicided, was at the head of the police department. Hudson ran a beat until December 24, 1881, when he was promoted to the patrol squad service. On May 7, 1885, he was appointed a detective under Chief Wappenstein. Colonel Hudson, father of the subject of this sketch, was then chief of police.

Young Hudson's career as a policeman came near being brought to a sudden close soon after its beginning, by a bullet from a burglar's pistol. It was about four o'clock in the morning of October 5, 1881, that word was brought to the Central Police Station that burglars had just rifled a cigar store on the corner of Longworth and Smith streets, and had entered the yard of another house. Two officers were sent to the point designated at once, and on their arrival they saw three men standing in the moonlight under the walls of a dwelling house. The officers started in pursuit, and commanded the men to halt; but the latter, instead of obeying, scaled the fence in the rear of the yard, and started through a dark alley towards Fifth street. The "blue-coats" ran after them, firing as they ran. Officer Hudson, who was patrolling his beat on Fifth street at that time, heard the shots, and, following the direction of the sounds, he arrived at the entrance of the alley just as the thieves emerged from it. Hudson seized one of them, but the fellow jerked away, and leveling his revolver discharged it point blank in the brave officer's face, the bullet grazing the cheek under the left eye. Stunned for the moment, and blinded by the powder, Hudson fell back, but soon recovered, and being joined by his fellow officers a hot fusillade ensued between police and rogues, the battle finally ending in favor of the former. Two of the burglars were captured and escorted to Central Station, where they gave the names of Charles Naylor and John Walker. Naylor was a Cleveland crook, while Walker belonged to this city. The former was slightly wounded in the left arm.

Hudson ran a patrol wagon during the riots in this city, and took an active part in the pitched battle which took place between police and mob at Sixth and Freeman avenue, and in which two brave officers fell victims to the senseless fury of the rioters.

The young detective has a long list of important arrests to his credit. One of these was the capture in this city of the fiend David Williams, a colored Hercules of Jellico, Tenn., who coolly discharged the contents of a loaded shotgun into the body of John Glass, a fellow workman, after the latter had bared his defenseless breast to his enemy. After committing the murder, Williams escaped the angry mob that was searching for him, and came to this city, where he was found by Hudson, assisted by Detective Toker, who figured in the capture.

A big case, in which Hudson figured prominently, was that of the notorious crooks and ex-convicts, Burch and Sinclair. These fellows were trailed to a room in this city by Detective Hudson, who, with the assistance of another officer, arrested them. Sinclair was a desperate fellow, and while crossing a canal bridge, on the way to the station house, threw a steel "jimmy," which had been hidden in his coat, into the water. The instrument was recovered however, and, with other burglars' tools, was used in evidence against the pair. Again, at the station, Sinclair made a fierce attack on Hudson, to whom he rightly attributed his capture, but was quieted by a blow in the eyes. It was found that Sinclair's real name was William Osgood, a New York thief. Burch was known as James Leonard in Chicago, where he was a professional "worker." Both had been sent to Joliet from Chicago for burglary on a three years' sentence. There was plenty of evidence that the men had committed a number of burglaries in this city, and, at last, one of them "squealed," and a great deal of the property stolen by them was recovered. The men also stated that several sets of burglars' tools had been at different times manufactured for them in this city, and gave G. W. Shepherd as the name of the man who had made them. This person, who resided at Fifth and Broadway, and was ostensibly a peddler, had already excited the suspicions of the police, and he was immediately arrested by Hudson and Jackson, who, before making known their identity, pretended that they wanted some burglars' tools made, with which Shepherd promised to supply them. A comical story was told by Burch and Sinclair, in regard to an attempt made by them to rob a house on the corner of Laurel street and Central avenue. When arranging with Shepherd for the manufacture of their tools, the pair incautiously discussed the proposed robbery of the house mentioned. Their plans worked well that night, and they were just about to obtain entrance to the residence when they heard stealthy footsteps approaching. In a moment they had vaulted over the fence, but were surprised to see the man, whose approach had alarmed them, turn and dash down Central avenue at a professional sprinter's gait. It was afterwards found that this third party was Shepherd, who had taken advantage of their discussion in his presence of the proposed robbery, and had concluded to play the thief himself. Burch and Sinclair had taken him for an officer and started to run, as it happened, towards him, while Shepherd, on seeing them appear so suddenly, made a like mistake, and flew in mad haste from the presence of the men whom he thought to be "cops."

The notorious bunko woman, Mrs. Lena Knecht, is probably as well known by the Cincinnati police as any criminal of her sex. Her peculiar "turn" was what is known as the "raffle racket." She called on unsuspecting persons, generally ladies, and, representing to them that they had drawn a lottery or raffle prize, offered to secure it for them for a consideration. She found plenty of victims from whom she secured from fifteen to fifty dollars. Detective Hudson first arrested her several years ago for this work, and she was sent to the "Works" for nine months. Since then the female "bunkoist" has become notorious in this and other cities.

For the last two years Hudson has, besides his other work, attended entirely to the "policy players." His success in this particular line was demonstrated by the fact that at one time there was not a "policy-shop" in the city. At that time, however, the policy men, when convicted, were heavily punished. One of them arrested by Hudson was fined $500, and spent three months in the workhouse.

The oldest detective in the department is Edward J. Moses, who has already passed his fifty-first mile-post. He was born in Cincinnati, and comes pretty near knowing every man, woman, and child in his native town—information which is sometimes priceless to a man of his calling. There are few smart "crooks" in the country that Eddie Moses does not know. There isn't a "flim-flammer," "shell-worker," "confidence man," or "short-card manipulator" whom he cannot call by name. As a rule, and for the reason just named, the majority of them steer clear of Cincinnati, and have been doing so since Moses joined the Police Department, about four years ago. While he has achieved no particular distinction for notable arrests, still he has performed excellent service in ridding or in keeping Cincinnati rid of some of the worst of miscreants with which large cities are generally infested.

Billy Jackson's bright, brown eyes first gazed sleepily on the surrounding world on April 2, 1863. Smoky old Pittsburgh was the birth-place of the youngster, but soon after the conclusion of the fraternal war his parents removed to Cincinnati. The embryo Vidocq received a fair education in the city public schools, and at sixteen left them to learn the trade of a machinist in Lane and Bodly's shops, where he was employed until 1882, and where his fine physique was developed. But the young man's love for adventure made this monotonous occupation irksome, and he resolved to see something of the world. Two years were spent in roughing it. He was a miner in Leadville, a driver in San Francisco, a tourist in Salt Lake City, the Mormon capital, and finally a traveller in Europe.

Jackson began his professional career in 1884; at that time Colonel "Larry" Hazen, now the Superintendent of the Cincinnati Detective Department, was the manager of a private detective agency. The subject of this sketch became a "fly" in the "Big Chief's" corps, and worked for him almost two years. He then, after easily passing the same examination which a candidate for a position on the Cincinnati police force has to pass, became a patrolman in the Bremen Street District, and, after running every "beat" in the territory, was transferred six months later to the First District. In May, 1887, Jackson was put on the city detective force, and has been one of the most valued men of that able corps since his appointment.

Jackson's training in Hazen's private agency was of great service to him, so that the young man was by no means a tyro in the business when he was appointed to the city force. Indeed, it was chiefly to the ability he displayed when a private "fly" that he owed his public appointment.

One of the first important cases in which the young detective was engaged, was the tracing and successful apprehension of a gang of porch-climbers, who infested Cincinnati in the early part of '88. Although the credit of this capture must be divided among several members of the detective department, none of them were more instrumental in running down these bold thieves, than Billy Jackson.

For two months the residents of the hills had received nocturnal visits from the burglars, and so energetic and indefatigable were these fellows in making their midnight calls, that the citizens were in a constant state of apprehension. House after house was visited, the habitations of the more wealthy residents being chosen, and hundreds of dollars worth of money, jewelry and other property was carried off, but the indentity of the thieves remained a mystery. Only houses with porches were visited. These porches were scaled, and entrance to the house obtained by means of the second-story windows, when the thieves had only to select such articles as struck their fancy, and make their exit the same way by which they had entered.

The police were eager to capture these fellows, as their constant presence in the city, as shown by the continued depredations, was a reproach to the department. "Beer" Bailey, one of the gang, was caught in the act of robbing Judge Taft's house, and was convicted for his crime, but he resolutely refused to "peach" on any of his "pals." Finally Jackson and his conferres obtained a knowledge of the identity of the "porch-climbers" to their own satisfaction at least. It remained only to prove it to others, or, in other words, to get the gang "dead to rights." This was the hardest part of the work. Thirty-six hours were spent by Jackson with three associates in "shadowing" the suspects, the detectives during that time doing almost entirely without food or sleep. At the end of that period, on the afternoon of January 25, 1888, seven persons were arrested, five of whom were found to be connected with the gang which had so long infested the city. Burglar's tools were found in their possession, and conviction was only a matter of time. Among the captured were the notorious Fred Friend and Sam Toulster, leaders of the band of thieves; Miss Condon, the "fence," and several other thieves of local repute. "Porch-climbing" in this city was broken up for a time, and at least suburban citizens could sleep without fear.

Another and more recent case in which this detective figured, was that of McDonald, Lane and the woman Lowry. The first two were caught in the act of robbing a house on Westwood avenue, Fairmount, where they secured $200 in money and $50 worth of jewelry. The latter was recovered, but the money was never found. When tried in police court the fellows received very light sentences—a fine of $50 each and thirty days in the work-house. In ways known only to the "fly force," it was learned that McDonald and Lane were the "workers" in a professional gang of thieves that had been "doing" the city for several weeks. It was further discovered that their "fence" was McDonald's wife, who had given her name at the place where she was stopping as Belle Lowry. This woman was found and arrested, and two trunk loads of stolen property were taken from her room to police headquarters. But the detectives were not satisfied. They thought there must be more. They had Mrs.

McDonald searched by the Matron of the House of Detention, who carefully examined every article of clothing worn by the former. On lifting her bustle the searcher was struck with the idea that it was too heavy for ornamental purposes. Closer investigation revealed the fact that this necessary adjunct of woman's apparel was stuffed with stolen property of the most valuable description, consisting of gold watches and jewelry. Their value was at least $3,000. Jackson figured prominently in the capture and conviction of these people and in the recovery of the property stolen by them.

Detective Jackson's memory for a criminal's face is perfect. Let him once see a rogue and he never forgets him. It is this that has made Jackson as much feared by the "crooked" gentry as any "fly" in the city. This faculty was made prominent at the meeting of the Grand Army veterans at Columbus, Ohio, in 1888. The crowds there during the two or three days of the meeting were enormous. Several corps of detectives from the large cities of the country were there to aid the Columbus force in defending the visitors from thieves and sharpers. Cincinnati, of course, sent her quota. Of all those present Billy Jackson is credited with running in the largest number of crooks of notoriety. Soon after the close of the G. A. R. Encampment the Columbus authorities sent to Cincinnati police headquarters the photograph of forty-four "good" men captured there during the meeting, together with a letter of thanks for services rendered. Especial mention was made of Detective Jackson, and high praise accorded him in the letter.

CHAPTER XI.

PATROL AND MOUNTED POLICE.—THEIR INTRODUCTION INTO CINCINNATI, AND THEIR EFFICIENCY.—TRIBUTE TO EDWARD ARMSTRONG.—EVERY-DAY DRAMATIC SCENES ENACTED BY THE PATROL.—SKETCH OF SUPERINTENDENT DUFFY.—WIDE AREA OF CINCINNATI SUBURBS, AND THE NECESSITY OF MOUNTED POLICE TO PATROL THEM.

"THE Patrol Wagon," or, as it is called in the slang of the masses, "The Wagon," as exemplified in Cincinnati, is the highest achievement of American efforts to improve police service. It had its origin in Chicago during the riots of 1877, and there and in the Queen City it has had its best development. The ambulances and police vans of eastern cities are comparatively inefficient and far less picturesque.

Chicago, as said, was the first to adopt the patrol service, and Cincinnati came next, thanks to the foresight, public spirit, and liberality of Mr. Ed. C. Armstrong, who himself equipped, and for a time maintained, the first wagon used here. Mr. Armstrong established Company No. 1, December 5, 1881, and supported it from his own means until August, 1883, when the Common Council passed an ordinance appropriating money to reimburse him, and, further, $20,000 to equip four more companies and erect one hundred signal stations at the street corners. This was the highest compliment that could have been paid the lamented citizen, whose best monument in many a mind will be forever the splendid branch of the service which he inaugurated. "No. 1" had effectually demolished all old prejudices—had spoken for itself and conquered public sentiment by its eloquent deeds. The second company, now "No. 5," went into commission in September, 1883, and was stationed at the corner of Oliver and Linn streets. The third, "No. 3," began duty November 13, 1883, on Race street, below Elder. The fourth, now "No. 2," went into harness December 9th, and the fifth, "No. 4," threw open the doors of its pretty house on New Year's day, 1884. The "wagon" grew rapidly in importance and in value until it is, as claimed, the most brilliant branch of the municipal organization, or at least ranks with the Fire Department.

The city government, however, previous to 1886 failed to secure proper sites for the patrol houses, and as the Board of Commissioners had adopted the policy of having all real estate used, so far as possible, held in fee by the city, matters moved slowly, but now the following companies are in first-class condition: No. 1, 86 George street; No. 2, 8 McAlister street; No. 3, 648 Race street; No. 4, 545 West Sixth street; No. 5, Camp Washington; No. 6, Walnut Hills; No. 7, Price Hill; No. 8, Olive street; No. 9, Columbia avenue and Crawford road.

It is not putting it too strongly to say that the patrol houses are kept in absolute neatness. Up to July 1, 1887, the property was in the general control of the Board of Police Commissioners, who still make an annual inspection, but throughout the year it is now in the direct care of a Committee on Buildings and Improvements. These committees have been as follows: July 1, 1887, to January, 1888, George R. Topp and James Boyle; January to August, 1888, James Boyle and Dr. T. C. Minor; August, 1888, to the present, James Boyle and Louis Werner. The former takes especial care of Nos. 1, 2, 3, and 6, and the latter of Nos. 4, 5, and 7, the outlying houses also being divided among them. The ordinary station-houses and houses of detention are also divided up among these two commissioners. Captains of patrol companies, like lieutenants of districts, are held to a strict personal accountability for the houses under their charge.

To a non-cosmopolitan, or to the reader who has not visited a large city, the system can be described in a very few words. The patrol-houses are kept in constant readiness like those of the Fire Department. When any officer of a beat requires assistance, or when an accident has happened, he merely steps to a sentry or "signal" box on the nearest corner, enters it and calls the nearest patrol wagon. It is out of the house, when haste is necessary, and on the ground of action in a few seconds. In ordinary cases from three to four men ride on the patrol and are ready to assist the officer who called them in any way. In the instance of a riot or a raid on lawless places, a wagon or several wagons go to the nearest station and carry re-enforcements rapidly to the scene. A large force can be concentrated rapidly in any part of the city. The wagons also rush to fires according to their districts, and aid the firemen, if necessary, and hence are officially known as "Police and Fire Patrol," though the bulk of their service is in the former way. The horses are the best and swiftest that can be picked, and the wagons built for combined lightness and strength. They have the most luxurious springs known, and are provided with stretchers, tourniquets, and other surgical instruments, in the use of which the crew are trained, that the wounded may have temporary relief where found, or *en route* to the hospitals. Medicines and extra arms are also in the outfit. Strange to say luxurious as the ride is, it is a very hardened member of the criminal class who does not prefer a walk to the station to the shame and publicity of the "Hoodlum Wagon."

To an observer of modern police methods, the morale of the patrol service is its most striking feature. A "wagon," with its clanging gong, its galloping horses, carries more terror to the hearts of a mob than a hundred marching men, though its complement of officers be but four. Nay, the mere announcement that it has been sent for is sufficient to subdue before defiant law-breakers, who resist the blue-coated representatives of order, armed though they be with revolver and club, but who are merely footmen. It must be something on the same principle on which the word that "cavalry is coming!" has on many noted battlefields sent panic into the ranks of before unbroken regiments. And how fast the "wagon" comes when sent for! A whisper over the telephone from the signal box on the corner, and a hush of expectancy settles down on the crowd who have gathered around the arrested and the arresting. If it be an "emergency" call, the bystanders have not long to wait. Fast as blooded racers can run—everything on wheels whipping out of the way, and pedestrians hurrying to the safety of the sidewalk at the "clang, clang" of the warning bell—the compact, strongly-built, easy-riding vehicle comes. The horses need no urging. Their driver is all nerve. As the squad approaches the scene of trouble a glance of experienced eyes shows the general nature of the case. The halt is as sudden as that of troopers. There is a wheel, a backing up to the curb, a springing out of agile, stalwart men, a lifting in of prisoners. Again the gong signals, and all hands are on their way to the station before one can gather his breath. The scene is essentially intensely dramatic by day, and at night has the added effect of gleaming headlights and swinging lanterns. All this in the case of an ordinary arrest.

Even if it be the pitiful sight of a drunkard being taken in, the modern method is a long step forward in civilization. Who that remembers does not recall with horror the too frequent sight upon the streets of Cincinnati of some poor woman, reeking with rum, and perhaps shrieking blasphemy, dragged between two officers along the sidewalk, followed by a morbid group of gaping men and boys—alas! even by little children.

It is, however, on occasions of great public disturbance or disaster that the patrol service is pre-eminently the best arm of the Police Department. In removing the dead and dying from a fallen building or from the field of riotous battle, it is quick, merciful, efficient. In the great riots of 1884, the wagons were soon on the scene, and at least one of the brave fellows who manned them and carried to the hospital those who were wounded by the merciless fire from the military in the garrisoned jail, laid down his life for duty. Gallant Patrolman Joe Sturm of the "Fours" was shot dead as he stood at his post assisting in quieting the restive horses. In the excitement of that hour the fatal shot was supposed to have come from the mob; but as it is true that nearly all bullets that carried death with them in those terrible days came from the guns of the soldiery, so the source of Sturm's fatal wound will, like that from which the gallant Desmond met his fate, remain always in doubt.

The patrol wagons have in themselves, when they appear on occasions of public parade, their most eloquent advocates. As, four abreast, they clear the street from curb to curb before the advancing column, civic or military, they seem to be the best embodiment yet found of the idea of law and its enforcement; of humane principles and their practice.

The superintendent of patrol is Thomas A. Duffy. He ranks as a lieutenant, but his duty is to look after the workings of the patrol system, the mounted police, and transportation service. All orders from the superintendent of police to the patrol department must be transmitted through the patrol superintendent. His office is always at such patrol-house as the police superintendent may designate. He is compelled to visit and inspect each patrol company as often as twice a week, and is responsible for the enforcement of the rules and the proper discipline throughout the patrol department. The mounted police, their horses and equipments, are under his immediate control. On the first day in the months of January, April, July, and October the superintendent of patrol makes out a requisition for all feed and supplies necessary in his department during the ensuing quarter, and after this requisition is approved by the mayor and Board of Commissioners he makes the purchases thus authorized. Mr. Duffy was born in Cincinnati, on the 16th day of May, 1851. He received a common school education, and is regarded as a long way above the average in intelligence and prudence. His father was a blacksmith, and in his early youth Tom worked at the forge. At the tender age of fourteen years he went into the army as a teamster, and while he did not particularly distinguish himself he established a reputation as a steady and trustworthy boy. At the close of the war he learned the trade of boilermaker, and worked at this business until 1874, when he was appointed patrolman. In this capacity he served until December, 1880, when there was a change in the administration, and he was relieved from duty. In May, 1881, however, he was again appointed as a patrolman, and served in the ranks until 1884, when he was promoted to a lieutenancy. In November, 1885, he was appointed superintendent of patrol, which position he has con-

THOMAS A. DUFFY,
Superintendent of Patrol.

tinued to hold until the present time. Since this appointment Lieutenant Duffy has not performed any active police duty, but when a patrolman and a lieutenant he did some very effective work. One thing worthy of special mention was his capture of the notorious safe burglar and general crook "Dayton Sammy," and his equally notorious pal, "Kid" Kelly. The arrest was made by Duffy, shortly after the crooks had picked the pocket of a well known citizen, and it was made on the description furnished by the victim. Duffy was highly complimented for this piece of work by his superior officers, and received several very flattering notices in the local press.

The lieutenant is one of the finest looking men in the department, which, considering the appearance of the present force, is a very high compliment. He is married and has an interesting family. In politics he is a Democrat, but he never took any active part in any of the contests of the ballot. He is attentive to his duties, and prides himself on being at the head of the best police patrol system in the West. He has the confidence of his superiors, and is altogether a model officer.

A few years ago there was a policeman's beat in the vicinity of Lick run, out among the numberless quarries and dairy farms to the west of Mill creek, whose boundaries measured nine miles. Just to walk around it meant a tramp of nine miles, while, if the officer on duty were to attempt to go over it thoroughly, he would have had to go twenty-seven miles. Of course there were parts of that district in which a policeman was not seen from year's end to year's end. It was a physical impossibility for one officer to begin to patrol the beat. About four years ago it was divided, but matters were not then particularly improved, save that the officers could make a semi-annual round, whereas they had formerly been content with an annual inspection.

And this gigantic Lick run beat was not alone in being unguarded. There were beats almost as large in all the outlying portions of the suburbs, and they were practically without police protection. All this is now changed, and the introduction of mounted policemen has done it.

In places where policemen were once a veritable curiosity, they are now to be seen not only daily but hourly. Remote parts of the city, which were once terrorized by nomadic rowdies, have become peaceable, and the law is observed because its minions are always at hand to insist upon it. In suburban quarters, where cases of wanton lawlessness were daily reported by the sufferers, all is quiet. No matter what may be the inclination of a rough, he knows that the only safe thing he can do when retribution is so near and certain is to behave himself.

To the looker-on the squad of mounted police is the most striking part of the force. In parades as its members lead the long lines of blue-coated, brass-buttoned officers, with their horses sometimes gaily caparisoned and full of life, or as they travel up and down to keep the crowds in order, they become the cynosure for all eyes. Horse and rider seem to be one, and they cannot but impress the spectator with an idea of strength. And the animals in this branch of the service soon learn to be as exact in their deportment and as official in their bearing as the men. They have been so trained that when their riders dismount they will stand still, or upon the word of command, will follow after like a devoted dog. It is a familiar and pleasant sight in the suburbs to see one of these cavalry policemen walking on the pavement stretching his legs for exercise, while his horse walks sedately at his heels looking neither to the right nor to the left, but bearing himself in every way as a being quite above the ordinary skittishness of the equine kind. Notable among these intelligent animals is a horse on Price Hill that has stood still where its master left it in the midst of screeching fire engines and the shouting, surging crowd attracted by the fire. In spite of the hub-bub all about it, and the unearthly ear-splitting noises that would almost send a human being into hysterics, that horse kept its place unmoved.

It is almost needless to say that the efficiency of the mounted police is greatly enhanced by the patrol wagon system. When a mounted officer makes an arrest it can be easily seen that he would have more or less difficulty in conducting his prisoner to the station. In the first place it would take him from his beat for an unduly long time, and then he would not only have his prisoner to guard but his horse to look after as well. So when an arrest is made the officer goes to the nearest patrol box, summons the wagon, and in four or five minutes at the most, he has handed the prisoner over to the patrol squad; the wagon dashes off to the station, and he is again upon his rounds. An officer in this way has been able to arrest three or four offenders at once. On foot he can rarely cope with more than one. A man on a horse carries more moral force with him than the footman.

The mounted police force in Cincinnati is as yet in its infancy, for it was only inaugurated a little more than two years ago. Its complement is not yet full, as it is intended to eventually have a squad of fifty. That is the numerical strength of this branch of the service in both Chicago and St. Louis, New York having about eighty men. Cincinnati, with its great territory and vast outlying suburbs could use as many men as New York to good advantage, and if ever Hamilton County and Cincinnati become one that is the way in which the city will be policed.

Thomas McDonough has the honor of being the first mounted officer in the city. He is a superb horseman, and as he dashed up and down Gilbert avenue, the beat upon which he was placed, he presented a fine appearance. The aristocratic residents of Walnut Hills, riding to and fro in the cable cars, made much of this policeman, and they were so delighted with his work that there came a call from that favored suburb for more like him; and it was not long before a good part of the police work in that part of the city was done by policemen on horseback. The second mounted officer was assigned to Race street. He was Officer Hammersly, an old army cavalry man. Race street had just been paved with asphalt, and was then the only thoroughfare in the city that was inviting to the owner of horses other than those of the Norman family. Every young man—and old one, too—who owned a fast horse tried him on the long level stretch of the unbroken asphalt. All kinds of amateur races were indulged in, much to the danger of pedestrians and the drivers of slower vehicles. The city ordinances against fast driving were daily and nightly set at naught. The policemen on the street seemed powerless to stop the boys from speeding their horses, as the offenders would be out of sight in less time than it takes to tell it. When this thing had gotten to be an intolerable nuisance, Officer Hammersly appeared on the street mounted on a well-formed bay horse that seemed able to take its part in the racing business with credit; and when the fast drivers tried their usual tricks, they found that the policemen not only followed, but overhauled them. An arrest or two was made, and then the racers concluded that it was no use to try to get away from that active officer and energetic horse. Since then Race street has not been a deadly terror to pedestrians.

Colonel Dietsch, Chief of Police, says that "the mounted police are an unqualified success. Their orders are to regularly traverse the length and breadth of the suburbs. They are not merely to keep on the principal streets and be ornamental, but they are to go into the by-places, the little cross streets, and the alleys. They are to show themselves in all parts of their territory as often as possible, but unexpectedly and irregularly. Thus the citizen will be inspired with a feeling of safety, while the thief or the possible rough will be inspired with a feeling directly to the contrary. Since the adoption of this system the falling off in the number of cases reported from the suburbs is wonderful. Seldom is heard the misdeeds of roughs or the ravages of cattle turned loose upon the community, as was once the case. Good order and safety have been established, and at the same time the number of arrests reduced."

This commendation from the chief of police is deserved, and Colonel Dietsch is to be complimented upon the force, for it was formed at his suggestion; and he has been untiring in making it all that it is possible for it to be. Of course, the greatest care is taken in selecting men for the service. In the first place, a previous knowledge of horsemanship is essential. U. S. ex-cavalrymen are given the preference. Then a man must not be more than five feet and nine to ten inches in height, nor must his weight exceed one hundred and sixty pounds. He must be a lover of horses, for it is only by kindness and gentleness that a mounted officer can hope to bring out all the good qualities in his animal, making him respond to his wishes as though he were a part of his rider. If he does not constantly improve, it indicates that he does not take a proper pride in his work, and had better be relegated back to the ranks of the footmen. Finally, if he is a good officer, it avails him not if he grows fat—the fate of ninety out of every hundred policemen. He must keep under one hundred and sixty pounds, or off he comes from his horse, and a lighter and presumably more active man takes his place in the saddle. These horsemen report at the Ninth, Tenth, and Walnut Hills stations, where there are stables for the animals. The men take care of them personally, so that they are individually responsible for their well-being.

"This horse Frank of mine," said one of the officers who patrols Price Hill, "is like one of my children, and it seems to me that he knows as much, too, meaning no reflection on the children, sir, for they are all a father's heart could ask."

Although more is required of the mounted men than of the rank and file of the force, yet they receive exactly the same pay. The horseman brings more experience and special training to his work than the officer on foot, and the risks he takes are much greater. However, he is allowed more clothing than the unmounted man, as the wear and tear on his garments are greater, he receives one additional pair of trowsers a year, and is given overcoats of a special pattern. These overcoats are shorter than is customary, but they have long capes that come over the knees of the wearer. Their regular uniform, while it is made of the blue police cloth, is cut after the manner of the cavalryman's uniform, with an abbreviated coat buttoned up clean to the neck in front, looking like a girl's stylish jacket. They go on duty at two in the afternoon and retire at 11 P. M. Before long it is hoped to extend the service so as to have it continuous throughout the twenty-four hours. They do not carry clubs as do the other policemen, but are armed with revolvers which are conveniently carried in the holsters in front of the saddle. The weapon can be drawn a good deal quicker there than if it were in the customary place in the hip pocket, as two or three fellows have found to their dismay when they attempted to "get the drop" on the officer. The mounted officer also carries a dark lantern and handcuffs. These are put on a prisoner to render him harmless when the policeman alights to summon the patrol wagon at the signal box. However, this little arrangement, while humiliating to the evildoer's dignity, relieves the officer from any apprehension of an attack or an escape. In fact escape from a mounted policeman is impossible, as no pair of legs can outrun the pursuing horse.

Cincinnati has suburbs more extensive than most American cities. They are measured by the square mile. The day is not far distant when the last slow policeman on foot will disappear from them, and the swift officer on horseback take his place. This would be a decided improvement in many ways. Not only would the work be better and more expeditiously done, but the cost would be less, as one man could then do the work of three. In the parks there is no question but that the mounted policemen will soon replace the present watchmen. The latter may be faithful men, but they find it impossible to cover the great territory given them, and outrageous cases of assault and robbery are frequently reported. Especially has this been the case during the summers in Eden Park. The introduction of horsemen into the police department has proved of such general utility and has met with such popular favor that the system will soon be greatly enlarged. And if the larger mounted police squad of the future is as capable as is the present small one, there is no doubt that it will be the "crack" company of horsemen in the country.

CHAPTER XII.

POLICE RELIEF ASSOCIATION.—WHY A RELIEF FUND WAS ESTABLISHED.—HISTORY OF THE ORGANIZATION OF THE PRESENT FUND.—OFFICERS OLD AND NEW.—THE CONSTITUTION AND BY-LAWS.—POLICEMEN'S BENEVOLENT ASSOCIATION.—THE ROLL OF HONOR.—DEEDS OF HEROISM THAT OFTEN MAKE THE RELIEF ASSOCIATION A NECESSITY.

THERE are few occupations in life liable to be more monotonous, few liable to be beset with more danger, than that of the faithful patrolman. Day after day or night after night he may traverse the same beaten paths, view the same familiar scenes, look into the same faces, without an interruption. Anon a cry for help is heard; a fire breaks out in a building filled with the helpless; at the dead of midnight the door of some dwelling is found open, suggesting the presence of that worst of all miscreants, a burglar. It is then that the monotony dies and danger takes its place. The faithful officer does not reconnoiter, he sends no messenger when comes the sudden summons. Always ready, he goes himself, and by that route which is the most direct. If a deadly assault is being made, he takes no account of the odds against him in attempting to defend. If there are stairs left in a burning dwelling, or there are ladders at hand, smoke and flame do not stand in his way where a human being is in danger of being consumed. He knows the desperate character of a burglar, that he will kill to escape identification or capture; but this knowledge does not deter him from boldly entering the open doorway, and running the miscreant to earth. There is a long roll of honor in the possession of the police authorities of Cincinnati to prove that there are many patrolmen in the department who are faithful, not only when their life is monotonous, but when the hour of peril comes. There is also a long list in the history of the Cincinnati police of names of officers who have been faithful even to being desperately wounded, faithful even to death. It was for these and for their dependents, and for the officer whom sickness has overtaken, that a relief fund was created, an idea as humane in its conception, and altogether as necessary, as a soldier's pension. The allowance from the fund is not munificent. It is only ten dollars a month to those patrolmen or officers of higher rank, who, while in active service and in the performance of duty, shall have become disabled.

The commissioners, as a board, are authorized by law to create a relief fund, by assessing upon each member of the force a sum not exceeding fifty cents, the same to be deducted from each month's salary. This sum is paid into the city treasury to the credit of the fund, and can be applied in no other way than to relieve sick or disabled policemen or their families, or to the expense incurred in a policeman's funeral, or as a pension to those who shall have been honorably retired from the service. The fund does not depend entirely upon assessments made each month upon the officer's salary; by law it is increased by fines and forfeitures from policemen, rewards, fees, proceeds of gifts and emoluments that may be allowed by the board, paid and given for or on account of any extraordinary service of any member of the force. All moneys arising from the sale of unclaimed property, also, go to swell this humane store. The relief fund is not a new thing for the police department. In various ways it has existed for a number of years. It was, however, reserved for the present Board of Commissioners to enter upon a course of action regarding this fund which was systematic and business-like. This the board was authorized by law to do, for therein it was provided that the commissioners should be trustees of the fund, and have the power of investing its surplus in United States, State, County or City bonds. Among the first acts relative to this fund, was one by which the board forbade "symposiums" or pic-nics from which large sums had hitherto been realized. This decision was reached because on such occasions there had been practically enforced contributions from citizens. Besides, the moneys derived from these amusements had not always been placed in the relief fund, but had been diverted to other purposes.

The amount the commissioners took charge of on April 1, 1886, was $7,795.79. On the first day of January, 1889, that sum has been swelled to $10,189.38. The Board of Commissioners act only as trustees of the money. The making of the rules and regulations for its disbursement rests entirely with the members of the force, who are authorized to elect on the first Wednesday after the first of January, a Board of Seven Directors from their own number, who shall be known as the Board of Directors of the Police Relief Fund. They are entrusted with the entire management of the fund, subject of course to the approval of the Police Commissioners.

The commissioners authorized the deduction of the assessment of fifty cents from the first pay-rolls in 1886, and ordered it paid into the fund. Subsequently they referred to Commissioner Topp the questions relative to the preparation of rules and regulations, disbursements, etc. Mr. Topp held that such rules and regulations should be prepared by the members of the force, and so the matter was allowed to rest. Directors of the fund continued to act under the rules and regulations of the Police Relief Association, which had been organized under a State law passed in 1880. This law differed from the present one, in that it did not recognize the right of the Board of Police Commissioners to control the fund.

On January 7, 1887, Commissioner Boyle called the attention of the Board to the questions arising under the law relative to the fund, and it was determined to make the matter a special order of business January 11, 1887, on which date it was ordered that further consideration be laid over until such time as the Police Relief Association shall be ready to submit to the commissioners a report. April 1, 1887, the association submitted for approval a draft of a constitution and by-laws, which was ordered referred to Commissioner Topp for examination, and for incorporation into the Manual.

On the 9th of the same month Mr. Topp reported back the draft, stating that the proposed articles were practically those of the old Relief Association, and not strictly conformable to law. The board ordered that the draft be referred back to Mr. Topp, with power to formulate the proper rules and regulations.

The clerk of the board, Mr. Warren, submitted to Commissioner Topp a form in accordance with existing laws, and a series of by-laws. Owing to various causes the matter was allowed to rest until January 24, 1888, when Commissioner Boyle, impressed with its great importance, called the attention of the board to the matter, and it was ordered that Commissioner Topp be instructed to confer with the association. He thereupon submitted to the association Mr. Warren's draft, which was explained, corrected, and amended to suit the views of the association. At this juncture arose the important question as to who are contributors to the Police Relief Fund. Early in 1886 the board had decided that only those who had come up to the required physical standard were contributors, but on February 7, 1888, the directors of the fund submitted to the board a resolution that, in accordance with the law which stated that the superintendent, inspector, detectives, lieutenants, patrolmen, court officers, station-house keepers, and clerks composed the force, all should contribute monthly dues to the fund. The matter was referred to Commissioners Boyle and Dodds, who reported agreeing to the resolution, especially as its subject matter had been approved by the city solicitor, and the board referred the matter back to the directors to incorporate this view in the proposed constitution. On February 21, 1888, the Relief Fund directors presented a copy of a constitution and by-laws to the board, and it was referred to Commissioners Boyle and Dodds. These gentlemen met in conference with a committee from the directors, from which conference resulted the present constitution and by-laws of the Police Relief Association. The decision of the conference was submitted to the board March 9, 1888, which ordered that six hundred copies be printed and distributed to the members of the force. April 4, 1888, the question of acceptance or rejection was balloted on by the members of the association, resulting in a cordial endorsement of the conference decision. Two days later the result was reported to the board, and April 24 the board sigified its approval, and from that date the disbursement of the fund has been under the rules and regulations thus adopted.

In the constitution there are eleven articles. The first, second, and third recite the name and object of the police relief fund, and the time for the election and number of members of the board of directors. Article IV. provides for the seven directors, choosing a president and secretary, and limits the payment of any money, save for investment by the trustees, except upon the order of the board of directors, signed by the president, countersigned by the secretary, and approved by the police commissioners. In articles V. and VI. the facts are set forth that discharged policemen can have no interest in the fund, and that those who are honorably retired can have only such interest as the commissioners may approve. Article VII. provides for the monthly assessment of fifty cents on each member's salary, and Article VIII., that all fines and forfeitures from members of the force, all rewards and fees, and the proceeds of gifts and the sale of unclaimed property shall be turned into the fund. Article IX. makes the Board of Police Commissioners the trustees of the fund, and Article X. stipulates that no member of the force who, in consequence of partial disability, is assigned to a position to which a salary is attached lower than the one he received prior to his disability, shall be excluded from the pension which may have been awarded him. The last article sets forth that the superintendent, inspector, surgeon, chief of detectives, lieutenants, sergeants, patrolmen, substitute patrolmen, court officers, stationhouse keepers, and clerks are members of this relief association.

The by-laws are elaborate, and are divided into forty-four sections. In a conventional way they indicate the time and manner of holding the meetings of the association, and make known the duties of the board of directors, the president, secretary, and treasurer, and of the several committees. Those sections defining how the benefits shall be disbursed are herewith presented to the reader in full:

"The benefits derived from the police relief fund shall be given to members of the association when sick, when disabled from the performance of duty, for funeral expenses, for relief of their families in cases of death, and for pensions when honorably retired from the force.

"All applications for sick benefits shall be made to the board of directors, and said benefits shall commence from the date of the report of such sickness, provided that no relief shall be granted in cases of sickness of less than four days successive duration.

"There shall be allowed for four or more successive days of sickness relief at the rate of one dollar and twenty-five cents per day.

"In extraordinary cases, on a vote of five of the seven directors, the board of directors may pass a resolution authorizing a donation not to exceed fifty (50) dollars, in addition to the sick benefits, said appropriation to be approved by the Board of Police Commissioners.

"It shall be the duty of each member of the association, upon his becoming sick or disabled, or being rendered unfit for duty, to report in person, or by message, or in writing to the officer to whom he may be assigned for duty, in order to be entitled to benefits.

"The report of the police surgeon of the sick time of each member of the force made to the secretary of the association on the first and third Mondays of each month, shall set forth the name and rank of the sick member, the date and duration of the sickness, the total number of days time lost; also, in plain and popular language, the name and character of the disease or disability. He shall also state in said reports if benefits should be allowed or withheld from such member, and if recommending a non-allowance of benefits, his reasons therefor.

"All applications for benefits from members sick and out of the city must be accompanied by an affidavit or certificate from the attending physician, or both when required by the relief committee, stating the nature of the illness, the date and duration of the sickness, the total number of days under his care, that the sickness is not feigned or caused by dissipation, self-abuse, immoral conduct or violations of law.

"The board of directors having approved the list of sick benefits, shall, when countersigned by the president, be transmitted to the Board of Medical Examiners, who shall examine and report thereupon to the police commissioners.

"All applications for disability or distress consequent thereupon shall follow all the rules as laid down in cases of sickness.

"For funeral expenses the board of directors may appropriate for carriages, band, and incidentals attending the funeral services, a sum of money not to exceed fifty (50) dollars.

"On the death of a member of the association, the sum of three hundred (300) dollars shall be appropriated by the board of directors to be paid to the widow of the deceased, or such other member of his family as the board may designate, subject to the approval of the police commissioners, except in the case of the death of the superintendent of police, the inspector, surgeon, chief of detectives, detectives, court officers, station-house keepers, and clerks, when there shall be appropriated the sum of two hundred (200) dollars.

"On the death of a member of the association it shall be the duty of the president or secretary to notify the Superintendent of Police, requesting that he furnish the proper escort at the funeral.

"Pensions being granted upon the recommendation of the Mayor and the approval of the Police Commissioners, it shall be the duty of the president (or in his absence of the vice-president) and the secretary of the Board of Directors, together with the president of the Board of Police Commissioners, to sign and attest monthly all warrants for pensions. The official notification of the clerk of the Board of Police Commissioners shall give the proper authority, which notification shall be entered upon the records and filed with the papers of the association by the secretary.

"It being further provided by law (sect. 1902, O. L., 1886, p. 56), that pensions may cease on restoration to duty and full pay, the official notification of the clerk of the Board of Police Commissioners that a pension has ceased will give proper authority to the president and secretary to decline signing such ceased pension warrants, and such notifications shall be entered upon the records and filed with papers of the association by the secretary."

The commissioners in their capacity as trustees of the Police Relief Fund have been exceedingly careful, scrutinizing every detail of expenditures, knowing that in a few years the demands upon it will be heavy. This has been the experience of the New York Police Relief Association. There more than a quarter of a million dollars are annually paid out of its relief fund. The board in Cincinnati have found that without any extraordinary epidemics, and with the members of the force comparatively young, the monthly sick benefits may reach three hundred and fifty dollars, and not be less than two hundred dollars. So far the death rate is about four per annum.

A fund which will yield an annual income of not less than two thousand dollars is needed at once, and two thousand dollars is only the interest on fifty thousand dollars in Government four per cents.

The first officers of the association under the new organization were:

President—Lieutenant C. W. Fisher.
Vice-President—Sergeant E. C. Hill.
Secretary—Lieutenant Adolph Smith.
The City Treasurer is the custodian of all moneys.
Directors—Lieutenant Edwin C. Rockwell, Sergeant Joseph Wilmer, Sergeant Louis Schmitt, and Patrolman John H. Menke.

The association is now governed by the following Board of Officers, chosen the first Wednesday in January, 1889:

President—Sergeant Louis Schmitt.
Vice-President—Sergeant Henry Leitz.
Secretary—Dr. John Draper.
Directors—Dr. John Draper, John Whitaker, Charles Crossley, James Casey, Henry Lietz, Louis Schmitt, Edw. T. Rockwell.

Independent of the regular association, authorized by law, is what is known as the Policemen's Benevolent Association, recently organized, and not under the control of the Commissioners. Its annual dues are but twenty-five cents a year, and membership is voluntary. At the death of any member two dollars are assessed all around for the benefit of the family of the deceased. It now numbers three hundred and eighty members, and is officered as follows:

President—Lieutenant O. M. Fisher.

Vice-President—Lieutenant Newton Kendall.
Secretary—James Weatherby.
Treasurer—Clerk John R. Bender.

The Trustees are: First District, Edwin Howard; Second, T. J. Doherty; Third, Lieutenant Godfrey Pistner; Fourth, T. C. McMillen; Fifth, Lieutenant E. C. Rockwell; Sixth, Sergeant Henry McMullen; Seventh, Lieutenant Samuel B. Hall; Eighth, Lieutenant Edgar Robinson; Ninth, Lieutenant Patrick Curran; Tenth, Louis Schmitt; Police Court-room, John Whitaker; Headquarters, Thomas McGovern; Patrol Service, Mike Welsh.

The annual election occurs the second Wednesday in October.

To be placed upon the roll of honor is an achievement of which the Cincinnati policeman feels as justly proud as did the ancient Grecian athlete of his crown of laurel. It is a delicate acknowledgement of bravery, carrying with it at once a distinction and a reward. Empty thanks are but poor recompense to a man who has risked his life, and he who has done this in the effort to save another is too generous to accept of pecuniary reward. The consciousness of having performed a noble deed is, perhaps, the best requital; but there is in all men a something which looks beyond self-consciousness for approval. When a policeman engages in a desperate combat with law-breakers, in which his life is freely risked, he experiences a keener satisfaction in reading the report of his brave act in the newspaper, than in the successful arrest and placing behind the bars of the law-breakers. It is a pardonable feeling, and the Board of Police Commissioners displayed rare tact and good judgment in recognizing this when they instituted the roll of honor more than two years ago.

A policeman often takes his life in his hands in the discharge of his duties, and the fact is often overlooked in the daily paper. A child may be snatched from under the wheels of a wagon or street car; a runaway team seized and stopped from a possible career of destruction; an obstacle is hastily removed from the track just as a fast train thunders by; fire and smoke, with all the unseen but probable dangers are often dared by the rescuing policeman, or a drowning human being is saved from the hungry floods.

The Roll of Honor takes full cognizance of acts like these. Its insignia is as much of a desideratum in the heart of a Cincinnati policeman as was the cross of the Legion of Honor in the hearts of the devoted followers of the "Little Corporal." It has been found to possess many advantages over other methods of recognition. For its possessor it stands for courage, and is a mentor that bids him do no unworthy act to tarnish the bright record.

The Roll of Honor, or the diploma awarded in connection with the roll of honorable mention, is conferred at the first public gathering of the entire police force, following the report of the commissioner which makes the award. The last award was made January 1889, on the occasion of the bestowal of the Morgan medal. The presentation was made in the presence of the entire Police Department and by the Mayor, and the occasion was made impressive and memorable by the attendant speeches and other appropriate circumstances.

The rules governing the bestowal of this valuable prize are very strict, and there is not the slightest possibility of its being received by a man whose life has not been absolutely risked in the discharge of his duties. When a policeman achieves some deed which, in the opinion of his superior officer, entitles him to recognition, the case is fully reported to the superintendent by the lieutenant in charge of the district where the incident occurred. The superintendent in turn presents the matter to the Board of Commissioners, who refer it to the Committee on Morals and Discipline. If this committee, after investigation of the affidavits relating to the act, reports favorably to the bestowal of the roll of honor, the whole board then formally passes upon it, and the policeman's name is placed upon the roll of honorable mention, and in due time he receives his diploma.

The roll of honor is a work of art as may be seen from the engraved sketch. It is lithographed on heavy paper of the finest quality, and is presented inclosed in a handsome natural wood frame, measuring twenty-nine inches by twenty-four. It is in colors, giving an accurate representation of the paraphernalia of a policeman's make up. The club in cherry-brown, and the cord

ROLL OF HONOR.

and tassel a bright scarlet; the belt in olive-green; the helmet in dark navy-blue, with the silver number of the owner in front; the pistol and handcuff in steel-gray; the dark-lantern in brown; the whistle and fire alarm box key in silver-gray, suspended with the bronze-tinted patrol box key from a gilt chain, are all faithfully reproduced in colors and quarter natural size in the engraving. Everything is artistically grouped, and branches of laurel leaves are gracefully entwined, making the effect at once appropriate, striking, and elegant. It is a handsome object intrinsically valuable as a work of art, and priceless as a souvenir of a brave deed.

One of the earliest bestowals of the Roll of Honor was upon patrolman Patrick Coffey, whose deed is still pointed to with pride by his brother officers as a rare instance of unswerving fidelity to duty and courageous purpose. About 2.30 o'clock on the afternoon of December 14, 1886, while patroling his beat, officer Coffey, of the Fourth District, observed two fellows, who were subsequently identified as Michael Welsh and John Brennan, assault and attempt to rob a peddler on Race street, between Second and Front streets, a neighborhood of notoriously bad repute. Officer Coffey hurried to the rescue of the peddler, who immediately made off and left the policeman to cope single handed with the highwaymen. Both were desperate criminals, and would not hesitate to sacrifice life to escape imprisonment. When the officer seized them they turned upon him and began one of the most desperate struggles of which the police department has any record. One of the thugs tripped the officer, and at the same time the other dealt him a powerful blow on the side of the head, felling him to the pavement. In falling Coffey broke his arm at the elbow, but nevertheless he did not relax his hold upon his prisoners, and managed to regain his feet, but not before he was kicked several times in the chest and had a rib broken. One of the men succeeded in loosening Coffey's grasp, and then turned upon him to prevent his beating the life out of his "pal." The officer immediately recovered his grip and held it in spite of the struggling, biting, and kicking of his prisoners until passers-by and a patrol wagon came to reinforce him, when the two highwaymen were taken to the station-house. Coffey was so badly injured that he had to be carried home in the patrol wagon, and it was some weeks before he fully recovered.

Another brave possessor of the Roll of Honor is Henry Kramer, of the Cumminsville District. Officer Kramer, while patroling his beat, observed a door, which had become loosened from its fastenings, fall off the car of a passing freight train. The door struck the ground with such force that it rebounded over upon the Cincinnati, Washington and Baltimore railway tracks. An express train was thundering along at forty miles an hour on this track, and was scarcely three hundred feet away when Mr. Kramer sprang forward, and, by a herculean effort, raised and threw to one side the heavy obstacle. So close was the train upon the officer that the locomotive actually brushed his coat as it shot by. Even the engineer thought the policeman had undertaken a hopeless task, and desperately whistled to him to get off the track, at the same time setting his brakes. The train was too close to be stopped, however, and had it not been for brave Kramer's act a frightful calamity would have resulted, for the scene of the obstruction was a high embankment.

"But I wanted to get that door off the track," said Kramer afterward, when asked why he did not heed the engineer's warning whistle.

It was a simple declaration, but it stamped the man a hero who bravely undertook to avert danger to others without a thought of himself.

To quote an eye-witness: "There are few men who would have risked their lives so cheaply. If the door had not been taken off just in the nick of time, the train would have struck it and gone plunging down the embankment with its human freight."

Charles Bocklett and Julius Beiser, policemen of the Third District, were each awarded the Roll of Honor for a joint act of bravery that deserves special mention. On the night of September 6, 1887, the stables of the Western Transfer Company, situated on McMicken avenue, were discovered to be on fire. The flames had gained considerable headway before it was learned that a man was in the burning building. The imperiled person was young Ruckstuhl, clerk of the company, who slept in a room over the office. Several firemen essayed a rescue, but were driven back by the flames and smoke. Volunteers were called for, but none responded, and for a moment it seemed as if the young man was doomed. Policemen Bocklett and Beiser, however, bravely made a dash through the wall of fire and disappeared. Several seconds passed before they emerged, but they were empty handed. "We know where he is," they shouted back to the encouraging cheers of the crowd, and again they darted into the seething mass of fire and smoke, the roar of the flames drowning the plaudits of the crowd. When they again appeared, it was with the unconscious and almost lifeless form of young Ruckstuhl borne between them. They had saved him, though not without severe burns to themselves. It was one of the bravest acts ever recorded in the history of the Police Department.

Instances of acts of bravery could be multiplied on these pages if the limited space allotted to the Roll of Honor would permit. There is room only for the catalogue as it appears at police headquarters, and which is as follows:

James Flannagan, August 24, 1886, at the burning of No. 114, rescued a woman from the fire.

Frank C. Morgan, August 25, 1886, at the corner of Fourth and Race streets, stopped a team of runaway horses.

Henry Eckerstaff, September 16, 1886, at the corner of Fifth and Walnut streets, stopped a runaway horse attached to a baker's wagon.

Thomas McDonough, November 16, 1886, on Gilbert avenue near Grant street, stopped a team of runaway horses attached to a coal wagon.

Patrick Coffey, December 14, 1886, on Race street, between Second and Plum streets, accomplished an arrest in spite of personal injuries.

Louis Becker, January 8, 1887, at the corner of Fourth and Race streets, stopped a runaway horse attached to a buggy.

Louis Kussman, January 29, 1887, at the corner of Abigail and Spring streets, made an arrest while being assaulted by a villanous gang.

James Casey, January 31, 1887, near the corner of Sixth and Walnut streets, stopped a runaway team belonging to the U. S. Express Company.

John Donnelly, February 14, 1887, at the burning of No. 611 Main street, checked a street car team maddened by the music and banners of a procession.

Patrick J. White, March 17, 1887, at the corner of Fourth and Vine streets, checked a street car team maddened by the music and banners of a procession.

Sergeant William Leukering, April 21, 1887, on Freeman avenue near Findlay street, stopped a runaway team attached to a wagon.

Frank Seaford, June 1, 1887, at the fire at No. 902 Central avenue, rescued a woman.

James Casey, June 5, 1887, on Sycamore street between Sixth and Seventh streets, stopped a runaway horse attached to a buggy.

Cyrus O. Hames, July 15, 1887, at Tusculum station stopped a two mule runaway team.

Joseph Burman, July 29, 1887, at the great fire on State avenue and Gest street, rescued a woman.

Albert Simons, July 30, 1887, near the corner of Sixth and John streets, stopped a runaway horse attached to a wagon containing a man and woman.

John J. Doherty, September 1, 1887, on Fourth street between Walnut and Main, stopped a runaway horse attached to an express wagon.

John B. Anderson, September 2, 1887, on Eastern avenue near Torrence road stopped a runaway horse attached to a wagon, containing a woman and two children.

John Kratz, September 4, 1887, on George street east of Plum street, stopped a runaway team attached to an ice wagon.

Charles Bocklett and Julius Beiser, September 6, 1887, together, at the fire of the Western Transfer Co.'s stables on McMicken avenue, rescued a man after making two attempts.

Henry Kramer, September 27, 1887, removed an obstruction from the C. W. &. B. R. R. at East Cumminsville, in front of a train approaching him at the rate of forty miles an hour.

Jacob Schilling and Frederick Werner, October 1, 1887, together, with great bravery and coolness, at Robinson's Opera House, in the midst of a panic caused by a false alarm of fire, restored calm and quiet.

Jacob Fisher, October 22, 1887, at the fire at No 492 Central avenue, rescued a woman.

William Berning, November 1, 1887, on Vine street near Fourth street, stopped a runaway horse.

John Miller, March 8, 1888, at the corner of Central avenue and Second street, stopped a runaway horse attached to a delivery wagon.

Robert Nellis, April 3, 1888, on George street, between Elm and Plum streets, stopped a runaway team.

Philip J. Roach, June 9, 1888, at the great fire on West Sixth street, near the Southern Railroad bridge, rescued Mrs. Annie Water.

James F. Malloy, August 1, 1888, at Gilbert avenue and McMillon street, stopped a runaway team hitched to a milk-wagon.

John Wambsgans, August 23, 1888, on Baymiller street between Findlay and Poplar, stopped a runaway horse attached to a buggy.

James Ellis, August 23, 1888, on Elm near Twelfth, stopped a runaway horse attached to a buggy.

On December 25, 1888, at the fire of the ropewalk of Charles Jacobs Cordage Company, and other buildings located between Budd street and the Cincinnati, Hamilton and Dayton Railroad tracks, running west from Harnet street, James A. Hemmings rescued Mrs. John Riley and three small children from the second floor of No. 41 Budd street, which at the time was burning in the rear, and every room of which was filled with dense smoke.

CHAPTER XIII.

CENTRAL STATION AND POLICE TELEPHONE.—THE OLD, THE TEMPORARY, AND THE NEW QUARTERS.—DUTIES OF LIEUTENANTS AND SERGEANTS.—THE DISTRICT IN WHICH THE UNSOLVED BALDWIN MYSTERY WAS DISCOVERED.—REVIEW OF THE STARTLING CRIME AND THE PART THE POLICE PLAYED IN IT.—OFFICERS NOW IN CHARGE OF THE DISTRICT.—POLICE SIGNALING THEN AND NOW.—THE OLD DIAL AND THE LIGHTNING TELEPHONE.

NINTH Street Station was a term familiar to Cincinnatians for years. It is the old name for the capitol of the First District. Every one knew where "Ninth street" was. To many the mere mention of the term brought remembrances that were anything but assuring. The place was also known as Central Station, being in connection with the regular police headquarters, and the place of detention of all important prisoners. It was a dingy old den, a veritable hole in the wall. Dark, with low ceilings, ill-ventilated, sultry in summer and damp in winter, a day's confinement there was almost sufficient punishment for minor crimes. Central Station was reached by passing through a narrow entrance on Ninth street, being located in the basement of the old City Hall, recently torn down to make room for a more substantial and modern structure. The station-house, proper, was about thirty feet long and fifteen feet wide, with a small apartment back of the desk for the private office of lieutenants and sergeants. In the rear of this were the male and female apartments for prisoners, separated only by a temporarily constructed board partition, reaching half way to the ceiling, and scarcely shutting off the view from one apartment to the other. There were four rows of six cells each, rudely constructed but strong and stubborn to an occupant. Behind the department for females was a small room, eight by ten, containing a solitary cell, this was known as the "fly cell," in which many noted murderers, burglars, counterfeiters, and desperadoes in general have been incarcerated. There have been but few notorious criminals in the United States in the past fifty years who have not at one time or another breathed the foul air of the "fly cell" at old Central Station. It was in this place that George Palmer, who, with William Berner, in 1884, killed Kirk, made the confession at midnight which sent him to the gallows, Berner to the penitentiary for twenty years, indirectly burned the Court House, and caused the deaths of upwards of fifty people and the wounding of as many more. Behind the "fly cell" was another dark and forbidding apartment used for storing arms and ammunition. In one corner of Central Station was a table with telephone, lock boxes and other attachments for the accommodation of newspaper reporters, and right in this corner were chronicled most of the murders, fires, accidents, and other sensational episodes that have occurred in Cincinnati during the last decade. Adjoining the reporters' corner was the Police Telephone Exchange. Within the walls of this Central Station a murder was committed on a Sunday afternoon about ten years ago. Colonel Thomas Snelbaker, subsequently a theatrical manager in Washington city, shot and killed Policeman Chumley while the latter was standing at the lieutenant's desk. During the terrible floods which visited Cincinnati for three successive years, Central Station was the rendezvous of all classes of people, and, in addition, room was made for soldiers and extra policemen on duty at the time.

The court-house riot of 1884 brought hundreds of soldiers to Cincinnati, who made Central Station their headquarters. Immediately above Central Station was the police court, a large, roomy place, but poorly arranged for the purpose, poorly constructed, and owing to its location above a transient prison, an unhealthy spot in general. Across a narrow, dark hall from the police court-room were the offices of the chief of police, chief of detectives, and inspector.

When the old city hall was torn down and this historical old station house removed from sight forever, the police department was transferred to the building near the corner of Fourth street and Central avenue, now used as a temporary city hall. In the basement, with an entrance on Central avenue, is the present Central Station. Although temporary, it is in every way far superior to the old quarters. The officers, lieutenant's desks, and special officers' departments are large and roomy, and every detail for comfort, convenience, and business arranged as admirably as though the place were adopted as a permanency. Of course the newspaper men followed the police and are conveniently located in one corner of the station house. The cell-rooms are in the rear of the offices. The lieutenants have a nicely furnished private office, and in the same apartment are the offices of the chief clerk of the police department and his assistants. Overhead and on the next floor is the police court-room, a narrow, inconvenient place, but the best that the building affords. On this floor are also the offices of the superintendent of police and his clerks. The chief has a large, comfortable office, with every desirable convenience. It adjoins the office of the chief of detectives, who as a rule has his subordinates before him twice a day. Across the hall the inspector of police has an office. The police department, in its present quarters, taken as a whole, is admirably located, and there is nothing that money can buy omitted to make it complete in all its details. The old quarters were in striking contrast, but no more so than the present temporary location will be to the new quarters now in course of construction on the site of the old city hall.

The entire west wing of the new City Hall will be given up to the police department. On the first floor will be the police court room, offices of chief of police, chief of detectives, police court clerks, police department clerks, halls, corridors, bath-rooms, and other adjuncts. On the next floor will be the offices of the police commissioners and police library. The third floor will be devoted to a large and spacious police gymnasium, and the place of detention for women and children. For this new wing, which will be entirely cut off on the first floor from the City Hall proper, an extra appropriation of $250,000 was granted by the legislature. This appropriation was granted only after a hard fight made by the Hamilton County delegation. With these additional funds provided, the plans as mentioned above will be executed, and when finished Cincinnati will have as fine and convenient a police department as any city in the United States, or for that matter in the world. The city formerly boasted of her fire department, which maintains at present its old-time efficiency, but of late years her police department has been elevated to the highest standard, and as Cincinnatians point with just pride to their "finest," it would seem eminently fitting to provide the "finest" with apartments commensurate with their standard of efficiency.

The boundaries of the first police district are as follows: beginning at Third and Walnut, along the west side of Third street to Canal; along the canal to Clark, to Baymiller, to Seventh; along the north side of Seventh to Smith; along the east side of Smith to Third; along the north side of Third to Walnut. Sixty-nine policemen report at the Central Station; three lieutenants—Fisher, Gill and Schmidt; sergeants—Borck, Carroll, Wilmes and Ewbanks; two station-house keepers; fourteen special officers, and forty-six patrolmen, assigned to regular beats.

The duties of a lieutenant of police under the non-partisan board are multitudinous. When not engaged in inspecting his district, or in discharging some other official business which may call him away from his desk, he must be at his station house during all of his hours of duty, and he must see that the station house is always kept open to receive prisoners, attend to calls, and answer applications from citizens. He must visit every part of his district daily, note the condition of the streets, side walks, street lamps, obstructions, nuisances, and all non-compliance with city ordinances, and with the provisions of city ordinances he must be as familiar as with the English alphabet. He is supposed to learn of any contagions that may be prevalent in his district, and it is his duty to report the same at once to the superintendent. Any negligence which may expose the city to fire or any matters pertaining to the Board of Health which have been neglected he must notice and report to the same officer. For the conduct, condition, faithfulness, and efficiency of the officers of his district, whether sergeants, patrolmen, or station-house keepers, he is held responsible. He calls the roll of officers subordinate to him, and communicates to them all orders and necessary information, and he notes and reports all absentees. He inspects the patrolmen and other subordinates, reforms any negligence in attire or cleanliness, or any improper personal habit. If there is any sickness among his men, any unfitness for duty, he reports the same to the superintendent. Not less than twice a week he is required to instruct patrolmen as to their duties at fires, riots, in making arrests, or hearing complaints as to nuisances on their respective beats. It is among his duties to see to it that each officer is provided with a manual, and that he observes the rules it contains. The lieutenant must divide his district into beats, for day and for night, and so arrange that the whole territory can be covered by the patrolman on duty. If any officer under his command shall fail to discover a homicide, burglary, or serious breach of the peace committed on his beat during his patrol duty, against that officer he must prefer charges. It is the lieutenant's duty to receive into his custody all persons arrested for any crime or misdemeanor in his district, and unless they are otherwise disposed of, to see that they are conveyed to the police court for trial. He must also keep a record of the name and personal description of all persons furnished lodgings at his station house. It is his duty to keep a daily record of burglaries, robberies, larcenies, amount of property stolen, assaults, disturbances, fires, dangerous places, accidents, with the cause and proofs, and all other matters connected with the police department in his district. He is compelled to keep a "time roll," showing the pay per diem of all members of the force in his district, an alphabetical list of all persons released from the workhouse, a "general complaint book," in which is entered every complaint preferred, a "register book," for name, ages, etc., of lost children, and an "arrest book," containing the names of all persons arrested, charges preferred, residence, age, color, sex, nationality, occupation, whether married or single, religion, and education, together with the name of the arresting officer. The extra duties done by his men are also a matter of his concern, and the amount of money due them, a record of which he must communicate to the chief clerk of the department on the fifteenth of each month. It is his duty to

LIEUT. C. M. FISHER.   LIEUT. T. F. GILL.   LIEUT. ADOLPH SCHMIDT.
First District.

receive moneys collected for licenses by men reporting at his station house, and make out a true return of them to the chief clerk. Among his duties is that of keeping a record of all pawnbrokers, second-hand dealers, junk shops, intelligence offices, all drinking saloons, gambling houses, houses of ill fame, and policy shops located in his district. In case of a riot or of any unlawful gathering in his district he must at once summon all the men possible, proceed to the scene of the disturbance, and be vigilant in his efforts to restore order. He must at the same time notify the superintendent of the police of the disturbance. He must practice economy in the use of fuel, and other articles necessary for comfort in a station house. The cleanliness about the station house is also a matter of his concern.

The sergeants act as lieutenants in the absence of the lieutenant, and when not serving in this capacity have general charge of the men on their beats, assisting them in their duties. Acting on the theory that men are never fitted to command until they have learned to obey, the commissioners in the rules they have prepared for the government of the patrolmen have insisted upon the utmost respect being shown by all subordinates to their superiors in command and to their orders. Insubordination is never tolerated on the Cincinnati police force.

Cassius M. Fisher was born in Campbell County, Kentucky, September 23, 1854. He was a farmer boy, and it was not until he was nineteen years of age that he decided that farming was not his vocation, and came to Newport, Kentucky. He engaged in various business enterprises until 1880, on the sixth of January of which year he went on the police force. He was assigned to the second district, and during his term as patrolman and officer he has been stationed at Hammond street, Fulton, Corryville, Third street and Central. He was appointed sergeant on the 1st of May, 1886, and on the 22d of June, 1886, he was made lieutenant.

Lieutenant Fisher is a fearless man and determined. These traits, combined with executive ability and great coolness, make him one of the great officers of the police force. His peculiar fitness for police work was shown soon after he went on the force.

In 1883 he was assigned to the Deer Creek beat, then the most dangerous beat in the city. Under the history of Hammond street, the condition of things before Fisher came there will be fully described. The Deer Creek gang traveled in crowds of from fifteen to forty; and never were Grecian bandits in the fastnesses of their native mountains bolder or more desperate than these wretches in the narrow and dirty lanes that branch out from "Dublin" street. The police officers traveled four together, and were shot at and "bowldered" every night. Robbery and violence were carried on under their very eyes, and they did not dare to interfere. Once the patrol wagons were driven in headlong flight from this district.

Fisher adopted new tactics. Appointing himself commander of the four men, he ordered them to cease rapping as they went around, because this gave the gang warning. They skulked in the shadows of the houses, hid their badges and helmets, and waited their chances. As soon as a shriek of "Murder!" or "Watch!" would come from some traveler who was being held up, they would leap out and begin to club right and left. Soon over forty of the gang were in the work-house, seventeen were in the penitentiary, and the rest were completely cowed.

Some of the methods of the gang were interesting. An illustration of this is the way they treated a certain Major Ewing, of Nashville, brother-in-law to Stanley Matthews. One night two of the gang were at the Highland House with the two Cronin girls, about as tough women as there were in the town, but rather pretty, and able to look respectable when the occasion demanded. The two men were "Red" Finnerly and John Brummagen. Major Ewing sat at the same table with these four, and they drew him into conversation. He was a stranger and fond of horses. Finnerly, who hung around the horse market, soon interested him. When the time came to go home, they said they were going down town, and the Major said he was going the same way. They led him down into the fastnesses of the gang—an easy thing to do, as he was a perfect stranger—and then one of them throttled him while the woman he was with picked his pockets of a fine gold watch and $175 in money. The Major complained to

Fisher, whom he met on a corner as he was making his way home. Fisher arrested the four, but the Major did not appear against them, dreading the notoriety. These same two Cronin girls acted as stool-pigeons for the gang frequently. Nearly every night one or the other of them would lead a "sucker" down into the darkness of "Dublin" street, whence he would presently emerge, hatless, coatless, moneyless, watchless, and breathless—glad to get away with his life. Then the gang would hold high revelry on the proceeds of the evening's work. But six months after the advent of Fisher this was broken up, and the Deer Creek gang sank into innocuous desuetude, from which the few remaining leaders have never been able to revive it.

Fisher was among the first on the scene at the great riots, and saw men killed on each side of him in the tunnel. He was also in the squad which so daringly captured the three cannon from the mob. When the struggle against the flagrant violations of the law began in 1886, Fisher, newly made a lieutenant, showed himself to be fearless and tireless in the discharge of his duty. It is due to him in a great measure, as well as to Lieutenant Schmidt, that Longworth street was reduced to at least a semblance of order and decency, and that gambling dens in full blast became a thing of the past. Lieutenant Fisher's life has been as eventful as that of any police officer, and whenever perilous duty is to be performed, Fisher is one of the first men to be called upon. He plays no favorites, and has the respect of his men, despite his strictness and even occasional severity.

Lieutenant Adolph Schmidt first saw the light February 2, 1851. When but fifteen years old he was apprenticed to a carpenter and joiner, and as a carpenter he worked for ten years, when Mayor G.W. C. Johnston made him a member of the Cincinnati police force. He served successively in the Tenth and Fifth Districts, and was then transferred to the First. For three years he was entrusted with the most difficult beats in the city, and was always recognized by his superior officers as among the most trustworthy of patrolmen.

In 1881 Mr. Schmidt surrendered his mace and badge and resumed work as a carpenter. For five years he continued to shove the jack-plane, and then as the non-partisan police commissioners came into power his love for a patrolman's duty returned. He applied for a position under the new order of things, and May 21, 1886, his application was granted. Six weeks afterwards he was made a sergeant, and three weeks later, his sterling qualities having become conspicuous, he proudly donned the shoulder-straps.

Superintendent Deitsch, for a long time previous to his promotion, had been considering the advisability of creating the office of a night chief of police or supervising lieutenant. As an experiment Lieutenant Schmidt was appointed. While the commissioners fully appreciated Lieutenant Schmidt's worth, they never took kindly to the new office, and after considerable parleying it was abolished. Six months of service in this position, however, had shown him to be an officer of no mean ability, and he was straightway given the responsible place as a joint commander at Central station, a position which he has ever since held.

Lieutenant Schmidt has made as many successful raids on gambling houses and houses of ill-fame as any other officer in Cincinnati. With some assistants in 1876, he effected an entrance into the notorious Empire gambling house and captured ninety players. While lieutenant of the Hammond street district he invaded the haunts of the Deer creek desperadoes, and the arrest and imprisonment of the entire Nuttle gang was the result. One hundred and eight persons were arrested from the Morris' cock-pit in January, 1887, by a detachment of officers, Lieutenant Schmidt in command, and all of the prisoners, with three exceptions, were fined twenty-five dollars and costs. Lieutenant Schmidt's father was also a good officer, serving under Mayor Len Harris. He died in 1870, while in the active discharge of his duties as a policeman.

Thomas Francis Gill is the youngest of the police lieutenants. He was born on the 22d of February, 1860, in this city. After receiving a common school education he was apprenticed to the carriage trimming trade. He spent some years at this and then began to travel about the country, living with relations in various cities and gaining a large experience, which has been particularly valuable to him. Just before going on the force he was clerk at the St. James Hotel. In October, 1884, he was appointed a patrolman. In July, 1886, he became a sergeant, and in July, 1887, he was promoted to the rank of lieutenant. All these promotions have been owing to his able and faithful discharge of duties. Ever since he was made a sergeant he has remained at Central Station, and last spring he was one of the two night chiefs appointed to assume command alternately in the absence of Colonel Deitsch. Gill was early in his career as policeman appointed to run what was then a very tough beat, around the neighborhood of Lincoln Park. There were several organized gangs of desperadoes which haunted that district, ready at all times for any kind of crime, from murder and highway robbery to stealing a door-mat. They bore such suggestive names as "The Dirty Dozen" and "The Tearers," the latter gang numbering about forty. Early in 1886 these gangs were rampant. In a few months Gill had made such inroads in their numbers that few of the gangs were left. Many were in the penitentiary, many in the work-house, a goodly number had left the city, and the shattered remnants hung about their old haunts, grumbling and uneasy, like bees about a dismantled hive. It was his effective work here that first brought him into prominence and led to his rapid promotion. He also displayed his bravery during the election riots. Gill is quick in his movements, sharp witted, an excellent detective, a good executive, and a fairly well educated man. He stands in the first rank of the good lieutenants, and his loss to the force would be felt for a long time.

John Wesley Carroll is a native of Springfield, Ohio. He was born there on February 2, 1852. When he was seven years old his parents removed to Cincinnati, where, after receiving a common school education, he was apprenticed to the plumbing and gas-fitting trade. He continued to work at this until his appointment to the police force. In 1875 he enlisted in the First Regiment of the Ohio National Guard, and soon began to be distinguished as the best drilled man in the regiment. He rose through all the grades until he became captain of Company H. When the new Board of Police Commissioners came in and began to consider the discipline and drill of the force, it selected Carroll as drill master. He received his appointment to the force with the rank of sergeant on March 17, 1887. Ever since then he has been the drill master, and to his instructions the force owes its ability to execute all the evolutions known to military science. He is thoroughly competent, being drilled as few men are even in the regular army. May and June, 1887, he spent at Hammond street. The rest of the time he has been attached directly to the chief's office, or at the Central Station, where for five months of 1887 he acted as lieutenant. He was the only officer of the First Regiment who received special mention for work done during the riots, and he also conducted himself honorably when the regiment was ordered to the Shawnee mines during the coal strikes of 1877.

Sergeant George Ewbanks was born at Fayetteville, Ohio, in 1857, and was brought up on a farm until 1873, when he came to Cincinnati and learned the blacksmith's trade. May 21, 1886, he became a patrolman, reporting at Third street station. He was made a "special," and served as such until promoted to a sergeantcy on February 1, 1888. He has served at Central and Bremen street stations, as well as in the Oliver street district. Sergeant Ewbanks is one of the finest looking men on the force. He stands six feet one-half inch, and weighs 231 pounds, and is finely proportioned, his muscles being so compact and hard as to greatly deceive the observer. He is married, dearly loves hunting, and spent five winters, before joining the police force, in the great swamps of Mississippi hunting and trapping.

William F. Borck is a policeman by inheritance, as it were, his father having been an old and honored member of the force; a man who dropped dead at his post of duty in the Oliver street station-house. Borck was born on May 3, 1862, in this city, and, as soon as he was old enough, learned the carriage trimmer's trade. On the 19th of July, 1886, he was placed on the police force at Oliver street. He was afterward assigned to Patrol 4. December 13, 1887, he was transferred to Bremen street. On

SERGT. J. W. CARROLL.   SERGT. JOS. WILMES.   SERGT. GEO. EUBANKS.   SERGT. W. F. BORCK.
First District.

January 4, 1888, he was made a sergeant, and on the 1st of February was transferred to Central Station, where he now is. Sergeant Borck is a most meritorious officer, a man of pleasant manners, kind-hearted, yet very just and equable when duty is concerned.

Joseph Wilmer was born on the 20th of November, 1860, in Cincinnati. He was employed in several large stores in the bottoms before he became a policeman. On the 22d of August, 1886, he went on the force, and was assigned to Oliver street. On the 1st of November, 1886, he was transferred to Central Station, where he has been ever since. On February 1, 1888, he received deserved promotion to a sergeantcy. On the 1st of July, 1888, he was detailed to detective duty, along with many other officers, on account of the Centennial. So efficient was he found, that when the necessity for the special assignment of detectives had disappeared, he was still retained, and detailed to watch the banks on Third street. Sergeant Wilmer is a brave man, and his bravery came very near costing him his life one night in September, 1887. He was standing near the corner of Oak and McMillan streets when he heard a cry for help at that corner. He rushed up and found five men holding up a sixth. He at once attacked them, and they, turning their attention from their intended victim, began stabbing him viciously with their knives. Wilmer resisted as well as he could, but was soon overpowered. He received seventeen cuts, several of which were very deep and dangerous, one extending from the left arm-pit to the navel and narrowly escaping the abdominal cavity. After weeks and weeks of suffering and dangerous sickness he finally recovered, and at once began the pursuit of the gang which had attacked him. He sent every one of them to the work-house for long terms, and, in addition, sent up nine others of the gang who were implicated in other crimes.

Nearly ten years have elapsed since the night when Harry Baldwin was found dying in an alley from a bullet fired by an as yet unknown hand. But time has not dimmed the horror of it, and the haze of mystery which surrounds the event still excites the interest of the curious and the uneasiness of the nervous.

So many and so romantic are the tragic incidents which cluster about that mysterious bullet, fired on the Sunday morning, March 16, 1879, that wonder at this prolonged interest ceases when the tale is told.

Harry Baldwin was the only son of Ammi Baldwin, once a prominent insurance man, then cashier of the Third National, and later of the ill-starred Fidelity. He came of a luckless family. His father was found dead one morning, about a year and a half ago, when disgrace and ruin had compassed him on all sides. His uncle took a fatal dose of poison, when certain exposure of some crooked transactions in the Third National made him take a hasty choice between death and facing dishonor. Harry Baldwin himself was murdered, as every school child knows.

He was a tall, muscular, fine-looking young fellow, whose manly beauty made him admired of many women. That he was fond of wine and also of these women, against whom all society bars its doors, cannot be gainsayed. But early in 1879, he reformed, and married Miss Wiswell, daughter of one of the most prominent families of this city. The young couple took up their residence with the bride's parents, and, so far as is known, life's pathway was strewn with flowers. Baldwin had a fine position as travelling man with a prominent firm, and the salary enabled him to provide for his wife handsomely. Early in March he bade his wife farewell, to start on a trip, with no thought that never again would domestic happiness be his.

The early morning sky of Sunday, March 16, was clear and cold. The stars were shining brightly, and on Vine street and other gay streets of the city the revelers were holding high carnival. Every gambling house was in full blast, the saloon doors were wide open, and from the houses of ill fame came the clinking of glasses mingled with the pealing laughter of women and the hoarser shouts of drunken men. Everything was "wide open" in those days, and some of the streets at three o'clock were as well filled with people as Vine street now is at midnight.

At a quarter to one o'clock patrolmen Adolph Schmidt and James Howard were standing at the corner of Court and Elm, when a pistol shot rang out upon the air. It came from the direction of Ninth and Elm, and was evidently the discharge of a heavy weapon. As that corner was a "tough" corner, the officers hurried down towards it. Their attention was attracted by a group of men on the crossing at Ninth and Elm, half a square above Kitty Bennett's house of ill repute, which was at 297 Elm, at the northwest corner of the alley between Eighth and Ninth. The officers hurried up, and found a crowd of about fifty people collected, in the midst of whom stood two private watchmen, Doran and Hertig, holding a third man, whom they recognized as William Schaller, the brewer. The watchmen explained that Schaller had fired off his pistol in the air in front of Bennet's, and that they, being in the saloon next door, had rushed out and grabbed him. Schmidt walked up to Schaller, and reaching in his back pocket, pulled out the pistol which had caused all the trouble. Stepping over to the lamp-post, Schmidt looked at the revolver, and saw that it was a thirty-two calibre. This little incident was what saved Schaller from a life sentence in the penitentiary, or possibly from the gallows. On this one observation hung a man's life.

The watchmen turned Schaller over to the officers, who started down Ninth street toward the station-house with him. His friends followed and all explained the occurrence and pleaded with the officers. Schaller said he was celebrating his birthday, and being a little under the influence of wine, had made the rounds of the houses, and finally by a dare from Kitty Bennett had fired the revolver. He urged the disgrace it would bring on his wife and family, and finally prevailed over Howard and then over Schmidt. They thought that the firing of a revolver at night was an every night's occurrence at any rate, and then, too, in those days much greater license prevailed. So Schaller was let go. Then one of his friends, a man who was collector for the brewery and lived in Newport, said the revolver was his, one that he carried for protection in his every night trips across the river, and that he had loaned it to Schaller. After a little persuasion Schmidt gave it back to him.

The officers continued their rounds while Schaller and his

friends went up to the Washington Park Exchange. An hour later, that is, at a quarter to two, Schmidt and Howard were once more walking down Elm street. They had passed up that way a short while before, but had observed nothing strange. This time they saw two men dragging a third, seemingly with great difficulty, along the sidewalk opposite Bennetts. As they came up they recognized the two private watchmen, Doran and Hertig, as the men who were doing the dragging.

"What have you there?" said Schmidt.

"Oh, a drunken man we found in the doorway just below here," answered one of the watchmen. The regular policemen took the drunken man in charge as was their duty. He was a heavy man, weighing somewhere near 225 pounds. His vest was partly torn open, his cuffs were rumpled, his watch chain hanging loosely from his pocket, his trowsers were unfastened, and his suspenders had been loosened from them. Altogether he looked like a man who had been scuffling and had sat down to think it over and sleep off some of his drunk. The officers and watchman hauled him along and in a few minutes were assisted by a man named Hogue, whom they pressed into the service. As the Central station was near at hand they soon arrived there and stretched the drunken man out on the floor in front of the desk. Lieutenant Roberts and the four men comprising the day watch were in the station house at the time. They all gathered around, remarking how well dressed the drunken man was, and laughing at the muttering noises he was making as though trying to speak but too much overcome to do so. His face was dirty, and on his temple was a little cut, like an abrasion of the skin from which a thin stream of blood had trickled down to his cheek and dried. Presently Hogue said:

"Why, this is Harry Baldwin, Wiswell's son-in-law."

Lieutenant Roberts told Pickett, the station-house keeper, to put him back in the cell-room, instructing him to lay him on the floor lest he should fall off the bench and hurt himself. Then the lieutenant marked S. K. (safe keeping) on the slate under Baldwin's name, and asked the watchman to go to Wiswell's house and tell them that Baldwin was there.

The two officers and the two watchmen left the station house together, the officers to go home, the watchmen to go to Wiswell's house, which was on Ninth between Race and Elm. They rang the bell until Mr. Wiswell appeared in a second-story window. They told him that his son-in-law was in the station house dead drunk. He muttered something and slammed the window. Nor did he send any word to the station house or make any attempt to rescue his son-in-law.

The next morning, at six o'clock, when Pickett went to wake the "safe keeper," he found Baldwin still lying in a stupor. An hour later and he was still in the same condition. An hour later Dr. Muscroft, the police surgeon, was called in. He entered the cell, made a superficial examination and ordered him sent to the hospital. When he arrived there and a physician came to his bedside, Baldwin was no longer in a stupor.

He was dead! And furthermore, he had died from a bullet wound in the temple. The slight abrasion that had excited no attention was a mortal wound. The incoherent and indistinct mutterings were the efforts of a dying man to speak and explain who had killed him.

Harry Baldwin had been murdered!

Chief of Police Reilly startled Schmidt from his sleep with this announcement at 10.30 Sunday morning, and into that officer's mind at once rushed the Schaller incident. Schaller was arrested, and the work of weaving the chain of circumstantial evidence about him at once begun. But one fact in the evidence of Schmidt broke the chain beyond repair. Schaller's pistol was a 32-calibre. The bullet found in the brain of Baldwin was from a 22-cartridge

Schaller was soon afterward dismissed. Then the questions arose: Who did it? When was it done? Where was it done? To none of these queries has a satisfactory answer ever been given. The Baldwin mystery is wrapped in as profound gloom as that which enveloped it on that cold Sunday morning.

His hat and valise were found near the mouth of the alley which runs through the square between Eighth and Ninth streets and Race and Elm. Baldwin himself was discovered by the watchman in a sitting posture, with his legs straight in front of him, in the doorway of the grocery on the east side of Elm, at the southeast corner of that same alley. Across Elm street, at northwest corner of the same alley, is the house of ill-fame of Kitty Bennett. Here is a complete diagram of the scene of the murder:

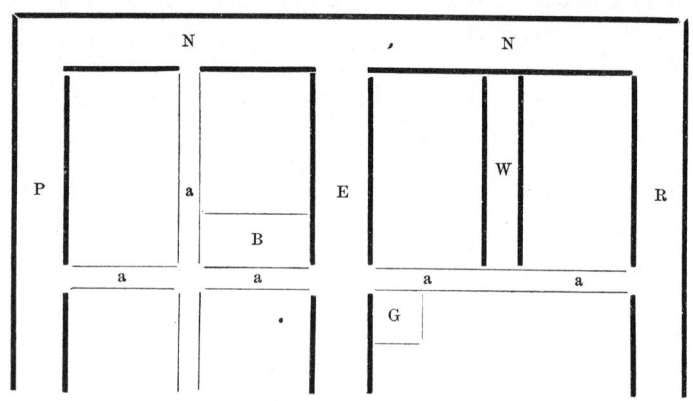

E.—Elm street.   N.—Ninth street.
R.—Race street.
P.—Plum street.   a a.—Alley.
B.—Kitty Bennett's.
G.—Grocery, in the door of which Baldwin was found.
W.=Wiswell's lot, fronting on Ninth street, and opening through a gate in the fence at the rear in the alley.

Suspicion settled on no one person. Everyone who had anything of intimacy with Baldwin was suspected. It was discovered that Baldwin had come home from his trip, entered a barber shop, valise in hand, had been shaved and then had gone out. This was at 7.30 Saturday evening. Those who saw him between that time and a quarter to two o'clock, have never come forward and acknowledged it. It was almost proved that he was at one time intimate with a woman in Bennett's house. Did he go back there, under fear of threats, or to wilfully renew relations which marital honor bade him forget. And did the woman, after bitter reproaches, pick up a revolver—a 22-calibre is a woman's revolver, never a man's—and shoot him ? Or did some man find him in the house and in the room of this woman and shoot him through jealousy? Baldwin's clothes bore the evidences of a struggle. Did Schaller and his friends enter the house just after the shooting, and while the women were doing all in their power for Baldwin, and did his half-drunken condition suggest to wily Kitty Bennett a deep scheme? Did she dare him to shoot when he got out in the street, hoping thus to divert suspicion and make the shooting appear accidental? And was Baldwin conveyed across to the doorway of the grocery after the excitement had cooled down? Certain it is that soon after the murder, Kitty Bennett and all the girls that were there in the house left the town. Would she go to such lengths to protect a friendless and destitute woman of the town from justice? Does it not seem more probable that if he was killed in the house a man did it?

A little over a year after Baldwin's murder, his beautiful young wife, who had slowly pined away under the strain of the excitement and under the shameful stories attending it and finally died, leaving an only child, born after the father's death. So that Harry Baldwin and his beautiful wife, but a short while before as happy as youth and love can make mortal men, now fill unhappy and murder-enshrouded graves. Who will deny that the same red right hand which fired death into his brain, slew also the wife?

This is the Baldwin mystery, as deep and thrilling as any story of romance or real life, unsolved and seemingly unsolvable. So impenetrable does it seem to the police that when you ask them who killed Baldwin, they reply: " The murderer of Baldwin is dead." But there are those that live who can tell; and strange though it be that a secret in the possession of more than one should be kept for nearly ten years, it would be stranger still if the day does not come when suspicion will be driven aside by the clear light of certainty. And when that day comes who will stand revealed? Who knows?

A quarter of a century ago the only mode of communication between the various police stations was by messenger, an officer being detailed to carry whatever official documents or information that might require prompt delivery. Necessarily this system was slow and cumbersome, and retributive justice travelled with an exceeding slow foot. As an illustration the following sample of work done in the old days may be useful to serve as a criterion for judging the service of to-day : a murder has been committed in an extreme end of the city. The officer detailed in the district learns of it a half hour later from some spectator. Proceeding to the scene he learns the name of the murderer, who has escaped. Retracing his steps he goes to the station-house and informs his superior officer. He in turn despatches a messenger to police headquarters with an official communication notifying his chief of the facts, and giving a description of the fugitive. A general alarm is necessary, and a couple of officers are hunted up and started on a journey to the nearest stations. Giving the information they return to headquarters and report. The officers in charge of the first stations notified, despatch a messenger to the next and proceed to make a round of their respective districts, notifying each patrolman as he is found, to look out for the murderer. Thus from five to eight hours are consumed in notifying the force. Compare this irritatingly slow method with the one in use at the present time. Within five minutes after the commission of such a crime a patrol wagon with its complement of officers is dashing toward the scene, every man knowing exactly what has taken place and what is expected of him. In the meanwhile the news has been flashed to every police office in the city, and within a brief hour every man on duty knows that a murder has been committed and that the criminal is at large.

Twenty-five years ago it was a common thing in a rough neighborhood to see a police officer forced to release his prisoner and flee for his life, after making a gallant resistance against overwhelming odds. Pitched battles could be fought in the streets by opposing factions, to the terror of law-abiding people, and perhaps hours would elapse before a sufficient number of police could be brought to quell the brawlers.

To-day almost every house contains a valuable police assistant, and a patrolman needing help to defend himself against an attacking force, is soon relieved by a wagon load of fellow officers. Warring factions are soon dispersed by the same means, and a street filled with fighting men is cleared as if by magic.

What has accomplished this wonderful change?
Electricity.

The famed spark of Franklin and of Faraday has been so utilized by men of science, that it is really one of the most efficient arms of the police service. The flashing lightning of the telegraph, travelling with inconceivable and almost immeasurable speed, has in thousands of instances been the means of apprehending criminals who deemed themselves secure, seated within a train flying from the scenes of their crimes toward chosen hiding places. Keeping abreast with the development of science, the police have adopted the latest invention in the electric art— the marvelous telephone. In this city the police telephone system has been more elaborately constructed than in any other place in the world, owing to the unexampled enterprise and generosity of the general telephone company of Cincinnati, of which it is a branch. Prior to 1866 the messenger system was in vogue in this city. In that year the department took a step that startled the sober old-fashioned citizens. It adopted the " dial system " of telegraph between the stations. At the time this was considered the *ultima thule* of the art of telegraphic communication, because of its so-called simplicity. The system consisted of a general circuit, uniting all the stations and other public points, such as the hospital and fertilizing companies' office. At each station was a large box containing a dial, around which moved a needle. The circle was divided into spaces containing the letters of the alphabet and the Arabic numerals. This needle moved synchronically with any other on the circuit, and the parties wishing to communicate were thus enabled to spell out their messages to each other. The first superintendent of this department was Evan A. Saunders, who was familiarly known as " Teddy." His was a wearisome position, because of the failure of the various lieutenants to grasp the simple ideas on which the system was based. The instruments were continually getting out of order, and " Teddy " was forever in hot water. As a result, in 1867 the then Chief of Police, Robert McGrew, addressed the following communication to the mayor in his annual report: " The police telegraph is out of order to such an extent that very little benefit has been derived from it. I think, however, that in the hands of some competent person it may be made very useful to the department."

During Mr. Sanders' administration an arbitrary code of signals based on the numerals was adopted as a means to facilitate the quick transmission of communications. Each lieutenant was furnished with a book containing these signs, known as the "manual." The manner of operating the machines can be imagined after reading the following rules taken from that book:

"Dial Communications.

"1. The use of the dial becomes necessary where no provisions have or can be made for telegraphing by means of bell signals.

"2. The switches must always be thrown back when not in use.

"3. Never touch the needle with your hand

"4. In words where the same letter occurs twice (as in will), drop one of them, (thus: wil.)

"5. When sending messages—after calling a station and securing an answer thereto, and having given signal and receiving the answer 1 repeated, pull forward both switches, let the needle go at least three times around the dial and stop at the uper white key, the instrument will then be ready for use.

"6. Always stop the needle at the upper white key at the end of your communication, and either white key at the end of every word, as most convenient.

"7. When receiving messages, after having received and answered signal 1, pull the right hand switch toward you, then press down the upper white key and hold it down until the clicking inside the dial-box ceases, then release the key quickly, the needle will be ready for use.

"8. Be particular when receiving messages to keep the left hand switch thrown back.

"9. To stop an instrument of the station, communicating with you, press upon the key on the right hand side of the box (do not rap your key).

"10. The mark T on the dial plate is to indicate outside circles or letters, and the mark ⊥, the inside of figures.

From the arbitrary signs the following are selected as samples :
    8.—Did you call the station ?
  23.—I understand you, all right.
    5.—I don't know.
  57.—Give me the correct time.
368.—Have you any lost children ?
564.—Is the Chief's clerk in his office ?
749.—Send a surgeon here forthwith.
874.—There is a large mob in the district.
2523.—Where is the fire ?
2539.—The bells are tolling for a funeral.
2634.—Manslaughter.
2626.—Lunacy.
2635.—Murder.
2679.—Burglary.

Regular calls were made during the day and night for the benefit of the reporters of the daily press, the call for news being "4-2-3." In case an item had developed itself the answer in the affirmative was given, and the reporter hastened to the station indicated. In some cases a trifling item was sent over the "dials" and copied at police headquarters. It is related of one lazy reporter who was connected with a German daily, that he had the hardihood to request that the celebrated Schilling tragedy be transmitted in detail to him by this method. Another anecdote is related regarding the general knowledge possessed at that time of electrical instruments. A stringent rule prevailed that no one should manipulate the instruments but the officer in charge of the station. One Sunday afternoon, when the lieutenant in charge of the Central Police Station was temporarily absent, an outside station began to ring furiously for him. The turnkey "Sandy" Batt, a herculean colored man, recognizing the signal became alarmed, and ran around the neighboring park looking for his superior officer. He returned without finding him, and the bell was still tapping like mad. Growing desperate he ran to the instrument, and throwing open the closet in which the battery cells were kept, stooped and shouted into the jars.

"De lieutenant aint hyar, his done gone out, sah !"

At that instant the bell ceased, and Sandy arose satisfied that his words had been heard. In after years he firmly avowed that he was the first who had thought of the telephone. This wonderful instrument came a few years afterward.

Mr. Edward C. Armstrong succeeded Evan Sanders during the seventies. He was of a progressive spirit, and took the utmost interest in the improvement of the efficiency of the department. Such rapid strides were made that it seemed entirely rejuvenated, and to this day he is called the father of the police telegraph system. When the telephone was invented and introduced, Mr. Armstrong was one of the first to recognize its true value and to introduce it for practical use at the time when it was considered a scientific toy. In 1878, one year after, Bell had obtained his patent, Mr. Armstrong had eight lines working in the police service. On the 30th day of August, 1879, a contract was signed with the Cincinnati Suburban Telegraph and Telephone Association, whereby it was agreed to remove the dial system and substitute telephones. Thirteen days later this was done, and the distinction achieved of being the first police department to take such action. As was well said at the time, the introduction of the speaking machines almost doubled the efficiency of the force. Mr. Armstrong watched carefully the developement of this branch of the service and supplied every necessity demanded. The operating force consisted of Chas. D. Armstrong and Wm. H. Devine, Jr., the latter after succeeding to the superintendency on Mr Armstrong's retirement. During the past years of the telephone service a careful record was kept of all calls received. In the first three months, 52,448 messages were transmitted, and in the following year no less than 363,080, or about one thousand a day. In 1870, 10,385 calls were sent over the dials. The progress of electrical improvement has kept pace with it. The services of Professor Gilliland, a colaborer of Edison, were engaged to design an operating switchboard, which remained in use until 1888. At present the service is the finest and best equipped in the United States. The introduction of the patrol system, for which Mr. Armstrong was also responsible, has added an immense amount of work to the operating department, and has necessitated the employment of an additional operator to attend to the work alone. In addition to being connected with all the station-houses and telephone exchanges, the Central office has six circuits on which one hundred and sixty-seven street boxes are connected. Each of the eight patrol houses are also connected. Calls for a patrol wagon are answered in a fraction of a minute. Should the summons be received from a box or from a private telephone, it is the work of but a second to tap a button that releases the horses in the patrol house, throws open the doors, and jingles an alarm bell. A hasty message through the telephone, and the squad is on its way to the place indicated. During the day and night incessant calls are received from patrolmen on duty who are required to report every hour. As they do they are checked off by the operator on a huge ruled sheet, the precise moment of the call being given. This sheet undergoes the inspection of the superintendent of police the next morning, and the delinquent is detected and reprimanded. The amount of business transacted can be imagined from the following table submitted by superintendent, Thomas J. Sullivan, in 1888.

The number of messages received during the past year for patrol wagon calls was	10,605
General messages	372,445
Officers on beats	130,305
Total messages handled during the year	513,355

During the year of 1888 the apparatus in the operating room was almost entirely changed by Superintendent Sullivan, so that at present the service is almost perfect, the loss of time being reduced to the minimum. The operating force is divided into two reliefs, doing twelve hours duty each. The first consists of Harry N. Adams and Jos. Sullivan, and the second of Harry White and Frank Nugent. These young men are veteran operators, and to their efforts is greatly due the good work of the department. Superintendent Sullivan, like his predecessor, Wm. H. Devine, Jr., began as an operator and was speedily promoted. One fact that has been generally overlooked is that by means of the present telegraphic system the entire police force can be mobilized at any point in the city within an hour. Three-quarters of the force can be notified within twenty minutes. This in itself is inestimable in the eyes of a chief of police who has gone through a strike or a riot. To the credit of the telephone department it may be said that it rendered the most valuable service during the court-house riot of 1883. By means of a solitary wire the defenders of that building, and of the jail, were kept in constant communication with police headquarters, and Colonel Reilly during the hottest of the fight directed his reserves and the patrol squads over this slender thread of iron, the only mode of communication outside the lines of the beleaguering rioters. The telephone service is now the strongest arm of the police department.

CHAPTER XIV.

SECOND AND THIRD DISTRICTS.—TERRITORY WHICH COMPRISES RAT AND SAUSAGE ROWS AND "OVER THE RHINE," THE TOUGHEST AND JOLLIEST PORTIONS OF THE CITY.—THE NOTORIOUS DEER CREEK GANG.—LIEUTENANT JOE THORNTON'S CLEVER CAPTURE OF A FORGER, AND THE MANNER IN WHICH HE RAN DOWN A "SWITCH."—HOW LIEUTENANT LANGDON TREED A BLACKMAILER.—WHAT A BUNDLE OF RAGS IN A STATION-HOUSE CONTAINED.—ANIMATED APPEARANCE OF VINE STREET SUNDAY NIGHTS.—THE HOUSE OF DETENTION.—SKETCHES OF LIEUTENANTS AND SERGEANTS.

THE history of the Second Police District, of which the Hammond street station-house is the headquarters, would be anything but the "annals of a quiet neighborhood." Since there has existed such a station as Hammond street, its police have patrolled the most criminal sections of the city. The station-house slate has had written upon it the names of some of the worst desperadoes that ever worked deeds of Stygian darkness within the limits of Cincinnati. The pages of its history are dark with the record of riot, murder, and bloodshed. In the dark and forbidding streets patrolled by its police, crimes without number have been committed. But a few years ago highway robbers roamed the fastnesses of Deer Creek and Sixth Street Hill as freely and fearlessly as Italian banditti tread the trackless wastes of the Appenines. Night after night the shouts of drunken desperadoes frightened the citizens wending their late way homeward. In the low-ceiled doggeries murders and robberies were plotted. The night air often echoed the sharp crack of pistol shots and the curses and moans of wounded men, while every street-light in certain sections has been reflected from the steel of glistening knives. The police patrolled the beats four together, and knew not what moment one of them would be stretched dead upon the ground. They often carried their revolvers in hand, ready at an instants' warning to answer with pistol shots a shower of boulders.

The "toughest" of all sections was the Deer Creek beat. Here, from 1880 until 1885, the Deer Creek gang ruled supreme. Always traveling in crowds of from ten to forty, they committed robberies night after night, "holding up" any one who chanced to pass that way. The shrill whistle of alarm and the quick roll of the patrol wagon rarely disturbed them, and seldom could one of their number be captured.

But the glory of Deer Creek has departed. Highway robbers no longer lurk in every shadow, and murder and violence are the exception, not the rule. The leaders of this gang are scattered indeed, and the remnants no longer have the courage of ancient times. Flanagan, Walker, Skelly, Doherty, and Kennedy are serving time at Columbus. "Cock" and Dan Nuttle and Jack Smith have died violent deaths, and McCormick ended his life in the penitentiary. The downfall of this gang came in 1885, and was due to the brave patrolmen who ran those beats.

Down in "the bottoms" was an almost equally desperate region. Here lived the roustabouts, the degraded negroes and whites, sewer rats who never saw the light of day and who hid away in foul dens and filthy lodging houses. Here was the harbor of refuge for the lowest kinds of thieves, assassins and debased women. Here are situated the great, low lodging houses, the Spencer House, Hogshead John's, the saloon of "Ruck" McKernan the counterfeiter. Jealousy and gambling were the passions which produced murderers and cutting affrays without number. Rat and Sausage Rows were and are yet to a certain extent names associated with all that is bloody and criminal. But here, too, the splendid discipline of the police has told, and this quarter of the town is becoming as safe as such a low quarter ever can be.

The Second Police District begins at Vine and the river front, extends east along the river to Parsons, to Third, to Hill, to Eden park, along the northwest side of Eden Park to Gilbert avenue, then north to Effluent Pipe, west to Hunt, along Hunt to

LIEUT. MARK LANGDON.
LIEUT. JOSEPH THORNTON.   LIEUT. EUGENE DIEHL.
Second District.

Sycamore, to the Canal, to Walnut, to Third, to Vine, to the place of beginning. It is the largest down town district, and was laid off as a district in 1872.

The Hammond street station-house was first established on the east side of Hammond street where the kitchen of the St. James Hotel now stands. Over it was a carpenter shop belonging to a Mr. Brooks, of whom the building was leased. It was established in 1853. Its officers then patrolled the territory included in the lines extending from Main to Hunt, to the river, to Washington street, Fulton, then the corporation line, to Main again. In the fall of 1870, the station-house was moved across the street to its present site, which was then leased property. Early in 1872 the property was bought, and it was decided to erect a building more convenient for use as a station-house. Temporary quarters were fitted up in the Fidelity block on Sycamore below Pearl. In 1874 the present station-house was completed. It is one of the handsomest in the city. The cell room is clean and has ample accommodations for all the prisoners that could possibly be brought there. The station-house itself is well fitted up—a large, light, high-ceiled room, with racks for the clubs and closets for changes of uniform. At the west side of the room a raised platform is railed in, and has on it a desk for the lieutenant and sergeant, and a case for the records of the station-house.

The Second District police force is composed of three lieutenants, Joseph Thornton, Mark Langdon, and Eugene Diehl; three sergeants, Luke Drout, Samuel T. Corbin, and Edward B. Newman; two station-house keepers, and forty-three patrolmen. Of the lieutenants Joseph Thornton is the oldest in point of service, not only at Hammond street but in the entire city, having been on the force continuously for twelve years. He was born on the 26th of March, 1846, in the house on Deer creek, near the base of Walnut Hills, in which Hoover, Washburn, and Davis murdered a man named Beaver for his money. It was one of the first murders committed in the city, and the murderers were hung in Deer Creek.

Young Thornton got the rudiments of an education at the Walnut Hills school, and then learned the trade of stonecutter

He worked at this until 1876. He was working on the Government Building when the idea struck him of going on the police force. On the 24th of August he was appointed patrolmen, and after running the Mt. Adams beat for six months he was made a sergeant. This was about the time of the memorable railroad riots.

The vicious elements of the city were bringing down censure on the heads of the strikers by committing acts of violence in their name. The car shops of the C., H. & D. R.R was at Sixth and Hoadley, and the lumber in an adjacent yard had been set on fire. The Hammond street police were ordered to the scene to protect the engines engaged in putting out the fire. Sergeant Thornton was placed in command, and the police hurried to the scene. A mob of several thousand was gathered about the place, and some of the leaders were urging the cutting of the hose. Thornton drew up his men and charged, driving the mob back; it returned to the charge, those in front pressed on by those behind. "Buck" Maloney, a moving spirit in the trouble, rushed forward, knife in hand, to cut the hose near the plug. Sergeant Thornton seized him, and, with the assistance of his men, brought Buck within the lines, after a hand-to-hand battle. This discouraged the mob, and the fire was soon put out. The sergeant kept his men on the scene for four nights afterward.

On the sixth of April, 1878, Sergeant Thornton was instrumental in the arrest of the sharpest forger that ever came to this city. It was just about three o'clock on that day, and the bank was preparing to close when a short heavy set German with a round fat face, entered the door. He was dressed like a well-to-do farmer, and his manners tended to confirm the supposition aroused by his dress. He walked up to the teller's window and presented a check for $1490 in favor of Fred Marker or bearer and signed by a well known business firm. The teller examined the check and was about to pay it. But something in the man's manner made him hesitate.

"Wait a moment" said he, taking the check into the back room where President Colville was sitting. Mr. Colville examined the signature, and compared it with other signatures of the firm in possession of the bank. He became convinced that the man had presented a very cleverly forged check. A messenger was at once sent over to the Hammond street station. He informed Sergeant Thornton of the president's suspicions. Thornton at once went over and going in the back way, placed the German under arrest. He felt quite sure, however, that this man was only the assistant of some sharper thief. Two officers were sent up the street in front of the bank to see if any suspicious persons were hanging around. Sure enough, leaning against a telegraph pole on the opposite side of the street stood a dark complexioned man with a mustache, and dressed in a blue business suit. This seeming business man was watching the door of the bank anxiously. The officers at once arrested him and took him to the station-house. He gave his name as John Doe. On his person were found diamond studs, breast pin and earrings, $2,500 in money, and $2,300 in government bonds. The two men were stopping at the Grand Hotel, and a search of their room brought to light, acids and other chemicals used in altering and raising checks. Doe's record was looked up and he was identified as a great English forger who had done many clever jobs in this country. He was very shrewd and pleaded his own case in court. But each of the men received a sentence of fifteen years in the penitentiary. Marker died there in April, 1882. About two years ago Doe was found to be dying of consumption and was released. The police have since lost all trace of him.

Another excellent piece of work which Sergeant Thornton did, was the arrest of a thief named James Shorton during the winter of 1878. Shorton was a young man of good family but of very dissipated habits. He was known to the police as a thief, but was regarded as a "snitch" or thief who tells on thieves. This was in reality a sharp dodge which he adopted to cover up his own tracks. On the afternoon of February 20, he told Chief of Detectives Waffenstein and two of his assistants named Duffy and Meade, that a gang of thieves were going to "weed" a few houses on Mt. Auburn. Late at night they went up there and stationed themselves at Mason and Auburn streets. Shorton told them to wait while he joined the thieves and told them that every thing was all right. He dissappeared in the darkness and returned no more. After waiting nearly two hours the disgusted detectives returned to the city.

Shorton returned to the city as soon as he left the detectives, and "jimmied" the front door of Fred Klimper's tailor shop at Fourth and Hammond, making four trips to the shop and loading himself down each time with fine goods. The police were informed of the robbery, and Sergeant Thornton set to work. He learned from the young daughter of Cohen, who then kept a second-hand clothing store at Fourth and Sycamore on the site of the Ortiz building, that she had seen a man carrying goods into Shorton's cellar that night. Thornton and officer Tighe at once searched the cellar, and after some time found a hole in the ceiling. Thrust in between the laths and the floor of the room above were all the goods from Klimper's store, besides a lot of other stuff stolen from various stores about town amounting in all to nearly $2,000 worth of goods. They then set out to find the young thief. He was seen standing at Pearl and Butler streets. The police approached him from both sides, and while Thornton made a feint at attacking him, Tighe rushed in and pinioned his arms. He was armed to the teeth, having a small rifle, a heavy revolver and a dirk. He just finished a good long term in the penitentiary a short time ago.

Sergeant Thornton also took a prominent part in the court house riots. He was put in charge of a squad of men to keep the crowd back from the Sycamore entrance. In the squad were officers Cass Fisher, now a lieutenant, Phil Nunn, John Connelly, Von Seggern, Luke Drout and several others. They were driven from their position and fought their way through the crowd to the Main street entrance to the tunnel between the jail and the court house. They entered here and were in the thickest of that frightful battle which was perhaps the most terrible event of the riot. The militia followed them in. There were two other entrances—one on Sycamore and one on South Court—along both of which the mob was coming. The Hammond street officers were thus between the militia on one side and the mob on the other. As soon as the militia caught sight of the mob, they began firing. The officers called to them to stop, but it was of no avail. Several of them were shot down and one was killed. Of the mob many were killed, and many more wounded before they finally fled.

Sergeant Thornton was appointed a lieutenant on the 28th of April, 1885, and stationed at Hammond street. He has never left that station-house, having served there the entire time he has been on the force. He has taken part in three riots, the one not mentioned being the attack of the mob on the Hammond street station, during the campaign of 1876. Thornton was in charge of the police guarding the line of march of a democratic procession. A colored man was stabbed on the sidewalk and shot one of the paraders at Sixth and Vine. The police took him to the Hammond street station, and beat back the infuriated mob which was trying to get at and lynch him. Mayor Johnston prevented a serious riot by inducing the ringleader, Jake Gardner, a coal dealer, to go away. Lieutenant Thornton has been a faithful officer.

Lieutenant Eugene Diehl was born on a farm in Newcastle county, Delaware, December 21, 1837. His parents were quite well off, and after he had finished the High School he was sent to a collegiate school at Charlottesville, New York. He only staid there a few months, and returned to his father's house to follow farming. He married, and when thirty-five years old, went to Philadelphia to keep a boarding-house during the Centennial Exposition. He remained in Philadelphia six months, and then came to Cincinnati to open a produce store. This he afterwards changed to a dry goods store. Not meeting with success in business, he went on the police force as patrolman at Hammond street. He remained there nearly five years, running the beat around Sixth and Walnut for three years of that time. He was raised from a patrolman directly to a lieutenant, in August, 1887, and transferred first to Oliver street for two months, then to Walnut Hills for nearly a year, and finally, last February, stationed at Hammond street, where he now is. Lieutenant Diehl is a thorough gentleman, an excellent officer, and is very faithful in the discharge of his duties. He has been eight years on the force continuously.

Lieutenant Mark Langdon first saw the light of day in a log house one mile south of Sharpsburg, now called Norwood, this county, on the 1st of July, 1848. He was hardly a year old when his father and mother died during the cholera plague of 1849. His grandfather brought him up, sending him first to the common school, and then to the preparatory school at Oxford. With eleven other boys of the school he ran away to enlist in the army at the age of sixteen. He was the only one of the boys who did enlist, and he served until the end of the war. A few years after the close of the war his grandfather died and left him considerable property. This he lost in a few years, and, being left with no money and a family, he went on the police force, in 1876, at the Walnut Hills station. In 1880 he was made a sergeant, and in 1881 was discharged for political reasons. At the end of a week, with the change of city administration, he was reinstated and assigned to the Hammond street station, being transferred soon afterward to Walnut Hills, and again made a sergeant. On May 5, 1881, he was made a lieutenant in charge of the Walnut Hills station. He resigned under Mayor Stephens and became a successful detective in Wappenstein's Agency. He again went on the force from May 5, 1886, and was made a lieutenant the same day. He alternated between the Bremen and Hammond street station-houses until June 1, 1888, since which time he has been stationed at the latter place.

Lieutenant Langdon has good detective ability, and is able to quickly grasp a situation when it is properly presented to him. During February, 1882, he was riding across the Eden Park bridge on a car, when he saw a man running up the road from the park entrance. He was bareheaded and from time to time looked over his shoulder. Lieutenant Langdon at once suspected that something was wrong and started after him. After a chase of a quarter of a mile he stopped him and placed him under arrest. It turned out to be Charles Wilson, a notorious burglar who had just done a small job on Gilbert avenue.

While in the employ of the Wappenstein agency, Lieutenant Langdon was detailed on a strange case of blackmail at Greensburg, Indiana. A wealthy quarryman of that place named Poole, was made the victim of an infamous blackmailer. Some unknown wretch circulated dodgers all over the town one night, which defamed the character of a member of Poole's family in a shameful way. Mr. Poole was naturally very indignant, and sent down to Wappenstein for a detective. Langdon was sent up and at once went to work. The only clue he had was the hand-bill, and the point of course was to first find out where the bill was printed. By knocking about the town and getting acquainted with the tougher element of Greensburg society, Langdon learned that a certain doctor of the town had confided to some friends over a "night cap" that he hated Poole. Langdon kept this fact in mind, and looked around for the printers of the bill. He considered that such work would very probably be done in a city, and as Indianapolis was the nearest and most convenient place of large size, he went there. After diligent search among the small printing establishments he found one which was suspected of doing that sort of work. He questioned the proprietor but could learn nothing. The bill was like a thousand others which might be printed, and there was no chance of fastening the printing of it through similarity of type. Then came one of those strokes of fortune which seemed rather parts of romances than of real life. Langdon was standing in the street considering what to do next. A bootblack came along and he stopped him. While the boy was polishing his shoes, Langdon talked to him and found that he was very clever, so he thought perhaps he might be able to help him.

"Do you know of any place around here where I can get some of this kind of printing done?" And Langdon showed him the hand-bill.

"Oh, yes," said the boy "right over there," pointing to the establishment which Langdon had just left.

"How do you know?"

"It's an old place. I put a man on to it about two weeks ago."

That corresponded to the time the dodger concerning Poole might have been printed.

"Would you know the man again if you saw him?"

"Mebby so."

"Is this his picture," said Langdon, displaying the photograph of the doctor which he had secured in Greensburg.

"That's him," said the boy.

This strange and almost incredible coincidence established the doctor's guilt beyond doubt. He had left Greensburg on a visit to the West, where he announced his intention of locating. Langdon started in pursuit, and after a long chase finally caught his man in Dayton, Ohio. The doctor confessed that the cause of his malicious attack was the fact that Mrs. Poole had refused his attention. The good people of Greensburg nearly lynched him, but he was rescued and landed in jail, and then in the penitentiary.

One winter night in 1878, a curious thing came under the observation of Langdon, who was then a sergeant in charge of Hammond street station. Officer Scarlett came in shortly after midnight, leading a curious figure. The night was bitter cold. The wind swept over the icy streets, and cut deep into the faces of belated pedestrians. Officer Scarlett saw a man standing in the shadow of a house, and moaning piteously. He walked up to him, and brought him out into the stronger light of the street lamp. The man was a forlorn spectacle. His ragged and dirty clothes afforded him no protection from the icy wind that was asweep. His head was hatless, and his thin dirty grey locks were unkempt. Under each arm he carried a dead white goose, while in his hand he clutched a bundle of rags tightly. From his talk it was evident that he was not in his right mind. The stalwart officer brought him to the station-house for the night. His name was put on the slate, and he was sent back into the cell-room. Officer Scarlett returned to his beat, and Sergeant Langdon was left alone before the blazing fire in the stove, the door of which was open. All at once he became conscious of a disgusting odor which pervaded the room. Looking about for the cause, he saw the bundle of rags still lying on the station-house desk where the old man had left it. He walked over, looked at it, and thinking it was nothing but a dirty handkerchief tied around a few filthy articles of clothing, he lifted it gingerly to throw it in the fire. Then he thought perhaps it

SERGT. E. B. NEWMAN. SERGT. SAMUEL T. CORBIN. SERGT. LUKE DROUT.
Second District.

would be well to look in it. He untied the knots and unrolled the rags, when before his astonished eyes were revealed a roll of bank notes, and some slips of that peculiar paper on which bonds are printed. In the foul and apparently worthless bundle lay $365 in greenbacks, and $500 in bonds. The lieutenant might have stolen it and none would have been the wiser. But he saved it until morning, when the old man's brother called and took him away. The geese had been stolen from a Catholic priest on Mt. Adams.

Lieutenant Langdon was in charge of one of the Gatling guns at the court-house riots, and while the gun was never fired, he distinguished himself in other ways. He is quite a fine pistol shot, and has never been known to flinch in the presence of danger.

Sergeant Luke Drout was born May 2, 1849, at the corner of Front and Parsons streets in this city. He went to school at St. Xavier's, and then learned the trade of tinner, which he followed until September 1, 1879, when he became a patrolman at the Walnut Hills station. On the 19th of July he was made a sergeant, and stationed at Hammond street, then transferred to Walnut Hills and finally changed back to Hammond. He has been on the force over nine years and has never lost a day. He has been through many perilous situations, having been shot at several times, but has always conducted himself bravely. There is no more trustworthy or efficient officer on the force.

Sergeant Samuel Corbin was born on the 23d of October, 1849, on a farm one mile from California, Kentucky. He left home in 1873, and became a street car driver on the Pendleton line, this city. He was then given a position as collector on the Mt. Adams elevator, where he remained until 1883. On the 12th of June, in that year, he went on the police force as patrolman at Hammond street, where he has always remained with the exception of three months at Central Station during last year. On the 10th of December he was made a sergeant. Corbin has for the most part patrolled the beat in "the Bottoms," where the police come in contact with the toughest and lowest element of humanity. Yet his heart has always remained warm and humane, as many an unfortunate can testify. "The Bottoms" is a place where sad scenes are an every day occurrence. In October, 1884, Officer Corbin came across a particularly distressing case, which pictures one of those tragedies in humble domestic life. The officer was walking along the river front when a fairly well dressed man walked up to him and said.

"Are you running this beat?"

"Yes, sir."

"I wish to tell you my story and to ask your assistance. My name is Robert Johnson. I am a cooper by trade at Lexington, Kentucky, and until two months ago had a happy home, a wife and two dear little children. Then my wife suddenly disappeared. I enquired for her, and finally learned that she had eloped with the colored porter of a Pullman car named Jackson. How she met him or what induced her to desert me and her children, I do not know. They came to this city and are here together. Will you help me find them?"

Corbin knew of a fine looking negro who was with a white woman in the lodging house over Pickett's saloon, at 91 East Front street. He went with the husband to this place and inquired for the woman. The negro was standing behind the bar, and sent up after her. Soon a slender young woman with a sweet face in which evil was not written, came into the bar-room. She was well dressed.

"Lizzie!" cried the young husband.

"Well, Robert" she said looking at him unmoved.

"Is this your husband?" asked the officer.

"He was once, but I'll never live with him again."

Johnson fell on his knees, and the tears fell like rain from his face.

"Not for my sake, Lizzie. But for the little ones who cry themselves to sleep each night. I don't ask you to live with me. I'll support you if you'll only care for the children."

"I'll never live with you again," said she in a dull monotonous voice, turning her head away.

"Did I not give you everything you wanted?" pleaded Johnson.

"Yes."

"Did I ever wrong you in any way?"

"No."

"Then why not return to your children?" But she never answered him, and soon hurried away to return up stairs again, leaving him sobbing on his knees. When he saw she was gone, he turned with a wild cry of rage on the negro. But the officers held him back and took him outside. He walked along sadly, stooped and broken. Next day he returned to his desolate home. The woman lived on at the lodging house, growing paler and thinner each day, until finally in the fall of the next year she died of consumption. She never asked for her husband and children but died as she had lived, the victim of her strange infatuation.

Sergeant Corbin distinguished himself in the court-house riots, being one of the officers who captured the cannon from the mob. He is quiet and unostentatious in manner, but of a brave and determined disposition.

Sergeant Edward B. Newman is a Cincinnatian born and bred. He came into this world on the anniversary of Washington's birthday, 1862, in Gano street. After receiving a common school education, he went into the coal business with his brother. Then he became a carpenter's apprentice and finally a journeyman carpenter. June 7, 1886, he went on the police force, and was assigned to Patrol 6 on Walnut Hills. After running on the various patrols for about a year and a half, he received his appointment as sergeant on February 1, 1888, and was stationed at Hammond street. It was he who in February, 1884, during the floods went down with his brother to the fallen tenement at Pearl and Ludlow, and took out in a skiff ten of the drowned bodies of the inmates. He has three brothers in the fire department.

The Third District comprises that part of the city known as "Over the Rhine," so called because of the fact that it is separated from the rest of the city by the canal, and is almost exclusively inhabited by German-Americans. Its boundary line extends from the corner of McMillen street and the canal, along the canal to Sycamore street, to Hunt street, to Montgomery road, to Liberty, to Price, to Boal, to Sycamore, to Dorsey, to Baltimore street, to Mulberry, to Vine, to Clifton avenue, to Bellevue, to Ravine, to Brown street, and thence to the place of beginning. Several theaters and the most of the concert-halls of the city are located in this district. Vine street is its main thoroughfare, and on Sunday nights is always crowded with merry makers as well as by those bent on mischief. It is probable that Venice during her carnival rarely presents a more animated appearance than do the streets in the " Over the Rhine " district on the evening of the first day in the week. Its main thoroughfare has more places where liquor is sold than any other street of the city. It is necessary for the reasons already named that vigilant officers should be assigned to this district. The demand for the exercise of coolness and good judgment is well nigh constant. Forty such officers now report at the Third District Station-house, located on Bremen street between Fifteenth and Liberty streets. This police building was originally erected in 1870, but has since been entirely remodeled and now constitutes one of the best structures belonging to the department. It is in this building that the house of detention is located. Formerly there was room in its basement for lodgers, and as many as one hundred and fifty poor wretches have often found shelter there. When the recent alterations were made, however, and a house of detention was placed under the roof of the Bremen street station-house, the free lodging house had to go, and the "Poor Joes" who now wander in there are compelled to "move on."

The necessity for seperating the sexes in State penal institutions, and for classifying convicted criminals has long been recognized in this country. There are now few penitentiaries, the walls of which enclose both male and female prisoners; there is no well conducted prison where the worst of the criminal classes are suffered to mingle indiscriminately with those whose offending has been but slight. It was reserved for the present Board of Police Commissioners to bring about a reform in Cincinnati for even the temporary detention of offenders, whether petty or gross. The Woman's Branch of the Associated Charities, was the first to urge upon the commissioners the necessity for this reform, and out of that

LIEUT. HENRY HAMBROCK.
LIEUT. PETER BERG.   LIEUT. GODFREY PISTNER.
Third District.

urging grew the plan for a house of detention now located at the Bremen street station-house. The Committee from the Board of Commissioners entrusted with the care of plans and location, consisted of Messrs Boyle and Topp, and by September 15, 1887, they concluded their work, and the history in Cincinnati of crowding male and female prisoners into adjoining cells, or of thrusting hardened wretches in with young boys, comparatively innocent, was ended. The house of detention is in charge of two matrons. In their care are placed all female prisoners and all boys under sixteen years of age, who are taken into custody, unless they are known to have been previously convicted of a felony. When an officer arrests a person whose destination is the house of detention, it is his duty to take the prisoner to the station in his district, and after reporting the arrest to the person in charge of the station to send for the detention 'bus. It is also his duty to remain in the station-house in charge of his prisoner until the 'bus arrives, when he surrenders his charge and is relieved from further responsibility. In no case, save one that is violent, is the person thus arrested to be locked up in a station-house cell.

The room in the house of detention occupied by a female prisoner depends altogether upon her offense, while the boys, unless disorderly, are all placed in the same room.

One of the oldest lieutenants on the force is Godfrey Pistner. He was born on the eighth of November, 1836, in a little village near the town of Aschaffenburg in the Kingdom of Bavaria. When about one year old Godfrey's parents immigrated to the United States, and the little fellow was of course taken along. The voyage was undertaken in a sailing vessel which was *en route* to Baltimore for more than eight weeks; from Baltimore to Cincinnati they came over the mountains in a wagon. Godfrey received his education in the public schools of Cincinnati, and when fourteen years old went to work in a hair factory. At sixteen, young Pistner traveled for A. D. Bullock & Co., and bought supplies in the different towns which he visited for that firm. When the war broke out he enlisted in the three months service. After the war, with John Kindle as partner, he went into business for himself, but in 1878, during a commercial panic he was unfortunate enough to lose the greater part of his fortune, so that in August of that year he was glad to accept a position on the police force which was then under the control of a commission. For ten years Lieutenant Pistner has been continuously on the force, and has not missed a single day from sickness, negligence, or any other cause. When he first became a patrolman he was detailed for duty in the Oliver street district, and proved to be such an able man that after a service of only nine months he was promoted to the office of sergeant. He successively served in the Sedamsville, the Hammond street and the Walnut Hills district, and then went back to the Oliver street district. He was appointed to a lieutenantship under Mayor Stephens on the eighth day of November, 1883. When the new police law was passed he was reappointed by Mayor Smith as a lieutenant, and in the summer of 1887, was transferred to the Bremen street district. During his career as an officer he has made important arrests, and has assisted in breaking up several notorious gangs of roughs who infested the western portion of the city. The worst of these was what was known as the Freeman avenue gang, occupying for headquarters an abandoned church property from which the members were wont to sally on nightly marauding expedition. During the riots of 1884, Lieutenant Pistner with a command of ten men succeeded in capturing some field pieces on which the mob had laid hands at the armory, and by this *coup de main* is believed to have saved the city a good deal of trouble. He was married in 1860, in Louisville, Kentucky, and is the father of four interesting children.

The subject of this sketch, at a tender age, left home to share the dangers to which his father as a soldier of the Union was exposed.

Peter Berg was born July 21, 1848, at Biebern, a little place in the Rhein Province in the Kingdom of Prussia. His parents emigrated to this country in October, 1853, and the lad of course came with them. They settled at once in Cincinnati, where Peter received his education in the public schools. When the war broke out the elder Berg enlisted in the Twenty-eighth Ohio, and when but thirteen years and six months old, his son followed him and joined the regiment in camp as a drummer. When, however, Colonel Moore, the commander of the regiment, saw the little drummer, he thought him too young to stand camp life and ordered him sent home. Peter came back to Cincinnati and worked at Gibsons & Co's. lithographing works at the corner of Walnut and Third streets until January 2, 1862, when he enlisted in the Sixteenth U. S. Regular Infantry Service, Co. A, Second Battalion, as a drummer. While not taking active part in the fighting, he had to go through all the hardships of the campaign, which he endured for three years, when he was honorably discharged. Shortly after Berg had joined his regiment his company was detailed for duty on the Tennessee and Cumberland rivers, and there it remained till the fall of the same year, when it again joined the regiment at Chattanooga, Tennessee, and took part in Sherman's campaign of 1864. Lieutenant Berg's discharge papers show that he was engaged with his regiment in the following battles: Buzzards Roost, Resaca, New Hope Church, Kenesaw Mountain, Marietta, Georgia, Peach Tree Creek, battles before Atlanta and Jonesboro. When he was about to receive his discharge, Peter learned that his father had been wounded at Piedmont, West Virginia, captured and taken to Andersonville prison. Straightway young Berg made his way to the neighborhood of Andersonville, when to his delight he learned that his sire had succeeded in making good his escape. Peter then returned to Cincinnati to be welcomed by both his parents. He worked for some time in a wholesale grocery, and then learned the carpenter trade at the works of the Cincinnati Cooperage Co. He followed this for a number of years or until in May, 1880, when he was appointed by Mayor Charles Jacobs, Jr., on the police force, and soon after was promoted to the position of sergeant. Another year and Mayor Means was inaugurated, when the Republicans had to make room for Democrats, and Berg was among the former. A few months after he left the police service he was appointed a despatch clerk under Postmaster Lodge. In this position he continued under Postmaster Witfield until a new National administration crowded him out, when Mayor Smith appointed him a member of the non-partisan police force. August 12, 1886, he was made sergeant, and on May 26, 1887, he was tendered a lieutenantship. Berg has been on duty in the Sedamsville, the Cumminsville, the Bremen street and the Central districts. He is now one of the lieutenants of the Bremen street station. While in the Sedamsville dsitrict he became conspicuous in the Major Goodspeed case, which created a profound sensation in Cincinnati. It was charged that Goodspeed tried to kill his wife in order to get possession of her fortune. Lieutenant Berg appeared as one of the State witnesses when the case was tried; Goodspeed was subsequently declared insane and committed to the asylum at Athens, Ohio.

Lieutenant Henry Hambrock is a native of Cincinnati, having been born in Bremen street on November 15, 1853. The boy was sent to school for a few years in the Tenth district, and when only thirteen years old was apprenticed to a cigarmaker, A. Meyems, on Vine street opposite the *Enquirer* office. Here the boy worked for five years as clerk and general assistant. He managed to pick up considerable knowledge of the trade, and he left Meyems to go to work for himself on Seventh street near Main. The panic of 1873 had a disastrous effect on his little shop, and he was compelled to give it up. He became a shipping clerk at Erkenbrecher's starch works on Canal near Race. One year later he became a member of Engine Company No. 5 of the fire department. To this company and the Hook No. 3 he belonged three and a half years. He next worked a year as a porter at Shillitos. Then three and one-half years as a laborer in the employ of the county commissioners. He was then appointed a government storekeeper, but lost the place two years later because of alleged "partisanship." Hambrock became a patrolman on May 4, 1886, but was immediately assigned to Cumminsville as sergeant. On July 31, 1886, he was made lieutenant and placed at Bremen street station, whence eleven months later he was transferred to Coryville. In January, 1888, the lieutenant accidentally broke an ankle running to a fire, and on recovery was assigned to the Third district.

While a fireman, Hambrock was noted for his daring exploits.

When Brock's Printing Works on Fourth near Elm were burning, and the huge building collapsed, Hambrock was one of the thirteen firemen who went down in the ruins. The squad were in the third story of the building when it fell, and the escape of any of them from death was miraculous. As it was, however, there were three killed, two mortally injured, and the others bear marks of the accident. Hambrock, who was a pipeman, was internally injured, and had his left arm crushed. Enoch Megrue, chief of the fire department, was buried in the *debris* of the fallen building for several hours, but was finally released comparatively uninjured. When Pelstrang's box factory on Canal near Walnut was consumed by the flames, Hambrock fell from the third story to a shed below, but was only slightly hurt. It was at this fire that the canal bridge, unable to support the weight of the people congregated on it watching the fire, broke in two, letting its burden of humanity into the water below. A number of persons were severely injured.

The lieutenant has an excellent police record. It was he who arrested Kathman, the incestuous wretch who ruined his own eleven year old daughter. Kathman was a shoemaker, and lived on Twelfth street near John. He was tried before Judge Buchwalter, and the jury pronounced him insane. Kathman was then sent to Longview, where he remained just six months, when he was set at liberty. Lena Knecht, the notorious "piano woman," was arrested by Hambrock in 1887, together with her paramour, Minnich. Both received heavy sentences.

Edward Leonard is a Cincinnatian born and bred. August 30, 1888, was his thirtieth birthday. His education was obtained in the public schools of the city, and two years were spent in Hughes High School. When seventeen years of age he became an apprenticed carriage trimmer in Gosling's factory, and for nearly twelve years remained with that firm. On May 6, 1886, he was appointed a patrolman by Mayor Smith, and reported at Central Station until July of that year, when he was made a sergeant, and transferred to the Tenth district. Here he remained for six months, when he was changed to the Coryville stationhouse. After more than a year spent in this district he was transferred to the Third district, and has remained there ever since.

Emil Linhardt was born in Poeston, Ontario, February 23, 1858. His father and mother were natives of Bavaria, Germany. When Emil was still a baby his parents moved to Cincinnati and permanently settled, and in Cincinnati the future officer was educated. When only eleven years old young Linhardt began to earn a livelihood as a "paint boy" in a safe manufactury. Subsequently he secured a place with Pape Bros. and Kugemann, picture frame manufacturers, and with them rose to the position of foreman. With this firm Linhardt remained twelve years, then went to the Southern Railroad repair shop, and then back to manufacturing picture frames. His second engagement was with Peter Reuhl & Co., on Main street, where he soon became foreman in the gilding department, and here, after two years experience, the mayor of the city found him and at once appointed him a patrolman. This was on May 25, 1886. He was on duty successively in the Seventh and First districts, and in the patrol-wagon service, when on February 1, 1888, he was promoted to a sergeantcy. Sergeant Linhardt is kind and obliging, uniformly polite, and right in the line of further promotion.

Sergeant Lewis Bedinger is known on the Cincinnati police force as the "Indian Fighter." He is a native of Germany, born on the 15th of November, 1845. When a lad of eight years he came with his parents to America, and a year later, by the death of his father at Clinton Furnace, Kentucky, he was thrown upon his own resources. After several shifts he reached Cincinnati, and in 1861, when in his sixteenth year, he enlisted as a soldier. As a member of the first battalion of the Eighteenth Infantry, he fought under old "Pap" Thomas at Chickamauga, and was a participant in the battles of Shiloh, Pea Ridge, Corinth, Perryville, Stone River, and in a skirmish at Hoovers Gap, was slightly wounded. His experience at the bloody battle of Chickamauga, September 19, 1863, was one that falls to the lot of few soldiers. He was standing behind a small tree, his left side toward the enemy, in the act of loading, when a minie-ball struck him in the shoulder and passed partly through his body. He started

SERGT. E. LEONARD.   SERGT. L. BEDINGER.   SERGT. E. LINHARDT.
Third District.

to retreat when a peremptory order to halt was heard. Although weak from the loss of blood, and tired from the day's exertions he continued to flee, when three bullets struck him, one cutting his haversack, one penetrating his canteen, the third carrying away the heel of one of his shoes. Notwithstanding the disadvantages under which he was laboring, he succeeded in eluding his pursuers, and finally reached Chattanooga, where his wound was dressed. He was out of the hospital and back in his company in time to take part in the battle on Mission Ridge.

The fourth of July, 1864, was a hot day, and the tired young soldier, having erected a small breastwork of rocks and timbers, fell asleep amid the heavy cannonading of the enemy. One of his comrades lay down with him, his head resting between Bedinger's feet. At 7 o'clock in the evening the young man was aroused by one of his friends violently shaking him.

"Are you hurt, Lewis?" was the first question put to him.

The young man was covered with blood from head to foot, and his shoes spattered with brain-matter. At his feet lay his companion, dead. A shell had struck the ground fifteen feet ahead of him, had come out about four feet distant, and had exploded, killing seven men and wounding thirteen; Lewis himself had miraculously escaped without as much as a scratch. Having been honorably discharged, Bedinger returned home, but active service on the battle field, full of danger and excitement, had too many charms for him, and on the 10th of April, 1865, he re-enlisted for one year in the Thirteenth Ohio Cavalry, Company F. His time expired, but Lewis still wished to remain a soldier. He joined the First United States Cavalry, and was sent to Los Angeles, thence to Sacramento, California. There the men mounted and started for Bidwell, California, to relieve Company G. of the Second California Cavalry. Thence dates his experience and renown as an Indian fighter. His first engagement with the "Redskins" took place at Townsend's Bluff, California, on the 30th of September, 1866; the second at Abbott Lake, in Oregon, about a month later. Bedinger, who was made a corporal at the Abbott Lake engagement, had charge of eight men, with instructions to head off a detachment of hostile Indians from gaining a rocky gap in the mountains. He succeeded, after killing a number of the warriors, and capturing several squaws. For this meritorious conduct he was made a sergeant. Subsequently he started from Fort Klamath, Oregon, with fifty men and twelve Indian guides on a scouting expedition. Lieutenant John F. Small was in command. On the 8th of September, 1867, in an engagement with one hundred and thirty Snake Indians which lasted for two hours, eighty-seven "redskins" were killed, and the rest, including squaws and papooses, were captured. Again honorably discharged, Bedinger returned to Cincinnati, and in 1873 became a patrolman, and on the river beats was as much of a terror to the "toughs" as he had been to the western savages. In 1876, he was made a sergeant. Four years later he resigned to accept a place in the water works department, and in 1886, he again returned to the police force. After four months of service as a patrolman under the non-partisan commission, he again became a sergeant. Since then he has been on duty at the First and Fifth Districts. The sergeant is a good story teller, an excellent officer, and a capital drill-master and disciplinarian.

The duties of the matrons of the house of detention combine those of an officer in charge of a station, and the station-house keeper. They serve on day duty each alternate month, and on night duty the other months, and they are assisted by one janitress. The difficulties under which the matrons of a place like the house of detention, must labor can readily be imagined. For this place women who are not only of good character, but who also have a large supply of patience and gentleness are required. The two matrons fill the requirements perfectly. They are Mrs. Pauline Fieber and Mrs. Margaret Meade. Both are widows, the latter being the relict of Detective Meade. They are middle aged women, and manage the affairs of the house of detention admirably.

CHAPTER XV.

FOURTH AND FIFTH DISTRICTS.—" SHANTY TOWN " DESCRIBED.—BRAVERY OF AN OFFICER IN FOLLOWING A DESPERADO.—INTERESTING INCIDENT IN THE LIFE OF THE NOTORIOUS CORDELIA WADE.—HOW THE QUIETUDE OF THE FIFTH DISTRICT WAS STARTLED IN 1874.—DETAILS OF THE SCHILLING MURDER, THE MOST ATROCIOUS IN THE CRIMINAL ANNALS OF CINCINNATI.

THE Third street station-house headquarters for the Fourth Police District, is one of the oldest in the city. It has stood on its present site ever since 1867. The building is a two story brick house, the entire front of which is made of doors with small stained windows in them. It was evidently formerly occupied as a store, but some years ago was purchased by the city. The front room is very cosy indeed, being kept spotlessly clean by the station-house keeper. Back of this room is a cell room, large enough to meet any emergency which might arise.

The force which reports here consists of three lieutenants, Jesse Lingenfelter, Patrick Currin and James Scahill; three sergeants, Joseph Burman, Martin C. Brennan and Henry Lietz, and forty-one patrolmen. The district covered is that bounded by a line beginning at the west side of Vine and the Ohio river, thence north to Third, thence along the south side of Third to John, to Fifth, to Mound, to Seventh, to Baymillar, to Gest, to Mill creek, to the Ohio river, and along the Ohio river to the place of beginning. It includes many low quarters of the city, where poverty and drunkenness breed vice and crime. The most notable " tough " sections are the Mill creek bottoms and notorious " Shanty town," where the shanty-boats are located. These boats swarming with women and men of the worst types, line the Ohio in this district. They are usually the especial care of the police, inasmuch as many of their inhabitants, called " river gypsies," are like their land prototypes, slow to recognize the difference between what is other people's property and what is their own.

This district is peculiarly the district for accidents. Scarcely a day passes, but that some one is reported killed or seriously injured, from the Third street station-house. The reason for this is that the district is full of factories, and also that it runs along the river front, besides including many railway crossings.

The most interesting features of the district, however, is that already named as Shantytown. Too indolent to ever rise above petty thiefts, too ignorant to recognize their own degraded condition, the inhabitants live on from year to year, half starved in both winter and summer, the only difference between their status in the two seasons, being the difference made by the atmosphere. As a rule in the vicinity of each shanty is a small garden which the woman, seldom a wife, who presides over the household, "tends" in a half hearted way during the warmer months. The man and the children when not idling are either engaged in stealing or in getting ready to steal. In winter time, each hovel is transformed into a scene of distress. The icy winds blow from the river, and pierce the shanties through and through. Vacancy occupies the cupboard, want stares from the blue faces of the human inhabitants, as many of whom as can are crowded into the beds while the rest huddle together for warmth.

It will be readily believed that in such a condition of society as this, the darker passions of jealousy, revenge and hate, are not easily stirred from their sluggish repose. Yet once in a while a murder is committed here, and when such a thing does occur, the horror and brutality of it are intensified.

Such a murder was committed early in 1885. Two shanty town men named Coales and Oliver, fell to quarreling on the river bank. Both were slightly under the influence of liquor. The quarrel arose out of a grudge of long standing, but which had a cause as trivial as the resulting quarrel was bitter. They met on the river bank about five o'clock in the afternoon. Curses and shouts were heard. Presently Oliver drew a dirk from his pocket, and with a swift slash almost severed Coales'

LIEUT. JOHN W. SCAHILL,
LIEUT. P. L. CURRIN. LIEUT. J. LINGENFELTER.
Fourth District.

head from his body. Then he turned and fled. Soon the police were on his track, and it was learned that he had rowed down the river in a boat. Two policemen followed him, and overtook him at Coal city, just as he was pulling out from the shore. They commanded him to stop, but he paid no attention. Crack! went the revolver of one of the policemen, and Oliver's left hand dropped the oar which it held. But still he managed to row to the other side, and disappeared in the bushes. A boat was hired and the police followed him. After several hours search, he was finally found in a miserable hut back in the woods. He was recently pardoned from a life sentence in the State Penitentiary.

Lieutenant Currin, was born the 15th of March, 1840, passed in due form the examination prescribed by the commissioners under the recent law, and was the second appointee under such enactment, receiving his commission the 29th of April, 1886. His original assignment was to the Third street district, but the changes consequent upon the Centennial caused his transfer to the Ninth, and thence to the Fourth. From the 15th of August, 1886, to March 21, 1888, he made a personal record of 148 arrests. The offenses were of all grades, from drunkenness to murder. Among the many on his pocket list was that of Teddy Cunningham, who is now serving a twenty years' sentence for rape. This is not his first experience in police work, as he served about a year under the administration of Mayor S. S. Davis. Like many others, he has a disposition to place life in the balance against duty. A fugitive from Tennessee justice, for murder, had been located here by the officers of that Commonwealth. He had taken lodging in a tumble-down house on one of the lower streets of the city. Currin, as the officer of the Third district was summoned, and found fully 500 people assembled about the place. Conspicuous among them were the Tennessee authorities, who appeared to feel ample respect for the killing propensity of their man, and so hinted when Currin asked them why they had not gone in and arrested him. Nothing daunted, he secured a ladder, ascended to a second story window, and through it saw the victim lying on a bed. He had pawned his pistols the day before to secure money for food, and acquiesced in the command to surrender with fairly good grace, backed as it was by a judicious display of weapons on the part of the plucky lieutenant, who has often thought since of what might have been, had not hunger deprived the Tennesseean of the power to harm.

Lieutenant Jesse Lingenfelter is one of the oldest men on the police force. He was born on the 2d of August, 1837, in Carrolton, Kentucky. About eighteen years ago he came to this city, where he has lived ever since. He was appointed to the force on the 21st of July, 1875, and in his long service of thirteen years, he has lost but seventeen days. He was first detailed at Central station. On May 24, 1886, he was appointed lieutenant, and was transferred successively from there to the Sixth district, then to the Fourth district, then to the Fifth, to the Ninth, to the Tenth, and finally back again to the Fourth, where he now is. This has given him perhaps the most varied experience of any man on the force. Before the patrol system was established, he was the officer appointed to transfer the prisoners from the Police Court to the jail. He held this place for three years, and during that time marched hundreds of handcuffed men whose names are known to all familiar with the annals of crime, in gangs through the streets to the county prison.

Lieutenant Lingenfelter, tells quite a thrilling experience he had one night about twelve years ago. He was patrolling his beat along Ninth street just below John. It was about half-past ten o'clock, and the street was completely deserted. A tremendous rain was falling, and the lieutenant thought to himself that this was an excellent night for gentlemen of the craft to be abroad. As he was passing Dr. Maley's residence, which was then below John street, he saw a man crouching under the abutment down the short flight of basement steps.

"What are you doing there?" said Lingenfelter.

"I am trying to keep out of the rain," answered the man in the basement.

"Come up and let's have a look at you."

The man attempted to discuss the subject, but presently sprang suddenly up into the street, revolver in hand. Lingenfelter grabbed him and whirled him around, making a successful snatch at the revolver. The desperado then drew from his pocket with the other hand a pair of knucks with long spikes in them. After a desperate struggle, Lingenfelter succeeded in holding him so that he was powerless, and then turning his revolver against him, made him throw up his hands. When searched, he was found to have on his person, in addition to the knucks and revolver, a jimmy, a pound of powder, a long fuse and all the other tools necessary to do a successful job of safe cracking. He was recognized as John Gates, one of the most successful safe blowers in the country. A work-house sentence of four years and a half. was given him on five charges. At the end of two years he escaped, however, by hiding himself in the middle of a cart load of dirt that was carried out of the work-house and dumped.

In his experience Lingenfelter has handcuffed many men, and says he can tell whether a man has ever been handcuffed before the minute he attempts to put the cuffs on him. One instance is especially striking. When John Doe, part of whose career is related in the sketch of Lieutenant Thornton, was arrested, he "made a strong bluff." His gentlemanly appearance, not unlike that of a prosperous bank president, helped him considerably, but the officers insisted in handcuffing him. At first he objected loudly, but finally submitted. Said Lieutenant Lingenfelter: "As soon as he turned his hands over for me to put the cuffs on, I knew he had had them on before. Why he laid his hands in them as naturally as a trained horse backs into the shafts."

Among the most interesting prisoners the lieutenant ever handled (and he had the pleasure of her society a score of times) was the beautiful, wayward, unfortunate Cordelia Wade. Those who were around the Central Station fifteen years ago will remember her well. She was then in her prime—a woman but little over twenty years of age—in whose dark eyes dwelt a dreamy expression, such as belongs only to those who are confirmed in the opium or morphine habit. Those who remember her five years ago, which was just before her death, will recall her worn and wasted face, which, when close to view, was seamed and scarred with the deep-cut traces of many a dark passion and many a wild debauch.

Cordelia Wade came of that old and highly respected family after which Wade street was named. She was a favorite daughter—the spoiled child of her parents. When she grew up to young womanhood, she became very beautiful—wavy brown hair, great dark, passionate eyes, stormy brows, straight nose, and pouting red lips. Her form was slender, and her carriage that of a queen. This last grace followed her to the grave, so that even the rough loafers about the station-house remarked her stately walk when vice had stamped out every other loveliness. She was a wilful girl, and when the man came along whom she loved and whom her parents disliked, she refused to give him up and met him clandestinely. Then followed the old, old story that half the women of the town can tell with drunken laughter or when tears stream from their sad eyes and despondency brings softness to their hearts. The time came when her parents drove her from their home, and then she went to her sister's door and knocked. To her she told the story, and the sister turned from her and ordered her to leave the house. Out into the streets she went to lead that woful life of the woman of the town. Soon she became a victim to the morphine habit, and then the story was not long. Step by step she went down until no woman was lower than she. Her fierce temper and revengeful disposition led her into brawls, and Cordelia Wade—or "Delia," as she was better known—became notorious for her swiftness to draw a knife and use it, too. She was arrested and sentenced to the work-house time and again. Soon most of her time was passed in prison. She would not resist the officers when they came to arrest her, but sit sullenly until her opportunity came, and then with a devil in each eye would attempt to stab one of them. Many a bitter struggle have they had with her, and many a time has an officer narrowly escaped with his life. To such degradation had this once beautiful and refined daughter of a respectable house sunk.

Once she went to Chicago on a morphine drunk, and when she was arrested there the reporters were so struck with her aristocratic appearance that they wrote a flaming account of the swell

Cincinnati society woman who had been found drunk with morphine on the streets. At that time, however, she was yet young, and had not yet fallen to the depths.

A scene which she created in Robinson's Opera House, now Harris' Theatre, is yet remembered. It was about twelve years ago, and some ephemeral play was being presented with "East Lynne," Ada Grey in the cast. The plot turned on the ruin of a young girl, and her being driven from home by her sister. Just as the sister had ordered her out, and the poor girl, hounded to bay, turned and denounced her for her cruelty, a woman whom many recognized as "Delia" Wade suddenly rose in the midst of the orchestra chairs and with a frightful oath shouted, "Give it to her! Give it to her! My sister treated me that way once, and I owe my shame to that. Give it to her!"

This wild, thrilling tirade threw the audience into consternation. The star lost her lines, the women grew pale, the curtain went down. Two policemen rushed down the aisle and dragged the woman away. The performance went on, but the incident will be remembered by those present when memory of all the surroundings shall have faded.

Down, down went Cordelia, tasting the cup of shame and wringing out the lees. Beauty fled, and naught of the woman that was remained but the flashing dark eyes, the wealth of brown hair and the queenly walk. At the age of forty she died a horrible death in the Infirmary, and no one knows or cares where she is buried. Her life was the drama acted which Hogarth once painted.

Lieutenant John W. Scahill was born in this city on the 25th of March, 1858. He was apprenticed to the carriage woodwork trade, and worked at it until October 20, 1886, when he went on the police force. He was assigned to the Central Police Station, but had a brief experience as patrolman. On December 12, 1887, he became a sergeant, and on the 1st of January, 1888, he was appointed a lieutenant. His rise has been rapid and has been due entirely to meritorious service. He has served in the Ninth, First, and Fourth districts, the last being his present location. He has been attentive to his duties and he knows them all.

Sergeant Joseph M. Burman was born in this city January 4, 1853. Before becoming a policeman he was a private watchman. After following this occupation for some years he was, on June 19, 1886, appointed to the force, and assigned to Oliver street, from which, after half a month's service, he was transferred to the Ninth district. February 3, 1888, he was appointed a sergeant and assigned to the Third Street Station. He owed his promotion, and also the placing of his name on the Roll of Honor, to his heroic rescue of a woman from a burning building. It was during the great Gest street fire, July 29, 1887. Burman entered one of the houses which was in flames and filled with blinding smoke, mounted to the second story and brought down in safety Mrs. Topmiller, who was lying sick there. It was a most daring and most gallant rescue, performed at the risk of his own life. No other eulogy is necessary. Lesser actions have won greater glory and greater applause.

Sergeant Martin Cody Brennan was born in December, 1844. He can never become President, as Dublin, Ireland, was the place of his birth. It is twenty-two years since he first landed in this country, and went to the coal region, near Scranton, Pennsylvania, to assist his uncle in sinking coal shafts. He drifted about the country a good deal, pursuing this occupation. Then he went to Philadelphia and married. This rather settled him, and he came to Cincinnati twelve years ago to make it his permanent home. He lived with old Mayor Moore as gardener for awhile, and on the 28th of April, 1881, went on the police force as patrolman. He was appointed sergeant about four years ago, and stationed at Sedamsville. In July, 1886, he was transferred to Third street, where he has since remained. In his career as policeman he has always shown himself to be brave and fearless in the discharge of his duties, often endangering his life in the enforcement of the law. He played an honorable part in the defence of the court-house during the riots. He owed his promotion to the sergeantcy to a desperate and skillful pursuit of four desperadoes, who were planning a robbery just outside the Sedamsville district.

Sergeant Henry Leitz was born in Milwaukee, Wisconsin, on

SERGT. JOS. M. BURMAN.   SERGT. M. C. BRENNAN.   SERGT. HENRY LEITZ.
Fourth District.

the 24th of March, 1860, and about a year afterward came to Cincinnati with his parents. He learned the trade of a blacksmith, and soon became one of the most skillful workers in iron in the city. On the 1st of December, 1886, he was appointed to the police force, and assigned to the Central Station. He was appointed sergeant on the 1st of February, 1888, and went to the Fulton Station; after two months he was transferred to his present situation. He is a man of quiet manners, but is noted for his determination as well as for bravery.

Oliver Street Station-house, the headquarters of the Fifth police district, is located on the north side of the great city stables which fill the square bounded by Liberty, Linn, and Oliver streets, in that part of the city known as "the West End." The stables were built in 1868, and the station-house—an afterthought—was incorporated in the building and opened for service on December 20, 1869. Though in some respects the situation is not as desirable as might be, yet the rooms are all on one floor, and the cell-rooms are the airiest and most comfortable of any in the city. Reached by a short flight of steps, the only outside door opens into the office, a room about twenty-five feet square, lighted by two great windows, kept scrupulously clean, and furnished with the usual paraphernalia of a police station. In the corner is a raised platform for the desk, the safe, the telephone closet, and the place of authority for the officer in charge. A big closet occupies most of the opposite side of the room. A stationary marble washstand fills the corner. The sides of the room are filled with big, comfortable chairs. The cell-rooms are east, reached by a door opening into a hall, used for the storage of the personal belongings necessary for the men. Then comes the first cell-room. This room is about sixty by twenty-five feet. Two rows of cells, five in a row, of lattice ironwork, occupy the centre of the room. As each cell will accommodate two inmates, this room will furnish quarters for twenty prisoners. A broad walk surrounds them and separates the two rows. The lattice work is strong, and the only way of escape for a prisoner would be to dig through the heavy wooden floor of the room, a thing not to be thought of under the circumstances. Still further east is the second cell-room, about eighteen by twenty-four feet in dimensions, and containing three cells, in one row in the centre of the room. Great windows give abundant light and ventilation.

Although headquarters for the largest police district in the city, the work done at Oliver street does not ap roach that at Central or Hammond street station houses, this section of the city being very quiet, and containing little of the elements that usually contribute to the Black Maria and the police court bench. Yet, occasionally, a great crime contributes to break the monotony that, as a rule, makes the life of a Fifth District policeman a peaceful if not a happy one. Seldom has there been recorded so revolting a crime, one so replete with horror, so full of brutal and barbarous incident, so hideous and ghastly in its conception and carrying out, as the murder of Herman Schilling, on the night of Saturday, November 7, 1874, in this the Fifth District. So frightful was it, that it is stated that rumor, which ever adds to the story of any event, fell far short of the facts in this case. The mind of one who remembers in recurring to the event, is, after an interval of fourteen years, sickened and horrified at the recollection. No array of strong adjectives, no powers of description, however realistic, can begin to paint this most inhuman of crimes in its true and real colors. From beginning to end it reveals a degradation of human nature, a brutality, a ghoulishness revolting and almost incredible. Once or twice in the annals of crime this butchery has been equaled, but never has it has been surpassed.

For some time previous to November 7, 1874, a young tanner named Herman Schilling, worked at the Freeberg tannery, on Livingston street and Gamble alley, just west of Central avenue. He boarded and lodged in a boarding house and saloon, owned by Andreas Egner, an evil looking man, hard, cruel, avaricious. His place was at 153 Findlay street, and the lot around it adjoined the tannery. Through the fence between the lots there was a gate which Schilling was in the habit of using. Egner had a son, Frederick, a bad, stupid, young fellow of about eighteen years, and a daughter, perhaps a little more than a year younger, bright, buxom, and rather pretty, with a thoroughly German countenance, in whose veins the hot, passionate blood of

LIEUT. BERNARD RAKEL.
LIEUT. JAMES J. HANRAHAN.   LIEUT. E. T. ROCKWELL.
Fifth District.

youth ran fast and red. Egner knew his daughter's worth, and proceeded to turn it into money. He made her attend bar, and the saloon of the Egner's was a popular resort. For the beer seemed to taste better if the pretty young bar maid drew it, and smiled on the drinker. Then, too, she would sometimes take a hand in a game of cards with the hangers on about the place. Her father abused her shamefully.

In the midst of such surroundings, with a father who had no higher idea of her than to use her as a decoy for trade, it is not surprising that she listened to the insinuating words of some of the younger and handsomer customers and fell. This was unsuspected by Egner, who was as anxious about his daughter's virtue as he was careless about protecting it. One night, however, he caught Schilling in her room. He turned all the brutal wrath of his sullen nature upon the young man. Nor did he spare the young girl herself, but added blows and kicks to his reproaches. Schilling left the house, and went to board with a certain saloon keeper named Westenbrock, at 126 Findlay. He was given the position of night watchman at the tannery, and slept in a little room just off the stable.

One day Egner, after upbraiding his daughter, knocked her down and kicked her heavily in the side. Being in delicate health the kicking compelled her to go to the hospital, where she died from the effects of it on the 6th of August, 1874. The rage of Egner burst out afresh against Schilling, and the day after her death he picked up a heavy oak barrel stave, ordered his son to do likewise, and the two went through the tannery gate, attacked Schilling, and would have killed him had not some men interfered. For this father and son were fined $50 and costs each before a magistrate, and put under bond to keep the peace. Then Egner began to make threats against Schilling's life, swearing to kill him, and describing various modes of accomplishing it, some of which he afterward employed.

Schilling had also gained the enmity of one George Rufer, also employed about the tannery, by having him discharged. Rufer was a brutal man, and as was afterward discovered an ex-convict and a bigamist. Rufer, too, swore to have his life. Saturday evening, November 7, 1874, Rufer came into Egner's saloon, and the two began pouring out imprecations against Schilling.

"Let's kill him this evening," finally said Rufer.

"All right," said Egner. And then and there the plan was arranged. Egner's son, Fred, who has already been mentioned, was in the barroom at the time, and was prevailed upon by threats to go into the plot.

The saloon was closed at half-past nine, and at ten the three men started forth on their mission of crime. In the tannery yard were several large and vicious watch dogs, which however were acquainted with the Egners, and did not disturb them. Rufer led, carrying in his hand a large stave sharpened to a point. They went through the gate into the tannery lot, and then to the stable, concealing themselves in a small harness room, just off the stable proper.

At half-past ten o'clock Schilling left Westenbrock's saloon where he boarded, and started for his bedroom in the tannery stable. He entered, all unconscious of the three pairs of murderously gleaming eyes that watched his every movement. He lighted a small lamp in the stable, and went over toward the stall of the horse, putting his hand on the animal's haunch.

Rufer crept from his concealment and stealthily advanced until he was but a few feet from his victim, then raising the stave high in the air, he brought it down with terrific force on Schilling's head. Three times he did this, the third blow felling the watchman to the floor. But Schilling had a hard head and rose to his feet to grapple with his assailant. Then old man Egner leaped out and rushed to the assistance of his coadjutor in crime. He had picked up a five-pronged pitchfork, used about the stable, which he proceeded to use with telling effect. He plunged it to the hilt in Schilling's abdomen and pulled it out. Five jets of blood followed it, deluging Rufer's trousers and soaking through to dye his underclothes red with blood. Twice more the ferocious old man plunged the pitchfork into the already lacerated abdomen, and each time drew a hideous half-choked shriek from his victim. "My God, you are murdering me," exclaimed the young tanner in German, and then he sank down unconscious. Rufer once more raised his stave and brought it down on Schilling's head a dozen or more times. The sound was afterward described as like that made by hitting beef with a hammer.

Young Fred Egner, all this time a spectator, now came forward and joined the two others who were standing over the unconscious man's body. The next question was what to do with the body. At first it was proposed to throw it in the vat, but Egner insisted that his favorite scheme of burning it in the furnace be adopted. The body was taken outside, the three men bearing it, carried along the buildings into the furnace-room at the farther end.

These furnaces were peculiarly constructed, and the fire in them was fiercely hot. Rufer attempted to push the body in at the door which he had opened, but found the opening too small. Egner grew impatient, ordered his son and Rufer to hold the body against the door, and then with an iron bar as a ram, crammed it through the hole into the raging white coals, beating and pounding it down until it was almost covered.

"Was Schilling dead at the time?" was afterward asked young Egner.

"I don't know," he replied. "I thought he was dead, because he did not speak." It may have been that he was not dead, and that the fire, burning into his vitals, revived for a moment the spark of life. If so, can anything more hideous be imagined than the excruciating suffering of that moment—the eternity of exquisite pain and mortal agony thrust into that one brief moment!

Rufer closed the door of the furnace, and the three once more came into the outside air.

"Good night," said Rufer, as he started away for home.

"Good night," answered the other two, coolly, and they went back through the gate, washed their hands at the hydrant, concealed the gore-bespattered clothes, and went to bed and to sleep. They were glutted to the full with vengeance and slept soundly. No dreams of that hideous scene in the stable, the swaying forms in the dim light, the dull heavy sound of the stave-blows, the spouting red streams that followed the pitchfork thrusts, the low moans of suffering, the entreaties for mercy—none of these things, as they afterward averred, troubled their sleep.

Early the next morning Westenbrock, Schilling's landlord, who also worked at the tannery, pounded on the stable door for admission, and pounded in vain. A young man, named Hollenbush, heard the pounding from his window across the way and went down. Said he: " I heard sounds of a struggle in there last night, and maybe he's murdered."

They both went for the police, who burst open the door—that is, the stable over where the struggle had taken place. In the stall, stood the horse trembling and shaking with fright. The walls and the floor were splattered and splotched with blood. A pitchfork, covered with dried blood and matted hair stood against the wall. On the floor lay a broom, also covered with blood, and a stave, the end of which had clots of blood and hair upon it.

A trail of blood led to the furnace-room, and in the furnace, the fires of which were dampened by the police, was found as hideous and ghostly a mass as ever human eyes looked upon. At first glance it looked like a half burned mass of bituminous coal. But on closer investigation, masses of crumbling human bones were distinguishable, strung together by half burned sinews, or glued one upon another by a hideous adhesion of half molten flesh. Boiled brains and jellied blood, mingled with coal. Skull burst like a shell, and the upper portion seemingly blown out by the boiling and bubbling brains. The brain all boiled away save a small piece the size of a lemon in the bottom of the brain pan. It was crisped and hot to the touch, the fibres seeming to writhe like worms. The eyes were cooked to bubbled crisps in the blackened sockets, and the bones of the nose were gone, leaving a hideous hole. The teeth remained, but could be crumbled in the fingers. The body had burst open at the chest, and the heart and the lungs had been entirely consumed. The liver was wasted, and the kidneys fried. So tightly were the teeth clenched that they seemed to give credence to the supposition that Schilling was still alive when thrust into the furnace.

The news of the terrible discovery spread, and an immense crowd, undismayed by the falling rain, gathered at the scene, eager to hear and see. The two Egners and Rufer were soon arrested by Lieutenant Jake Birnbaum and officer Henry Knappe, as many things pointing to them as the perpetrators of the crime were soon discovered. In fact the murder was as unskillful as it was brutal. The bloody trio were taken to the Oliver street station-house and locked up. Fred Egner soon gave in and confessed all, describing the commission of the crime minutely. In the trial that followed, he turned State's evidence, and escaped what he, too, deserved, the gallows. Rufer confessed also. But old man Egner held out.

"I had no hand in it," said he.

"Yes, but you had your fork in it," was the jeering retort of his accomplice, Rufer. Days followed each other, bringing to light new and more horrible details, until the whole crime stood revealed in its naked horror—black, devilish and inhuman beyond belief. Schilling was a young man of twenty-five years, and rather comely. Egner was old and his malignant character was revealed in his countenance. Rufer was thirty-five years old, with a dark record behind him, and a face fully as brutal as Egner's, while the younger Egner looked only stupid and cowardly. There is not much doubt but that he was little worse than a frightened spectator.

Such was the fearful tragedy that resulted from the infamy of a father in exposing his daughter to temptations under which she so early succumbed. The trial of Egner and Rufer resulted in a life sentence in the penitentiary for each. Egner, however, only served about seven years, when, under the supposition that he was dying from consumption, was pardoned by Governor Foster. Once out of prison his health was soon restored. That his murderous nature still remained with him, was clearly evinced when to a reporter who was sent to interview him after his return to Cincinnati, he said, "of you dont get off these premises right avay kvick I vill kill you too." He died a raging maniac January 24, 1889, near the scene of the awful tragedy.

Klein, the rapist, was also arrested in this district on February, 1879, and locked up at Oliver street, and, upon being searched in front of the desk, was found to have in his pocket, articles stolen from the house back of Newport, whose mistress he had outrageously assaulted a few days before, evidence which settled his guilt beyond question and caused him to be taken to Newport, over the river, where he was taken from jail and hanged by a mob the next Sunday night. Hulse, who had assaulted a little girl only a short time before the Klein episode, was also arrested in this district, and locked up here. Only a couple of squares or so away, at the corner of Linn and Dayton streets, at 5 o'clock on a calm, clear morning in February, 1878, brave officer Kunkle was shot dead by one of a party of burglars, whom he and two of his companions were pursuing, an episode that attracted wide attention, not only because of the deliberate murder of a brave man in the exercise of his duty, but because the crime was never brought home to the perpetrator. This shooting has remained a mystery to this day, though most people believe the guilty parties were arrested almost immediately, but were never identified, and were finally let go, because no positive evidence could be brought against them.

The Fifth District, is the largest in the city in area, covering about one-fourth of the city below the hills, excluding Cumminsville, and the extreme East and West ends along the river. Probably 40,000 people inhabit it. The boundaries are as follows: Beginning at the corner of Twelfth and Plum streets, thence following Plum street and the Canal to Addison street; west on Addison street to Spring Grave avenue; south to Queen City avenue; west to Mill Creek; north on Mill Creek to Hickenlooper's subdivision, thence west to the first toll-gate on the Harrison pike; south to the lower end of Lick Run; east to Mill Creek; south along Mill Creek to Gest street; east on Gest to Baymiller street; north on Baymiller to Clark street, and east on Clark and Twelfth streets, to the place of beginning. In this are some of the largest factories in the city, three fire districts, four great breweries and 372 saloons.

At present the force consists of forty-four patrolmen, with three lieutenants and three sergeants, as follows: Lieutenants, Barney Rakel, James J. Hanrahan, and Edwin T. Rockwell; Sergeants, Edward C. Hill, Louis Schmitt and J. H. Kiffmeyer.

Lieutenant Edwin T. Rockwell was born at Ripley, Ohio, March 9, 1860, but has lived in Cincinnati since he was three years old, and received his education here in the public schools. As a boy he was fond of travel, and managed to indulge his propensity in long trips to the south and southwest, with a show. He learned the trade of a shoe-laster, and, being a thinker, became a leader among his fellow workmen, whose condition he desired to improve. He joined the police force July 3, 1885, as a substitute, but in five days was made a regular patrolman. He left the force for awhile, but, July 7, 1886, was reappointed a patrolman, and, July 28, was promoted to be a sergeant. On December 12, 1887, he was promoted to a lieutenancy, and, having passed the regular sixty days probation, was confirmed as lieutenant on February 18, 1888. He stands five feet nine inches, weighs 190 pounds, and is married. In 1887 he was one of the ten men who received honorable mention for the Morgan medal, the possession of which is regarded as the highest honor by a Cincinnati policeman.

Lieutenant Bernard Rakel was born on January 26, 1855, in the little village of Lohe, near Lingen, a town situated in that part of Germany which was then the Kingdom of Hanover, but which to-day is a province of Prussia. When only one year old Barney had the misfortune to lose his father, and in consequence was in his youth subjected to many hardships. His education was confined to the schools of his native village. At seventeen, after he had learned the trade of a shoemaker, he resolved to try his luck in the New World. He crossed the Atlantic on the German Lloyd steamer "Ohio," and in 1872 landed in Baltimore, and proceeded thence to Cincinnati, where he has remained ever since. Failing to obtain work as a shoemaker, he finally secured a place in a tannery, and after serving six months left to accept a situation in the Mitchell chair factory. Here he worked but a fortnight, when all hands struck, and he was again in search of employment. This time his lot fell in with the proprietor of a furniture car, with whom he worked several years. Then he bought a car for himself, and until 1881 was engaged in moving the *penates* of Cincinnati from one house to another. In this year he was appointed a patrolman by Mayor Means, and straightway sold his furniture car outfit and bought a uniform. He was first detailed for duty at Coryville, but in October of the same year was transferred to the Bremen street district, where he remained for five years. In August 1885, he was promoted to the position of sergeant, the position to which he was reappointed when the present Board of Commissioners came into power. Soon after this recognition by the commissioners, he rejoiced at the opportunity of putting on the shoulder straps, since, on October 28, 1886, Mayor Smith recommended him for a lieutenantcy. He was then transferred to the Oliver street district, where he remained for a few days only, when he was entrusted with a joint administration of affairs at the Central Station. After six months service here, by the rule of rotation, adopted by the Board of Commissioners, he was transferred, this time to the Hammond street district. December 1, 1887, he was delighted at being sent back to his old " Over the Rhine " territory, comprised in the Bremen street district. Here he remained until July 4, 1888, when he was selected by the chief of police to take command of the city squad, detailed for duty at the exposition. The exposition over, he was returned to his old command in the Oliver street district.

During his career in the city's service, Lieutenant Rakel has made several important arrests, to which several criminals now in the Ohio Penitentiary can bear witness. Rakel was at the scene of the riots of 1884, and did good work for the cause of law and order. Through his efforts, aided by others, the attempt to set fire to a barrel of coal oil, poured into the jail at four o'clock on the memorable Friday morning was thwarted. On the second day of the riots he was where there was the most danger. The lieutenant is at the head of an interesting family.

Lieutenant James J. Hanrahan, one of the handsomest men on the Cincinnati police force—and still unmarried—was born in Cincinnati March 22, 1860, was educated in the public schools, and learned the shoemaker trade. In August, 1885, he became a substitute patrolman, was entered on the regular force September 8th following, and became a sergeant on July 27, 1886,

SERGT. LOUIS SCHMITT.
SERGT. JOHN H. KIFFMEYER.   SERGT. EDWARD C. HILL.
Fifth District.

and was promoted lieutenant July 18, 1887. He stands six feet one inch and weighs 203 pounds.

Sergeant John H. Kiffmeyer was born at Cincinnati, April 19, 1854, and was educated in the public schools. For some time he was a salesman. He entered the United States army, serving five years in the Third Artillery, being stationed mostly at Fortress Monroe. He was there in 1881 when President Garfield was shot, and was transferred to Washington, where for a part of the time he was on duty at the White House, and part of the time was on duty at the jail on guard over the assassin Guiteau. During one year he was detailed as one of the surveying party under Government direction, making maps of the Virginia battle fields for use of the War Department. On June 29, 1886, he was appointed a patrolman, was promoted November 15 following, and has since reported at Bremen, Central and Oliver street station-houses. He is married, stands five feet nine inches, and weighs 175 pounds. He was one of the ten receiving honorable mention in the competition of 1886 for the Morgan Medal.

Sergeant Edward C. Hill, the son of "Squire" Francis A. Hill, a well known citizen of Hamilton county, was born at Pleasant Ridge, near Cincinnati, June 1, 1846. He was raised on a farm, but came to the city when a young man, and became a salesman. He joined the police force June 1, 1884, under Mayor Means; was a patrolman, eight and a half months as a "special," then was at the Grand Central Passenger Station for a year. He was promoted to a sergeantcy in the spring of 1887. He stands six feet one inch, weighs 246 pounds, and has a soldierly, impressive appearance. He has been married twenty years.

Sergeant Louis Schmitt was born in Brooklyn, New York, October 14, 1856. He came to Cincinnati about seven years ago after having learned the carriage painter's trade. He worked at this trade until he went on the force, the 6th of November, 1886. After remaining at Central station for nine months, he was promoted to a sergeantcy the first of July, 1887, and was transferred to the Third district. After eight months there he went to Oliver street, where he now is a faithful, diligent and efficient officer.

CHAPTER XVI.

FROM SIXTH TO TENTH INCLUSIVE.—THE DISTRICTS WHICH COMPRISE CINCINNATI SUBURBS WHERE OFFICERS ARE EITHER MOUNTED OR ARE PROVIDED WITH A SUPERABUNDANCE OF LEG TALENT.—THE UNCANNY EXPERIENCE OF LIEUTENANT HEHEMAN IN ARRESTING A BURGLAR.—" BURKING " AND BODY SNATCHING IN THE SUBURBS.—HOW THE WORD BURKING CAME INTO USE.—THE STEALING OF THE BODY OF PRESIDENT HARRISON'S FATHER, AND THE AWFUL CRIME OF INGALLS AND JOHNSON.

THE Fulton station-house is located in a neat two-story dwelling house at the corner of Eastern avenue and Ferry street, where it has been since July, 1882, when the former station-house just at the railway track on Vance street was condemned because it was ready to fall down. The existence of a station-house in the East End antedates the war, and the Fulton District was established when that part of the city east of Washington street was included in the corporation limits.

The present station-house is as light and clean as any police building in the city, a state of things, however, which dates only from the fall of 1888. Previous to that time it was perhaps the dirtiest in the city. But through the efforts of the lieutenant and sergeant a marked change was brought about. It is not owned by the city, but is rented for $35 a month.

The Sixth District, of which this station-house is the headquarters is the largest and also the most peaceable in the city. Beginning at the river front and Parsons street, its boundaries run to Third, to Washington, to Fulton avenue, to Kemper lane, to Columbia avenue, to Woodburn avenue, to the Madisonville pike, to Observatory road, to the Corporation line, along the dummy track to Linwood road, then again along the Corporation line to the Turkey Bottom road and then to the river front. It extends along nearly eight miles of river front, and is over three miles wide in its widest part. It includes the villages of Fulton,

SERGT. M. O'HEARN.   SERGT. H. McMULLEN
SERGT. JER. NAGLE.   LIEUT. JAS. M. BRANGAN.
Sixth District.

Pendleton, Delta, Tusculum, Undercliff, O'Brienville, Mt. Lookout, and Tusculum Heights. The people in a large portion of it are very poor but not criminal, so that the four or five cells in the station-house are amply sufficient for all prisoners. The force which patrols this district is composed of one lieutenant, James Brangan, three sergeants, M. J. O'Hearn, Jeremiah Nagle and Henry McMullen, and seventeen patrolmen, divided into watches of three and six for the daytime and eight for night duty.

As has been stated the lieutenant in charge is James Morgan Brangan, an Irishman who was born in Cork on the 20th of May, 1852. When but a lad he went to sea, and for seven years sailed over the Atlantic and Arctic oceans, and the Baltic, Mediterranean and Caribbean seas. He has gone through many strange adventures, having been shipwrecked twice. His second experience of that kind cured him of his love for a life on the bounding deep, and in 1872 he landed in New York, and to remove himself from temptation came far away from his old mistress, the ocean, to Cincinnati. He ran on an Ohio river boat for a while, and then for twelve years worked at the construction of elevators until he we went on the force April 30, 1885. He was the first man appointed by the present Board of Police Commissioners. He was assigned to a beat in the Second District and after about four months was made a sergeant. On the first of July, 1887, he became a lieutenant and was stationed at Corryville, and then about a year ago transferred to his present place. His rapid promotion is tribute enough to his efficiency as an officer. He has never flinched in the face of duty and is one of Colonel Deitsch's most trusted assistants.

Sergeant Jeremiah Nagle was born in this city on the 6th of March, 1859. After several years experience as a private watchman, he was on the 23d of July, 1884, appointed to the police force, and two years later on the 24th of July, 1886, made a sergeant. His promotion was due to his excellent service on patrol wagon No. 2. He has had several narrow escapes from death while discharging his duties, but has won a reputation that makes criminals fear him. They know that Sergeant Nagle will not be trifled with.

Sergeant Michael J. O'Hearn was born on the 12th of February, 1861, in this city. He was originally proprietor of a grocery store, after leaving which he went into the employ of the Board of Public Works, and finally was appointed to the police force on the 19th of July, 1886, and assigned to the Central Police Station. He has run all the important beats in that district. On the 30th of June, 1888, he was promoted to a sergeancy and assigned to Fulton. With the opening of the Centennial he was assigned to the special detective force because of his ability in shadowing and arresting criminals. He has always been ceaselessly active, and is the ideal police officer in his alertness for the discovery and prevention of crime.

Sergeant Henry McMullen was born in Boston, Massachusetts, October 9, 1847. He learned the trade of brass moulder, which he followed until he went on the police force, May 16, 1884. He was assigned to the Hammond street station-house and remained there for two years. On the 17th of July, 1886, he was transferred to the Fulton Station, and four days later he was promoted to a sergeancy. He is the only officer in charge on the force who has not been transferred within the past two years and a half. He has endangered his life frequently in the service of the law, and has had several close calls. All who know him recognize him as faithful and determined.

The Walnut Hills, or Seventh Police District, comprises that territory bounded by O'Brienville and Columbia avenue on the east; by Eden park and Liberty street on the south; by the Reading road, Burnet avenue and Avondale on the west; and by Idlewild Station and the Corporation line on the north. Walnut Hills formerly formed the old Twentieth Ward, and for many years the police station was in an old two-story frame building on Gilbert avenue opposite Curtis street; the place is now occupied by a locksmith. Among the first policemen who reported at this old station was William Cane and Charles Crowley, both of whom are still living. Cane is a brick-layer, while Crowley keeps a saloon on McMillan street. The former was once a lieutenant of police.

The new station-house was built in 1874, H. Bevis being the

architect, and Frank Burns the contractor. The building, a two-story brick, cost about $6000, and is a handsome structure. The first floor is divided into two compartments, one of which is occupied by desks, etc., for the accommodation of the police, and the other contains the cells, of which there are six. The new building stands at the corner of Concord and Morgan streets. Thirty officers report there; two lieutenants, two sergeants, two station-house keepers, three mounted police and twenty-one patrolmen.

There is no officer on the force better known and liked in the district in which he serves than Lieutenant Samuel B. Hall of the Seventh District. Throughout his eight years service there, he has done his part towards preserving the peace in such a manner that the citizens have protested against his being assigned to any other district.

Lieutenant Hall was born in the little village of Decatur, Brown County, Ohio, on August 9, 1848. He was of English parentage, bnt his father, who, was a weaver, died before his son was born. The boy attended school in Ripley, Ohio, until the beginning of the war, when his mother moved to Cincinnati. Young Hall then went to work at the shoemaker's trade, and was employed in the factory of Stribley & Co. for fifteen years. On Jnly 5, 1881, he went on the police force, and ran a night beat in Walnut Hills for three years. He was then given a day beat, and on May 27, 1886, was made lieutenant of police. During his whole service in Walnut Hills, Lieutenant Hall has never lost a day. He is modest to a fault concerning his own achievements, and although he has sent several "good" men to the penitentiary, the lieutenant would be the last one to question concerning them. The district in which this faithful officer has always served is a peculiarly quiet one.

Sergeant Michael Duffy was born in the eastern part of Cincinnati on April 17, 1846. He attended public school until he was eighteen, and then went into the employ of James Griffith, carpenter and builder, at Hunt and Abigail streets. Here Duffy became a machinist. He afterwards worked for Robert Creighton & Co., of Fulton, and in the C. H. & D. and Southern

Railroad shops. Duffy was appointed on the police force on May 11, 1873, under Mayor Johnston, and was a patrolman in the Sixth District for five years. He was then made sergeant and served in the same district three years longer, until 1881, when he was appointed lieutenant and placed at Hammond Street Station From there he was transferred to Third Street Station, and thence to Bremen Street Station. At the beginning of Mayor Smith's administration, Lieutenant Duffy was dropped from the force, but six week's later, he was for a second time appointed patrolman and placed in the Walnut Hills District, where he has remained since. In October, 1887, Duffy received the appointment of sergeant.

One of the cleverest bits of work ever done by the police was the capture and conviction of four expert burglars who broke into and robbed Andrew Barge's dry-goods store in Columbia, carrying away $1,500 worth of stolen property. The main credit for the capture belonged to Sergeant Duffy, who arrested Charley Holthouse, Martin Maloney, Joseph Leppard, and the Eckert brothers. These men were all convicted and all sentenced to five years in the penitentiary except Maloney, who, being under age, was let off with three years. The property stolen by the quartette was found hidden on Mt. Adams.

Ney, the horse thief, burglar, and forger, who ran a successful criminal career in the east end for a long time, was captured by Duffy, and is now serving a fourteen years sentence at the Columbus penitentiary.

James Harp, who shot and killed Weber in McGill's drug store in Newtown, was sent to the "pen" for ten years by Duffy, who arrested him.

Duffy served through the riot with honor, and commanded forty-five men in defense of the court-house.

Sergeant Robert King was born in Stirlingshire, Scotland, September 15, 1853. He came to this country early in life, and followed the occupation of teamster until he went on the Cincinnati Police Force, June 7, 1886. He was assigned to the Walnut Hills Station-house, and after a little over a year's service there was made sergeant, August 10, 1876. Sergeant King is a

SERGT. ROBERT KING. SERGT. M. DUFFY
SERGT. F. W. SHAFER. LIEUT. SAMUEL B. HALL.
Seventh District.

thorough police officer, and deserves his rank as much as any officer on the force.

Sergeant Frederick William Shafer was born in Delhi, on April 25, 1855. When he was but five years old his parents moved to Walnut Hills. The lad continued in school until he was thirteen, when he began to learn the trade of bricklaying. In the first year of Mayor Jacob's administration he became a member of the Cincinnati Police Foree, and was a "sub" at Hammond Street Station for two months, whence he was transferred to the Fifth District, serving there as a "regular" for one and one-half months. Walnut Hills Station was the next to which Shafer was assigned, but after a little over a year's service there he was discharged from the force on account of his political views.

The young man went back to his old trade, bricklaying, and pursued this occupation until June 29, 1886. He was again placed in the Walnut Hills District, and has remained there since. On January 18, 1887, Shafer was made a sergeant of police.

When he was a "sub" at Hammond Street Station he had a thrilling experience with a mob, in which he ran a narrow escape from being killed. It was during the usual October election, and at the polls at Pike and Pearl streets, illegal voting was attempted. A U. S. Marshal called on Shafer to arrest one of the "ballot-box stuffers"—a request which was at once complied with. When the young officer started off with his prisoner, the crowd gathered around him threateningly, and Shafer was compelled to fight his way through. Three shots were fired at him, but fortunately missed their mark. He took his prisoner to the station, and afterwards saw him sent to the penitentiary for five years.

Sergeant Shafer is a powerful fellow, with ruddy face, blue eyes, and brown mustache.

It was in 1871 that the territory known as Corryville was made into a separate police district; about the time that the Twenty-third Ward was laid out. Before this the blue-coated "peace-makers" found their way on the hill from Bremen Street

Station, and still earlier, a marshal with two or three assistants maintained order in this locality.

But in '71 an old one-story frame structure on Vine, between Corry and Charles streets was rented and used as the Eighth District Station-House. This old building was torn down and on its site a hardware store erected. There were no lieutenants in the district then, only two sergeants instead. The first two were Louis Pope and Isaac Stokes, the latter of whom is now a turnkey in the same district. Mike Miller, who now keeps a grocery at Vine and Corry streets, was the "keeper" of this first station-house. Miller afterwards served several years as an officer on the force, and will be remembered as the captor of Charles Hartnet, the wife-murderer of Walker street, who was hung at Columbus, O.

In 1872, the lot on which the present substantially-built brick station-house stands, was purchased of Frank Ries, a saloon-keeper at 1104 Vine. The building, which stands on the south side of Vine, between Corry and Charlton streets, was erected in '72-'73, under Mayor Davis and Chief of Police Bleaks. The station-house, proper, consists of "police-room," cell-room, and basement. The cell-room can accommodate eight prisoners.

The boundaries of the Eighth Police District are as follows: Beginning on the north at the line between the city and that of Clifton and Avondale to Burnet avenue; east and south on Burnet avenue to the Reading Road; south to Liberty, to Price street, to Boal street, to Sycamore, to Mulberry, to Vine street, to Mappis alley, to Ohio and Clifton avenues; thence northwest along Clifton avenue to North Elm street, to Cross street, to Ravine street, along the brow of hill to where the line of McMillan street completed would meet, down the hill to Canal street, and along the canal to the place of beginning.

Lieutenant Edgar Robinson has had a varied, adventurous and interesting career. He was born in Buffalo, N. Y., on November 7, 1844. When but three years of age his parents removed to Columbus, Ohio, and it was there that the boy received all of his "schooling." At the age of fourteen, then tall and stalwart, he began to learn the machinist's trade. Three years were spent in the car-shops, after which Robinson "fired" a few months on an engine on the Central Ohio Railroad, at that time running from Zanesville to Columbus. Then he was given an engine, and for twenty years after followed the responsible calling of a railroad engineer.

When the civil war broke out he was in Martinsburg, Va., and was forced into the confederate service. He soon deserted, however, and escaping to the North entered the One Hundred and Eighth Ohio Volunteers, with which he did faithful work for the Union cause. His knowledge of engineering was of service to the government, and the young man was repeatedly the engineer for train loads of Union troops passing through dangerous parts of the South.

In 1874 he left his engine to take charge of the old National Theatre of this city. Three years were spent industriously in the interests of this erstwhile popular house, but in 1877 he sold out and went back to the "throttle." While a railroad man, Robinson was employed most of the time on the Baltimore and Ohio Railroad. In 1883 he began to travel for the French Furnace Company of Boston. About this time he invented the Robinson adjustable balanced valve for locomotives and stationary engines. Other inventions followed, and the lieutenant now receives a handsome royalty on his patents, about twenty in number.

Lieutenant Robinson went on the police force on July 14, 1886, as a patrolman in the First District. On August 22, of the same year, he was made sergeant, and transferred to the Eighth District. Two months after, he was again promoted and made a lieutenant in the "Oliver Street" District. On January 1, 1887, he went back to Corryville Station, where, with the exception of a few months spent in the Ninth District, he has since remained.

Lieutenant Robinson is the tallest man on the police force, his height being six feet four inches in his stocking feet. He is a thorough man of the world, his long and varied experiences having given him an education far beyond anything to be acquired from books.

Charles F. Geist was born August 10, 1861, in Cincinnati. He attended public school and the intermediate department, but left his books to take a position with the Western Union Telegraph Company. After spending two years in the telegraph service Geist was employed successively in the employ of Shapley, Stoover & Co., W. J. Littell & Co., F. Eckert & Co. On June 4, 1886, he was appointed on the police force, and assigned to the Third District. Eighteen months after, he was assigned to patrol squad 4, and on February 1, 1888, the young officer was made a sergeant of police.

Geist is a hard working, faithful officer and a credit to the force. He is unmarried. Among the "good collars" credited to the sergeant may be mentioned that of Lena Knect, the famous "piano woman," whom he once arrested and sent out to the "Works" for a long term.

Sergeant Thomas F. Bartley was born in 1855. He received an ordinarily good education, and, when he reached his majority, became a street-car conductor—an occupation which he followed for several years. On July 30, 1881, he was appointed on the Cincinnati Police Force. He was reappointed by the present Board on May 25, 1886, and on January 30, 1888, was promoted to the position of sergeant and assigned to the Eighth Police District, where he is at present located. Bartley is married, and lives on St. Clair street near Vine.

Sergeant Daniel Adams is of German parentage, and was born on June 18, 1884, in Cincinnati. He attended school in Storrs township until eleven years old, when he went to work in a saw-mill. Various occupations employed his time until the beginning of the Civil War, when he enlisted in the 79th Regiment Ohio Volunteers, Twentieth Army Corps. Adams returned from the war in 1865 and resumed his old place in a saw-mill. Here he worked for several years, serving as foreman a large part of the time. Then he became foreman in Louis & Milton Glenn's works, and, three years later, a sawyer at James Mack's mill.

On December 20, 1875, Adams went on the Cincinnati Police Force and served almost ten years, when he was discharged on account of his political views. He was reappointed on July 19,

SERGT. D. ADAMS. SERGT. J. GEIST.
SERGT. T. F. BARTLEY. LIEUT. E. ROBINSON.
Eighth District.

1886, and was made sergeant on December 20, 1887. He is now stationed in the Eighth District, where he was assigned July 1, 1888.

It is a peculiarity of the outlying districts in Cincinnati's scheme of police protection that they reach out into measurements that can only be compassed by resort to square miles as a basis of calculation. The Ninth or Sedansville district demonstrates this fact clearly. It extends from Mill Creek on the east, to what is known as Bold Face Creek on the west. The latter is an insignificant stream, the channel of which lies about midway between Sedansville and Riverside. To the north the boundary line is Fairmount's old corporate limits, and on the south the river. These lines embrace the heavy manufacturing and distilling interests, lying west of Mill Creek, much railroad property and all of the fast growing suburb of Price Hill, the extent of which is marked by Cedar Grove Academy. It is one of the old districts, and a study of the record of arrests shows the moral standard of the inhabitants to be above the average, for but few are made for any cause. This vast territory is competently patrolled by a force of twenty-eight men, three of whom are mounted and who remain at disposal until ten o'clock at night. The commissioned officers are Lieutenant Newton Kendall and Sergeants William Luekering, John Nealis and W. E. Watson. The lieutenant and senior sergeant stand the day watch.

Lieutenant Newton Kendall was born at Georgetown, O., on January 26, 1849. He received a good common school education and his parents early removed to Cincinnati. He was appointed on the police force May 4, 1880, under Mayor Jacob's administration, but was discharged on April 21, 1881, immediately after the election of Mayor Means. This dismissal was of course owing to political difference. During the two years following Kendall was a private watchman at the Highland House. He then became the proprietor of the "Black Horse Exchange," a famous resort in Fifth Street Horse Market. On October 28, 1886, Kendall was appointed on the police force again as patrolman, and was immediately promoted to the office of sergeant. On June 22, 1887, he was made lieutenant and is at present assigned to the Ninth District.

Among the many important arrests made by Kendall, may be mentioned John Coleman, "Kid" Walker, and Henry Schroder, for burglary; Mike and William Skully, for larceny; James Grant and Charley White, for cutting to kill, all of whom were convicted and sent to the Penitentiary.

Lieutenant Kendall is a tall, handsome man, quiet and gentlemanly in his manners. His intelligence and daring have made him one of the most valuable men on the force.

Of the sergeants, Luekering was made a patrolman for the Ninth District the 6th of May, 1886, and the ensuing August was raised to the rank he now holds. His name was among the first to be placed on the roll of honor for heroic conduct in stopping a runaway team at Freeman avenue and Findlay street, April 21, 1887; a woman with two little children, one an infant in a perambulator, was directly in the way of the flying horses. A street car had stopped her progress and to attempt to go back was death. The officer saw the danger, and placing himself in the road seized the reins as the frantic animals rushed by. He was dragged from his feet. The iron-shod hoofs of one of the horses struck him in the breast and side, seriously injuring him, but he held to the advantage he had gained. The injury confined him to the house for some time, and now he declares that he has had all the experience he desires in that line. Luekering was born the 8th of October, 1849, and was prepared for life as a molder. He drifted into the army, where he was a member of the 8th U. S. Cavalry. He is married and rejoices in the possession of three children.

John J. Nealis, the second sergeant, was born in this city the 14th of January, 1861, and now at the age of 27 years is one of the youngest men on the force. He won distinction early. He was admitted to the ranks as a patrolman the 19th of June, 1886, reporting from the First to the Ninth District Station. He was made sergeant in November of the same year.

William Edward Watson is a Cincinnatian by birth and education. He was born on Laurel street, on June 13, 1854. After attending the public schools for a few years, Watson, at the age of fourteen, left his city home to become a farmer boy. Nearly

LIEUT. N. KENDALL.
SERGT. W. LEUKERING.   SERGT. W. WATSON.   SERGT. J. J. NEALIS.
Ninth District.

five years were spent in Butler county, Ohio, engaged in this arduous but healthful occupation, after which he returned to Cincinnati and went into the pork-packing business in the establishment of Simms & Enyart, Race and Canal streets. Young Watson worked faithfully here for four years, and then returned to farming, choosing Clark county, Ohio, as his home. In the spring of 1883 he went to Dakota and became the foreman of a large wheat farm in that territory, but after seven months he tired of the monotonous life and the freezing climate, and returned once more to Cincinnati. On July 2, 1886, he was appointed a patrolman, and ran a beat in Central District until December 12, 1887, when he was promoted to a sergeantcy and transferred to the "Oliver street" District. Thence, in February, 1888, Watson was removed to the Ninth District, where, with the exception of four months spent in Chief of Detectives Hazen's office during the progress of the Centennial Exposition, he has remained.

Watson has a well-filled "record-book," which bears the name of many a crook of note who has fallen into the hands of this nervy young officer. Among them is that of "Nat" Mason, a well-known thief, who has spent two long terms in the penitentiary.

The history of the police force as connected with the territory comprised in Cumminsville, properly begins in 1873, when this suburb became a part of Cincinnati. Before this time there was a so-called police force, consisting latterly of a marshal and two assistants. These officers had little to do except on Sundays or holidays, when large, boisterous crowds would gather in front of the old Millcreek House, then a favorite resort for the citizens, sporting and otherwise, of Cincinnati. The huge old building, which still stands a hundred feet back from Spring Grove avenue, has been the scene of many a wrestling match, its lawn the scene of sprint-races, or cock-fights. But now it appears lonely by day and ghostly by night. It has had its day, and soon its walls will be razed and a building more modern in style will take its place.

The building at the corner of Spring Grove avenue and Hoffner street, now occupied as a station-house, was first used for police purposes in 1868. During the term of Gabriel Dirr as Mayor of Cumminsville, the building was leased from the Spring Grove Avenue Railway Company. Two or three cells were placed in the cellar below the structure, but these were scarcely ever used, as, for the last twenty years, Cumminsville has been quiet and peaceable. When Cumminsville was annexed to Cincinnati its territory became the Tenth Police District. The same old building has been used since it was leased in 1868. Three years ago an addition was built to it and cells placed above ground. The quaint old structure was built by one Ephraim Knowlton, a rich grocer, as a lodge-house to his premises, on which still stands the palatial mansion which he with his family occupied for so many years. Knowlton sold the premises to the Spring Grove Avenue Railway Company.

There are at present twenty-two officers and patrolmen in the Tenth District—two lieutenants, two sergeants, two station-house keepers, and sixteen patrolmen. The district is bounded as follows: Commencing north of Addison Street and Camp Washington; east to Miami Canal; northwardly to Spring Grove Cemetery, to Linden avenue, to Dane street; north on Dane to Corporation line; west to West Fork creek, south to Mill creek, to Addison street.

Lieutenant William Heheman was born on June 7, 1855, in a house which stood at Fifth and Vine streets on the site of the present Wiggin's Block. His parents, who were Germans, came to this country when young. Young Heheman was sent to school at the Holy Trinity Church on Fifth street, but when twelve years old left his studies and worked three months as a baker's apprentice; then he became a bill clerk in D. F. Woodruff's iron-store on Race street, where he worked five years, leaving it to enter the employ of the Mosler Safe Company. After two years he became a shipping clerk at Woodrow and Stewart's wholesale railroad supply house, and three years later passed the examination which made him one of the "finest." This was on July 1, 1883, during Mayor Stephen's administration. Heheman ran the old River Road beat in the Ninth District for nine months, and was then made a sergeant. Ten months later he was transferred to Hammond Street Station, and after five months' service, to Central Station, where, after fourteen months' service, he was made lieutenant. In this capacity, Heheman now served two months each in the First, Third, Fourth and Fifth Districts, and after other short transfers was placed at the Tenth District a year ago, where he still remains. Heheman has served under fifteen different lieutenants.

Lieutenant Heheman had one "uncanny" experience which is worth relating. It was on a dark, rainy night in November, 1887, that he was making his rounds, when at Eighth street and Freeman avenue, he noticed a light moving around in a house near by. As it was about three o'clock A. M., the officer's suspicions were naturally aroused, and stealing across the street and up the steps, he stooped down beside the stairs and awaited developments. Shortly the light appeared and Heheman saw at the head of the stairs a man, white-faced and of wild appearance, approaching him.

"What are you doing here?" cried the officer, suddenly rising from his stooping posture.

"Hush! Do not disturb me; my daughter lies dead in that parlor."

Heheman apologized and went away. Thinking it over, he became suspicious and walked back to the house.

"Here again?" said the bereaved father, who was still wandering aimlessly about, carrying the lamp.

"Yes," replied Heheman; "how do I know you are straight? I am an officer." And he exposed his uniform, hidden under his rubber coat and hat. "Show me the dead girl."

"Willingly," was the grave answer. Slowly a side door was opened and the man approached a long, narrow object, which rested on a bier in the centre of the room. It was a coffin, and in it lay the dead girl.

"I am satisfied," muttered Heheman, and he left at once. He walked only a short distance, however; a superstitious interest seemed to hold him to the place.

Pretty soon he saw a man walking hastily along the pavement opposite, with some object trailing behind him. Approaching,

Heheman found that the man was carrying a ladies' circular cloak, and that his pockets were loaded with silverware. Before he could reach the thief, however, the latter pulled his gun and stuck it under Heheman's nose. After threatening the officer's life if he made any "breaks" the thief again started off, but too late. The lieutenant's turn had come; he had the drop, and the burglar was taken to the station. The prisoner was found to be Thos. Barry, *alias* Wm. Eggleston, a desperate burglar. Barry was given a fine of $200 and six months in the "Works" for carrying concealed weapons, and was afterwards indicted and sent to the penitentiary for four years on a charge of receiving stolen goods.

Lieutenant Heheman is stalwart, active, and in the prime of life. He has brown hair and keen gray eyes.

Sergeant William Krumpe was born October 24, 1862, on Stark street, Cincinnati. He received a liberal education, passing through the public schools and the intermediate departments, and attending Hughes High School for a period. He left his books when fourteen to learn the painter's trade, first entering the shops of the Spring Grove Avenue Railway Company. Here and in the shops of the Consolidated Railway Company he spent six years, and then worked four more years in the Cincinnati, Hamilton & Dayton Railroad shops. On October 16, 1886, Krumpe was appointed on the police force, and was assigned a beat in Corryville. On November 8th of the same year he was transferred to Cumminsville, where he has since remained. The young man was made a sergeant on July 1, 1887.

Krumpe has been for the most part assigned to outlying districts, and cannot, therefore, count so many arrests as if he had served in down-town districts, where crime is more common. Still he has made a good record. Among his arrests was that of Henry Kahan, a burglar, who was wanted in Clinton county for robbing a farmer's house. Sergeant Krumpe is of medium height, well built, and of determined character.

Sergeant Michael Rigney was born on Baymiller street, near Court, Cincinnati, May 11, 1861, and was educated both in the public and parochial schools of the city. When but fifteen years old, owing to the loss of his father, he was obliged to earn his

SERGT. M. RIGNEY.   SERGT. J. W. WINTERS.
SERGT. W. H. KRUMPE.   LIEUT. WM. HEHEMAN.
Tenth District.

own livelihood, which he did at first in a daily market, and later, as an iron moulder, in the Blymyer Manufacturing Company. With this company he remained till May 24, 1886, when Mayor Smith appointed him a patrolman. His first service was in the Sedamsville District, where he attracted sufficient attention to invite a promotion, which came in the form of a sergeantcy, in February, 1888. He was then transferred to the Cumminsville District. Sergeant Rigney has a good future before him, if it is to be judged by his fidelity in the past.

John Winters was born in Rushville, Indiana, June 13, 1848. When but ten days old he was brought by his parents to this city. For the six years previous to going on the police force, he worked in a fire-kindling factory. On the 4th of December, 1886, he was appointed to the force and assigned to the Fourth District, where he remained until the 1st of July, 1887, when he was appointed a sergeant and assigned to the Ninth District. On the 10th of February, 1888, he was transferred to the Tenth or Cumminsville District, where he has been ever since.

GHOULS AND THEIR WORK.

The robbing of the grave of the father of General Benjamin Harrison, President of the United States, and the sensational developments in the finding of the body in the Ohio Medical College, was the ghastly event that led to the passage of an Ohio law regulating the manner in which medical colleges should be provided with material for dissection.

On Saturday, May 25, 1878, John Scott Harrison, son of General William Henry Harrison, was found dead in his bedroom at the old homestead, below North Bend. On the twenty-seventh his mortal remains were interred under the shadow of the tomb of "Old Tippecanoe," his father. Public apprehension had already been aroused by the robbing of graves, and even the vicinity of North Bend had suffered. As an extra precaution, the grave was dug to an unusual depth, carefully walled up with brick, and when partially filled, a large stone, which required several men to handle, was placed over the metallic case, and the whole covered with cement, then a guard was placed over the grave, to be kept there thirty days.

But only the day after, the grave of a young man named August Devins, only a few feet from that of John Scott Harrison, was rifled of its contents. John Harrison, a brother of General Benjamin Harrison, and George Eaton, a nephew, at once proceeded to Cincinnati on a hunt for the stolen body. With a search warrant, and accompanied by Detective Tom Snelbaker, Constable Walter Lacy, and Deputy Constable Cullen, they went to the Ohio Medical College and began a thorough examination, which they were about to abandon, finding nothing, when Snelbaker discovered a windlass and rope. The rope ran down through a long chute to the cellar. The detective took hold of the rope. It was taut.

"Here's somebody!" he exclaimed, and began to turn the crank. Finally a naked body came to view, suspended by the neck at the end of the rope, and it was laid on the floor. The face and head were wrapped up in an old tattered shirt.

"That is not the man!" said John Harrison. "The young man was a consumptive, and terribly emaciated," and, sickened at the sight, he turned to leave the place. Snelbaker advised him to have the head uncovered to leave no doubt. Harrison assented, when the cloth was removed. The face of an old man was then laid bare, with closely cropped white beard. There were bruises about the head and body from the rough handling in dragging from the grave, and the face was discolored from the hanging. It was a pitiful, horrible sight. Suddenly the son's face blanched with an awful suspicion, which grew to certainty, and he moaned, "It's father!" reeled, and would have fallen but for the assistance of his companions.

It was the desecrated remains of an honored father whom he had seen buried but a day or two before. The remains were removed to an undertakers. General Ben., his brother, and Carter Harrison were summoned; the janitor of the college and his assistant were arrested, and the best detective talent in the country was secured. Meantime the remains were removed to North Bend and reinterred. The Harrisons spared no expense to find the desecrators of their father's grave, and the matter was investigated by the Grand Jury and County Prosecutor Lewis

W. Irwin. The janitor and assistant were, however, finally discharged from custody, as no evidence against them could be found. The grave robbers were never caught.

In crime's vocabulary there is no word fraught with more meaning than is that derived from the name of a man who on January 27, 1829, was hanged in Edinburgh, Scotland. The word is "burking;" the name of the man, William Burke. In an old book printed in Philadelphia in 1839, and containing "accounts of celebrated trials and remarkable cases of jurisprudence," a history of the awful crime of Burke is fully set forth. From that history the following extract is made:

" The trial of Burke and of his mistress, the McDougal woman, took place in December, 1828, before the Right Honorable the Lord Justice Clerk and Lords Pitmilly, Meadowbank, and Mackenzie. At twenty minutes to ten the prisoners were brought in from the Tolbooth Prison, and placed at the bar.

Burke was a native of Ireland, rather below the middle size, and stout, and was of a determined, though not particularly sinister expression of countenance. He had high cheek bones, gray eyes, sunk in the head, a short snub nose, a round chin, hair and whiskers of a light sandy color, and a complexion of nearly the same hue. His companion was of the middle size, but thin and spare, though of large bone. Her features were long, and the upper half of her face was out of proportion to the lower. She was miserably clad. And this twain were arraigned under an indictment for a crime until then unknown—that of killing people for the purpose of selling their bodies for dissection. The indictment, stripped of some of its legal verbiage, reads:

1. On one of the days between the 7th and 16th of April, 1828, within the house in Gibb's Close, Canongate, Edinburgh, that "you, the said William Burke, did wickedly and feloniously place your body or person, or part thereof, over or upon the breast or person and face of Mary Paterson or Mitchell, who was lying in the said house in a state of intoxication, and by covering her mouth and nose with your body or person, and forcibly compressing her throat with your hands, and forcibly keeping her down, notwithstanding her resistance, preventing her from breath-

ing, you did suffocate or strangle her, and Mary Paterson or Mitchell was wickedly bereaved of her life by you, William Burke; and this you did with the wicked aforethought of disposing of, or selling the body of Mary Paterson or Mitchell to a physician or surgeon, or some person in the employment of a physician or surgeon as a subject for dissection.

2. Further, that between the 5th and 26th days of October, 1828, within a house in Tanner's Close, Portsburgh, Edinburgh, occupied by William Haire or Hare, you, William Burke, did then and there wickedly and feloniously assault James Wilson, commonly known as "Daft Jamie," and throw yourself upon him, he having sprung up, and you did struggle with him and bring him to the ground. The indictment goes on to describe the same method of lying across the victim's face and strangling him, and for the purpose of selling the body.

3. Further, that on the 31st of October, 1828, in the house occupied by Burke in Portsburg, Edinburgh, you, William Burke and Helen McDougal, did wickedly and feloniously place or lay your bodies upon the person and face of Madgy, or Margery, or Mary McGonegal, and by grasping her throat, and keeping her mouth and nostrils shut, did suffocate or strangle her, with the wicked aforethought and intent of disposing of or selling the body for purposes of dissection.

So Burke made a business of it, and it came to be called Burking.

The Lord Advocate chose the last indictment for the first proceeding, as it implicated both prisoners.

In this trial the man Hare, in whose house Burke had murdered "Daft Jamie," and who, no doubt, was in collusion with Burke, told how he had suffocated the woman. Burke brought her into the house himself and plied her with rum until she was intoxicated. He had invited the witness that afternoon to come down and see the "shot" he had for the doctors, and he went. The old woman fell or was pushed over a stool. She was too drunk to get up further than on her elbow. Burke stood astride of her a moment, and then laid himself down upon her, his breast being over her head; she cried, and then moaned a little.

He put one hand on her nose and mouth and the other under her chin and stopped her breathing. This was continued for ten or fifteen minutes, when she appeared quite dead. Hare was all the while sitting on a chair, looking on. Burke then stripped the body of its clothes, and put it in a corner under some straw. The wife of Hare and the McDougal woman ran into the passage way when they heard the old woman's first moan. They did not see the killing, but knew it was going on. The body was removed by a surgeon's porter the next morning.

Burke was convicted and sentenced to be hanged on the 28th of January, 1829. The woman McDougal was acquitted. Burke confessed in jail to the murder of Mary Paterson and Daft Jamie, and several others, and likewise implicated Hare.

All Edinburgh came to see the hanging of this monster, and the windows and tops of the houses about the place of execution were black with people. As the hangman was about to adjust the rope shouts arose of "Burke him! Burke him! Give him no rope!" And there were cries of "Hare! Hare! Where is Hare? Hang Hare! Burke Hare, too!" When the culprit was cut down one general and tremendous huzza was given, and the crowd dispersed.

The crime thus given a name in Scotland soon found its way into this country, and finally into this city or its immediate vicinity.

On the night of Friday, February 15, 1884, a little cabin on the Blachley farm, just at the outskirts of the village of Avondale, was discovered to be on fire, and before anybody could reach the spot it was almost totally destroyed. It had been occupied by a negro family, consisting of Beverly Taylor, his wife, Elizabeth, and Emma Jane Lambert, a little adopted daughter, eleven years of age. The cabin belonged to Mr. Mills, of Avondale, of whom Taylor rented, and he was about the first to discover the flames and to hasten thither. No trace of the family could be found. It was at first supposed that the members were away at the time of the fire, and that their whereabouts would shortly develop. But the next day they did not make their appearance; nothing was heard concerning them, and so a search was instituted among the ruins. The ashes were thoroughly sifted by Marshal Joseph A. Brown, of Avondale, his assistant Walter Lynch, and neighbors without result. The Taylors had a married daughter, a Mrs. McCrea, living in Cincinnati. Inquiries of her were also fruitless. Her father had not been to see her for some days. The old man had been observed about the premises the evening of the tragedy, and five persons, presumed to be negroes, had also been seen prowling about the place by Mrs. John P. Murphy and her brother, who were walking out to their home in Bond Hill, three miles beyond. The lady had expressed her fear of the prowlers, but her brother had reassured her by saying that he was armed. They had passed the spot about ten o'clock, and were walking out from the end of the street car line.

Marshal Brown at last hit upon the idea that the Taylor people had been murdered for dissection material. He went to the medical colleges and made known his suspicions. Dr. Cilley, of the Ohio Medical College, told him that no such bodies had been brought to the institution in which he was interested, when, discouraged, the marshal went home. Subsequently the doctor remembered that two negroes had brought, in an express wagon, three bodies to the college at eleven o'clock on Friday night, and that he had agreed to give them fifteen dollars a piece for them and no questions asked, as was the custom. The negroes were not known to him except as "Jack" and "Harrison." Dr. Cilley had examined the bodies and noticed that they were considerably bruised, which he had at first attributed to rough handling in shipping. Still he was not led to suspect foul play, and he so informed the marshal. The marshal looked at the remains and instantly identified them. Coroner Muscroft was notified, and ordered a *post mortem* examination, which was made by Drs. Cilley, Kebler, and Walker. They found wounds about the heads, and discovered that the skulls were fractured. Marshal Brown's suspicions fell upon a colored man by the name of Allen Ingalls, a laborer, who had been known to furnish medical colleges with bodies for dissection. Only a year before the body of a young man had been found in a wild place called "The Devil's Hole," near the Zoological Garden. There was a bullet hole through the head. Ingalls had been seen skulking in the vicinity of the body, and it was then supposed that he knew of its whereabouts and was watching a chance to remove it. This negro, Ingalls, had assisted in the search among the ashes for the remains of the Taylor family. The more Marshal Brown watched him the more certain was he that he knew something about the crime. Ingalls was at last arrested on suspicion on the Thursday evening following the cabin fire. The same evening the marshal caused the arrest of Jeff Lout, a cousin of Ingalls' wife, Richard Ingalls, a brother of Allen, and one Ben Johnson, all of whom occupied the same house with Ingalls on South Crescent street, Avondale. Johnson gave the most satisfactory account of himself, and was the least suspected. Marshal Brown was positive, however, he had the guilty among the four. He then appealed to Colonel Reilly, chief of the city police, for assistance, and Detective Jim White was detailed on the case at four o'clock Friday afternoon. Then Dr. Cilley gave the detective the important information as to who the expressman was who had brought the bodies to the college. His name was Robert B. Dixon, then living at 434½ West Fifth street, and he, too, was arrested. He aid he could identify the negroes who had hired him to haul the bodies in from Avondale, where they were lying in bags in a fence corner. Dixon was taken to the Avondale jail by Detective White, and suddenly brought face to face with Ingalls, whom he instantly recognized as the man who had hired him. Ingalls weakened, and admitted that Ben Johnson was his accomplice. Johnson was also made to face Dixon, and he too was recognized, when, throwing up his hands in terror, he exclaimed, "You've got me! You've got me!"

This was remarkably quick work. The marshal had bagged the right men in less than a week. Detective Jim White had been detailed at four o'clock P. M. on Friday, a few hours later had arrested Dixon and taken him to the Avondale town hall, where the prisoners were confined, and at eleven o'clock the evening of the same day, just one week from the hour of the delivery of the bodies to the college, the burkers had confessed their guilt.

On the next day, Saturday, Ben Johnson confessed to Sheriff Hawkins and a reporter. He said "Jack" was the name Ingalls went by at the college, and that his assumed name was "Harrison." They had called on the Taylor family about four P. M. on the fatal Friday, when Ingalls told old man Taylor that he would bring him some good whisky that night, and Taylor, who was crippled with rheumatism, seemed greatly pleased. Ingalls then went down town and, as he afterwards confessed, hired the expressman, Dixon, to meet him on the Avondale road about nine o'clock at the last lamp-post. This was near the cabin. About half-past six o'clock, Johnson said, he and Ingalls stole up to the cabin, and through the window saw the three victims sitting about the fire-place. Ingalls took a heavy club from one of the bags he had brought, and together they opened the door and rushed in. Ingalls struck the old woman first, then the old man, and lastly the little girl. The onslaught was so terrible and sudden that the victims did not have time to move. The old man tried to rise after being struck, but he (Johnson) forced him back and choked him, and Ingalls finished the bloody work by hitting them all several additional blows. The bodies were then stripped, placed in the bags, and taken to a fence corner near by to await the wagon, which came up about 9.30. The bodies were thrown in, and Ingalls, lighting his pipe, got in and sat on one of the sacks and smoked during the ride to the college. Johnson's confession was corroborated by Ingalls, but at the preliminary hearing in the town hall he pleaded "not guilty." Johnson pleaded "guilty," and the two were then committed to the county jail. On April 17, 1884, the grand jury indicted both men for murder in the first degree. Ingalls, however, cheated the gallows, and hanged himself to the bars of his cell window with a strip of blanket a few days later. Johnson was tried in one of the little sheds built for court-rooms about the jail, convicted, and was hanged.

CHAPTER XVII.

THE ROGUES' GALLERY—A UNIQUE DESCRIPTION OF A DEPARTMENT WHICH OFTEN FURNISHES THE UNMISTAKABLE TRAIL—THE PART INSTANTANEOUS PHOTOGRAPHY IS TO PLAY IN POLICE BUSINESS—HOW IT CAN DEFEAT THE ROGUES WHO OBJECT TO HAVING THEIR "MUGS" PLACED ON FILE.

The thought of being compelled to undergo the process of being photographed for the Rogues' Gallery is next to falling in the hands of his sworn enemies, the police—the *bete noir* of the professional. So obstinately fixed is this feeling in his mind that in most cases, when it lies within his power, he will resist such a proceeding until every physical method of defeating it is exhausted, and in many instances his resistance is successful, much to the disgust of the patient operator. Dragged in the posing chair and deprived by the strength of his captors of all power to struggle, it is a favorite device to resort to the exasperating expedient of distorting his features by muscular contractions, and thus prevent the anxious officers handing his features down to future generations as a perpetuation of his infamy. From the standpoint of the criminal such resistance is highly commendable, for the photograph is one of the most powerful instruments in the hands of the police to compass his arrest and to deter him from future depredations in the place where his features are thus made familiar to the officers of the law.

It is the rule, and there are but few exceptions, that it is only the professional criminal who thus resists the efforts of the police, and his reasons are given above. The novice in the paths of crime, who, upon committing an offence, perhaps his first, is deemed worthy of posing for a picture for future reference, generally does not comprehend the true magnitude of the operation or else gives way to the universal vanity of the human kind, and poses to the best advantage. Oftentimes it has been noted that this feeling has so far mastered them as to impel the asking of the question whether or not the picture was a good one. Especially is this true of the female criminal, and an imperfect likeness, detracting from their beauty, as the unfinished photographs for the gallery generally do, is received with natural anger.

Under the present administration the photographs of criminals are secured in the ordinary way patronized by the public. It having been determined that a picture is wanted of a person in custody, he is marched between a couple of officers to a patrol wagon and driven to an up-town photograph gallery. Entering through a private passage, used only by the police, the subject is ushered into the operating-room through a rear door. Unless notified in advance, it is often the first intimation that he has of the forthcoming operation. If it be distasteful to him he is informed that, if necessary, coercion will be used, and is advised to submit without resistance in order to avoid the hard knocks that are sure to follow. Two plates are then exposed, the subject being taken with his hat and with uncovered head, the same rule being followed with women. Should the subject prove refractory a scene occurs, the officers striving to hold the struggling criminal until the operator can secure a good picture and the criminal striving equally as hard to prevent it. Thus it continues until one or the other is defeated.

Although the instantaneous process of photography has been developed so far that it has become practical to the highest degree, yet it has not been introduced into this important branch of police service beyond a few isolated cases of attempts at "snapping" the faces of refractory prisoners by enthusiastic amateurs, which uniformly proved lamentable failures. It has been suggested to the Police Commissioners to put into operation a secret camera, which can be so situated that the photograph of a criminal can be taken without his knowledge, or even without giving rise to a suspicion in his mind that he is undergoing that dreaded ordeal. It is claimed for it that a natural expression, or a variety of them, can be secured in contradistinction to the fixed stare of the usual photograph. The cost of establishing and maintaining such an apparatus would be small indeed in comparison to the valuable aid it would be to the department.

Whence came that singularly appropriate title, the Rogues' Gallery? Its inventor is not known, but the felicity of the appellation is simply charming. It came, of course, with the invention of Daguerre, for the annals of crime do not show a single case where the painter's art was summoned to assist in securing the features of criminals for record purposes, and no doubt it will last as long as the camera. As previously stated, it is one of the most powerful engines in the service of the law for the detection and prevention of crime. It is a fundamental principle that law was made not to punish but to prevent crime, and in fulfilling this laudable end the Rogues' Gallery is peculiarly effective. Under the mutual agreement existing between the police departments of |the leading large cities of the United States, copies of the pictures of dangerous criminals are exchanged and kept on file in the Rogues' Galleries, where the local detectives have constant access to them. Constant scrutiny enables the officers to become familiar with the faces before him, and the features of the criminal is stamped indelibly on his mind to be recalled by the sight of the original on meeting with it.

Thus it will be seen that the motive of the professional criminal in resisting the process of being photographed is a powerful one, for it practically has the effect of introducing him to thousands of men whose hands are against him during life, and his constant fear when at liberty is that he will be recognized and arrested because of the fact that his picture is in the Rogues' Gallery, and that therefore it is dangerous for him to be at large. As the latter is often the case, the value of the photograph in preventing crime will be recognized, as the old adage says: "An ounce of prevention is worth a pound of cure."

The popular idea of a Rogue's Gallery is a very crude one, caused, no doubt, by the general unacquaintance with the inside workings of the police machine. The impression that prevails most, formed, no doubt, by the notion of a photograph gallery, is a large room, the walls of which are covered with the pictures of criminals. Nothing could be more remote from the thing as it exists. In the office of the chief of police are two wooden cabinets, each six feet in height by four in width. One is fastened to the wall, while opposite it, at the other side of the room, the other stands upright. The standing cabinet has glazed doors opening from the center, while the other, of more improved design, has a solid door swinging from the side. The keys secured from Private Secretary Draper, for the cabinets are always locked, the doors are swung open, revealing one hundred pictures. These are of the size known as *carte de visite*, and are slipped into slanting grooves in vertical strips fastened to the leaf which is hinged to the door outside. The picture desired can be taken out by merely lifting it from the grooves. Should a picture further inside the case be wanted, the leaves can be swung outwardly like those of a book until the desired one is found. In other words, the cabinet contains a huge book, filled with pictures, and resembles the familiar album of the parlor. The wall cabinet is designed after that in use in New York, and can receive two thousand pictures.

On the upper right hand corner of each card is gummed a tiny tag, bearing a number written in indelible ink. This number corresponds to a similar one in a record kept by the chief's private secretary. The book is a valuable adjunct to the gallery, which would be almost useless without it. As to the working of the gallery. When a criminal is ushered into the presence of Secretaries Draper and Byrne, after being photographed, his appearance is carefully noted, and a printed blank corresponding in size to the photograph card, is filled out with a description of the subject, and a brief synopsis of his crime. In order that its worth may be comprehended a *fac-simile* is given:

Name—John Smith, *alias* Newman.
Born—England (London).
Residence—Cincinnati, O.
Age—Thirty-five years.
Weight—167 pounds.
Height—5 feet 9 inches.
Eyes—Hazel.
Hair—Brown.
Beard—None.
Mustache—Brown.

ROGUES' GALLERY.

Complexion—Dark.
Build—Heavy.
Occupation—Blacksmith.
Married—Yes.
Date of arrest—January 3, 1889.
Arrested by—Detective Hazen.
Charge—Burglary.
Sentence—Fourteen years in Ohio Penitentiary.
Photo. taken—January 4, 1889.
Marks—Right hand deformed by burn; mole on neck, near left ear; size shoe, $7\frac{1}{2}$; hat, 7.

This slip is gummed to the back of the card, and serves as a ready guide to the identity of the criminal, and dispenses with an examination of the bulkier record. In the latter is kept a more complete discription, and a brief history of the criminal acts for which the offender has been arrested. In order to keep this record abreast of the times, the utmost care and constant watchfulness is required, additions being made as the criminal runs his eventful career. An evil to be guarded against, is overcrowding with useless pictures. The gallery contains at present, 1,725 pictures of various lawbreakers of this and other cities, and even countries, who are still in the land of the living. When the fact that a criminal, whose picture is in the gallery, is known to have died or "croaked," as the slang of his pals would term it, the card is taken down as being of no further value. It is laid away as a relic, and the vacant space filled with the counterfeit presentment of a newer and possibly more dangerous member of the great family of criminals. Thus only the useful is retained as in the business world, where the survival of the good is the rule. To illustrate the manner in which the gallery performs its silent work. A citizen hurries excitedly into the chief's office, aud declares that a few moments before a daring thief entered his store, and stole a valuable package of goods

" The rascal did it before my very eyes;" he exclaims, " why, sir, his impudence stunned me."

" Then you saw him did you?" asks the Superintendent.

" Certainly I saw him; why he—

"Would you know him if you again met him?" interrupts the chief.

"I think I would" replies the latter, looking about him as if to recognize the fellow in the silent clerks.

"Well, then, step this way," remarks the chief as he gives an order to open the cabinets. Face after face is scanned until at last, perhaps, the victim explodes with, "There's the villian; I swear it."

The secretary merely extracts the picture, glances at the number, and then turning it over, reads, "John Smith, daylight sneak and burglar."

"So it's Johnnie is it?" asks the chief, "well sir, we'll have your man shortly." A call, and a detective enters. To him the chief speaks: "Here is a picture of a thief who robbed this gentleman. It's John Smith."

"Oh yes; I know him well," returns the officer.

"Get a warrant for his arrest, and bring him in at once" comes the command.

The next morning the robbed confronts the robber in the Police Court, and after sentence has been inflicted the latter goes slowly to his cell, ruminating on the vicissitudes of life, and wondering how it was that he was found out so quickly after the commission of the offense. Again the mail brings a photograph of a criminal, who is wanted in another city, together with a letter of advice regarding the criminal's haunts. It is given to a detective, and within a day or two the fugitive is trapped and returned to the scene of his crime. At another time a picture will be received with the announcement that the original of it is held on suspicion, and a query as to whether his identity is known. The secretary compares it with the thousand in his case and discovers mayhap a similar card. Within an hour the telegraph flashes back a message that may read as follows: "man referred to is Charles *alias* 'Blinky' Morgan. Arrested here in May, 1886, for housebreaking. Is wanted in New York for same offense." Within twenty-four hours an officer is ready to start from that city, armed with a warrant for the luckless lawbreaker, who bitterly curses the hour his "face was given up to the coppers," as he terms the procuring of his picture.

The gallery at police headquarters has been greatly improved within the past three years, and is now up to the highest grade of excellence in that line. Hundreds of pictures of thieves with traveling propensities have been added, and the faces of many "crooks" of national reputation secured.

A few selections embrace those of Horace Hoven *alias* "Little Horace" and Wm. Thompson *alias* "Slimmy" Williams, two "bank sneaks," recently arrested for the robbery of the People's Bank of Denver, Col.; "Old man" Yowell and his gang of educated pickpockets, captured at the Columbus Exposition; Sophy Lyons *alias* "Levy," whose reputation is international, her exploits having been sounded even in the French capital. She was arrested here twice within the past ten years, the last time being in 1886. A more skillful and daring shop-lifter and blackmailer never lived. "Molly Matches," the *alias* of John Larney, a gifted pickpocket, and bank sneak also appears in it. It was here that he was arrested and from here he was sent to Galesburg, Ill., to answer for a robbery of a bank there, getting ten years in prison. "Little Louise" Jordan *alias* Bigelow, a noted female pickpocket, beams complacently from beside her companion, Mrs. Anderson, also a pickpocket. They were arrested in May, 1886, and escaped through the medium of a straw bond. Both are noted the country over for their deeds. "Old Man," or John Dennis, a hoary-headed thief, whose repeated robberies of hotels has given him a national reputation, is an occupant of a niche, while his confrere in crime and equal in years, Theophilus George, the leader of a clever gang of pickpockets, captured in President Cleveland's train at Atlanta, Ga., appears in another. Two of Sophy Lyons' pupils, George Moore and Frank Smith, arrested in St. Louis with her, occupy places near her photograph. The likeness of Victor F. Ward, a notorious scoundrel, who was a finished swindler when the war began, is a recent addition. He was captured in this city last summer, while working a swindling scheme, and his venerable features now adorn the gallery. The pictures of the murderers, Berner and Palmer, who caused the famous riot of 1884, two boyish faces, look out from the old cabinet side by side. Then there are "Dayton Sammy," a pickpocket; "Red" Austin and "Dave" Murray, noted confidence men; "Red" Heyl, a noted burglar; Etta Lewis, the "typewriter," a daring girl swindler and confidence woman; "Shang" Campbell, an Eastern pickpocket of high degree; "Bart" Kelly, a sleeping car and hotel thief; "Bob" Crawford, a hotel sneak; Billy Hoolihan, *alias* "Sutton," a safe blower; "Dutch" Alonzo, a noted pickpocket; Kate Fitzgerald, a kidnapper, who stole a child in this city many years ago; George Gardner, *alias* "Miller," an accomplished confidence man; Jim Anderson, a solitary safe blower and burglar of local fame; Mrs. Christianna Anderson, a diamond robber; Lizzie Dugan and Mary Smith, New York "pennyweighters," or jewelry store sneaks, now in the Columbus penitentiary; "Horsehead Bill" Barnet, an aged but active safe blower; "Bob" Wright, general thief and murderer of a woman in this city; William and Josie Freefield, confidence operators from Boston; George Norris, a "hoister" or male shop-lifter and jewelry sneak; Ed. Sloan, *alias* Freeman, a highly educated and polished hotel and depot sneak thief; the "Galway Slugger," or Dan Callahan, a "strong-arm man," or safe blower's accomplice, who stands guard; Robert Milroy, a "change racket" operator and general thief; and Daniel Madden, a youth now serving a life sentence for a criminal assault on a little girl.

These are but a small fraction of the thousands shut in by the doors of the gallery, yet almost any one would form the subject for a romance of the criminal type. With the rapid progress of improvement in the photographic art, as regards instantaneity, and the recent introduction of the famous Bertillion system of bodily measurements, the art of obtaining a minute description of a marked man has received a notable impetus, and the day is not far distant when it will be impossible for the enemy of public property—the professional thief—to disguise himself so as to deceive his sworn enemy, the detective, aided as he is by that mute servant—the Rogues' Gallery.

CHAPTER XVIII.

THE POLICE REPORTER.—NECESSITY FOR VERSATILITY IN HIS MAKE UP.—ACTING IN THE ROLE OF CONSOLER AND DETECTIVE.—A VERITABLE GENERAL WHOSE ARMY IS MADE UP OF ONE MAN.

MANY other things might be overlooked in a history of the police department, with less loss than a sketch of what is termed "the police reporter." Journalists, from their self-raised pedestal, may view him as an insignificant and necessarily tolerated member of the great profession, but those familiar with newspaper work daily wonder how he survives the strain and manages to keep up with the surging rush of events. His range of subjects is wide—in fact, one might say with truth, almost boundless. A sudden call may take him to the slums, and he hardly has time to scrape the mud off his shoes before his business brings him in contact with some high dignitary or prominent social light. There is no time for preparation, coaching of manners or arrangement of dress. He is a minute man, and whatever the summons, he must obey with trained promptness and with a mind that moves with lightning rapidity. As he hurries along he must cast his programme. When he reaches the door, the introductory explanation must be at his tongue's end. Even more than that, he must have ready several plans of campaign. The person he is to see may be of an unapproachable nature, or perhaps there is something in the case that impels the interested parties to preserve silence. He must storm the citadel and break down this reserve. Probably he may encounter too much volubility, a readiness that is suggestive of bias and self-interest. This he must carefully sift, and then corroborate from other sources. He takes every chance on the kind of person he is to meet, and must be prepared for skillful parries as well as rude and positive rebuffs, for the police reporter's visits are rarely gratifying to the recipients. His paths lie mostly in the sinister shadows rather than among the flower gardens of life. Crime, tragedy and misfortune are the great monsters in whose footsteps he must follow and carefully note the work of sadness and horror. With the mourners he must mourn in order to loosen their tongues about some possible misdeeds of the deceased, and skillfully enwrapped by his expressions of sympathy is often a trap for the sorrowing relatives. He must buckle himself close to the criminal, and be ever on the alert for some admission of guilt, or slip of the tongue. Often he comes in conflict with persons as sharp as he, and then the edge of the famed Saracen's blade must be dull in comparison with the keenness of his mental weapons. The police reporter goes out with the assumption that every hand is against him, holding himself ready for a regular combine of circumstances to defeat him. He has but one object in view, and that to get the item. No matter what the physical labor or the galling insults, he must surmount every difficulty and submit to every affront until success has rewarded his efforts. The stern supervisor at the city editor's desk is a relentless master, with whom no explanations, excuse, or even palliate failure. In the bright lexicon of the police reporter there must be no such word. He must thread his way through the intricacies of a crime, give every movement of the criminal and reveal the motive, as if supernatural agencies were at his command, and he could read thought as easily as the child's primer. He must cross-examine with the adroitness of a legal wonder, and draw his conclusion with the consummate acumen of a judicious Solomon. Deeper even than the detectives must he delve into the hidden workings of crime, for within a few hours he is compelled to lay before the public not only a detailed account of the act, but an analysis of the motives and impulses. Gathering what he can from the movements of the authorities, he must outstrip them in the great effort to touch bottom and direct the machinery of justice. By the world he is considered a person without compassion, or how could he put in print the things that rend the heart-strings or bring shame to the household? The sufferer never considers that with the police reporter it is a matter of business, and that he would never have been called upon to exert his energies had not somebody else made the occasion. His best friend must be as a total stranger, for, in his duty to the paper he cannot shield the guilty, however close the bonds between them.

Of the horrors of life—those which are graphically described in the morning prints, and which a majority of the readers doubtless skip—he must be an eye-witness. While the vital fluid pours forth in a sickening flood, and the dying gasps come slower and slower, he is standing, figuratively, with his notebook in hand, chronicling every moan. When the body lies stretched upon the cold slab of the morgue or hospital, his eyes follow those of the surgeon as the knife of science cuts its horrid path through the soulless clay. His duty forces him to be present when the suicide's rope is cut, or the mutilated remains of the despondent mortal lie in all the horror of self-crime.

When the fire-bells call, it is imperative that he respond, for while the flames may not be dangerous to property, there is the ever-present liability of accident. The destruction of an insignificant shanty may develop into a holocaust. At the last moment unwary inmates may fall victims to their own carelessness, or brave firemen may perish in the fearful element they are fighting.

Such is the work of the police reporter and the responsibilities it carries. He has been spoken of as an individual. There are others just as keen as he—all anxious to get the best account of an event and "scoop" the contemporaries. Beyond and outside of his work in getting an item he must excel his fellow-workers in the same line. This may be done by sheer labor or skill, and if these means fail he must put on the fox's skin. He must be cunning as well as adept, sly as well as painstaking, and good fortune or luck must be a guardian spirit that illuminates his pathway and solves his difficulties.

The police reporter is justly held in high esteem at his office. There are not many who are envious of his position—but few take his assignment but with reluctance. Owing to its many responsibilities, the place calls for the best talent on the staff. Several of the police reporters have found their training so thorough and comprehensive as to enable them to step at a moment's notice into the highest of the editorial chairs.

With the police department the police reporter is necessarily closely identified. Often he is of valuable assistance in tracking a criminal or spreading the network for a capture. Sometimes, too, he is a check on the more exuberant of the force, who fear more to see their misdeeds spread forth by his trenchant pen, than to receive the stern admonitions of their superiors. It is also a fact that the reporter's praise is frequently more desired than the best of commendation the deserving officer can receive at headquarters.

It is a matter of pride that the information branch of the Police Department of this city is by far the most complete and trustworthy in the country. There can scarcely anything of a criminal nature occur that does not reach the authorities and the reporter at the same moment. While the energies of the former may be devoted to the capture of the criminal, those of the latter are bent on detailing the crime and unraveling any attendant mystery. The lines of both are cast together, and rarely is their work not in harmony. The reporter, forced to brave the most inclement weather and difficulties calculated to weaken the stoutest heart, knows how to appreciate the officer who is exposed to the same dangers and discouragements.

The leading dailies of Cincinnati have at police headquarters what is called a "day" and a "night" man. These two divide the twenty-four hours, and are expected to write up every accident or crime that occurs in the allotted space of time.

The present staff of reporters who attend to police business is equal to any that has ever represented the newspapers at police headquarters. They are all bright, active young men who cover that wide field of news completely. The *Commercial Gazette* and *Enquirer* have two men each—one for day stations, the other for the night run. The other papers are represented by one man each, none of them making such a specialty of police news. Following are the names of these reporters:

Commercial Gazette—(Day Stations), Edward H. Anthony. (Night Stations), James T. Gardiner.

Enquirer—(Day Stations), James W. Faulkner. (Night Stations), Charles Hodges.

Times-Star—Louis T. Heck.
Post—Walter Dunbar.
Volksblatt—Geza Berger.
Volksfreund—Gus. J. Karger.
Frei Presse—Charles Gerth.
Anzeiger—Alfred Reiser.

Mr. Anthony is a young man, barely past thirty, and has been in the newspaper business about eight years. He started in as an assignment reporter on the *Enquirer*, and distinguished himself by his remarkable clearness in detecting the aroma of a news item. Four years ago he left the *Enquirer* for the *Commercial*, and since that time has been constantly at day police work. He is also quite a politician, and now represents his district in the City Board of Aldermen.

Mr. Gardiner started his newspaper career with the *News Journal* seven years ago. He soon afterward became connected with the *Sun*, and after its demise was immediately offered a place on the *Commercial Gazette*. He left that paper for the *Enquirer*, but returned to it soon afterward, and has been doing the night-station work ever since. There is no more painstaking reporter than Mr. Gardiner. He knows a news item when he sees it, and will not rest until he has the full particulars in his possession. His style of writing is direct and connected rather than ornamental.

Mr. Faulkner has been a reporter for about four years, getting his first experience on the *Times-Star*. He gained his first reputation as a newspaper man by a series of brilliant dialect sketches, which were copied from one end of the country to the other. He left the *Times-Star* for the *Enquirer* two years ago, and has continued his good work. He is an excellent writer, and controls a style that can be graphically descriptive or very amusing, as he chooses.

Mr. Hodges has been connected with the *Enquirer* ever since his arrival here, five years ago. He came from Nashville, where he had been managing editor of the *American*. He has a wide acquaintance in police circles and is an excellent news-gatherer. He has profited by years of experience and has a minute acquaintance with police business.

Mr. Heck is a young newspaper man, starting in on the *Post* about two years ago—at the close of his college course. His special line is descriptive writing, and he has done some remarkably good work.

Mr. Walter Dunbar is also a young newspaper man, having been in the employ of the Scripp's league only a few years. He is a new accession to the corps of police reporters, but makes strong and frequently successful efforts to penetrate the secrets of Colonel Deitsch and Chief of Detectives Hazen.

Mr. Berger joined the staff of the *Volksblatt* three years and a half ago. He was born in Presburg, Austria, and began life as an actor. He drifted to America and became one of the great comedy stars of the German stage. He grew wearied of the constant travel which his profession involved and entered the newspaper business. He is one of the most talented writers on the *Volksblatt*, and does much of the fine German writing which appears in its columns.

Mr. Karger has been on the German press of this city about five years. He was originally a reporter for a German paper in Columbus. He is a man of excellent education, of wide reading, and writes good German. He began here as a reporter for the *Frei Presse*, but went to the *Volksfreund* a year ago.

Mr. Gerth was first employed as a reporter for the *Zeitung*, but about two years ago went to the *Frei Presse*. He gets all the police news for that paper and does it in a creditable manner.

Mr. Reiser, of the *Anzeiger*, has been police reporter for that paper for nearly three years. He is a man of pleasing address and does his work well.

ADDENDA.

Peter J. O'Hara, who was awarded the Morgan Medal, obtained the prize when ninety-one men were entitled to compete and was one of six men who before the mental and manual examiners had obtained a percentage of ninety and more. These men were P. J. O'Hara, F. W. Arnim, J. W. Carroll, James Casey, and W. T. Bebb. On the first ballot of those who examined the papers Mr. O'Hara received the prize.

He was born in London, England, October 17, 1864, and became a Cincinnati patrolman August 27, 1887.

At the annual parade inspection May 29, 1889, at the Cincinnati Ball Park, the feature of the occasion was the presentation of a stand of colors by General A. Hickenloper in behalf of the following-named companies and citizens who had contributed towards its purchase: Ætna Insurance Company, Adams Express Company, Bofinger & Hopkins, A. E. Burkhardt & Co., Browning, King & Co., D. H. Baldwin & Co., Fechheimer Bros., Geo. Fisher, Gibson House Company, A. Hickenloper, Henderson & Achert Lithographing Co., A. Lotze's Sons & Co., Liverpool, London and Globe Insurance Company, Laidlaw & Dunn Co., F. H. Lawson & Co., Macneale & Urban, Mt. Adams and Eden Park Railway Company, Robert Mitchell Furniture Company, George W. McAlpin Company, Mabley & Carew, H. B. Morehead, Phœnix Insurance Company, Putnam, Hooker & Co., H. and S. Pogue Company, John Shillito Company, J. and A. Simpkinson & Co., Singer Manufacturing Company, Henry Strauss, Stern, Mayer & Co., Daniel Stone Company, Van Antwerp, Bragg & Co., Vorheis, Miller & Ruppel, John Van Range Company.

The remarks of General Hickenloper on this occasion were as follows:

GOVERNOR FORAKER, MR. MAYOR, COMMISSIONERS AND MEMBERS OF THE CINCINNATI POLICE FORCE:—

It certainly affords me pleasure to acknowledge the compliment of being delegated by some of your prominent citizens to say a few words in their behalf and perform such personal and pleasant duty as that which has been assigned to me to day. Government is the power by which communities are ruled, and under our form of government is composed of three separate and distinct departments: Legislative, Judiciary and Executive. The first provides the form, the second interprets, whenever interpretation becomes necessary, and the third executes the laws, each separate and distinct in its functions but when working in harmony forms a perfect whole. At the very earliest establishment of civil government and the department which you gentlemen represent came a realization of the necessity for the creation of some agency or the organization of some force with power sufficient to protect the lives and property of citizens, and force obedience to all laws irrespective of the wishes of the individual or the interests of any class. Failure upon your part to do this dwarfs the dignity of your position, and to just the extent of such failure defeats the object and purposes of your organization, one of which has grown with the growth of civilization and the increase of population from the village constable and town marshal on up through the varied phases of partisan and municipal creations to such a perfectly organized and thoroughly disciplined body of men as there are now before me, which, in moral, intellectual and physical perfection, stands the peer of any similar organization in the United States. Such perfection, however, came not by chance, or is the mere incident of increase of population, but as the legitimate result of wise and judicious non-partisan legislation, administered and carried into practical effect through the untiring efforts of honest, impartial and intelligent commissioners, the appointment of capable experienced and thoroughly disciplined officers, and the selection of men peculiarly fitted for the per-

GEN. ANDREW HICKENLOPER.

formance of duties requiring the possession of physical strength, intelligent self-control and courage of the highest order.

No longer does the force serve as an asylum for the broken-down politician or embrace within its numbers weak and inefficient striplings or the portly man whose entire physical strength is barely adequate to the task of propelling his ponderous body slowly along his beat. But in their places now stand strong, resolute, honest men, the very perfection of physical manhood, with clear complexions and bright eyes, backed by a knowledge of duty and a degree of general intelligence that merits and commands the respect of every law-abiding citizen. Such being the generally recognized condition of the non-partisan police force of the City of Cincinnati it has appeared to many citizens vitally interested in the fame and prosperity of our city proper that they should through me express to the chief executive and the members of the Police Commission their appreciation of the wonderful change which has been wrought in such a brief period of time through the intelligent and impartial administration of the delicate and difficult duties of such a trust. They have also commissioned me to present through your Honor, as the chief executive, to Colonel Deitsch and officers and men of his command this beautiful stand of colors, the emblem of liberty, unity and strength, as a slight token of their appreciation of his own and their devotion to duty, in the full confidence that so long as they remain in the possession of such men they will never be dishonored by any mean, unworthy or cowardly act.

The colors are dark blue, six feet by six and a half, with a gold fringe, the Cincinnati Coat of Arms in the centre, over which are the words "Cincinnati Non-partisan Police," and under which are the words "Presented by the Citizens." It constitutes a beautiful tribute to the soldierly-bearing of the best body of men ever organized—the Queen City of the West.

ROSTER OF THE FORCE.

AS ORGANIZED MARCH 31, 1890.

Mayor,
JOHN B. MOSBY.

Police Commissioners,

JAMES BOYLE, *President,* . . . . Term expires April, 1890.
THOMAS C. MINOR, *Vice-President,* . . " " " 1892.
MILO G. DODDS, ... " " " 1890.
LOUIS WERNER, ... " " " 1892.

Clerk of the Board,
SAMUEL B. WARREN, ... Appointed October 20, 1886.

Messenger,
JOHN C. CALLAHAN, ... Appointed April 1, 1886.

MEDICAL DEPARTMENT.

Police Surgeon,
C. L. ARMSTRONG, M. D., ... Appointed April 7, 1886.

Medical Examiners,
C. L. ARMSTRONG, M. D., . . . Appointed April 7, 1886.
N. P. DANDRIDGE, M. D., . . . Appointed November 16, 1887.
ASA B. ISHAM, M. D., . . . Appointed April 8, 1886.

INSTRUCTION DEPARTMENT.

Mental and Manual Examiners,

JEREMIAH KIERSTED,	Appointed April 23, 1887.
H. H. TINKER,	Appointed June 21, 1887.

Official Instructor,

SAMUEL B. WARREN,	Appointed Feb'y 14, 1889.

Gymnasium Instructor,

DENNIS RYAN, *Patrolman*,	Detailed April 1, 1889.

EXECUTIVE DEPARTMENT.

Superintendent,

PHILIP DEITSCH,	Appointed June 23, 1886.

Inspector,

GEORGE D. HADLEY,	Appointed April 17, 1886.

Clerks,

J. R. BENDER, *Chief Clerk*,	Appointed January 17, 1885.
JAMES S. WEATHERBY, *Property Clerk*,	" April 22, 1886.
THOMAS G. MCGOVERN, *Report Clerk*,	" July 28, 1886.
JOHN DRAPER, *Superintendent's Clerk*,	" April 22, 1886.
CHARLES S. VICKERS, *Complaint Clerk*,	" July 19, 1886.
PHILIP P. STREIFF, *Pawn Clerk*,	" July 2, 1886.
FRANK M. COPPOCK, *Legal Clerk*,	" June 30, 1887.

DETECTIVE DEPARTMENT.

L. M. HAZEN, *Chief*,	Appointed May 4, 1887.
HENRY HALL, *Clerk*,	" July 23, 1887.
DANIEL A. CALLAHAN,	" May 4, 1887.
R. A. CRAWFORD,	" May 4, 1887.
JOHN SCHNUCKS,	" May 4, 1887.
WILLIAM A. TOKER,	" Sept. 10, 1887.
JOSEPH WAPPENSTEIN,	" May 7, 1887.
CHAS. HUDSON, *Special Clerk and Acting Detective*,	" Sept. 21, 1887.
EDW'D J. MOSES, *Special Clerk and Acting Detective*,	" Sept. 21, 1887.

COURT DEPARTMENT.

Court Officers.

JOHN A. WHITAKER, *Chief*,	Appointed	April 26, 1881.
MARTIN J. BRENNAN,	"	January 2, 1886.
DENNIS K. CREED,	"	March 2, 1885.
JOHN KUNZ,	"	July 2, 1886.
ALFRED LIKENS,	"	February 5, 1887.
RICHARD MORRIS,	"	July 15, 1886.
JOHN G. PEIFFER,	"	July 2, 1886.
JOHN M. THOMAS,	"	April 10, 1889.
A. G. JENNINGS, *assigned to Detention 'Bus*,	"	September 21, 1889.
L. A. JUDD, *assigned to Detention 'Bus*,	"	November 12, 1887.
JOS. A. SULLIVAN, *assigned to Prison Van*,	"	January 12, 1887.
JOHN ZIMMERMAN, *assigned to Prison Van*,	"	March 7, 1887.

PATROL-WAGON DEPARTMENT.

Superintendent of Patrol,

THOMAS A. DUFFY, { Appointed Lieutenant July 1, 1884.
" Sup't of Patrol Nov. 1, 1885. }

Veterinary Surgeon,

DANIEL BAILEY, ... Appointed July 1, 1887.

LIEUTENANTS.

Berg, Peter	Ninth	District	Station	Appointed	June 5, 1888.
Brangan, James M.	Fifth	"	"	......	"	July 1, 1887.
Currin, Patrick L.	Fifth	"	"	......	"	April 30, 1886.
Diehl, Eugene	Fourth	"	"	......	"	August 5, 1886.
Fisher, Cassius M.	Sixth	"	"	......	"	June 30, 1886.
Gill, Thomas F.	Fifth	"	"	......	"	July 7, 1886.
Hall, Samuel B.	Eighth	"	"	......	"	May 27, 1886.
Hanrahan, James H.	Third	"	"	......	"	July 1, 1887.
Heheman, William	Second	"	"	......	"	August 2, 1886.
Kendall, Newton	Third	"	"	......	"	October 28, 1886.
Krumpe, William H.	Tenth	"	"	......	"	August 14, 1889.
Langdon, Mark	First	"	"	......	"	May 25, 1886.
Lingenfelter, Jesse	Fourth	"	"	......	"	May 24, 1886,
Pistner, Godfrey	Third	"	"	......	"	Novemb'r 8, 1883.
Rakel, Bernard	First	"	"	......	"	October 8, 1886.
Robinson, Edgar	Seventh	"	"	......	"	Novemb'r 9, 1886.
Rockwell, Edwin T.	First	"	"	......	"	Febru'ry 18, 1888.
Scahill, John W.	Second	"	"	......	"	Febru'ry 24, 1888.
Schmidt, Adolph	Third	"	"	......	"	May 2, 1886.
Thornton, Joseph	Second	"	"	......	"	April 28, 1885.

SERGEANTS,

Adams, Daniel	Ninth District Station			Appointed	July 19, 1886.
Arnim, Frederick W.	Seventh	"	"	......	" October 22, 1887.
Bartley, Thomas F.	Sixth	"	"	......	" July 30, 1881.
Bedinger, Louis	Second	"	"	......	" July 21, 1886.
Borck, William F.	Sixth	"	"	......	" June 19, 1886.
Burman, Joseph M.	First	"	"	......	" June 19, 1886.
Carroll, John W.	First	"	"	......	" March 17, 1887.
Chase, Frank R.	Fourth	"	"	......	" June 8, 1887.
Clawson, William W	Third	"	"	......	" June 7, 1886.
Corbin, Samuel T.	Fourth	"	"	......	" June 11, 1883.
Drout, Luke	First	"	"	......	" October 28, 1878.
Duffy, Michael	Sixth	"	"	......	" April 6, 1881.
Eubanks, George	Tenth	"	"	......	" May 21, 1886.
Geist, Charles F.	Eighth	"	"	......	" June 4, 1886.
Hannon, Frank J.	Second	"	"	......	" February 1, 1888
Hill, Edward C.	Fifth	"	"	......	" June 1, 1885.
Kiffmeyer, John H.	Ninth	"	"	......	" June 29, 1886.
King, Robert	Eighth	"	"	......	" June 7, 1886.
Leukering, William	Tenth	"	"	......	" May 6, 1886.
Linhardt, Emil	Third	"	"	......	" May 25, 1886.
McMullen, Henry	Seventh	"	"	......	" May 5, 1884.
Nagle, Jeremiah	Seventh	"	"	......	" June 20, 1883.
Nealis, John J.	Fifth	"	"	......	" June 19, 1886.
O'Hearn, Michael J.	Second	"	"	......	" July 19, 1886.
Rigney, Michael	Fifth	"	"	......	" March 24, 1886.
Schmitt, Louis	Fourth	"	"	......	" Novemb'r 6, 1886.
Sinking, James H.	Third	"	"	......	" July 23, 1887.
Watson, William E.	Eighth	"	"	......	" July 2, 1886.
Werner, Frederick	First	"	"	......	" April 30, 1886.
Wilmes, Joseph	Tenth	"	"	......	" August 23, 1886.
Winters, John	Ninth	"	"	......	" December 4, 1886.

PATROLMEN,

Ackerstaff, Henry	District	3	Appointed	June 12, 1886.
Albrecht, Louis	"	9	"	May 31, 1889.
Allen, James A.	"	1	"	July 19, 1886.
Allen, James T.	"	1	"	March 11, 1889.
Ambrose, Robert	"	5	"	February 18, 1889.
Anderson, Jacob	"	5	"	December 1, 1886.
Anderson, John B.	"	7	"	September 29, 1886.
Apgar, George	Patrol	4	"	February 12, 1887.
Arand, Edward	District	5	"	June 29, 1886.
Aufderheide, Bernard	"	4	"	January 28, 1887.
Austerman, Louis B.	"	7	"	September 1, 1888.
Ayers, James K.	"	9	"	February 27, 1888.

ROSTER OF THE FORCE.

Bachman, Anton	District 3	Appointed	June 19, 1886.
Bachman, Jacob	" 1	"	August 14, 1889.
Baehr, William F	" 7	"	November 3, 1886.
Baeuerlin, August	" 4	"	October 26, 1887.
Batter, Michael	" 1	"	August 11, 1888.
Bay, John	" 6	"	May 1, 1886.
Beal, John	" 7	"	October 9, 1886.
Bebb, William T	" 4	"	October 9, 1886.
Bechtel, Louis	" 7	"	November 3, 1888.
Becker, Louis	" 1	"	August 11, 1886.
Beiser, Julius	" 3	"	November 17, 1886.
Belch, Kendrick L	" 10	"	October 9, 1886.
Benzig, Adolph C	" 10	"	December 14, 1887.
Berlekamp, John	" 5	"	May 1, 1886.
Bernhardt, Jacob, Jr	" 8	"	August 15, 1888.
Berrigan, James	" 3	"	May 25, 1889.
Best, Frederick J	" 5	"	October 8, 1888.
Betz, James H	" 6	"	September 29, 1886.
Blanchard, Charles	" 9	"	September 29, 1886.
Blice, Charles L	" 4	"	December 10, 1888.
Blum, Louis	Patrol 8	"	February 16, 1887.
Bluett, James	District 1	"	February 16, 1887.
Bocklet, Charles	" 5	"	May 18, 1887.
Boeckman, Frank	" 2	"	June 11, 1884.
Boehm, Henry	Patrol 3	"	June 9, 1886.
Boehm, Valentine	District 8	"	August 16, 1881.
Bogart, John A	" 6	"	November 2, 1888.
Bohnett, Charles A	" 10	"	March 24, 1888.
Bonfield, James	Patrol 7	"	June 21, 1886.
Booth, Amos S	District 10	"	February 16, 1887.
Boulware, James M	" 5	"	July 2, 1887.
Brand, John H	Patrol 8	"	October 4, 1884.
Brennan, Martin C	District 4	"	April 26, 1881.
Brenneman, John M	" 1	"	September 3, 1886.
Brockman, William	Patrol 1	"	October 9, 1886.
Brothers, Christ	" 3	"	April 26, 1881.
Brown, Anson C	District 8	"	September 1, 1888.
Brown, George H	" 1	"	August 9, 1889.
Buchanan, E. C	" 7	"	September 29, 1886.
Bulmer, William	Headquarters	"	June 19, 1886.
Buns, Frederick W	District 3	"	August 11, 1888.
Burck, John	" 2	"	August 21, 1886.
Burke, Thomas	Patrol 4	"	June 7, 1886.
Burke, William	" 4	"	June 1, 1885.
Burkolder, John H	District 2	"	November 2, 1888.
Burnet, James C	" 2	"	May 20, 1886.

Cady, Henry J	Patrol	7	Appointed	June 1, 1885.
Calnan, John	District	1	"	May 9, 1887.
Campbell, John A	"	5	"	June 19, 1886.
Carey, William	"	1	"	October 20, 1885.
Casey, James	"	2	"	September 8, 1886.
Clavin, Luke P	"	7	"	May 23, 1889.
Coffey, Patrick	Patrol	4	"	June 24, 1886.
Coleman, John	"	2	"	June 7, 1886.
Colina, Edward	District	5	"	October 9, 1886.
Collins, Jasper	"	6	"	February 12, 1887.
Collins, Jeremiah	"	9	"	April 4, 1888.
Conroy, Peter J	"	1	"	June 16, 1873.
Conway, Alva	"	3	"	December 27, 1887.
Copelan, William	"	3	"	March 7, 1887.
Copeland, William E	Patrol	4	"	May 22, 1887.
Cramer, Jos. H	District	2	"	October 8, 1887.
Crance, August J	"	2	"	September 10, 1888.
Crim, David C	"	1	"	December 27, 1886.
Crosley, Charles A	"	6	"	May 22, 1886.
Crowley, James	"	7	"	August 16, 1881.
Curlis, Posey L	"	2	"	March 30, 1889.
Dahling, John H	District	9	"	October 20, 1886.
Daly, Edward	Patrol	5	"	June 2, 1881.
Davis, Frank T	District	1	"	September 12, 1885.
Dean, Edward	"	1	"	February 14, 1887.
Deigh, Byron S	"	2	"	December 12, 1889.
Delaney, Jeremiah	"	1	"	October 8, 1887.
Denman, D. G	"	7	"	September 8, 1886.
Diers, Henry	"	1	"	September 3, 1886.
Doherty, John J	Patrol	6	"	June 9, 1886.
Doherty, Terrence J	District	2	"	January 12, 1886.
Donnelly, John	Patrol	1	"	January 11, 1883.
Donohoo, Levi A	District	2	"	February 10, 1887.
Donohue, Corn. A	"	4	"	September 17, 1887.
Downey, John	Patrol	4	"	June 1, 1886.
Drain, John E	District	10	"	September 23, 1886.
Durst, Frank S	"	1	"	September 5, 1888.
Dwyer, James	"	2	"	August 6, 1887.
Dwyer, John	"	8	"	January 14, 1888.
Eckert, Frank	District	9	"	February 18, 1889.
Eggleston, James E	"	1	"	July 23, 1875.
Ehrnschwender, John	"	2	"	May 31, 1889.
Ellis, James	"	9	"	January 14, 1888.
Engelke, William	"	3	"	October 26, 1887.

ROSTER OF THE FORCE. 407

Farrell, John	District 2	Appointed	August 28, 1886.
Farrell, William	" 1	"	July 6, 1887.
Fayen, John	Patrol 1	"	June 1, 1886.
Fellerman, Henry	District 1	"	August 2, 1889.
Ferber, Gustav	Patrol 3	"	September 18, 1884.
Fink, Adam	District 6	"	December 14, 1887.
Fink, Charles	" 7	"	July 10, 1885.
Finn, William	" 8	"	July 19, 1886.
Fisher, Frederick	" 6	"	May 25, 1886.
Fisher, Jacob	" 10	"	July 20, 1887.
Fitzpatrick, Rees	" 6	"	September 29, 1886.
Flanigan, James	Patrol 6	"	September 16, 1885.
Flannelly, Martin	District 4	"	December 9, 1889.
Flemming, James A	" 4	"	October 8, 1887.
Forbus, Millard F	" 5	"	February 18, 1889.
Fosher, Clinton	Patrol 9	"	July 2, 1886.
Forster, Joseph	District 9	"	February 18, 1888.
Francis, John R	" 4	"	July 7, 1886.
Fricke, Louis	" 4	"	June 3, 1889.
Fricke, Henry	" 4	"	February 16, 1887.
Gibbons, Jeffrey J	District 2	"	February 12, 1887.
Glazer, George B	" 8	"	November 10, 1886.
Goedieke, Charles	" 3	"	July 7, 1886.
Goepper, Edwin S	" 2	"	May 14, 1887.
Goff, Martin W	" 4	"	October 8, 1887.
Good, George E	" 4	"	September 19, 1889.
Graff, William H	" 3	"	January 18, 1888.
Greeneberg, Frank	" 8	"	May 21, 1886.
Grimsley, Charles M	" 4	"	October 5, 1887.
Grimm, John	" 3	"	October 1, 1887.
Gross, William	" 5	"	June 1, 1886.
Grundhoefer, Edm	" 5	"	October 8, 1887.
Gwynn, Clarence	" 8	"	May 22, 1886.
Haines, C. O	Patrol 9	"	April 30, 1886.
Haines, C. W	District 7	"	April 4, 1888.
Hale, John	" 2	"	December 28, 1886.
Haley, John	" 7	"	March 3, 1888.
Haley, Patrick J	" 2	"	October 9, 1886.
Hamant, Robert	" 9	"	June 15, 1887.
Hamersly, John	" 4	"	July 17, 1886.
Hanks, William B	Patrol 1	"	May 12, 1881.
Hanley, Edw	District 6	"	June 26, 1886.
Hanley, Timothy	" 4	"	May 14, 1887.
Hannan, Peter	" 8	"	November 10, 1886.

ROSTER OF THE FORCE.

Hannon, Michael............	District 9.........	Appointed	February 18, 1889.
Hardinger, John.............	" 8.........	"	June 11, 1886.
Hartfiel, Rudolf................	" 8.........	"	March 11, 1889.
Hartzel, Alfred................	" 3.........	"	November 3, 1886.
Heck, John...	" 5.........	"	December 11, 1886.
Heinrich, Ernst W............	" 7.........	"	July 16, 1887.
Hellwig, John H..............	" 4.........	"	October 26, 1887.
Hempfling, Conrad...........	" 3.........	"	June 16, 1886.
Hendricks, John..............	" 9.........	"	January 3, 1887.
Hennekes, John A...........	" 3.........	"	May 12, 1884.
Henry, Frank..................	" 2.........	"	February 16, 1887.
Henry, Nicholas..............	" 8.........	"	January 18, 1888.
Herrmann, Theo. M.........	" 1.........	"	December 31, 1887.
Herzberger, Frank............	" 1.........	"	May 1, 1886.
Hess, Frederick...............	" 5.........	"	September 29, 1886.
Hildebrant, J. J...............	" 6.........	"	February 1, 1887.
Hill, Benjamin S.............	" 10	"	September 3, 1887.
Hipple, William H...........	" 5.........	"	July 11, 1887.
Hogan, William...............	" 4.........	"	September 29, 1886.
Hollowell, Clement L........	" 5.........	"	January 24, 1889.
Holzlin, Jacob.................	" 7.........	"	October 26, 1887.
Hooker, John C...............	" 7.........	"	May 21, 1886.
Horn, Thomas.................	" 4.........	"	April 10, 1889.
Howard, Edward A	" 1.........	"	May 9, 1883.
Huesman, George H.........	" 3.........	"	January 18, 1888.
Hugloucht, John..............	" 7.........	"	September 7, 1887.
Hutchison, Addison...........	" 5.........	"	February 18, 1889.
Hutchinson, Edw. T..........	" 6.........	"	May 14, 1887.
Hyatt, Charles B..............	" 9.........	"	January 7, 1889.
Jackman, Charles E..........	District 3.........	"	June 15, 1886.
Jackson, William H..........	Headquarters....	"	June 1, 1886.
Jahn, William H..............	District 5	"	December 17, 1888.
Jones, Charles H..............	" 2.........	"	September 7, 1887.
Jones, Henry H................	" 7.........	"	June 8, 1887.
Jordan, William...............	" 2.........	"	May 3, 1889.
Juegling, Henry, Jr...........	" 5.........	"	October 26, 1887.
Kane, Michael J...............	District 3.........	"	March 30, 1889.
Keating, George M...........	" 1.........	"	July 16, 1887.
Keefe, Frank...................	" 5.........	"	July 23, 1887.
Keidel, August E..............	" 6	"	May 1, 1886.
Keith, George W..............	" 9.........	"	March 30, 1889.
Kelly, Robert J................	Patrol 8.........	"	Seqtember 10, 1887.
King, William H..............	District 1.........	"	May 3, 1881.
Kleiman, William H..........	" 7.........	"	February 1, 1888.
Klein, Peter.....................	" 4.........	"	September 1, 1888.

ROSTER OF THE FORCE. 409

Kleinjohn, Charles............Patrol	5........	Appointed	May 1, 1886.
Klusman, Louis.................	" 9........	"	August 28, 1886.
Koehler, George J............District	5........	"	August 6, 1881.
Korb, George.....................	" 1........	"	April 4, 1888.
Kosterman, Fred'k H..........	" 4........	"	February 18, 1889.
Kraft, William, Jr...............	" 5........	"	May 25, 1889.
Kramer, Henry....................	" 5........	"	July 2, 1886.
Kramer, Louis...................Patrol	7........	"	July 19, 1887.
Kratz, John.....................Headquarters.....		"	May 25, 1886.
Krebs, John.....................District	5........	"	February 18, ¶888.
Krey, Charles.....................	" 8........	"	June 29, 1886.
Kruse, Frank.....................	" 2........	"	October 28, 1886.
Kuhfers, Conrad C...............	" 2........	"	September 10, 1888.
Kussman, Herman...............	" 3........	"	December 14, 1887.
Lamping, Frank................District	5........	"	October 26, 1887.
Laue, Louis C.....................	" 8........	"	January 14, 1888.
Lavin, Patrick.....................	" 4........	"	February 12, 1887.
Leder, Charles F................	" 4........	"	July 11, 1888.
Lembert, Joseph.................Patrol	7........	"	December 29, 1886.
Lennon, James...................District	7........	"	May 3, 1881.
Leytze, Charles...................	" 3........	"	October 1, 1887.
Lill, Charles......................	" 3........	"	October 16, 1886.
Lillis, Joseph.....................	" 2........	"	December 17, 1887.
Lind, Charles.....................	" 7........	"	October 16, 1886.
Littman, Henry..................	" 5........	"	Nov. 10, 1886.
Lockhart, Dustin B.............	" 6........	"	October 15, 1887.
Lottes, Thomas...................Patrol	5........	"	October 9, 1886.
Lowenstein, Henry..............District	8........	"	October 1, 1887.
Lynch, Frank E.................Patrol	1........	"	June 29, 1886.
McAdams, Charles W..........District	2........	"	June 11, 1886.
McCane, Amos...................	" 10........	"	July 16, 1887.
McCarthy, John E..............	" 2........	"	March 4, 1884.
McGrann, John J...............Patrol	6........	"	October 28, 1886.
McManus, James................District	4........	"	February 18, 1888.
McMillen, Theoph. C..........	" 4........	"	November 17, 1886.
McNamara, John................	" 10........	"	January 28, 1887.
Mahon, Martin...................	" 5........	"	April 30, 1886.
Mangold, Frank..................	" 9........	"	February 23, 1888.
Manley, Patrick F..............Patrol	2........	"	July 30, 1881.
Martin, John....................District	10........	"	January 3, 1887.
Mathes, Joseph B...............Patrol	7........	"	August 21, 1886.
Menke, John H..................District	4........	"	May 20, 1886.
Messerschmitt, Charles........	" 1........	"	September 3, 1887.
Meyer, William B...............	" 2........	"	August 15, 1888.

Name	Assignment	Appointed
Miller, John	District 1	Appointed June 19, 1886.
Miller, William	" 3	" January 27, 1888.
Miller, William L.	" 4	" November 3, 1886.
Moffitt, William	" 1	" January 30, 1888.
Molloy, James F.	Patrol 6	" August 28, 1885.
Morten, Henry	District 10	" January 5, 1889.
Mount, James D.	" 1	" January 12, 1887.
Muhle, John B.	" 2	" October 23, 1889.
Muhleman, George G.	" 5	" August 28, 1886.
Muller, Frank.	" 9	" March 11, 1889.
Murphy, Daniel E.	" 5	" October 26, 1887.
Mutter, Conrad	" 4	" February 9, 1887.
Neely, Thomas	District 3	" September 17, 1888.
Nellis, Robert	Patrol 7	" May 3, 1886.
O'Brien, James	District 2	" January 18, 1888.
O'Conner, Michael	" 9	" October 26, 1887.
O'Gara, Michael	" 2	" May 31, 1889.
Ogden, Sidney W.	" 4	" March 30, 1889.
O'Hara, Peter J.	" 7	" August 27, 1887.
O'Neil, Thomas	" 10	" June 2, 1886.
Orth, Reinhardt	" 4	" May 19 1886.
Otting, Bernard	" 10	" October 20, 1886.
Packer, Charles	Patrol 2	" May 18, 1886.
Pettit, John T.	District 1	" August 21, 1886.
Pfeifer, John	" 1	" November 3, 1886.
Phelan, Larry	Patrol 8	" July 10, 1885.
Pickens, Clifford	" 3	" June 2, 1886.
Piles, Alfred	District 3	" July 2, 1887.
Poppe, John	" 1	" December 31, 1888.
Potts, Fred'k W.	" 5	" September 29, 1886.
Pouder, Henry	" 10	" October 26, 1887.
Prickett, John C.	" 1	" December 14, 1889.
Primrose, Oliver F.	" 1	" March 1, 1888.
Purcell, Patrick F.	" 9	" October 1, 1887.
Purdon, Douglas	" 4	" February 26, 1887.
Rawlins, Louis	District 9	" February 12, 1887.
Rearden, Dennis	" 6	" July 14, 1886.
Reisinger, Valentine	" 3	" May 29, 1885.
Reiss, Frank	" 2	" November 7, 1887.
Besler, Lafayette	" 1	" October 16, 1886.
Renkert, Louis	" 1	" July 9, 1887.
Richardson, Rich. J.	" 3	" August 21, 1886.
Richards, Herman	" 5	" May 19, 1881.

ROSTER OF THE FORCE. 411

Riddel, Thomas	Patrol 8	Appointed	August 21, 1886.
Rieck, Charles J	District 3	"	January 21, 1888.
Riesenbeger, Henry H	" 3	"	December 14, 1887.
Roach, Philip J	" 9	"	August 28, 1886.
Ruberg, Henry	" 9	"	October 16, 1886.
Ryan, Dennis	" 2	"	November 23, 1883.
Ryan, John	" 2	"	January 24, 1889.
Ryan, Joseph	" 5	"	April 17, 1889.
Ryan, Michael	" 3	"	June 19, 1886.
Samples, John	District 3	"	July 1, 1886.
Satters, William	" 5	"	May 7, 1887.
Seaford, Frank	" 5	"	October 11, 1886.
Scarlett, Edward	" 7	"	June 1, 1886.
Scellen, Walter C	" 2	"	March 13, 1889.
Schaefer, John	" 2	"	March 9, 1887.
Scherloh, Otto	" 3	"	September 22, 1886.
Schilling, Joseph	" 1	"	December 27, 1886.
Schmaltz, Charles	" 8	"	August 16, 1885.
Schmedes, Bernard	" 3	"	September 5, 1888.
Schmidt, Frank	" 4	"	June 15, 1887.
Schmudde, William H	" 3	"	July 19, 1886.
Schneider, Peter	" 9	"	June 4, 1886.
Schorr, Adam	Patrol 3	"	December 20, 1886.
Schrader, Frederick	District 2	"	May 21, 1886.
Schroeder, John	" 8	"	June 1, 1886.
Schwach, Joseph	" 1	"	October 28, 1886.
Schweitzer, John	" 10	"	April 27, 1887.
Schwinher, John	Patrol 2	"	May 14, 1887.
Scott, Craig	District 5	"	October 6, 1886.
Seidholz, Louis	" 3	"	June 15, 1886.
Shafer, Frederick W	" 7	"	June 29, 1886.
Shumate, Perry N	" 5	"	October 15, 1887.
Simmons, Harry L	" 1	"	September 19, 1889.
Simms, Albert	" 2	"	June 4, 1886.
Slattery, James	" 4	"	October 9, 1889.
Slattery, Michael	Patrol 6	"	October 2, 1885.
Sloan, Frank	District 5	"	March 30, 1889.
Smallwood, S. N., Jr	" 10	"	December 31, 1888.
Smethurst, Samuel	" 1	"	September 20, 1886.
Snyder, Clarence B	" 3	"	December 1, 1886.
Spiegel, Nicholas	" 2	"	December 29, 1886.
Springmeier, Louis	" 1	"	June 19, 1886.
Spurlock, Harry	" 4	"	January 26, 1889.
Stebbens, Charles	" 2	"	February 18, 1889.
Stegner, John P., Jr	" 8	"	January 14, 1888.

Steidinger, George J............District 5.........Appointed October 8, 1887.
Stenger, Aloysius.................   "   2.........   "   May 14, 1887.
Stevens, George...................   "   9.........   "   December 14, 1887.
Stottman, Theodore..............   "   5.........   "   July 1, 1886.
Sullivan, Dennis...................Patrol   9.........   "   February 18, 1888.
Sweeney, James....................District 4.........   "   April 7, 1888.
Sweeney, John A.................Patrol   2.........   "   March 9, 1887.
Sylvester, Anthony...............District 1.........   "   July 28, 1887.

Theidick, Frank A...............District 3.........   "   August 21, 1886.
Toal, John.........................   "   6.........   "   November 17, 1886.
Townsley, Alfred L..............   "   4.........   "   December 13, 1889.
Turner, Ernest C.................   "   2.........   "   June 8, 1887.

Von Bargen, Henry..............District 1.........   "   February 18, 1889.

Walsh, Michael.................Patrol   2.........   "   June 17, 1886.
Walz, Gustav A...................   "   3.........   "   October 29, 1886.
Wambsgans, John...............District 8.........   "   January 29, 1887.
Weaver, Charles T...............Patrol   9.........   "   May 22, 1886.
Weber, Charles....................District 4.........   "   August 28, 1886.
Weber, Nicholas..................Patrol   5.........   "   September 10, 1887.
Wessels, John B...................District 1.........   "   July 13, 1887.
Westerkam, Edw. A.............   "   3.........   "   November 12, 1888.
White, John B.....................   "   1.........   "   March 8, 1888.
White, Patrick J.................Patrol   1.........   "   September 29, 1886.
White, Willlam S................District 1.........   "   October 9, 1886.
Widmeyer, James................   "   4.........   "   November 3, 1886.
Wiening, Christian...............   "   3.........   "   May 20, 1886.
Wilhelm, Edward................Patrol   1.........   "   April 4, 1888.
Williams, Orason O.............District 1.........   "   June 29, 1887.
Wilson, Frank L..................   "   10.........   "   May 22, 1886.
Wimsey, Thomas J..............   "   3.........   "   February 9, 1887.
Witte, Herman J.................   "   1.........   "   April 10, 1889.
Wolf, John H......................   "   2.........   "   July 19, 1886.
Woodruff, George W............   "   5.........   "   July 2, 1887.
Worthman, Andrew.............   "   7.........   "   September 3, 1887.
Wyenandt, Emil W..............   "   9.........   "   January 18, 1888.

Yager, John.......................Patrol   5.........   "   September 30, 1886.

Zeilman, George..................District 4.........   "   June 19, 1886.

SUBSTITUTE PATROLMEN.

Batsche, Anton....................District 1.........Appointed August 31, 1889.
Conrad, Thomas J................   "   1.........   "   November 13, 1889.
Dwire, Joseph.....................   "   1.........   "   March 15, 1890.

Hearn, Edward U............District 1.........Appointed March 19, 1890.
Horner, Frederick E............ " 1......... " December 3, 1889.
Horstmeyer, Henry............ " 1......... " November 13, 1889.
Johnson, Isaac W............... " 1......... " March 15, 1890.
Matz, Adam...................... " 1......... " November 27, 1889.
Palmer, Charles A............... " 1......... " January 29, 1890.
Shaffer, William................ " 1......... " January 27, 1890.
Thompson, Hill................. " 1......... " November 13, 1889.

STATION-HOUSE KEEPERS.

Bartsche, Edward.............District 9.........Appointed June 16, 1886.
Berry, John..................... " 10......... " November 8, 1886.
Clark, John..................... " 4......... " March 5, 1887.
Curren, Timothy................ " 7......... " June 15, 1886.
Ennis, Dennis................... " 2......... " July 1, 1886.
Etter, Lawrence................ " 9......... " June 6, 1886.
Guynan, Barth.................. " 5......... " June 11, 1886.
Haller, Christian,.............. " 1......... " May 26, 1886.
Haucke, Rudolph............... " 1......... " June 12, 1886.
Henderson, Archibald......... " 4......... " May 12, 1886.
Homer, James H............... " 8......... " May 6, 1881.
Kleisler, George................ " 3......... " June 11, 1886.
Meischke, Charles.............. " 6......... " June 1, 1886.
Nash, David..................... " 6......... " June 15, 1883.
Sayre, Henry.................... " 3......... " May 25, 1886.
Schultz, Jos...................... " 2......... " June 12, 1886.
Schwegler, Victor............... " 10......... " December 22, 1888.
Stokes, Isaac.................... " 8......... " May 20, 1886.
Welsh, Michael................. " 2......... " March 8, 1890.
Wright, Charles................Gymnasium...... " June 7, 1886.
Wunder, Spence................District 5......... " June 12, 1886.

PLACE OF DETENTION.

Fieber, Pauline................Matron.............Appointed September 9, 1887.
Mead, Margaretta............ " .... " September 9, 1887.
Schuch, Catharine............Janitrix............. " August 17, 1888.

Police Telephone and Signal Service.

T. J. Sullivan............Superintendent...........Appointed May 12, 1885.
Harry Adams............Operator.................. " October 12, 1883.
Frank Nugent............ " .... " September 1, 1886.
Joseph Sullivan.......... " .... " July 1, 1887.
Harry White............. " .... " December 18, 1886.

INDEX.

A

	PAGE
Armstrong, Dr. C. L.	138, 141
Armstrong, Edward C.	286
Adams, Daniel, Sergeant	258
Anthony, Edward H.	392, 393

B

Bender, John	53, 196
Boyle, James	100
Borck, W. F.	170, 272
Bedinger, L., Sergeant	170, 314
Brockman, W.	170
Byrne, William J.	195
Berg, Peter, Lieutenant	310
Burman, Joseph M., Sergeant	328
Brennan, M. C., Sergeant	328
Brangan, James M., Lieutenant	349
Bartley, Thomas F., Sergeant	358
Berger, Geza	393, 394

C

Cincinnati, Original Site of	20
Cincinnati, Village Incorporated	23
Cincinnati, First Mayor	23, 25
Cincinnati, City Incorporated	26
Committee of One Hundred	36, 98
Coppock, Frank M.	165, 168
Clawson, W. W.	170, 175
Crawford, Ralph	202, 203, 210
Callahan, Daniel A.	203, 217
Carroll, John W.	271
Corbin Samuel, Sergeant	303
Currin, Patrick, Lieutenant	323

D

Dunn, James	53
Deitsch, Philip, Colonel	86, 103, 178, 240
Dodds, Hon. Milo G.	100

INDEX. 415

	Page
Dandridge, N. P.	138, 139, 146
Dun, Walter A., M. D.	139, 147
Draper, Dr. J.	192
Duffy, Thomas A., Lieutenant	234
Diehl, Eugene, Lieutenant	297
Drout, Luke, Sergeant	303
Duffy, Michael, Sergeant	351
Dunbar, Walter	393, 394

E

Ewbanks, George, Sergeant	272

F

Floods of 1883 and 1884	71
Fisher, C. M., Lieutenant	267
Faulkner, James W.	392, 393

G

Gordon, James S.	100
Gill, Thomas F.	270
Geist, Charles F., Sergeant	358
Gardiner, James T.	392, 393
Gerth, Charles	393, 394

H

Hazen, Lawrence W., Chief of Detectives	44, 202, 203
Hawkins, Morton L., Colonel	55
Hadley, George D., Captain	162, 187
Hill, E. C., Sergeant	170, 345
Hall, Harry	195
Hudson, Charles	203, 223
House of Detection	309
Hambrock, Henry, Lieutenant	312
Hanrahan, James J., Lieutenant	342
Hall, Samuel B., Lieutenant	351
Heheman, William, Lieutenant	366
Hodges, Charles	392, 393
Heck, Louis T.	393, 394

I

Isham, A. B.	138, 139, 145

J

Jackson, Billy	226

K

Kiersted, Jeremiah, Colonel	165
Kiffmeyer, John H., Sergeant	345

INDEX.

	Page
King, Robert, Sergeant	352
Kendell, Newton, Lieutenant	361
Krumpe, William, Sergeant	368
Karger, Gus. J	393, 394

L

Langdon, Mark, Lieutenant	298
Leonard, Edward, Sergeant	313
Linhardt, Emil, Sergeant	314
Linginfelter, Jesse, Lieutenant	324
Leitz, Henry, Sergeant	328
Luekering, William, Sergeant	362

M

Mayors...23, 25, 26, 27, 29, 32, 34, 39, 41, 44, 45, 47, 49, 50, 52, 53, 60, 79,	92
Meara, Thomas, Lieutenant	53
Moore, Arthur G., Colonel	86, 103
Mosby, John Borden	92
Minor, Dr. T. C.	100
Morgan, Robert J.,	100, 169
Morgan Medal	169
McGrann, John	170, 173
McGovern, Thomas G.	200
Moses, Edward	203, 226
McDonough, Thomas	239
McMullen, Henry, Sergeant	350

N

Newman, Edward B., Sergeant	305
Nagle, Jeremiah, Sergeant	349
Nealis, John J., Sergeant	362

O

Owen, Law	87
O'Hearn, M. J., Sergeant	170, 350
O'Hara, Peter J	395

P

Police, First Chief	22, 34
Police, First Night Watch	23
Police, duties of	26
Police, First Marshal	27
Police, First Station House	29
Police, charge in selecting	32
Police, pay of	30, 32, 33, 34
Police, Chiefs of	22, 27, 29, 30, 31, 32, 34, 39, 42, 44, 45, 47, 49
Police, Superintendents of	49, 50, 52, 53, 60, 86, 103, 178

INDEX.

	Page
Police, early Boards of Commissioners..........40, 41, 47, 49,	53
Police, present Board of Commissioners..........55,	96
Police do Military Duty	44
Police Officers, how appointed	131
Police Medical Examiners	131
Police Uniform	136
Police Gymnasium	155
Police School of Instruction	150
Police Mental and Manual Examiners	165
Police Patrol Wagon	234
Police, Mounted	238
Police Relief Association	243
Police Roll of Honor	252
Police Station Houses, Central	260
Police Station Houses, Second	289
Police Station Houses, Third	306
Police Station Houses, Fourth	319
Police Station Houses, Fifth	331
Police Station Houses, Sixth	346
Police Station Houses, Seventh	350
Police Station Houses, Eighth	356
Police Station Houses, Ninth	361
Police Station Houses, Tenth	366
Police Matrons	318
Police Districts, First	263
Police Districts, Second	289
Police Districts, Third..........289,	305
Police Districts, Fourth	319
Police Districts, Fifth..........319,	331
Police Districts, Sixth	346
Police Districts, Seventh	350
Police Districts, Eighth	355
Police Districts, Ninth	361
Police Districts, Tenth	365
Police, Duties of Lieutenants	263
Police, House of Detention	309
Pistner, Godfrey, Lieutenant	309

R

Riots, Pro-Slavery..........31,	39
Riots, Bedini	34
Riots, Know Nothings	38
Riots, Wendell Phillips	39
Riots, Berner	57
Riots of 1884	59
Riots, Court House and Jail..........59,	71

INDEX.

	Page
Riots, Strike of Freight-handlers	84
Reis, Julius	57
Rockwell, E. T., Lieutenant	170, 341
Rittweger, Philip	202
Roll of Honor	252
Rakel, Bernard, Lieutenant	341
Robinson, Edgar, Lieutenant	356
Rigney, Michael, Sergeant	368
Reiser, Alfred	393, 394

S

Spencer, Henry E., Mayor	32
Snelbaker, David T., Mayor	34
Smith, Amos J., Mayor	53
Stevens, William A.	57
Stephens, Thomas J., Mayor	60
Smith, Amos, Jr.	78
Scahill, J. W., Lieutenant	170, 173, 327
Strieff, Phil	200
Schuncks, John	203, 210
Schmidt, Adolph, Lieutenant	269
Schmitt, Louis	345
Shafer, F. W., Sergeant	355

T

Taylor, M. T., Mayor	34
Topp, George R.	100
Tinker, H. H., Captain	165, 167
Toker, William A.	203, 220
Thornton, Joseph, Lieutenant	293

V

Vickers, Charles S.	201

W

Wappenstein, Charles	53, 203, 221
Warren, S. B.	100, 161
Werner, Louis	100
Wilmes, Joseph	170
Weatherby, James S.	199
Wilmer, Joseph, Sergeant	275
Watson, W. E., Sergeant	362
Winters, John, Sergeant	371

—A— Striking Contrast

CHAPTER I.

THE BROTHERS.—A HOME IN THE FOREST.—DOMESTIC HAPPINESS.—THE GUARDIAN SWAMP.—PURSUERS AND PURSUED.—CAUGHT IN A QUAGMIRE.—THE TABLES TURNED.—HOW THE BANDITS SAVED THEIR CARTRIDGES.

There is a theory that a man's home, the one small portion of the earth's surface he has made peculiarly his own, will always bear the stamp of his individuality, and furnish thus an unfailing clue to his character and his mode of life.

An ideal home once stood in a forest glade near a town in Texas, for which its over-ambitious founders had chosen the name of Paris. The glade was a mere islet of clear sward in the midst of an ocean of greenery. For miles about it in every direction extended a virgin forest, almost tropical in the luxuriance of its vegetation. The patriarchal trees stood so closely together, that their interlacing branches formed a roof of foliage through which the sunlight was filtered into dimness. Vines twined chokingly about their trunks, and wove themselves through the warp of the branches. Long streamers of Spanish moss hung from every limb, like dust-covered banners in some crumbling castle's hall. Underbrush hid the ground from view. Tall ferns waved high their graceful fronds. Among them gleamed the coral berries of "Solomon's seal," the crimson cardinal flower, and the livid blossom of the "Sachem's pipe."

The place was deathly still save for the drowsy hum of myriads of insects, the rustle of dead leaves as the venomous moccasin wound his way among them or the lizard flashed by, a gleam of livid green and tarnished gold. Yes, there was life in the place, but such life as hides from the light and seeks its prey in darkness.

The air was heavy and damp; the soil seemed fairly to steam; the dull, earthy odor of rotting leaves was everywhere. In truth the place was one vast swamp, full of quicksands, quagmires, pools of stagnant water hiding fathomless depths of slime—a treacherous place where death lurked for the unwary passer by.

It had a beauty of its own but it was the beauty of a Lamia—melancholy, ominous, full of terrible suggestion.

There was but one safe path through this, labyrinth to the firmer ground and more open woods about the glade beyond. Of all the world but five men knew its windings. The dwellers in the glade asked nothing of society—at least in the way of companionship, and they rather shunned wide acquaintanceship apparently; it was an innocent foible enough, one not to be cavilled at.

But what a contrast was the glade to the swampy forest that hid it from the outer world! Here all was bright, cheerful, open to the sky. The wide stretch of sward was gilded morning and evening by the unobstructed sunlight; the brilliant flowers in the carefully kept parterres received the full fervor of the luminary. In the centre of the glade stood a low, picturesque house, with doors and windows opening upon a wide, vine-shaded verandah which ran all around it—a typical southern home. On the verandah were hammocks and low chairs inviting the lounger. Children's toys were scattered about.

Let us enter. Within are everywhere tokens of good taste and culture, and surroundings indicative of wealth. The piano stands open with good music on the rest; a bit of dainty embroidery half finished, the needle still in it to mark the last stitch is flung carelessly across a low table; beside it lies open, where the reader dropped it, a book printed in the German character. Goethe's "Faust" in the original; flowers are everywhere. It is such a house as any one might envy, here in the heart of the forest.

Let us seek its occupants.

They are gathered on the verandah, a pleasant group to look upon. Two brothers and their wives, all in the prime of life, their children clinging about them.

The wives are fair matrons, their brows unclouded by care as they cling lovingly to their stalwart husbands. The children, rosy with health, clamor for caresses. The two men have just returned from a long journey, and their families are welcoming them home. It is a scene upon which we will not intrude.

As we turn away we hear a gentle voice ask:

"But why *did* you walk all that distance in the heat? Where are the horses?"

"Oh, they're all right, Annie," answers the elder man. "We didn't walk *all* the way. You see, we met some pleasant fellows on the road, and had rather a jolly time with them. Circumstances over which they had no control alone prevented them from making us a visit."

He laughs pleasantly and favors with a fraternal wink his brother, who joins in his quiet merriment. There is evidently some private joke between them.

The wives look a little curious and slightly piqued, as wives do under such circumstances.

It is in our power to penetrate the brothers' little mystery, and it is worth our while to do so. It will enable us to read their characters more clearly, and so help the story of which we may as well say at once they are the principal actors.

Three hours before, these two quiet gentlemen had stepped out of a train from the north at the little station at Paris. A man who had been holding two magnificent horses, evidently awaiting them, whispered a few words as they prepared to mount. Both men's brows grew dark. While exchanging a few hurried sentences they looked carefully to their revolvers, for both were heavily armed; then they swung themselves into their saddles and galloped away towards the forest.

"The hounds must never reach the clearing alive."

"They never will, curse them! They are but three. They have scarce an hour's start of us and unfamiliar with the path; they can move but slowly. We are sure to overtake them, and then——"

They rode on in silence.

Reaching the border of the forest they struck into a narrow path, so well-known to them that they did not check their speed. Soon they found traces of the men they were following—broken branches and hoof-marks deeply indented in the soft sod. Steadily they rode until they reached a point where the path seemed to end.

"They cannot have gone beyond this safely, unless they have information that none but the 'Youngers' could give them."

"Oh, that's impossible; they must have turned off. See, here is where they have passed. The fools have headed straight for the big quagmire. Come on."

"But we can't get the horses through the brush."

"Ours can do it if theirs did, and here are their hoof marks. They can't be far off."

They forced their horses into the thicket, and pressed on following the hoof marks. Soon they found the steeds that had made them, unguarded and tethered to trees. Dismounting, they fastened their own steeds securely but in such fashion that a turn of the hand would set them free again. They did this skillfully and quickly, like men at an accustomed task. Then looked at the strange horses critically. They were fairly good ones, so they re-arranged their tethers, fastening them just as they had already done those of their own horses.

"The shooting may stampede them, and they may be worth keeping. Their present owners are not likely to have any further use for them."

A chorus of agonized cries woke the echoes of the woodland: "Help! for God's sake help! We are drowning."

"By heavens! they're in it. We can save our cartridges!" and the two pushed eagerly forward in the direction of the cries.

Bursting through the screen of foliage, this sight met their eyes. In a treacherous swamp whose green surface apparently of solid turf was but a thin crust concealing unfathomed depths of semi-liquid mud, three men engulphed to the waist were struggling for their lives. They were the men the brothers had been following. They had ventured on the treacherous surface unconscious of danger, had broken through, and were now facing death in one of its most awful forms—they were slowly being buried alive.

Their white, horror stricken faces gleamed with joy as they saw help coming, and the voice of their leader was steady and cheerful as he sang out:

"You're very welcome just now, gentlemen. If one of you'll get back to our horses you'll find a lariat on my saddle."

The brothers laughed—not pleasantly.

The younger started as if to go to the horses. Then he paused and seemed to meditate. Then he turned back.

The sinking men regarded him with angry wonder. Minutes were precious to them. Every one that passed brought death an inch closer.

"Gentlemen," said the man on the bank deliberately, "you are asking a rather important favor of us. We are poor men, and business is business. What are we to get for this job?"

"Curse you!" yelled one of the sinking men in his agony of suspense; "don't stand there; run for the lariat!"

"You don't answer my question. Come, old man, let's go! These fellows are no good."

In awful terror the poor wretches promised everything for their lives. The two men on the bank listened with indifference. The yells and struggles grew frightful; death had climbed to their breasts now.

"Oh, well," said the elder brother, "we might as well pull them out. Go and get the lariat."

The sufferers could hear every word. Imagine the agony of suspense with which they listened to the men who could save them if they would.

"Well, that's rather cool. If you're so anxious to help them, go and get it yourself. I'll be hanged if I wade through that cursed brake again."

"Humanity, my boy, humanity. 'Do unto others,' you know."

"Well, there's something in that. Hi there, you! Which way did you say that horse was with the lariat? Eh! I can't understand. Stop thrashing around, can't you."

The men could only point with agonized eagerness in the proper direction.

How fearfully the ooze had gained during the minutes passed in this dreadful mockery, for mockery it was.

Suddenly an access of rage seemed to take entire possession

of the younger brother. His face grew fiendish, as he shook his fist at the drowning men.

"You fools; don't you know us yet? We're ——," he mentioned two names, and as the sufferers heard it a yell of despair arose from that black pool such as human ears seldom are tortured by.

"*We* save *you!* Rot, you curs, rot! So, you thought to nose out our home, did you? To seize our wives and children, and hold them as hostages for our good behavior? And all to boom your dirty little business at Topeka! To give you a name in the country! You miserable, cowardly beasts, drowning's too easy a death for you. Come, old man, let's go."

"Oh, hold on. Let's see it out. It's a sight for sore eyes."

They stood and watched the wretched men. The ooze was up to their necks now. They could struggle no longer, but their shrieks, in which curses and supplications were horribly mingled, never ceased. But the bravest of them at last composed himself to say quietly:

"Gentlemen, I won't say you're not right, and I might act as you have. But if you are men, end this! You have your pistols, and are perfect marksmen. For God's sake, put us out of our misery!"

The men on the bank seemed to assent. They drew their revolvers and took careful aim at the spokesman and another man. The first shut his eyes and calmly awaited death; the other yelled in protest, so strong and so illogical is a coward's love of life. The shot did not come. The brave man opened his eyes. He saw the two brothers fairly shaking with laughter. They had simply been adding a refinement of torture to this dreadful death. He opened his mouth to curse his tormentors or pray to his Maker; who can say which? Ere the first word was spoken the black ooze choked him. It was up to its victims' chins. They threw their heads far back for one brief moment's respite. The last moment had come. With horrible slowness the white faces sank from view. The hands were still in sight for an instant, the fingers clutching convulsively at empty air. Then they dropped helplessly and were seen no more. A few black bubbles arose and pitted the slimy surface as they broke. All was still. Three irregular black patches on the green surface alone remained to recall the tragedy just enacted.

"Let's walk the rest of the way home and send back for the horses. It will be an all day's job getting the five of them through the brake, and we're late as it is."

The brothers turned away. Said the younger: "Best not mention this at home. The notion that any one knew the path would make Annie and Zerelda nervous all summer, and there's no use in having them worried. Confound it, I'd give something to find out just how much those agents *did* know and where they got their information."

Then they talked of home matters, their wives and children, as they rapidly threaded their way through the swamp, eager for the welcome which they knew awaited them.

This horrible story is no romance. It is a simple, unexaggerated recital of but one of many such incidents in the lives of those two quiet gentlemen, those loving husbands, those tender fathers we saw on the verandah of that pleasant house in the glade. If any index to their characters is to be found in their surroundings according to theory, it must be sought not in that home but in the morass which made it a safe refuge, fair enough on the surface, but hiding in its depths untold blackness and corruption, bearing disease and death in its atmosphere—sheltering deadly serpents and noxious beasts of the night. For these two men were the most daring, cold-blooded, cruel and murderous criminals who ever disgraced the land that bore them.

For years they kept the whole West in terror. They robbed and murdered whenever and wherever they saw fit, and between crimes led quiet, easy, untroubled lives. Neither ever felt the touch of an officer, nor stood at the bar of justice, nor saw the inside of a prison even for a moment. And this but little more than a decade ago in our own well-governed land. "Impossible," say you, dwellers in well policed cities! Impossible! There are such men by scores at your very doors. Nothing keeps them down but that organized police which protects you day and night, and which few of you value at its true worth. These two men and their careers were what they were simply and solely because, in the wild country where they lived there was no police such as that of your city. Had there been their careers could not have lasted for a week, even if they had ever dared to enter upon them.

In such reflections lie the moral which, by itself, makes worth the telling the story of audacious crime printed in these pages— the history of FRANK and JESSE JAMES.

CHAPTER II.

BIRTH AND PARENTAGE OF THE JAMES BOYS.—THEIR FATHER'S DEATH.—REMOVAL TO KEARNEY.—SWEET ANNIE RALSTON.—WITH QUANTRELL'S BAND.—THE CENTRALIA MASSACRE.—ROBBING THE RUSSELLVILLE, GALLATIN, AND CORYDON BANKS.—AT KANSAS CITY.—THE FIRST TRAIN ROBBERY.—FRANK JAMES' MARRIAGE.—THE GAD'S HILL ROBBERY.—A PRIVATE DETECTIVE'S BLUNDER.—THE MUNCIE ROBBERY.—THE DETECTIVES' RAID ON THE SAMUELS' HOMESTEAD.

The James brothers were born in a reputable home, sons of a clergyman deservedly esteemed by all who knew him, and a mother who, let us say at once, was not a consciously wicked woman. Hers was a wild, fierce nature; she had absolutely no moral training, she was so thoroughly devoted to her boys that whatever they did the deed seemed right in her eyes, no matter what the law, or the gospel either, might say to the contrary.

In the year 1838 Robert James, a single-hearted young Baptist clergyman, journeying in the course of his pastoral duties through Scott county, Kentucky, met in a pioneer's cabin where he had sought hospitality, the daughter of the house, the belle of the country for miles around, Zerelda Cale. She was a bold, frank, and fearless girl, of remarkable beauty, and of very decided character. Her rude upbringing in a part of the country which was then perhaps worthy to be called "the dark and bloody ground," had given her that self-reliance which, coupled with lack of education, is often a more dangerous than a valuable trait.

Robert James was carried away by her dark Southern beauty, and the frankness with which she returned, or seemed to return, his affection. He was so different from the rough, uncouth men she was used to, that he attracted her, and she believed she loved him.

Never were two people more utterly unsuited to each other. His people were not her people, nor his God hers. Still they were married, and began their married life in Robert's home on the banks of the Kentucky river. For two years they lived in harmony, until Frank James was born in 1841.

The child was christened by its father after a member of the wife's family, and the fact is significant. It indicates the stand Zerelda took in regard to this, her first born, from the very first —a stand which many undisciplined women are prone to take, and which almost invariably makes mischief. The child was hers, exclusively. The father must not interfere with it. Any attempt at discipline or correction on his part was resented as a personal insult. To do her justice, she was a devoted mother according to her lights. The child weaned her away from her husband, and she had no love to spare for the man who had won merely her girlish fancy.

Then came misfortune and poverty to add to her feeling of indifference, a flavor of contempt, for such women have neither sympathy nor respect for a man who cannot "get along," no matter why. The winter of 1842-3 was an exceptionally severe one, and Robert James lost most of his stock. He had no other wealth, and this loss was ruinous. They sold all they had, and with a little over a hundred dollars for all their wealth sought better fortune in Missouri. Settling in the town of Liberty, in Clay county, Robert James soon won the respect of his neighbors and was made pastor of a flourishing church. A college was established and he was urged to become its president. He declined the office on account of the pressure of his pastoral work, but became a valued member of its board of trustees. He was engaged in congenial work; was honored and respected—a man of standing and weight in the community. He would have been happy had it not been for his wife. She took no pride in his successes. They were as nothing to the ignorant woman. Whatever her husband might seem to the world, he was to her always the "slack and shiftless" man who, failing in Kentucky, was wasting his time in Missouri, neglecting his opportunities, and not "making money."

In the winter of 1845 another child was born, a delicate weakly boy, who for a long time was not expected to live. He was named Jesse after Zerelda's father—the husband was not considered in that household. Expenses, of course increased, and the strain of petty deprivations and annoyances was constantly felt.

Then was, indeed, Robert James's home made a hell to him, by the constant complaints and reproaches of his wife. Money was her constant theme. It was all she thought of, all she cared for. His work, his aspirations, all that he cared for were continually jeered at. She taught his children even to despise him, to pay no attention to his wishes or commands, and so to look upon all men who led such lives and held such views as he as worthless dreamers, whose example was to be sedulously avoided. The James boys were taught contempt for honest living at their mother's knee.

In 1849 came the news of the discovery of gold in California. Robert James, driven to desperation by his wife's pitiless tongue, joined the vast army of those who made haste to be rich. They never saw him again. Two years afterward he was found in a gulch near the present site of Sacramento, dead from starvation amid boundless wealth. He had discovered a rich "placer"; one dead hand grasped a mighty nugget of virgin gold; in the other was a faintly pencilled scrawl—"What shall it profit a man if he gain the whole world, and lose his own soul?"

What a message from the dead!

Its lesson was utterly lost on the widow's coarse nature, and was never taught the James boys.

So they grew in years and stature, utterly lawless, not even knowing the meaning of restraint, save as they experienced it at the Liberty public school. They earned a fearful reputation for mischief, uncontrolled temper, and wanton cruelty. Even then their names were sounds of terror in Missouri.

Local legend tells of a school fight, in which, being attacked by a number of their mates, their devilish temper and thirst for blood so broke out that they would have killed two of their antagonists had not the whole school set upon them as if they were wild beasts, borne them to the ground by sheer weight of numbers, and never dared to leave them until they were unconscious, and incapable for the moment of doing further injury.

How their mother's heart swelled with joyful pride when she heard the story. How she petted and praised them, never tiring of dilating upon their "lickin' the hull eight of them." It was the first of many "heroic" exploits in which she was to rejoice thereafter.

In 1857, Mrs. James married again; her second choice was Dr. Reuben Samuels, a man of some means, and much better suited to her in character and disposition than her first husband. The whole family removed to a house he owned near Kearney, Missouri. All Liberty breathed a sigh of relief when the two boys, one a stripling of sixteen, and the other a not over strong child of twelve departed from among them.

Kearney was a smaller and wilder place than Liberty, and here the boys did entirely as they pleased. Reckless enough their lives were, and lawless enough, but probably no whit worse than those of most of the other youths of the neighborhood. No one, in fact, thought much of their doings, and Frank was rather popular than otherwise. The moral tone of that part of Missouri was decidedly low during the period just preceding the civil war. Every boy and man went habitually armed; every petty dispute meant shooting; every one fought for his own hand.

"They followed out the simple rule, the good old plan,
That they shall take who have the power, and they shall keep who can."

Jesse James killed two men before he was fifteen. Joy and pride swelled his mother's heart.

Frank James was not doing so well. In fact he was even then dominated by a gentler female influence than his mother's. A gentleman named Ralston had settled at Independence, a short distance from Kearney. He had a daughter Annie, a beautiful and gentle girl, whom Frank met when both were little more than children. Mr. Ralston was a man of the highest respectability and considerable means. No better evidence of Frank James' reputation and social standing at this time could be adduced than the fact that his acquaintance with Annie, which soon became very close, met with no opposition from her father. In fact Frank James, before the beginning of the war was merely a wild, reckless boy. But Jesse was even then considered irreclaimably bad. It is grim satire now, but the story goes, that the younger brother's conduct caused Frank much mortification at this time.

The civil war broke out. In this community, divided in sentiment as to the great question involved, every semblance of law was at once swept away. Quantrell appeared and organized a guerilla force nominally in aid of the Southern cause.

Dr. Samuels and all his family were ardent and outspoken Secessionists, and Frank, then twenty years of age, joined Quantrell. This step was taken with the full approval of Annie Ralston, to whom he seemed now, more than ever, a hero. At their parting their love first found speech, and their troth was plighted Jesse, too, was anxious to enlist, but the guerillas refused to take him on account of his youth.

Thenceforth was Frank James utterly delivered over to the devil. The band was simply a gang of thieves and cut-throats, whose military organization was a mere pretence to cover a war upon both parties alike whenever booty was to be gained or lust of deviltry satisfied. These scoundrels were not worthy of the name even of guerillas. It is doubtful if Quantrell himself ever really held a regular commission from the Confederate Government. They terrorized the whole country about Clay county. Blood and fire marked their track wherever they rode.

In such ranks Frank James first met Cole and Jim Younger, George Shepherd, Clell Miller, Jim Jarrette and Bill Anderson, his associates in crime in after years, and gained wonderful ascendency over them. They recognized in him the cleverest, most daring, most blood-thirsty of all Quantrell's band. He soon rose to be its leader's most trusted lieutenant. He was not a man to stop half-way in anything he undertook.

Now came an event which roused all his evil passions, and gave to his worst acts of cruelty—to his mind at least—the semblance of righteous vengeance.

Missouri was, as we have said, divided in sentiment, and Unionists were not lacking in and about Kearney. They had also organized in armed bodies. These were duly enrolled State militia, and turned their arms only against the enemies of the Union. But they were recruited from very much the same class as was Quantrell's band, and the justice of the cause they fought for was hardly sufficient to sanctify some of their proceedings.

As we have already said, Dr. Samuels was an outspoken advocate of the Southern cause. He had the courage of his convictions and a large vituperative vocabulary. He exercised these gifts so well on every possible occasion that he soon became a marked man. Early in 1862 the Union militia determined that Dr. Samuels must be abated.

Accordingly, one morning, a body of them called upon him at his home and announced to him their intention of immediately hanging him. He attempted to remonstrate—with a shot-gun—but his efforts were unsuccessful. He was dragged to the orchard and there hung to a limb of one of his own apple-trees before the horrified eyes of his wife, who, shrieking imprecations rather than prayers, had followed the executioners. When they thought their work complete, the Unionists turned back to the house, leaving the doctor dangling.

They had not reckoned on the spirit of the mother of the James boys.

She showed herself a heroine. Without help, without even a knife, aided only by two sharp-edged stones, she found means to cut the rope. She did not faint, she did not even cry out (for the house was not far away, and the raiders would return if they heard her) as her husband's lifeless body dropped heavily and helplessly to the ground. She worked to revive the hanged man. After long effort she succeeded. Bidding him flee, she returned to the house, that the Unionists might not return to the orchard in search of her, and so discover his escape.

Meanwhile the raiders had made havoc of her home, and twice hanged Jesse to the rafters to "scare" him. They little knew Jesse James.

They rode away at last, dragging with them Mrs. Samuels

and her young daughter Jessie, whom they carried to the jail at St. Joseph, where they were long incarcerated.

Jesse James, burning for revenge, sought Quantrell's camp and told his story. He was admitted at once to the band, and from that hour he and Frank devoted themselves to vengeance. Their lives seemed to have but one object—hunting down and killing the men concerned in the outrage, and every one who might be supposed to sympathize with them. When the band raided Lawrence, Kansas, and killed every man in the place, Jesse boasted that he had slain thirty-six with his own hand.

It would be tedious to catalogue the sickening series of murders committed by the James boys while with Quantrell. Let one instance serve to show what all were like, the "Centralia massacre."

Centralia was a small village in Boone county, Missouri, a way station on the Wabash road. On September 23, 1863, a federal ambulance train was drawn up near the station laden with wounded men who were thence to be transported by rail to St. Joseph. No attack was apprehended, and the ambulances were but scantily guarded. Suddenly Quantrell's band dashed into the town, scattered the guard, and in pure wantonness overturned the ambulances. Of course some of the wounded were killed by the shock, but this was merely incidental. The rest, after the guerillas had sacked the town, would probably have been left to live or die, as chance might decree, had it not been for Jesse James.

When the rest of the band rode off, he detained his brother and Bill Anderson and suggested the slaughtering of the wounded men.

This was too much, even for Frank, and he objected strenuously.

"Bah!" said Jesse. "It's easy to see you don't know what being strung up feels like—nor being shut up in St. Jos. jail like your mother and sister."

"Well, killing these Yanks isn't going to help matters any, besides its dangerous. You know we're in a fearfully tight place here, and if we're taken such a job would settle our cases at once."

Then Jesse called Frank a coward, which the elder brother naturally resented. A quarrel seemed imminent but Bill Anderson, a good natured fellow, and somewhat of a humorist in his way as will be seen, interposed to smooth things over.

"Oh, come, boys, what's the use of quarrelin'? It's dreffle fer brothers to disagree. Jesse didn't mean nothin', Frank. Shake hands and let the boy have his way. What's the odds? Cartridges is plenty. 'N' I say, what a chance to mystify the rest er the boys—lettin on as we three killed fifty Yanks all by ourselves. We needn't say nothing 'bout their bein' wounded."

Frank hesitated. Jesse had been a good brother to him, and why should he deny him the little gratification he craved. Besides the joke on the rest of the boys would be rather a good one. He put fresh caps on his revolvers.

The three leisurely approached their helpless victims. One, a slightly wounded sergeant, greeted them cheerily enough, for he had as yet only known civilized warfare, with:

"Well, gentlemen, you see our fix. We're a pretty useless lot of prisoners, so I suppose you'll take our parole. The train will be along pretty soon, and we'll get into hospital up at St. Jo. all right. If you could manage to get us a little water ——"

Crack! A shot from Jesse's pistol pierced his brain. Then crack! crack! crack! as fast as hammers could be drawn back and triggers pulled the three revolvers sped soul after soul. Some of the men shrieked for mercy, but many were too brave or too dogged to speak, and many more were already so near to death as to be indifferent or unconscious.

So, while reloading, it occurred to Jesse that he was spoiling his own sport by undue haste.

On the next round he selected his victims with care, picking out the strongest and most conscious. Some, while the hot and smoking muzzle of his revolver was painfully pressed against their foreheads, he would assure that nothing but his pure kindness of heart induced him to put them beyond the reach of suffering; others he feared were cowards, and therefore unworthy to live; others still he pretended to listen to, as if their plaints made him hesitate in his purpose. All he slew, after prolonging their torture by every means his devilish ingenuity could devise.

Meanwhile Frank and good-natured Bill Anderson were not idle, and at last all the wounded were dead.

To Bill Anderson's everlasting credit be it said, that he robbed Jesse of his last victim. While the young fiend was playing on the soldier's hopes and fears, Anderson, who had one chamber still charged, mercifully killed the sufferer, and thus remonstrated:

"What's the use o' bein so durned aggravatin, Jesse?"

Just then a bugle's note called the humorists back to duty. They found their comrades formed up in order of battle. A company of Iowa volunteer cavalry had appeared on the crest of a hill to the north of the town. Though much inferior in strength, numbering not more than forty men all told, it ventured to charge the guerilla force.

It was a foolhardy enterprise. It ended disastrously. The company was exterminated, not a single man escaping.

Quantrell's band rode away unscathed, leaving Centralia a heap of embers, among which lay over a hundred corpses in the blue uniforms.

Such were the scenes in which the James brothers played leading parts until near the close of the war when Missouri became thoroughly dominated by the Union forces. Then Quantrell's band found its occupation gone, and began to disintegrate. Jesse James went to Texas, and led a wild life there for three years. Frank followed his leader with a remnant of the band, now avowed outlaws and bandits, into Kentucky, and shared its predatory fortunes, until in an encounter with forces sent against them by the authorities, all his gang but one were killed like wolves. That one was Frank James. He escaped without a scratch. He finally made his way back to Kearney.

For some time after, with Jesse away, and Frank keeping discreetly quiet, Missouri heard nothing of the James boys. But ere long Jesse returned, and, drawing around them a number of their old associates of Quantrell's band, the brothers began their extraordinary criminal career.

Their "prentice hands" they tried in Russellville, a small town in Logan county, Kentucky. On the afternoon of March 20, 1868, Frank and Jesse James, with four followers, all heavily armed and superbly mounted, dashed into the town at the top of their horses' speed and made straight for the bank. The suddenness of their appearance, their fiendish yells, the random but incessant fire from their revolvers, and the mad recklessness of their riding, left the confused citizens no time for thought. A couple of cool and determined officers, armed according to custom and trained to feel that such emergencies are "all in the day's work," could probably have stopped the raid at once; a single well-aimed shot, disabling man or horse, would have done it, by delaying them for the few minutes necessary to enable the townspeople to recover their wits and rally in overpowering force. But organized police were unknown in Russellville. Unchecked for even an instant, the band reached the bank. The James brothers rushed in, finding the cashier, a mild mannered individual named Harris, alone in his office.

A command to "open that safe," backed by the dumb eloquence of two levelled revolvers, met with instant obedience. Frank ransacked the vault, while Jesse kept Mr. Harris in order without the slightest trouble. It took very few minutes to secure all the money, some $14,000, and then the successful robbers relieved the cashier of their unwelcome presence, swung themselves into their saddles, and were clear of the town before its inhabitants had fairly realized what had happened. Mr. Harris took this opportunity to faint away, thus rendering it necessary to resuscitate him before the truth could be learned. When at last he did speak, and the people of Russellville realized that about all the ready money in the place was being borne towards Missouri at a very rapid rate, it did not take long to organize an energetic pursuit. It was kept up for nearly two weeks without any striking success. George Shepherd's horse gave out, and he was captured, tried and sent to the penitentiary for three years, but the rest got off safely with their booty.

It cannot be truthfully said that the robbery roused any deep feeling outside of the immediate neighborhood of Russellville. The complaisance of the cashier had made his murder unnecessary, and no special atrocity had marked the raid. In fact, the whole affair came to be regarded rather in the light of a good joke on the stalwart yeomen of Russellville by the citizens of other places, who in fact were rather inclined to think that they would like to see any such game played on them.

Within a few weeks the good people of Gallatin were gratified. One afternoon, just before the close of banking hours, the same gang robbed the bank there in exactly the same fashion. But this time they added murder to robbery. Captain Sheetz, the Gallatin cashier, was made of sterner stuff than his Russellville confrére, and refused, spite of all threats to in any way aid in robbing the depositors. He was killed in cold blood, and the deliberate villians paused long enough to write and fix conspicuously on his breast, this legend:

"HE DIED OF OBSTINACY."

Having secured about $8,000 the murderers rode away. The pursuit was close. Shots were exchanged, but to the disadvantage of the pursuers, two of whom fell. Finally the pursued made good their escape.

There was no apathy, no laughing this time. The cruel murder of Captain Sheetz had roused the whole country. It became too hot to hold Frank and Jesse James.

They fled—to this day no one knows certainly where. The probabilities are that they made for Jesse's haunts in Texas and Mexico, and under assumed names started and led for a while moderately decent lives. It is supposed that at this time they discovered the forest-glade near Paris, where they subsequently made their home.

But it was not long before they were heard of in Missouri after a fashion that made the country ring with their names. In the spring of 1869, a great political meeting was held at Corydon. It was a widely advertised affair; many well-known men were to address it, and the farmers for miles around attended. Many of them took the opportunity to bring into town such money as they had accumulated since their last visit for deposit in the local bank.

So the day was a busy one in that institution, and when the political meeting was called to order in the afternoon, Cashier Hinman was about the only man in the bank who could not spare the time to attend it. He was the soul of business, and until the day's transactions were all booked, and the cash balanced to the last penny, the affairs of the country must take care of themselves so far as he was concerned.

He missed a great intellectual treat. The speakers were most eloquent, the audience most enthusiastic, especially when one local favorite began to sing the praises of the "beautiful town in which we are to-day assembled—Corydon, the fairest gem that decks the swelling bosom of our mother land—a town where law and order reign, where such atrocities as have disgraced the records of less favored towns are impossible. Who ever heard of a raid or a bank robbery in Corydon? Why, gentlemen, at the first whisper of lawlessness our hardy yeomen would rise in their might and sweep the ruffian horde——"

Where the "ruffian horde" was to be swept to no one will ever know. The speaker was interrupted here, and never regained the thread of his discourse.

A tall man, sitting on a magnificent horse in the outskirts of the crowd, called out in a voice clear and loud enough for all to hear, "one moment, sir. The Corydon National Bank has this very day been robbed of $40,000, and—I've got the money. Good day, all." The tall horseman and a companion dashed away with a ringing laugh.

For an instant astonishment kept the crowd silent. But there were many there who knew that tall rider, and a dozen voices shouted :

"It's Frank James. After him !"

Oh ! then, and there was mounting in hot haste, but no one was particularly anxious to start sooner than the rest, and the James boys had a good five minutes' headway—quite enough for them, mounted as they were.

A strip of woodland checked the pursuers. They had time to think of the unpleasant consequences likely to befall people who, uninvited, might press too closely on men as quick at the trigger as the James boys. Many evolved a belief that Frank's announcement was simply an audacious joke, and turned back "to see if the bank had really been robbed." The more determined pushed on, but uselessly. A fortnight later, they returned crest-fallen, without either the James boys or the $40,000.

For Frank's statement had the merit of exact truth. The doubters found the business-like Mr. Hinman in a most unbusiness-like attitude, gagged and bucked in scientific fashion, lying in a heap on his office floor, dumbly guarding an empty safe, a vacant counter, and a rifled money drawer.

He told his tale, with much indignation at the unbusiness-like method of drawing money that had been pursued. He had been so busily engaged, he said, that he had failed to notice the entrance of two strangers, and their approach to the receiving teller's window where he was at work. He heard a pleasant " good day, Mr. Hinman," and, looking up, saw them watching his proceedings with apparent interest. He was counting the cash. He responded to their greeting politely, but told them that the bank was closed for the day, and that he was so unusually busy that they must excuse him from conversing, and resumed his count.

"What was my surprise and indignation," continued Mr. Hinman "when, for reply, one of them pointed a revolver at my head, and in a most peremptory and offensive tone told me to keep my "trap" shut, and hand over that money! I was speechless with indignation at such a demand, but some inner voice seemed to warn me that remonstrance would be useless. In short I ——"

"You handed over the money," broke in an impatient listener with something of a sneer.

"I honored their draft," corrected Mr. Hinman with dignity.

"Well, you're an infernal coward," answered the other hotly. " I'd have died sooner."

"Perhaps so; you are not a man of a business turn of mind. Heroism did not at the time strike me as likely to be profitable, and I have not altered my view since. I fail to see how the fact of my being killed would have in any way improved matters. My body would not be a particularly available asset, and the expenses of my funeral, which the bank, in common decency must have assumed, would have been an additional item on the wrong side of the ledger."

There was nothing to say in answer to this argument. Mr. Hinman took his pen, opened the big customers' ledger, turned to a new page and headed a new account:

"FRANK AND JESSE JAMES"
"*IN ACCOUNT WITH*"
"THE CORYDON NATIONAL BANK."

Then he made the first entry under it. It was on the debit side, and it read:

"To overdraft (unsecured) . . . $40,000."

Having thus to a certain extent legitimized the transaction and "balanced his cash," Mr. Hinman felt relieved.

So the James brothers had gained another small fortune with almost ludicrous ease, and for over a year they found it unnecessary to exert themselves further. But at the end of that time Missouri was horrified by another bank robbery, with murder for an episode. Columbus was the scene of the crime, and the method was the same that had proved so effectual at both Russellville and Gallatin. The four Youngers, Bill, Cole, Jim and John, took part in the raid, and the bandits gained the bank with their usual impunity. But they had timed their visit badly; both the cashier and the vice-president were in the bank, the vault was locked, and the officers sternly refused to reveal the combination. It cost the cashier his life (the vice-president escaped through an overlooked side door with no more serious injury than a pistol bullet in his shoulder), but the funds of the bank were saved. Unable to open the vault, the murderers were fain to content themselves with the loose cash lying in the drawer. It amounted to only $230, and they showed their contempt for the paltry prize by using the bills as wadding and "firing them back at the mean skunks."

Strange to say, this crime seemed to rouse but little attention. The ruffians escaped unmolested, almost unpursued. The "James boys" had made robbed banks and murdered cashiers commonplace in Missouri. The bank officers congratulated themselves on the safety of their funds, appointed a new cashier, and business went on as usual.

So did the business of the James brothers. Their next enterprise was less bloody and more remunerative. In the autumn of 1871 a great county fair was held at Kansas City. It was the event of the year, both for the town and the country for miles around, the greatest fair Missouri had ever seen. Exhibits and exhibitors poured in, and the town was crowded with strangers. Among them were three rough farmer-like men, who walked the crowded streets unnoticed, although they were three of the most famous men in the State. The fair was to last a week, and Wednesday was its greatest day. Crowds besieged the treasurer's office, buying tickets of admission or paying entrance fees for their exhibits. Nearly $10,000 were taken in, and when at last the lull came, and the treasurer had counted the receipts, he felt at peace with all mankind—expansive, sociable, inclined to pass his well-earned leisure time in friendly chat with some one whom he could impress with the magnitude of his office. The money was left carelessly lying on the counter in full view; he was pardonably proud of the show it made.

Just then the three farmer-like looking men rode slowly up One of them leisurely dismounted and lounged over to the office.

"Fine weather, pardner," was his countrified salutation.

"Yaas," replied the treasurer with condescension; "kinder hot, though—onseasonable it seems to me."

"Big day for you, I reckon."

"Fair, fair; nothin' to complain of. Thar's nigh ten thousand dollars in that pile."

"Sho! What an all fired heap of money! I sh'd think you'd be skeered o' bein' robbed. 'N thet reminds me, I heer'd only awhile ago that them James boys was kinder cavortin' 'round again."

"Oh, dern the James boys! I don't take any stock in half the yarns they tell about them." And the treasurer settled himself on his elbows for a good chat. "It don't stand to reason. Now do you s'pose I'd, f r instance, be such a gosh blasted fool as to hand over that pile to a hull caboodle of James boys without a fuss, with all these folks within ear shot. Why one single yell 'd send 'em kitin', and any fool could give that."

"Wall, I s'pose so, I s'pose so. But jest s'posin' I was ter jam a gun in your face and say ' I 'm Jesse James. Hand over that ar money, what 'd you say ?' "

"Say !" laughed the treasurer. "I'd tell you to go climb a sage bush. I'd ——"

A revolver's muzzle stopped his mouth, and Jesse James's natural voice hissed out: "You old fool, hand over that money, quick, without a word, or ——"

There was no need to complete the sentence; the money was in his hands. He regained his saddle and, with the two other farmer-like looking men—Frank James and Jim Younger,—rode rapidly away.

Imagine, if you can, the sensation that followed. The unfortunate treasurer had a hard time of it, and the Kansas City *Times* only voiced the general sentiment when it editorially condemned his carelessness, and to make its point stronger went very far towards justifying the robbers.

It is evident that the James boys had not even taken the trouble to leave Kansas City from what follows. That very night two men rode up to the *Times* office and sent up a message to the editor, Major J. N. Edwards, asking him to favor them by stepping down stairs for a moment, as they had something of importance to communicate to him and could not leave their horses. Major Edwards, probably anticipating an item, complied with alacrity.

The two strangers greeted him most courteously. "Major," said one, "you have been so uniformly fair in your treatment of two much maligned men, that they feel that they owe you a debt of gratitude. I am Jesse James, this is my brother Frank. We beg you will accept and wear this as a slight token of our friendly feelings towards you." He handed the editor a package, and with a cordial pressure of the hand, and a hearty "Good-night, old man !" the two strangers rode away.

The package contained "an elegant gold watch and chain."

Somewhat ungratefully the editor at once notified the authorities of his adventure, but he was not destined to have the capture of his friends on his conscience. The "police" of Kansas City were not at that time what we understand by the term.

Shortly after, in October of the same year, the James gang robbed the St. Genevieve bank of $5,000. The robbery was a very ordinary affair—for them—without sensational incidents. It made no especial stir.

More than a year rolled quietly by. In the rush and hurry of Western life the James brothers and their deeds were almost forgotten. So far was this true that in June, 1873, the James' and the Youngers' came back almost openly to Kearney, and no attempt was made to interfere with them. Almost co-incidentally with their arrival a Chicago, Rock Island and Pacific railroad train was wrecked in the neighborhood, and the express car robbed of some $4,000. Frank James was about to be married, and probably wanted a little pocket money for his wedding trip.

For during all these years he had been in communication with Annie Ralston, and the girl's love for and faith in him had never once wavered. Her infatuation was complete; knowing his character perfectly well, she clung to him in spite of all. It almost seems that there must have been some good in a man who could inspire such an attachment. Let that be as it may, his love for her was genuine and undoubted, and in her eyes that atoned for much.

Frank had the effrontery to formally ask her father's approval of the match. Mr. Ralston rejected his advances with honest indignation, and treated the bold suitor to a torrent of plainer language than he was wont to patiently endure. But Frank took it quietly enough, merely warning the father that his consent was asked merely as a matter of form, and that they would marry without it when the time was ripe.

"Very likely, as you are a thief," was all Mr. Ralston's response, and the two men parted. Annie was at once forbidden, on pain of being exiled forever from her father's home and heart, ever to see, write to, or even think, of Frank James again. She knew her father's stern character. She knew he fully meant all he said. But she had counted the cost long ago. She lived only for Frank James, and when he should call her she was ready to give up home, friends, honest repute, everything, and go to him. In this month of June, 1873, the call came, and found her ready. She was at Kansas City, and at once went by rail to Kearney. Frank James met her at the station, alone, in strange guise for an expectant bridegroom, his weapons belted about him. There was one quick embrace, then the girl was swung lightly to her lover's saddle, and clinging behind him, she was carried to his mother's house, where Mrs. Samuels received her son's choice with a loving welcome, doubtless, after the manner of mothers, thinking her a very lucky girl.

Here they were married. It was a strange wedding party,— Jesse, the Youngers, and others of the murderous band were its only witnesses; but all were kind to the gentle girl, and she was happy anywhere with Frank. Soon he took her to his forest home in Texas, and here they began an almost idyllic life "under the greenwood tree." Frank's absences on lawless expeditions were frequent, but time and again he returned safely, and she grew to have such faith in his prowess and good fortune that she felt no anxiety or doubt about his safety. Nor was she altogether deprived of female society. Zerelda Minn, a cousin of the James boys, a beautiful and cultivated woman, a school teacher in Kansas City, frequently spent weeks with her, and Jesse was no infrequent visitor. Soon Jesse and Zerelda fell in love and married, and the two families lived together in perfect harmony. It seems a strange assertion to make, but it may well be doubted if two happier wives could have been found than Annie and Zerelda James. Their husbands were devoted to them, and had no secrets from them. Only the children were deceived as to their fathers' lives.

As a rule only the summers were passed in the forests. In winters they generally went to St. Louis or Louisville, and lived fearless and unmolested in the very midst of their enemies. There is no stranger feature in all this strange history than the almost ideal home lives of these two outlaws. But we may not dwell longer upon it.

Frank was not allowed to linger long by Annie's side immediately after their marriage. An important business enterprise was on foot and Jesse sent for him in September. The James brothers were about to make their first essay in a new form of industry—" holding up " railroad trains.

It was a grand conception, when one thinks of it, this of treating mighty express trains thundering with irresistible force along their iron ways, guarded by strong crews of train men, carrying hundreds of people, in the same fashion that the highwaymen of a century ago treated the lumbering English stage coaches. To confidently enter upon such an enterprise with their scant numbers showed the perfect confidence in themselves possessed by the members of the James gang, as well as their shrewd knowledge of average human nature. To say that there was little peril in these undertakings, would be sheer absurdity. A single hitch in the working of the scheme ; a single man among the passengers used to scenes of violence, reckless of his life, and " quick on the shoot;" a single shot wasted ; a defective cap ; a jammed cylinder—any one of a thousand perfectly possible accidents might readily ruin all and place the bandits in an instant at the mercy of an overpowering throng of suddenly emboldened passengers. But they did not hesitate. Execution followed closely on conception with them.

One afternoon in late September (1873), the gentleman who represented in his single self the station master, ticket agent, telegraph operator, freight and express agent,—a very Pooh Bah among railroad men,—at a lonesome little station called Gad's Hill, on the St. Louis and Iron Mountain Road, sat in his office cursing his fate, and longing for anything in the way of excitement. The weather was eminently suited to his mood, for it was about as stormy, wet, and altogether gloomy a day as ever bluedevils chose to disport themselves in. No one was out of doors who could possibly stay at home, and our friend had resigned all hope of human companionship, when five mounted men splashed up to the station, dismounted, and entered. They were entire strangers to him, but he was glad to welcome them ; they at least could talk and listen. They lounged about, cursing the weather, and chatting idly on all current subjects, now and then interjecting some apparently objectless question about the road. One of these was an inquiry at what hour the night express ought to be along.

"At eleven-thirty," yawned the agent, thinking of the length of weary hours he had still to pass.

After a while the strangers lounged out, thanking the agent for his shelter, and he relapsed once more into silent gloom. He little thought that what had passed was the prelude to a drama that would cure him of all further longing for excitement, and make Gad's Hill Station for a while as famous as its English namesake, where once a Prince of Wales played foot-pad and a certain fat knight did deeds of prowess on unnumbered men in buckram, as is duly set forth in the works of one William Shakespeare, or Francis Bacon, as the case may be.

Night settled down on the lowly station, and the weather grew worse and worse. The station master dozed away the hours, listening to the rush of the rain and blinking at his dog, who sympathetically blinked in return. As the night wore on the animal became strangely restless; he sniffed at the door, scratched at it, whined and barked uneasily, and finally made his master so nervous that he arose to end the annoyance by kicking the brute out-of-doors. As he opened the door he saw something that made him rub his eyes. It was a red light. Now, ordinarily a red light is not a specially remarkable nor alarming apparition, but this one was just where a white light should be, the signal to the coming express train that the track was clear. If it were left as it were, signalling "danger" through the night, it would stop the train needlessly, and our friend's subsequent connection with the Iron Mountain Road would be very temporary indeed. So, braving the storm, he started out to alter the signal. He had taken scarcely two steps when he was roughly seized by the throat and thrown to the ground, while a rough voice whispered its owner's amiable intention of cutting his heart out if he uttered a sound.

In a moment more he was securely bound, a gag was fixed in his mouth; he was carried back to his office and flung unceremoniously into a corner to reflect on the joys of excitement and wonder what would happen next. By the dim light of a lantern he had noticed that his assailants were five in number, and except that they all wore masks, bore a strong general resemblance to his afternoon visitors.

Soon he heard the distant whistle of the coming train, then the roar of its nearer approach, then the sharp, quick signal for "brakes," then the manifold noises that mark the sudden stopping of a heavy train running at full speed—then for a moment all was silent, save for the hoarse roar of escaping steam.

But for a moment only—then his ears were stunned by a perfect pandemonium of yells, masculine curses and feminine shrieks, punctuated with the sharp cracks of revolvers. Though not a person of extraordinary acumen, the station agent knew what was happening.

The moment the train stopped, two masked men leaped into the cab. One instantly seized the engineer by the throat, and presenting a cocked revolver threatened him with instant death if he dared attempt to move the train. The other stunned the fireman with a single blow, threw him from the engine, and rushed back to join his comrades, who were already in the passenger cars yelling like fiends, sending pistol bullets flying everywhere, and so completely terrorizing the sleepy passengers that they gave up their valuables on demand without a thought of resistance. The work was done systematically, though rapidly, and nothing was overlooked or spared. There is a somewhat apocryphal story to the effect that Frank James was gallant enough to allow a charming widow to retain a pair of valuable diamond ear-rings, which she tearfully declared constituted all her wordly wealth. We doubt its truth. It doesn't sound like Frank James. He was not a man ever to allow sentiment to interfere with business, and was, as we have said, a model husband. He might well doubt if even gentle Annie James would altogether approve of lenity to charming and tearful young widows, however much she might advocate mercy as an abstract quality.

After securing some $6,000 in money and miscellaneous property from the passengers, the robbers gained possession of the express cars, and realized some $14,000 from the money packages in the safe. Then, with a parting volley and an ironical cheer the band disappeared in the darkness leaving the train to pursue its way, only a few minutes late, and the passengers poorer in purse but richer by an experience which would be material for constantly growing stories during the rest of their lives.

We must be pardoned for treating this audacious crime after a somewhat light fashion. No bloodshed attended it, and the scenes in the cars during its progress were more ludicrous than tragic. Besides, it is not in human nature to feel much deep sympathy for people who could allow themselves to be robbed in such utterly unresisting fashion.

But, naturally, the victims saw nothing funny in the matter. Neither did the railroad, nor the express company. Corporations have neither souls nor sense of humor, and these knew that if they were thereafter to transact business safely or profitably in that part of the country they must at once put a stop to such crimes as this, and make examples of its perpetrators. A corporate and individual clamor arose which ended in a heavy reward being offered for the detection and conviction of the Gad's Hill robbers. Its principal direct effect was the tempting of one brave man to his death, but it may be noted that the James brothers perpetrated no more robberies as near home as this was.

The brave man referred to was John W. Wicher, said to be an agent detailed by a famous Chicago detective firm to find the hiding-place of the James boys. His idea was to obtain a footing in the Samuels' house, which he rightly judged would be the best place possible to get the information he wanted. He started out from St. Louis as a tramp, and consistently kept up the character until dusty, foot-sore, and ragged he arrived at Kearney. He had been guilty of not one single act, so far, inconsistent with his assumed character of an aimless vagrant looking for odd jobs of farm work. But at Kearney he seems for the time to have lost his head completely. He committed the fatal blunder of allowing it to be known that he was in search of the Samuels' house, by asking a boy to direct him thither. How he could have overlooked the fact that this must sooner or later reach the ears of the James boys, and at once arouse their suspicions, it is difficult to imagine. He must have had a poor opinion of their abilities if he for a moment supposed they would see nothing strange in the fact that an aimless wanderer, a stranger in the place, should know that there was such a man as Dr. Samuels in it, and single out his house particularly as his destination; and he must have realized that the least suspicion meant death for him. Still he committed the blunder, and atoned for it with his life. He reached the Samuels' house. The doctor wanted help. The sturdy tramp was engaged, and at once set at work. At supper he met Frank and Jesse James and Clell Miller. His task was successfully ended. He knew the retreat of the James brothers. His dreams that night were pleasant.

The bandits had probably no suspicion of the new farm hand. His story was perfectly straight and consistent, for he had no need to invent. For some time back he had been just what he appeared to be, a tramp, leading a tramp's life. Still for men in their position it was such an obvious precaution to verify as much of his story as possible, that as soon as he had retired the three bandits rode over to Kearney and asked questions of every one. Every thing they heard corroborated him, and they were about to return satisfied, when chance threw in their path the boy of whom Wicher had asked his one foolish question.

The boy's story was Wicher's death warrant. The three returned home as speedily as possible and made their way noiselessly to the detective's bed-side. Rousing him they charged him with being a spy. Half asleep, and off his guard, his very denial betrayed him. They made him dress, bound him hand and foot, and dragged him out of doors. All this was done very quietly. There was no use of implicating "Marm" and the "Doctor" in what they were about to do.

But the trampling of their horses roused the old man—they slept lightly in that house. Recognizing the tall figures of his step sons, he called out, querulously:

"What are you boys up to now? Who've you got there?"

"Your new farm hand, curse him. He's a detective and we're going to kill him."

It was Miller who thus replied.

"Shut up, you fool!" hissed Frank, with a curse, as the old man cried:

"Come now, none o' that. I don't want any such talk, or any such doin's 'round here, and what's more I won't have it."

"Oh, it's all right Doc. Clell's only trying to scare the fool. But he is a spy, for a fact, and we've got to get him shut up safely somewhere. Go to bed."

They rode off, carrying their victim with them. Three days afterwards the unfortunate detective's body was found by some sportsmen in a patch of woodland near Independence, just across the Missouri River from Kearney.

For the rest of that winter the James boys were unmolested. In the spring they sought, with their families, the rural joys of the house in the forest. They stayed late that year (1874), Frank being so much disinclined to leave his wife that in November Jesse grew impatient and started off alone. Returning to his old haunts he hunted up Clell Miller, and with him "Bud" and Thompson McDaniels, and John Hines perfected a scheme for robbing a Kansas Pacific train. Muncie, a small station in Kansas, about eight miles west of Kansas City, was selected as the scene of operations for more than one reason. It was very lonely, and the station agent was a man very amenable to reason.

Shortly before dark on a stormy December afternoon the five outlaws rushed into the station and, after an exchange of shots, overpowered the agent, who, strange to say, was only very slightly wounded. Night fell in the midst of the most terrific snow-storm of the winter. The wind was blowing fiercely, and the train eastward bound was fighting its way in the very teeth of the storm. The engineer's every sense was alert, and he slowed down at once the moment he caught the red gleam of the danger signal at Muncie, set by the bandits. It was just the place where a heavy drift might be looked for. Instantly two of the band were on his engine, and he and his fireman were at their mercy. Jesse James and Clell Miller at the same time uncoupled the express car (next after the tender as usual) from the rear part of the train, and then the engineer was compelled to move forward for about a mile, thus isolating the express messenger from all hope of aid. The car was entered, and the messenger forced to deliver up about $24,000 in money and a thousand dollars'-worth of jewelry. Then the band rode off through the storm, the fast-falling snow obliterating all traces of their flight.

This robbery aroused the authorities thoroughly. The hunt was up indeed, but for a long time there was nothing to guide the hunters but the universal conviction that only the James gang could have devised and carried out such a scheme. But after a while "Bud" McDaniels got drunk in Kansas City, and was arrested for disorderly conduct. When searched, a quantity of the stolen jewelry was found upon him. He was at once held on the charge of being concerned in the Muncie train robbery and delivered over to the Kansas authorities, who lodged him in the jail at Lawrence, there to await his trial. In May, 1875, he broke jail, but was mortally shot the next day by a farmer named George Banerman. Finding himself dying he made a full confession implicating all his comrades.

So, five months after the Muncie robbery the local officers, by a series of fortuitous circumstances which they did very little to bring about, at last discovered who had committed it. They set about securing them. The results of their work were ridiculously disproportionate.

Hinds was buying some ammunition in a shop at Independence when the local sheriff entered, and kindly informed him that he was his prisoner, before taking the precaution to secure him. Hinds naturally went away by the back door, and was seen no more.

"Clell" Miller was found at his home, partially disabled by a badly sprained ankle, by the sheriff of his county with a posse of twelve armed men. He tricked the official into helping him on with his boot, jammed the muzzle of his pistol into his ear, induced him to escort him past his posse to their horses, chose the best of the lot and calmly rode away, still keeping the sheriff at his side until he was out of range. And that was the last of him.

Can you imagine the very clumsiest member of a trained police force committing such blunders as these? Do you wonder at the immunity so long enjoyed by the James boys?

The attempt made to seize the brothers themselves after the Muncie robbery was a more terrible blunder still. It was worse than that—it was a barbarous, cowardly outrage, as bad as any crime the James boys themselves ever committed. But comment is unnecessary; a bare statement of the facts will sufficiently exhibit its character. It is well however to bear in mind that at the time it took place the brothers were merely under suspicion of being concerned in the Muncie robbery, and, as a matter of fact, Frank had nothing whatever to do with it. Moreover several of the other sleeping inmates of the house into which a death-dealing bomb was to be thrown at random—that was the civilized and highly legal device which commended itself to the charming representatives of law and order who undertook the arrest—certainly were and were well known to the officers to be absolutely innocent of any crime whatever, being merely helpless children.

It is characteristic of the James brothers, that after the Muncie robbery Jesse went straight to the Samuels' house, and Frank chose this time of all others to leave his forest refuge and join him there. So, on the night of January 27, 1875, both were at their mother's home.

About nine o'clock that evening a special train, made up of an engine and one car, drew up at the Kearney station. The passengers, eight stalwart men, heavily armed, descended, and having procured conveyances, were driven to a point within a short distance of the Samuels' house. Here they left their teams, and after a short consultation, crept cautiously toward the house, spreading their line as they advanced, and preceded at a distance of some fifty feet by one of their number who carried a small round missile of cast-iron—in short, a loaded bomb. Having safely reached a point near enough for his purpose, he hurled his infernal machine through the nearest window, which happened to be that of Mrs. Samuels' bed-room. It was a clumsy contrivance, with a too long fuze, and did not explode for an appreciable time. The delay was fatal to the man who threw it. The noise brought a tall form at once to another window, and a bullet from a rifle discharged at point blank range pierced his brain.

Then came a blinding flash of light, the roar of a mighty explosion, and then the shriek of a child calling on its mother in its death agony, and a wounded woman's inarticulate moans.

The bomb had torn off Mrs. Samuels' left arm, and killed her little son, Archie, outright.

Truly, these "officers of the law" had reason to be proud of their work!

The seven poured a perfect hail of lead into the dark and smoking house. Only two shots answered, but each disabled its man. At last the private detectives, for such they were, finding that their fire drew no further reply, ventured to enter the house. They found there only a dead boy, and an aged man dressing an aged woman's ghastly wound. These brilliant geniuses had left the rear door of the house utterly unwatched, and Frank and Jesse James had again escaped. After making an utterly useless search of the house, the detectives returned to St. Louis, proud, let us hope, of their heroic deeds.

The brothers lingered in the neighborhood until after Archie was buried, and their mother's recovery assured. Then they turned south. They made a farewell call on a neighbor, one Daniel Askew. He it was who had set the detectives on them. They called him out, and left him dead on his own threshold. That was their farewell.

It was only natural that the events of this January night should make the James boys more fierce and bloodthirsty than they had ever yet been, but it also seems to some extent to have "broken their nerve." Thereafter they never seem to have laid their plans with the old skill, nor executed them with the old boldness. Their next enterprise was an utter failure, and the beginning of the end of their career. We refer to the attempt to rob the Northfield bank.

CHAPTER III.

THE NORTHFIELD BANK ROBBERY.—THE SAFE WITHSTANDS ASSAULT.—MURDER OF THE CASHIER.—FLIGHT AND PURSUIT.—A NIGHT IN THE SADDLE.—THE COUNTRY AROUSED.—THE JAMES BROTHERS SEPARATE FROM THE OTHER ROBBERS.—FRANK JAMES WOUNDED.—AN IMPROMPTU HORSE-DEAL.—SAFE AT LAST.—DEATH OR CAPTURE OF THE REST OF THE BAND.—THE GLENDALE TRAIN ROBBERY.—THE BEGINNING OF THE END.—GOVERNOR CRITTENDEN'S PROCLAMATION.—DEATH OF JESSE JAMES.

September is the month of months in Minnesota. The temperature always so cool that blankets are a necessity at night even in midsummer, then gets a keener edge from the first hint of winter in the early frosts; the sky sometimes throughout the month is absolutely cloudless, and the atmosphere takes on such a peculiar, almost metallic, crispness that ordinary sounds are borne for miles across the great stretches of prairie farm land, which end only with the horizon. September 7, 1876, was just such an ideal day at Northfield. No breeze worthy the name of a Minnesota wind had stirred all day long, scarcely a flake of cloud had flitted across the sky, and the little town of only 2,000 inhabitants seemed wrapped in the autumnal calm. From a distance the only signs of life to be perceived were the hum of the little mills and factories, carried with unusual distinctness through the clear, dry air, and the smoke from their chimneys curling lazily upward. Within the village a few score farmers from the surrounding country, for whose produce Northfield was then and still is the main market, were making ready to return home, and the store-keepers had begun to reckon up the day's receipts. Three o'clock had passed, and the lengthening shadows of the small but pretentious business blocks gave silent warning that trade for the day was nearly over. A few villagers were passing through the streets, and at a corner on the main street, near the most imposing building in the town, its only bank, stood a knot of loiterers idly discussing local gossip. Inside the bank the cashier, alone save for his young assistant, had closed his windows against possible tardy customers. Many of the farmers had made deposits and the afternoon had been a busy one, but the cashier's work was nearly done. The books and the bulk of the cash on hand had already been locked up in the safe; a small amount of money, mainly in silver, which could be entrusted to the cash-drawer over night, was all that remained to be disposed of, and the cashier and his assistant were busy counting the little heaps of dimes, quarters and half dollars. The ticking of the big clock on the wall and the chinking of the small coin as it passed rapidly through the fingers of the two men relieved the silence of the bank just about as the ordinary noises of the town did the pervading quiet out of doors.

But suddenly the peaceful scene outside was turned to one of wild and exciting tumult. The loiterers near the bank caught the first sounds of the uproar. They heard a loud but confused disturbance down the main street near the western border of the town; then came the sharp crack of rapid pistol shots, followed by a clatter of horses' hoofs. Mingled with these fast increasing noises were wild yells and furious oaths. The pistol shots came faster and sharper; the curses grew louder and fiercer; there was a rush of horses galloping madly nearer and nearer, and down the street in a whirl of dust dashed a band of wild horsemen. On they came whooping and howling, cursing more frantically with every bound of their horses, and swaying almost clear of their saddles, as they sent bullets whizzing up and down the street, and flying at random into the stores at either side. The loiterers near the bank stopped only long enough to note that there were seven horsemen in the frenzied cavalcade. Then they rushed headlong for shelter, and other wayfarers followed their examples. In a twinkling every pedestrian had vanished; the marauding party had swept the street like a cyclone, and now they wheeled suddenly at the bank. The two men who had led the mad ride into the town swung from their saddles before their horses had fairly halted; their bridles were tossed to the nearest of the gang, and the first of the leaders to alight shouted,

"Stand close, boys; keep your heads, and shoot the first man who approaches!" Then the two men darted into the little bank.

The reader needs no introduction to them. They were the James boys. Their dash into Northfield and down the main street, spreading consternation on every side, had occupied not a tenth of the time it takes in telling, and the bank cashier was hardly aware of the commotion outside, when the desperadoes confronted him. He had just started from his desk to lock up for the night, when two revolvers flashed in his face, before he could think of his own weapon, much less get it from the drawer in his desk.

"Do not move, or you're a dead man," said Jesse, in the quiet tone peculiar to him at such critical moments; then, turning to his brother, he added: "See what's in the safe, Frank; I'll cover this fellow and the other," and he pointed a second revolver at the terrified assistant as he spoke.

"What do you want here?" demanded the cashier, involuntarily moving back a step.

"You stand where you are, and keep your mouth shut, or I'll close it for good," was Jesse's answer, and he shoved the revolver in his right hand so close that it touched the cashier's forehead. The cashier was a brave man, and he proved it to his cost. Frank James had been unsuccessfully trying to open the safe.

"The combination is set, Jesse," he said. "Bring that cur here and make him open it."

"Move backward to the safe and unlock the door," commanded Jesse. But the cashier made no step. "Move over and open that safe; quick, do you hear?" cried Jesse again, and still the cashier did not stir. He glanced unflinchingly from the pistol muzzle to the bandit's eyes, and stared him full in the face. He said nothing, and not a muscle in his features twitched.

"Bring him along quick; time is precious," called Frank again, still fumbling with the lock.

"Will you unlock that safe?" demanded Jesse. "You have not five seconds to live if you refuse. Will you unlock that safe,

I say?" He fairly hissed the words in the fearless cashier's face.

"I will not," replied the cashier, resolutely. "And I tell you men that if ——"

He never finished the sentence. His corpse rolled in front of Jesse James with a bullet through the brain and another through the heart. Jesse sprang across it to the safe where Frank stood. Until this time the trembling assistant cashier had remained transfixed with terror on the spot where he had stood when the bandits entered. Just then Frank turned to order him to unlock the combination, but the boy, partly regaining his senses, leaped at that moment through a window at the side opposite that on which the mounted bandits were guarding the bank. With a tremendous oath Frank James sent a bullet after the escaping assistant; it found its mark in his shoulder, but only slightly wounded him, and, while Frank was yelling to the guard outside, the lad made good his flight. Meanwhile Jesse had kept on struggling with the combination on the safe. It withstood every effort either to unlock it or force it. Frank rummaged the desks and drawers, and turned the tin boxes upside down. Less than twenty-five dollars could be found, nearly all in silver coin. With an oath Jesse finally gave up the combination, and turned to the work of ransacking the bank.

"The cursed thing won't work," he called to his brother, "and we have neither time nor tools to force it. Have you found anything, Frank?"

"Nothing but this pint of chicken feed; it isn't worth carrying off."

With another oath, Jesse caught up a handful of the silver and strewed it from end to end of the room; and then, snatching a second handful, he dashed it into the face of the murdered cashier.

"There's the infernal fool who made this day's work a failure," he cried, "I wish he were alive; I'd like to kill him over again." He fired another pistol ball into the corpse, and, after kicking it aside in a heap, started for the door with Frank, both smashing the glass around the counters and such articles of furniture as they could with their pistol butts as they went. This work took only a moment, but it showed the Northfield people afterward, how furious had been the impotent rage of the bandits thus baffled in one of most desperate and daring raids they ever undertook.

"Come, come, Jesse; the town will be at our heels in five minutes," cried Frank, at last; and, with another curse for the murdered cashier, whose corpse bore ghastly evidence of his sturdy devotion to duty, the robber-assassins hurried toward the door.

Although the raid on the bank, fruitless as it proved for the outlaws and with the shockingly tragic episode, had occupied hardly ten minutes, the town had already recovered from much of the consternation caused by the sudden and startling advent of the robber band; and some of the men of Northfield, realizing that they had a murderous gang of freebooters in their midst, though none knew the James boys or their companions by sight, had caught up the first weapons at hand and hurried in a small but determined body toward the scene of the outrage.

These men were just drawing near and had begun to string out in a semi-circle across the street intending to intercept the the flight of the marauders, when one of the mounted ruffians on guard in front of the bank opened fire on them. The villagers in turn fired several shots, and the renewed fusillade brought other villagers running through the street from both directions to join in the melee.

It was at this critical juncture that Frank and Jesse James, infuriated by their disappointment, and ready for any bloody work, appeared at the bank door. Quick glances at the rapidly growing force of villagers told them that more than they had bargained for was at hand. It would be a plunge for life through the crowd of Northfield men who had gathered, bent on taking the lawless intruders alive, or killing them if they tried to escape. There could be no doubt about the determined look in the faces of the townsmen.

"It's a run or nothing, old man," exclaimed Frank, as he sprang for his horse.

"Yes, but we'll make it; we've done harder things," replied Jesse, between his teeth, leaping into his saddle.

"Now for it, boys!" he yelled to the others. "Let 'em have it hot and heavy, and make straight for the western way out. Off we go!" and with a loud whoop he wheeled his horse right toward the crowd, then turned sharply toward the west, and at the same time opening fire with his revolvers on the crowd, led the gang on a dead gallop straight up the street. The rest began to yell, and firing right and left, dashed after him, Frank close behind, four of the others in a bunch at his horse's heels, and the seventh bandit, whose horse had reared just as they turned, a few paces further back. As they started off several shots were fired from the crowd, but the Northfield men, being for the most part thrown into confusion again by the sudden flank movement of the robbers and the shower of pistol bullets, nearly all shot wide of their marks. One man, with a rifle, standing close up to a building diagonally across from the bank, remained cool, however, and taking steady aim at the horseman who had become separated from the main body of the bandits, pulled the trigger of his weapon when the desperado came directly opposite. The horseman turned short in his saddle, threw up one hand convulsively, and fell over upon the neck of his animal. In an instant he had toppled to the ground, and the terrified horse went careering up the street riderless. One bandit thus paid with his life for the murder of the brave bank cashier. The outlaw was dead before the villagers could pick him up, the bullet having passed squarely through his head. But his comrades in crime never stopped or looked back to learn his fate; with each the business of the moment was flight.

The temporary lull in the firing, while the villagers bore away the corpse of the bandit who had fallen, gave the others a few valuable minutes start in their flight. They headed straight to the south-west, still galloping on at the highest speed to which their horses could be spurred, long after they had cleared the limits of the town. But fast as they sped, and furiously as they lashed their horses at every bound, the ride was none too fast or furious to make their safety sure. Within a quarter of an hour after the raid on the bank the whole town of Northfield was up in arms. Before the first surprise of the attack had subsided, men on the best horses in town were off at as hot speed as that of the bandits themselves, and right on their trail.

The first party of pursuers numbered about fifty of the coolest and most courageous men of Northfield. When it became generally known that the bank cashier had been shot down in cold blood, hundreds of others took up the chase. Even farmers on their way home, several miles from town, had heard the repeated firing and turned back to find out what it all meant. When they learned, not a few unhitched their horses and set off in the wake of the pursuers and the pursued. All headed due south-west in the direction taken by the fleeing ruffians. Before nightfall not less than 500 men, fully armed and well mounted, had joined the chase from Northfield alone, and still the bandits had the lead and kept it through the darkness.

No such excitement had been known in Northfield and the surrounding country since the pioneer days, when Indian outrages were numerous. Small additions were made to the pursuing force from every farm along the trail. The whole county was aroused within a few hours after the perpetration of the outrage. The telegraph had flashed the news to all the towns near Northfield and farther south. Everywhere the report of the murder created the bitterest indignation, and, though the details were meagre, the news that the notorious James boys and their dreaded gang had chosen Minnesota for the latest theatre of their bloody deeds spread such contagious desire for vengeance that by the next morning towns hundreds of miles from the scene of the murder contributed posses to the great chase after the desperadoes.

All night the bandits rode as they never rode before; now along the broad highway, now through cross-roads and by-ways; skirting streams and forests; across country in untried paths; through stubble-fields and clearings; whipping their horses mercilessly at every jump; plying the spurs till the flanks of the poor beasts streamed with blood, and bending low in their saddles as they still kept on in the desperate race for life all night long;—

and all night long, thundering behind them, often almost within pistol shot, always close behind, and sometimes gaining; still fresh, tireless, determined, came their pursuers. Many a wild night ride had that reckless outlaw band taken before, but none like this; many a night had Frank and Jesse James spent in the saddle fleeing from retribution, but never had the pursuit been so close, so hot and persistent, and never in their lawless careers had they known so well when hard pressed that capture meant not the danger of penal servitude merely, but short shift without jury, court or sentence. Perhaps if death had to come they would have preferred it in just that shape—sure and sudden; but that was an alternative they were not yet altogether ready for; and so, still leading as they always did, they urged their desperado crew still on and on toward the south through the long night.

They were still ahead, still uncaught; they had the advantage of utter recklessness, and their comrades were thoroughly kindred spirits. Never before, perhaps, had the James boys captained a band of desperadoes so trusted by them as those who followed their lead in the Northfield deviltry. In the gang were the Younger brothers, Jim, Bob, and Cole on whose courage and fidelity the James boys relied as implicitly as they ever relied on the qualities of any men but themselves. All the Youngers had been in former criminal escapades with them, and neither had ever been found wanting, or given cause for a suspicion of his loyalty. Clell Miller was their only comrade besides the Youngers. He was a wretch of particular daring and brutality, and had been tested before, but the James boys were especially sure of his faithfulness because they knew that he idolized as well as feared them. The seventh desperado, who fell by the rifle shot of the Northfield man, had been Bill Caldwell. On the whole, the outlaw chiefs did not lament his death. He was the one in whom they had least confidence, and was lacking in the dash and abandon which distinguished the others of the gang. "Good riddance; he was a coward anyway," had been Jesse's heartless comment on Caldwell's fate when the band was clear of the town, and it was found which one had been shot down in the village. So, taking mental inventories of their equipment for flight and of the character of their comrades, they pressed ahead well-satisfied that if escape were possible they would yet make it theirs.

Thus hour after hour they rode forward. Sometimes in the darkness their horses stumbled in ditches, or plunged against unseen hedges; the bandits were often near being hurled headlong in the uneven course over a country with which they were none too familiar; but the horses were always reined up again, the riders pulled themselves together with the consummate horsemanship of which they were masters, and long afterward they boasted that in that twelve hours' blind ride through the darkness, not one of the gang was unhorsed, though many times the beasts floundered on their knees and staggered like drunken creatures.

At last dawn came. Along the horizon, away to the left spread a gray mist, like an indistinct cloud of steam rising from the prairie; then the sun's rays shot through it suddenly like golden arrows, the mist dissolved into space, and the bosom of the plain sparkled with myriad diamond points of early frost. But the loveliness of the scene was wholly lost on the fleeing bandits; they cursed the daylight which would make it easier for their fierce pursuers to follow them. The robbers were then on a broad, well-made road, which led due west. They had finally so far outstripped their pursuers that they could not hear the gallop of horses or the shouts of the men, but it was certain that the posse, more familiar with the country than the James boys and their mates, and as well mounted, could not be many miles behind. Not a farm-house could be seen on any hand, and when the sun got a little higher, and the pursuing party sighted them, it would be a straight away race in the open. This the bandits by no means courted. The terrible strain of the long and furious ride had begun to tell upon their horses, which were already fagged, and their speed began to slacken materially, despite the unceasing blows which the riders showered upon them. In another half-hour at furthest the animals would be run out, and then the bandits must begin a hopeless fight on foot. Revolving this critical possibility as he urged his horse more mercilessly than ever, Jesse James' quick eye caught the outlines of a dark patch on the horizon far to the southwest. Instantly his face lighted up with revived hope, and, cursing terrifically, he called to the others:

"Keep it up fifteen minutes longer, boys. Ride as if the devil were after you! Yonder is a piece of woods, and if we make it we can give the hounds the slip yet!"

With a shout of exultation the others followed his example, and belabored their animals with renewed energy. Their efforts told well, for within the quarter of an hour fixed by Jesse in which to cover the distance, they reached the edge of the thick woods ahead. It was none too soon, for they had barely turned from the road into the forest, when Clell Miller's horse, reeling aimlessly through the underbrush, fell dead in his tracks, and at the same instant, Jesse, closely scanning the level road which they had just traversed, saw three tiny specks far back against the horizon.

"There the devils come!" he cried. "We must make for it through the brush afoot. Curse that beast of yours, Clell we can't drag his carcass with us, and it'll be the first clue to our trail for those fiends. But come on; lead your brutes as far into the trees as possible; then we'll leave them."

Suiting the action to the word he leapt from his own horse, and, almost dragging the animal after him, struck into the forest where the underbrush was thinnest. The rest followed in single file. The woods soon grew very dense, and, after forging ahead with difficulty for perhaps a quarter of a mile, Jesse stopped and put a bullet through his horse's brain. The other poor beasts were promptly despatched in the same way, and the bandits plunged on into the thick forest. Half an hour later the six fugitives found themselves in a narrow ravine, down which they made their way as rapidly as possible.

Leaving them to pursue their flight on foot through the forest for a time, the reader will better appreciate how dubious and perilous a flight it was, by taking a survey of the surrounding country, and the sudden uprising on all hands in the chase. To the west Sheriff Estes had set out with a strong posse as soon as the news of the murder reached him. He and his followers could not have been more than twenty-five miles from the spot where the robbers took to the forest, at that very time. Sheriff

Davis, of the county south of Northfield, also was in the field with a posse of well-armed and well-mounted men; and to these forces were added straggling contingents of pursuers from many intermediate points. Besides, the vanguard of the original pursuing party from Northfield, who had kept so hot on the heels of the robbers all night, reached the edge of the wood where Miller's horse lay dead, barely an hour behind the James boys and their confederates as they disappeared into the sheltering forest. All the odds were thus heavily against the fleeing robbers; for, eluding those behind, the chances were almost overwhelming that they would run into the arms of the avengers led by Sheriff Davis directly ahead. There was a strip of uneven and more or less wooded country for nearly two hundred miles to the south-west, and in keeping to this depended the band's faint chance of making good their escape. The strip was in many places less than a quarter of a mile wide, and the bandits were wholly ignorant of its course. Besides, closing in around them from nearly every quarter, were the numerous pursuing parties.

Still the James gang made the most of what chance there was, and forged on without stopping through the belt of woodland, creeping along the occasional clearings like the thieves they were, and burying themselves, whenever possible, in the deep forest, until late in the afternoon. Up to that time they had not seen a human being or caught sight of a single human habitation. Thoroughly worn out by their terrific ride during the night, and weakened by want of food, they at last halted just as the sun began to sink. It was agreed that they must find something to eat, or all hands would give out, and Frank James and Cole Younger started through the underbrush on a short foraging expedition. They could find nothing but acorns and nuts and a few wild berries.

Gathering up greedily what they could of these, however, they had started to return to the other bandits, when Frank James heard a rustle in the bushes not ten paces away. He crouched in the underbrush, and watched and listened. Presently he distinctly caught the sound of dry twigs crackling, apparently under a man's feet, and the next instant, through a break in the bushes, he saw a man with a rifle slung across his shoulder making his way toward where Frank and Cole Younger were stooping in the high grass. The man peered suspiciously at every tree and bush. The path he was following led within ten feet of where the two robbers lay. Frank raised his rifle silently, and was about to fire when he heard a faint hallooing at a distance. The approaching stranger answered the call lustily and quickened his pace down the path. It was evident that he was a member of a party out hunting, perhaps for the James band itself, which, indeed, was actually the case. Frank dropped his rifle as silently as he had raised it, fearing to fire lest he should draw to the spot the men whose call he had heard. Loosening a long heavy bowie knife from his belt, Frank breathlessly awaited the approach of the stranger. The latter was now within ten feet, and just then turned to peer into a thicket. Frank James raised himself with the swiftness of a springing panther. His right hand was lifted suddenly, and there was a bright flash in the air. The stranger gave a half bound, and with a groan fell dead in the very thicket through which he had been peering. With the dexterity of an Indian Frank James had thrown his bowie knife straight into the man's left side, and the keen blade had pierced his heart. This latest victim of the murderous outlaws was a man named Denman. The scouting party of which he had been a member did not learn his fate until the following day, and by that time the bandits had pushed on many miles from the scene.

All through the second day the bandits kept on their skulking flight along the strip of forest land. None of their pursuers came up with them and the day was without incident. They camped at night near Kilkenny, Minnesota. The next day passed in a similar manner and that night the bandits stopped for a few hour's rest in a gulch near Marburg, Le Sūeūr County. There they obtained corn and potatoes from a field and roasting them in the hollow of a dead tree, ate the first warm food they had tasted for three days. For a week they progressed in this way, sometimes almost within pistol shot of small parties of their pursuers, but never detected.

Several days later they surprised a Minnesota man on the edge of a clearing. He sat against a stump eating lunch. The bandits approached noiselessly from behind and seized him. He proved to be a brother of the murdered Denman and he was also hunting for the James gang. He was hurried into the heavy timber, and the bandits held a council what to do with him. Jesse James insisted that he should be killed then and there. Some of the others dissented, claiming that the deed would only lessen their chance of escape by still more inflaming the pursuers. As a compromise measure it was decided to take a vote. Six sticks with the bark on and six peeled were chosen, and each bandit dropped one with his hand behind him into Frank James' hat. The result showed four peeled sticks, which meant life for Denman, and two with the bark on, which were for death. The disgust manifested by Frank and Jesse James left no doubt as to which two bandits had cast the unpeeled sticks. Jesse's rage almost sealed the prisoner's fate despite the vote, for the bandit chief impulsively drew his revolver to shoot Denman after it was cast, but Denman begged so piteously on his knees and swore such a profound oath not to reveal his knowledge of the bandits, that Jesse listened to the pleadings of the Youngers and Clell Miller, and, after being disarmed, Denman was set free. Denman was no sooner out of the clutches of the bandits than he made his way back to the posse of which he had been an outrunner, gave the alarm, and within six hours had a hundred energetic men following this new and valuable clue to the robber's whereabouts.

By this time the bandits had nearly reached the end of the two hundred-mile strip of forest, and, realizing the risk of continuing further in such a large party under any circumstances, and more especially since in the Denman case their companions had evinced a quality of mercy which they considered altogether too dangerous a precedent, the James boys decided to desert the gang. There were two routes to choose from; one over a small hill, covered with a thick undergrowth of shrubbery, leading to the west from the strip of country which they had been travelling, and the other, which led more south than west, apparently less closely grown with trees and, as far as could be judged from what was seen, running to marsh land. A toss-up gave the

James boys the marshy stretch of country. It had every prospect of being far the more difficult in which to dodge the pursuing parties, but, without complaint or hesitation, they set off at a swinging gait as the day began to wane.

While the Youngers and Clell Miller are over the well-wooded hill, congratulating themselves on the chance which had allotted the seemingly better route to them, we will follow the chief bandits on their less willing way.

"Luck seems to be with those fools," said Frank, before the others were well out of sight. "This is a nice piece of country we've got before us. We might as well head for a jail at once."

"Things don't always turn out the way they look," was Jesse's answer. "Luck hasn't played us many dirty tricks, so far, and I'm willing to trust it awhile longer. As for those chicken-hearted fools," he added, with one of his heartiest oaths, "we're cheaply rid of them. It saves the trouble of wasting powder and lead on the idiots. I felt like settling the whole lot after that Denman business."

"Yes; that was a fool job, curse them," said Frank.

"Fool job!" exclaimed his brother, again with a string of hair-raising oaths. "Fool job! It was lunacy. If every granger in the State isn't out with a gun after us by this time I've missed my guess. Why, they'll have bear traps set for us before to-morrow night."

"It is hell and no mistake," was Frank's rejoinder. "But, I say, old man, there's a bunch of trees three quarters of a mile beyond, and hardly a sage brush between. It's a nasty place for a chase and we'd better waste no time in getting to the woods."

"Let's take it on a run, then," said Jesse.

He broke into a dog trot as he spoke, and ten minutes later the woods were reached. It was none too soon, as the bandit brothers fully appreciated. The sun was nearly down and objects a quarter of a mile away looked hazy. Within that distance a horseman could be clearly distinguished, and that was just what the bandits discovered; not one only, but no less than six riders, who were galloping rapidly down a road which ran only a few rods from the wood. Jesse and Frank James waited to see no more. They scudded on farther and farther into the darkening grove, and were relieved to hear the six horsemen, who had come so near to overhauling them, gallop on till the echo of their horses' hoofs was lost in the distance.

The timber grew closer as the bandits advanced, and, after descending a sharp bluff, they found themselves stumbling along in very soft ground. As darkness settled down their way became more and more difficult, and half an hour later they were floundering through a Minnesota slough, half up to their waists in mud and water. Fearing that the quagmire might entirely engulf them, they moved with laborious slowness. Before they reached solider ground it was nearly daylight once more, and they were numbed through with the wet and cold. Two hours later they were following the course of a well-wooded stream, which, on account of its purplish clay banks, is called the Blue Earth river, though the James boys did not know its name. They kept down along the river all that day and the next. On the third day they had strayed a short distance from the stream in search of food, when they suddenly heard voices, whose possessors were so close that the bandits could almost reach out and touch them. Jesse and Frank were in a dense patch of hazel brush at the moment. They fell flat on their faces with noiseless quickness, and literally held their breaths. The voices came from three men at the edge of the brush.

"Yes; they've given us a mighty hard hunt, so far," said one, "but they can't get out of the State alive."

"No: since that clue to the trail that Denman brought back, it doesn't seem possible for them to get away," said the second voice. "What fools they were to let him go."

"What a fool he was to let them catch him, you mean," exclaimed the third voice, which seemed to belong to the youngest of the three speakers. "I only wish I had a chance at 'em with this little fowling piece, I'd——"

The remark was punctuated with the report of a gun, and simultaneously Frank James rolled over on his side, with his features set hard, but without uttering a sound. Jesse involuntarily drew his revolver, but Frank motioned him to lie still.

A loud laugh followed the report of the gun, and one of the voices called out, "Oh, you'd do wonders, you would; any fellow who lets his gun off when he stubs his toe always does wonders. Ha! ha!" Then the trio moved on.

"Are you hit, Frank?" asked Jesse, in a hoarse whisper.

"Yes; here in the thigh, old man," replied Frank; "see, the blood's oozing already. But it's only a flesher, I guess; no bones touched."

Jesse cursed till he grew purple in the face at this statement, and began tearing some wadding from the lining of his coat into strips while he yet lay prone upon his back. As soon as he dared he crawled over to his brother, and with the lint helped the latter to staunch the blood that was flowing freely from the accidental wound. Finally, Jesse rose and assisted Frank to his feet. To the satisfaction of both, it was found that Frank could walk, though with considerable pain, and they hurried back to the cover of the forest, roundly heaping blasphemies on the three searchers who, though the bandits did not know it, were three deputy-sheriffs.

Two days later the bandit brothers almost ran plump into a pursuing party of eighteen men. They had just emerged from a piece of woods when, across a field a quarter of a mile away, they saw the crowd of men, all mounted, and carrying rifles. One of the party evidently saw them also, for, dismounting to avoid fences, the entire crowd approached, firing as they ran. Another patch of woods gave the bandits a considerable lead, and doubling on their tracks they reached a marsh, into the high reeds of which they dove, and after working along on their stomachs some distance, they found an outlet which led under a shelving bank through to a good sized stream. They swam across, made their way to a second piece of woods, and crawling into a hollow log, lay there, drenched and shivering, till night-fall.

This experience caused Frank's wound to become much inflamed, while the pain greatly increased, and, being almost famished as well, the desperation of the bandits emboldened them to take openly to a good road which they came upon the next day. They had proceeded only a few miles when they were again driven to the woods by approaching horsemen. They passed another night and still another in the forest, but a day later once more found themselves upon a well-made highway leading southwest. The road turned due south a few miles farther on, and just at the turn they met a farmer. They were upon him before retreat was possible, and, as he did not seem startled at meeting them, they faced it out. He was leading a span of fine black horses hitched to the wagon in which he rode. Jesse called to him and asked if he would not like to sell the blacks?

"Don't mind, if I can get a fair figure," he replied, stopping his wagon.

"What do you call a fair figure?"

"'Bout two hundred apiece, I reckon."

"We'll pay five hundred for the pair? Untie them."

"Of course, it'll have to be cash down."

"Of course, it won't. You'll have to trust us. We're broke, but we're good for the money. Untie the horses, I say."

"Well, you fellers are cool ones, ain't you?" said the farmer, preparing to drive on. "Who the dickens be you, anyway?"

"My name is Jesse James, if you must know, and this is my brother, Mr. Frank James. Now, will you untie those horses, or must I? Five hundred is what I offered."

The farmer did not stop to glance more than once down the revolver barrel which was presented at his head. He got down, untied the span of blacks, handed the bridles to Jesse, and only stopped enough longer to tell his name and where he lived, in reply to the robber's question.

"From that farmer's accommodating manner toward the James boys," said Frank, dryly, "I guess we must be somewhere near the Missouri line, old man."

Splendidly mounted once more the spirits of the bandit brothers began to revive. Toward evening, after having ridden southward many miles along good roads, they stopped at a farm house, where they obtained a change of clothing and ate their first meal with knives and forks in a fortnight. The farmer, who was hospitable without being too inquisitive, and who had attained some surgical skill from practice in the war, also dressed Frank's wound, staying the inflammation temporarily and appreciably easing the pain.

Bright and early the next morning the James boys were again in the saddle, and, after several days of uneventful riding further toward the south-west, they reached the cabin, near the western edge of Iowa, of an old friend and kindred spirit in the person of an ex-guerilla. With him they found comfortable quarters for nearly a week. Then they set out again to beat the report of the Northfield outrage further south. They reached a town in south-west Kansas ahead of the report, with no very thrilling adventures on the way, and thence they hastened by rail to Paris, Texas. A stop was found necessary at Houston, however, long enough for a skillful surgeon to dress Frank's wounded thigh, which, owing to the renewed exposure, had become extremely painful again, and threatened gangrene. The leg was saved, but the operation caused a contraction of the ligaments, which gave Frank a pronounced limp for the rest of his life. It was a quick trip from Houston to the home in the heart of the forest, and once more the notorious outlaw brothers were hid, beyond hope of discovery, from the eye of the law. They remembered the Minnesota farmer whose fine span of blacks had proved such a boon in that perilous pilgrimage, and a few weeks later he received an envelope with a crisp five hundred dollar bill wrapped in a single sheet of plain, white note-paper, on which was written this laconic message:

"THANKS."

And thus ended unquestionably the most remarkable escape from justice in the history of criminal achievements in America. It is rivalled, though not surpassed, by some of the famous flights of England's highwaymen celebrities, Sheppard, Turpin and Paul Clifford; but their adventures are mostly legendary, not to say mythical, while the story of the James boys' wonderful and successful dash for liberty, as here related, is a recital of actual facts, amply verified by contemporaneous evidence. As the reader reflects upon the thrilling narrative and the astonishing immunity from arrest which the outlaw brothers maintained in that long journey toward the south, with literally the whole country at their heels, and sometimes hemming them in on every side, he may well exclaim, "How was it possible? Why should fortune have favored these wholly depraved wretches? It seems incredible!" Nor can he be blamed for this natural outburst of surprise. It does seem almost incredible. Why the fates should have helped the outlaws on their way is as utterly inexplicable as are all the freaks of fate. But to the other question there is an answer, and, by retracing the story to Northfield, the reader may find it. There the flight began; there the bandits took their dashing lead, breaking through the crowd of armed villagers far outnumbering them, but wholly unorganized to resist the sudden rush of the cool and murderous handful of desperadoes. Ah! of what priceless value then would have been a single squad of police, resolute, calm, carefully drilled. How they would have blocked the mad course of the murderous robbers, even before it began, shutting off escape as effectually as would a wall of iron! And how suddenly and inevitably would one platoon of police on horseback—as swift in pursuit of a criminal once sighted as fate itself—think how such a squad of mounted officers would have overhauled, dead or alive, that band of ruffian riders! But Northfield was not blessed with these faithful and skillfully disciplined guardians of your lives and homes, and so the outlaw horsemen dashed through the startled crowd of villagers, and began their great ride to safety. It was the same lack of well-organized pursuit by men trained to the business that gave Jesse and Frank James an outlet through all the excited countryside down the length of Minnesota, and so on clear down to the leaf-embowered hiding place in Texas, where they could laugh pursuers and pursuit to scorn.

The James brothers lay close in their forest home in Texas for some time after their return, for the news of their bloody work in Northfield had quickly spread throughout the west. Frank's thigh also began to trouble him again, making activity impossible even had he desired it. During this brief interval in the crimes of the outlaw chiefs, therefore, let us return to follow the fortunes of their comrades in Minnesota.

After making their way over the hill where they had parted

with Jesse and Frank James, and chuckling to themselves at having the better piece of country in which to hide, the Youngers and Clell Miller pushed on without adventure through the woodland region until late the following afternoon. Then they suddenly found themselves in a slough or marsh of very nearly the same character as that encountered by the James boys. Progress for Miller and the Youngers was extremely slow and fatiguing throughout that night. The morning of the next day, September 21, did not mend the situation. All around them stretched the vast morass, covered with tall swamp grass and broken only by clumps of osiers here and there. Food they could not obtain of any sort, and they were waist deep in the fever-breeding pools of the slough nearly all the time.

About the middle of the afternoon they gained a comparatively dry piece of ground thickly overgrown with willows. Beyond it the country seemed dryer, and while Bob and Jim Younger and Clell Miller, thoroughly exhausted, sank down to rest, Cole Younger volunteered to push on alone toward what looked like a piece of woods at some distance, in search of provisions. He had proceeded half a mile, when suddenly he saw a large party of mounted men, following the road through the morass not 500 yards away. He dodged down into the tall grass, but not quickly enough, for he heard a shout of exultation from the men on horseback, and, peering through the grass, saw them dismount and start rapidly right into the swamp toward him. Working his way along like a snake through the thick grass, he retreated swiftly toward the swamp island. The pursuing party pushed on steadily into the swamp, gaining on him, but unable to tell exactly where he was slinking along through the luxuriant grass. He reached the swamp island ten minutes ahead of them and gave the alarm. Further retreat was impossible.

Under cover of the willows the four bandits therefore began to gather such pieces of fallen trees as they could, and to heap upon them the soft peat of the marsh by the handful. It made only a rude and unsubstantial breastwork, barely three feet high, but it was their only hope of resisting the pursuing party; besides, the bandits had very little ammunition and wished to lie as long as possible without firing. They fell on their faces behind the low intrenchment just as a yell from the approaching party apprised them that they were discovered. The pursuers spread quickly in a circle around the swamp island and simultaneously opened fire upon the hiding place of the desperadoes. Bullets whizzed all around the latter, but none took effect. Then the attacking party closed in suddenly and the desperadoes were forced to return their fire. From that moment it was a brief but desperate battle. The Youngers and Clell Miller fought like wild beasts at bay. Many of the assailants were wounded and one killed, but they far outnumbered the bandits, who finally were crowded from the swamp island back into a long, narrow lagoon.

"Surrender and your lives shall be spared!" called the leader of the attacking party. The only reply from the bandits was another well aimed volley and one bullet shattered the leader's arm. Enraged to the point of frenzy at this the attacking party, renewing their fire faster than ever, dashed headlong into the morass towards the bandits. The conflict was short and bloody. Clell Miller was shot dead, Jim Younger's jaw was shattered, Bob was shot in the right arm, and Cole received six bullets in his body; but not until their wounds thus made it impossible for them to resist longer were the three brothers overpowered.

The scene of this sanguinary struggle was near Madelia, Watawan county, Minnesota. The Youngers were heavily ironed, and, being protected by the Sheriff with great difficulty from several attempts to lynch them, were taken to Faribault, Minnesota. They were promptly tried, and, on October 1, 1876, were severally sentenced for life to the Stillwater, Minnesota, Penitentiary. As this history is being written, eleven years later, the Youngers are still alive and serving their well earned terms at hard labor. With Bill Caldwell and Clell Miller killed while their crimes were yet fresh upon them, and the Younger brothers at last imprisoned, therefore, the James boys were the only members of the gang which perpetrated the outrage in Northfield who went scot free; yet they were the most desperate and dangerous of the lot; the ones who most deserved punishment, and the ones for whose capture the officers of the law were most eager.

Frank James' leg continued to give him much annoyance, and he was glad enough to gain repose and the attendant enjoyments of life with his wife and children for two years in the beautiful home in Texas to which none yet knew the path but himself, Jesse, their families, and the Youngers. Indeed, Frank had been greatly weakened by the arduous flight from Minnesota and its manifold deprivations and sufferings. His spirit after that experience never seemed to possess the same wild, dare-devil recklessness, and he more and more inclined to the quiet pleasures which he found with his family. Every absence and every criminal venture afterwards, at the risk of losing these with his life, intensified this feeling, until he contemplated departure with ill concealed aversion. Therefore, he was not sorry, even with the pain and life-long disfigurement that his maimed thigh gave him a plausible excuse for temporary sojourn in idleness at the forest home.

But on Jesse's restless spirit the Northfield affair and its subsequent hardships had produced an effect exactly the reverse. He was exasperated over its financial failure, vexed because of the wound received by Frank, and, altogether, had become bitterer in his feeling toward the law and society at large. He was silent, moody, unsatisfied. With the failure of his last murderous enterprise seemed to come indifference, for the time being, even toward his wife and children. He roamed about the villa in the glade with a gloomy face, and finally one morning, late in 1878, he abruptly announced his intention of going on another expedition. Despite his wife's entreaties and Frank's arguments, Jesse said hasty good-byes, and before night had threaded his way through the swamp, and again started northward.

A few days later the whole country was talking of the result of his determination, which is known on the records of crime as the Glendale train robbery. This quickly planned and executed robbery occurred on the night of October 8, 1878, but one month over two years after the Northfield raid. With Jesse James were Dick Little, Jim Cummings, Ed. Miller, and Tucker Bashaw, all notorious desperadoes. Near the little town of Glendale, Jackson County, Missouri, these ruffians met secretly in the woods on the night of October 8. In a deep cut just beyond the village they piled heavy timbers on the track of the Chicago and Alton Railroad, over which the north-bound night express was due about eleven o'clock. The obstruction was discovered by the engineer of the express train just in time to narrowly avert a terrible disaster. In the confusion of stopping, the six robbers, all heavily masked, boarded the train with drawn revolvers. Completely overpowering the trainmen and terrorizing the passengers by shooting right and left into the coaches, the robbers quickly made their way to the express car. Express messenger Charles Grimes was forced, at the point of Jesse James' revolver, to surrender the contents of the safe, and the mail bags also were rifled. Then, mounting their horses, which had been hid in a thicket near by, the robbers rode swiftly away in the darkness, carrying with them no less than twenty-seven thousand dollars' worth of plunder, mostly in bills and bullion taken from the express agent. So well had the train robbery been planned that not the faintest clue to the flight of the desperadoes could be found a mile from the railroad. At that point the hoof-marks of their horses ceased abruptly, and the robbers seemed to have vanished into air.

But all Jackson county echoed with the report of the bold crime within six hours, and countless search parties, the largest and most determined of which was led by Marshal James Liggett, began to scour that section of Missouri. The hunt proved fruitless, however, and the general excitement had essentially abated, when Marshal Liggett, whose efforts were continued untiringly, captured George Shepherd, formerly a member of the James gang, with whom he had been engaged in the bank robbery at Russellville, Kentucky, several years before. Liggett promised that Shepherd should not be prosecuted, and also offered him a large reward if he would undertake to ferret out the James gang and betray them to the officers of the law. To this Shepherd readily consented. He had a grudge of long standing against Jesse James, who, he declared, had robbed him of five thousand dollars, which should have been his share of the booty in a former robbery. He also claimed that Jesse had instigated the murder of Shepherd's uncle, who was killed by the James gang in a previous expedition. Being familiar with the haunts of several of the gang in Missouri, Shepherd easily came up with the Glendale train robbers within a week after the crime. After a council the desperadoes agreed to admit him to their schemes, against a vigorous protest by Jesse, who from the first was suspicious of Shepherd. Shortly afterward, having reached south-western Missouri, and divided the proceeds of the Glendale robbery, of which, by the way, Jesse took the lion's share, the bandits planned an expedition for the robbery of the Galena, Illinois, National Bank. Shepherd was present at their councils. No sooner was the raid decided upon than he left camp for the nearest town and notified Marshal Liggett by telegraph of the proposed expedition. Ed. Miller had been dispatched by Jesse to secretly follow Shepherd and report on the latter's movements. While Shepherd was in the telegraph office sending his message to Marshal Liggett, Miller galloped back to camp with news of Shepherd's treachery. It was promptly and unanimously voted that Shepherd should be shot down on sight. Late in the afternoon he was seen returning to camp on horseback, whistling blithely as he rode, and wholly unconscious that his plot had been discovered. Before he had got within the bounds of the camp, which was situated in a large sand pit, sheltered on all sides but one by high, tree-clad banks, the six bandits opened fire on the spy with their revolvers. Singularly enough not one of the practiced marksmen hit or even winged him. Instantly realizing that his treachery had been exposed, Shepherd headed his horse for flight. The others were after him like a whirlwind on their own horses. Jesse James was gaining on the traitor, when Shepherd turned in his saddle and sent back a bullet, which passed through Jesse's neck, knocking him from his horse. Ed. Miller was the only one of the robber band who kept on in the chase, but none of his rapid shots hit the fugitive. Being better mounted, Shepherd soon outstripped Miller, and speedily made his way back to civilization. He changed his name and remained in hiding for years in deadly terror of the James gang's vengeance, but they never captured him.

Jesse's wound proved to be a serious one. He was greatly weakened from loss of blood before the gang could convey him to Galena, where, in a deserted cabin on the outskirts, a doctor from Joplin was called to attend him, the doctor being led to and from the place blindfolded. Shepherd's treachery had balked the designs of the bandits regarding the Galena bank, and the gang was compelled to disperse to avoid the energetic search which Marshal Liggett was still conducting. Jim Cummings alone remained in the cabin with the wounded leader. Two weeks later Jesse's neck was sufficiently healed for him to venture forth, and he at once started for Paris, Texas, and the home in the forest again. He got through in safety, and was more content to remain than on his previous visit.

For two years thereafter, so far as the public knew, Jesse and Frank James refrained from deeds of crime. They lived in their delightful retreat amid the woods and vines and luxuriant flowers. Their lives were quiet, peaceful and, it is pleasant to believe, exemplary. Their names, at least, figured in no robberies or raids during that interval, and the busy western world, when it stopped to think of them at all, did so with a sense of relief coupled with a hearty hope that the bandits had retired from business permanently, or, better still, were dead. Uncharitable as was the latter feeling, it was the one held by law-respecting citizens generally. But one other sentiment prevailed regarding the outlaw brothers. It was one of hare-brained admiration by dime-novel-reading boys and naturally vicious characters, who always gloat on crime, no matter how dark the record, if committed with the boldness and intrepidity which had pre-eminently distinguished all the deeds of the James boys. Meanwhile, however, the officers of the law had not for a moment relaxed their efforts to hunt down the notorious desperadoes. Reports which occasionally gained currency that one or both of the James boys had died were wholly discredited in Missouri. Yet no trace could be found of the bandits. Clues were not wanting which promised well at first, but they invariably proved worthless when run to earth.

Near the end of their second year of inactivity, however, the bandits found reason to believe that their haunt was being watched. They had been making frequent trips into the country surrounding Paris, Texas, and long immunity from surveillance had, perhaps, made them incautious.

Finally, the incident which was described in the opening pages of this narrative, the encounter with three men who had penetrated far into the swamp by a path which they supposed unknown to all but themselves for the purpose of seizing their families as hostages during their absence, showed them both that they were closely watched and that the secret of their hiding place was at least partially known. The three men were silent in death, but it was not likely that their knowledge was confined exclusively to themselves. This precipitated a step they had long been seriously considering. It was to forsake the Texas home, and they proceeded to do so as speedily as possible. There were other causes for the change. Latterly the finances of the bandits had begun to run low, Jesse's share of the $27,000 from the Glendale train robbery nearly all having gone for current expenses during the long period of idleness. Besides, Jesse was again growing restless. His hatred of conventional modes of existence had been increased by morbid brooding during the two years, embittered by the ever-present memory of the bomb-throwing atrocity which he had sworn to avenge. This unrest was shared, though in a less degree, by Frank. Besides, their wives, alarmed by apprehensions for the safety of the bandits, when they learned that search parties were in the neighborhood, began earnestly to advocate a change of location.

At last everything was ready and the bandit brothers departed forever from the Texas home where almost the only happy hours of their lawless lives had been passed. The whereabouts of the outlaws were for a time again completely lost to the emissaries of justice.

It was not until the middle of July, 1881, that they were positively known to have engaged in another important and daring crime. This was the Winston train robbery. It soon became known from one end of the United States to the other, and created a tremendous sensation. On a dark and dismal night, the 17th of July, 1881, six strangers, all wearing heavy beards, and with coats buttoned close up to their throats, boarded the north-bound night express on the Chicago, Rock Island, and Pacific Railroad at Cameron, Missouri. Neither seemed to know the other. They took seats in the smoking-car, and smoked or buried themselves behind newspapers. Some miles further on three of them quietly made their way to the other coaches. When the train reached Winston, Davies county, a village of three hundred inhabitants, where a stop was regularly made for water, one of the heavily bearded men in the smoker rose from his seat as Conductor John Westfall entered the car door, and presenting a revolver, ordered the conductor to throw up his hands. Westfall, whose reputation for courage had caused the railroad company to give him the night express, which always carried valuable goods and large amounts of money, replied with an exclamation of defiance, and sprang at the other's throat; but his heroic conduct was no safeguard against the bullets of the revolver which the ruffian at the same instant discharged twice, and staggering back the brave conductor fell dead across a car-seat. One bullet had crashed through his brain, and the other had lodged in his breast. At the report of Jesse James' fatal shots (for it was the bandit chief himself who murdered Westfall), the ruffians in the other cars began firing promiscuously over the heads of the passengers. So great was the consternation caused by this concerted fusillade that, with a single exception, not a passenger made a move to resist the robbers. The one man who attempted to withstand the onslaught was John McCullough, a stone-mason, and he shared Conductor Westfall's fate, being instantly shot dead. During the confusion in the passenger coaches and the smoker, Jesse James rushed into the baggage car, and leveling a brace of revolvers at Baggageman Frank Stampler and Express Messenger Charles Murray, held them in subjection, while Frank, who had followed at Jesse's heels, robbed the safe and the mail-bags of seventeen thousand dollars in specie and greenbacks. Then, backing from the car, while they still covered the baggageman and the express messenger with their revolvers, the bandits leaped from the train. They were immediately joined by the other four desperadoes, and after further terrifying the passengers and the engineer by emptying their revolvers into the coaches and the locomotive cab, the robbers disappeared into the darkness. A heavy rain was falling, and it completely obliterated all trace to the trail of the James boys and their accomplices.

This piece of ruffianism with its atrocious double murder was the last straw that broke the back of public endurance. Not only were all the county officers in the vicinity of Winston stirred up to pursue the perpetrators, but public clamor assailed the doors of the State capital so vigorously that Governor Crittenden could not ignore the call. His administration had long been severely criticized because of seeming apathy toward notorious criminals, and to protect himself politically, if for no other reason, the governor was obliged to issue a proclamation offering heavy rewards for the capture of the Winston robbers and murderers. On July 25, 1881, he held a conference in St. Louis with representatives of the railroad and express companies. Three days later the rewards were offered. The proclamation was a somewhat remarkable document of its kind, and as such is worthy of preservation here. It read as follows:

STATE OF MISSOURI, EXECUTIVE DEPARTMENT.

Whereas, It has been made known to me as Governor of the State of Missouri, that certain parties, whose names to me are unknown, confederated and banded themselves together for the purpose of committing robberies and other depredations within this State, and,

Whereas, Said parties did, on or about the 8th day of October, 1878, stop a train near Glendale, in the County of Jackson, in said State, and with force and violence took, stole and carried away the money and other express; and,

Whereas, On the 17th day of July, 1881, said parties and their confederates did stop a train on the line of the Chicago, Rock Island and Pacific Railroad Company, near Winston, in the County of Davies, in this State, and did with force and violence take, steal and carry away the money and other express matters being carried thereon; and,

Whereas, Perpetrating the robbery last aforesaid, the parties engaged therein did murder and kill one William Westfall, conductor of the train aforesaid, together with one John McCullough, who was at the time in the employ of the said company, then on said train; and,

Whereas, Frank James and Jesse James stand indicted in the Circuit Court of Davies County, in the State aforesaid, for the murder of John W. Sheetz; and,

Whereas, The parties engaged in the robberies and murders aforesaid, and each of them, have fled from justice and have absconded and secreted themselves; now, therefore,

In consideration of the premises and in lieu of all other rewards heretofore offered for the arrest or conviction of the parties aforesaid, or either of them, by any persons or corporations, I, Thomas T. Crittenden, Governor of the State of Missouri, do hereby offer a reward of $5,000 for the arrest and conviction of each person participating in either robberies or murders aforesaid, excepting the said Frank and Jesse W. James; and for the arrest and delivery of the said Frank James and Jesse W. James, and each or either of them to the Sheriff of said Davies County, I hereby offer a reward of $5,000; and for the conviction of either of the parties last aforesaid of participating in either of the murders or robberies above mentioned, I hereby offer a further reward of $5,000.

In testimony whereof I have hereunto set my hand and caused to be affixed the great seal of the State of Missouri.

Done at the City of Jefferson, this 28th day of July, A. D. 1881.

THOMAS T. CRITTENDEN,
Governor.

MICHAEL McGRATH,
Secretary of State.

This proclamation was tacitly understood throughout Missouri as placing a price upon the heads of the James boys, dead or alive. How effectually this impression was acted upon remains to be told in one brief but darkly tragic chapter.

For a moment let the reader turn with us from the scenes of crime and bloodshed to a pleasing picture of home life in a pretty cottage. The cottage stands on a well-trimmed patch of greensward amid a well-tended garden. Delicate vines are trained on dainty trellises above the windows, and at the door grow beds of choice flowers. Some of them have already hung their heads before the chilling north wind—bowing, as all living things, even man himself, must bow soon or late to the relentless seasons—for with early November has begun the old age of the year. All about the cottage are signs of neatness and home-loving industry and care. It stands upon the brow of a gently sloping hill, and no other house is near. There is a back ground of many tinted woods above the hill, and below, beyond the hill's encircling belt of trees, lies a smoky, bustling little city. It is the city of St. Joseph, Missouri. Within the cottage is a family group in charming consonance with the inviting scene without. It is early evening, and they are gathered in a cosy sitting room, awaiting the welcome tea time. A man of medium height but well-built frame sits reading at a little centre table. His face is clean shaven save for a brown, drooping mustache. It would be a handsome face if the lines were less firmly set about the mouth and the skin less deeply bronzed, as though from continuous toil in blustering winds or under scorching suns. Two bright-faced children play about his knees. They laugh merrily, and punctuate his reading with childish appeals to papa. A frail, brown-haired little woman leans against the mantel and watches him and them with wifely pleasure mingling with maternal joy. Her face is intelligent, her small eyes are black and sharp, and her graceful figure is clad in a becoming house gown of dark brown stuff. She leaves the children and the man while she visits the kitchen, but, returning to the door in a moment, calls with a mischievous laugh:

"Tea is ready, Mr. Howard; come at once, please."

"All right, Mrs. Howard," answers the man, also with a laugh, but sharper and shorter than his wife's. Then laying down his book, with a mark to note the place, he says, gaily:

"Come, children, tea is ready and waiting; Mrs. Howard will be furious if we delay a minute longer," and catching up the children, one in each arm, with another of his short, sharp laughs, he bears them, shouting gleefully, to the room beyond.

The Howards, as we have looked in upon them early in November, 1881, had been living in the cottage near St. Joseph only a few weeks. Several weeks later two young men, who were called Charles and Robert Johnson, joined the little family circle. The Howards treated them with generous cordiality, and they seemed to be warm personal friends of Howard, or, perhaps, relatives of Mrs. Howard. The winter months sped away, and spring came with the Howards and their guests still living cosily in the little cottage. They made few acquaintances among their neighbors under the hill. Apparently they cared little about other society. They seemed a well-to-do household also, for none of the male members found it necessary to work. Howard was always busy about the cottage, however, making improvements here and there.

Finally one morning, when spring had well advanced (it was

the third of April, 1882, to be exact), Howard was busy making some minor changes in the sitting-room. Both the Johnson boys were helping him. They shifted the furniture and arranged it in new groups for the sake of variety. Then Howard thought he would hang in a different place a picture which was above the piano. It was high up, and he had to mount over several chairs to reach it. He always carried a brace of revolvers around his waist—"a habit," as he used to observe, laughing in his nervous way, "which I got in the pioneer days out west." The weapons interfered with his movement in reaching for the picture, and, taking off the belt, he laid it on the centre-table. Then he climbed up toward the picture over the piano.

"Now, one of you boys take the picture when I have drawn the nail," he said. As he turned his back he heard a "click!" With a sudden movement he started to turn again.

At the same instant Robert Johnson, having caught up one of Howard's own weapons, sent a bullet crashing through the back of Howard's head. A half curse escaped the victim's lips, and then they closed forever. He fell backward from the piano to the floor a corpse.

Half an hour later the Johnson boys walked quietly into the St. Joseph police headquarters, and, laying two revolvers on the chief's desk, exclaimed:

"We have just killed Jesse James! Our names are Charles and Robert Ford. We claim the reward offered by the State of Missouri.

* * * * * * * * * * *

Frank James surrendered to the authorities of Missouri a few months later. He had received a distinct assurance from the State administration, on his promise to quit the business of freebooter, that he should have absolute immunity from punishment. He underwent a sham examination and indictment for the Winston train robbery. The prosecution refused to prosecute, however, and the State administration thus made good its disgraceful bargain with the outlaw. In all the history of compounded felonies there is nothing to rival it. Missouri stands alone in the dark, unenviable distinction of this cowardly compromise with one of the most depraved, blood-stained, and utterly vicious villains that ever outraged law and order. Thomas T. Crittenden, the governor who permitted this notable abuse, saw his irretrievable error afterward, when too late, for he was defeated in his candidacy for re-election, and all his political hopes were forever blasted.

Frank James subsequently moved to St. Louis, and became a shoe clerk. Then he went to Dallas, Texas, to become a dry goods clerk. He was in great demand as an advertising freak. His leg continued to trouble him, and late in 1887 he was said to be dying of consumption. So far as was ever ascertained neither of the desperado brothers amassed fortunes at their lawless trade, both having spent their ill-gotten gains as improvidently as criminals always do.

The Ford boys, who, Judas-like, had sought Jesse James' confidence (and they were the only men who ever won it) only to slay him for a paltry reward, were put through the farce of a trial, but, as pre-concerted, were acquitted on a plea of self defence. Then they sought the cheap notoriety of the dime museum and the low class theatre.

Jesse James' corpse, after an inquest in which his widow and his mother, Mrs. Samuels, positively identified the body, was buried from Mrs. Samuels' home in Kearney, on April 6, 1882, three days after the murder. Thousands of persons attended the funeral. Not until the corpse had been viewed by numbers of persons who had known or seen the notorious bandit when alive, would many believe that the seemingly invincible desperado was actually dead.

The history is finished. There remains but one reflection on the careers of these most notorious of America's ruffians, who took more than three score human lives, captured countless hoards of money, and were so wonderfully successful that neither ever passed one hour behind prison bars; it is on the sociologic conditions which made their crimes possible; the sparsely settled country and unorganized state of community government, and, above all, the lack of drilled, organized, unflinching protectors of the peace. Such careers have been absolutely impossible for many years in the well-regulated and carefully policed cities and towns of the United States; and every day, with the rapid growth of municipal corporations, and the consequent increase of the most valuable adjuncts of civilization in them—the police departments—it is becoming less and less possible, even in the boundless west, for desperadoes to imitate, no matter how tamely, the unparalleled criminal careers of Frank and Jesse James.

And as the story closes, the mind reverts to our own way through life, and a feeling of satisfaction surrounds us as we realize that we are guarded on every hand by OUR POLICE.